Creative Problem Solving and Opportunity Finding

J. Daniel Couger

Decision Making and Operations Management Series

Paul Gray, *Series Editor*

Couger: *Creative Problem Solving and Opportunity Finding*

Gray/Jurison: *Productivity in the Office and the Factory*

Segev: *Corporate Strategy: Portfolio Models*

Segev: *Navigating by COMPASS: Corporate Matrix Portfolio Analysis Support System*

Creative Problem Solving and Opportunity Finding

J. Daniel Couger

Distinguished Professor

University of Colorado, Colorado Springs

bf

boyd & fraser publishing company

I(T)P   An International Thomson Publishing Company

Danvers • Albany • Bonn • Boston • Cincinnati • Detroit • London • Madrid • Melbourne
Mexico City • New York • Paris • San Francisco • Singapore • Tokyo • Toronto • Washington

This book is dedicated to Shirley, whose creativity has been an inspiration to me throughout our married life. Her continuous support and encouragement have been a major stimulus for my own creativity.

Executive Editor/Acquisitions Editor: DeVilla Williams
Production Editor: Jackie Bedoya
Production Services, Composition, and Design: Elm Street Publishing Services, Inc.
Manufacturing Coordinator: Gordon Woodside
Marketing Coordinator: Karen Grantham

 © 1995 by boyd & fraser publishing company
A division of International Thomson Publishing, Inc.

I(T)P   The ITP logo is a trademark under license.

Printed in the United States of America

For more information, contact boyd & fraser publishing company:

boyd & fraser publishing company
One Corporate Place • Ferncroft Village
Danvers, Massachusetts 01923, USA

International Thomson Publishing Europe
Berkshire House 168–173
High Holborn
London, WC1V 7AA, England

Thomas Nelson Australia
102 Dodds Street
South Melbourne 3205
Victoria, Australia

Nelson Canada
1120 Birchmont Road
Scarborough, Ontario
Canada MIK 5G4

International Thomson Editores
Campose Eliscos 385, Piso 7
Col. Polanco
11560 Mexico D.F. Mexico

International Thomson Publishing GmbH
Konigswinterer Strasse 418
53227 Bonn, Germany

International Thomson Publishing Asia
221 Henderson Road
#05–10 Henderson Building
Singapore 0315

International Thomson Publishing Japan
Hirakawacho Kyowa Building, 3F
2-2-1 Hirakawacho
Chiyoda-ku, Tokyo 102, Japan

End of chapter patent artwork courtesy of **Creativity!** journal, Austin, Texas.

2 3 4 5 6 7 8 9 10 MT 8 7 6 5

Library of Congress Cataloging-in-Publication Data:

Couger, J. Daniel.
  Creative problem solving and opportunity finding / J. Daniel Couger.
    p. cm.
  Includes index.
  ISBN 0-87709-752-6
  1. Creative ability in business. 2. Problem solving. 3. Creative thinking. I. Title.
HD53.C69 1994
658.4'03—dc20   94-30862

CONTENTS

Preface

Proving the academic respectability of creativity was one of my three major objectives in forming the Center for Research on Creativity and Innovation at the University of Colorado, Colorado Springs, in 1988. Few papers on the subject of creativity had been accepted in academic journals for the field of business and management because of the non-rigorous approach to research on the topic. Articles in the popular press were often trivial, giving the field a poor image. Yet, training programs on the topic of creativity and innovation were flourishing in business and industry. Companies were stressing creativity in an attempt to improve their competitive edge in the international arena.

The second objective for originating the Center was to prove the cost-effectiveness of creativity improvement programs in industry. While interest on the topic was expanding exponentially, many managers wondered how they could justify providing their employees with time for creative expression.

In five years, our Center produced 22 papers that were accepted in refereed journals and proceedings, including the best journals in the business field. We met our objective of proving the academic respectability of the subject. During this time, we also introduced creativity improvement programs in a number of firms, carefully monitoring the cost-effectiveness of the programs. The return on investment was highly significant, ranging from 200 percent to 600 percent.

The third objective in creating the Center was to develop a course on creativity that would be both interesting and meaningful. The first creativity course was offered at the University in fall 1991. I wrote this book for that course and used it for six consecutive semesters. I also used it as a key module in a graduate level course. As I experimented with different teaching approaches and continued to conduct research in the field, I continuously revised the book. I am quite pleased with the teaching results in my classes, as are my students. (The *Instructor's Manual* contains the results of my experiments in teaching approaches, culminating in my recommended approach.) This book has also been a key device in enabling individuals and teams to improve their creativity ability. I use the book for my industry workshops on the subject. Workshops and improvement programs were the source of the multitude of practical examples in the book.

Methodology

The Creative Problem Solving (CPS) methodology is a sound and systematic approach that enables individuals to resurface the natural creativity that we all possessed at age five. That natural creativity was pushed farther and farther below the surface as we progressed through the educational system. The bureaucratic activities in business and government, as well as management's lack of understanding of how to provide a climate to support our creativity, perpetuate the submersion of our native creativity. With knowledge of the key factors conducive to a creative environment, management can foster the creative abilities of its personnel. Within such a supportive climate, the CPS methodology enables us to resurface our basic creative ability—so that it flourishes!

Acknowledgments

I have some acknowledgments to make for support in my research and writing. Through Dr. Tudor Rickards at the University of Manchester Business School, United Kingdom, I gained access to the European creativity community. Drs. Scott Isaksen and Don Treffinger provided the same entree for me to the American creativity community. There is a small but strong network of creativity researchers/practitioners in Europe and North America. This summer I had the opportunity to visit Japan and present creativity lectures to the Asian community for the first time. Dr. Akira Onda was instrumental in introducing me to the Japanese view of creativity. My funding for the Center's activities came from Federal Express, United Technology, Texaco, and Microsoft. My thanks to the following individuals from those organizations: Scott Oki, Richard Legler, Jim Metzger, John Hammitt, Terry Snow, Jim Tollefson, Pat Flynn, and Doris Hellyer.

I'd also like to thank my colleagues who participated in the Center's research program, principally Lex Higgins and Scott McIntyre, my associate directors for the Center. I'd like to thank Kathy Abeyta and Karen Norris for their assistance in preparing the manuscript. Thank you to my students for their cooperation in experimenting with various teaching approaches.

Finally, I would like to thank the editorial, production, and design departments at boyd & fraser publishing company for insisting on such a high-quality text, and for encouraging first-rate design and graphics. I would also like to thank the many reviewers who helped shape the content and style of this book. I am especially grateful for the comments and insights provided by the following reviewers:

Carl Adams, *University of Minnesota*

James Buffington, *Indiana State University*

Dorothy Dologite, *University of New York–Baruch*

Charles H. Jones, *Boston University*

Donald J. McCubbrey, *University of Denver*

Mike H. Ryan, *University of North Texas*

J. Daniel Couger
Colorado Springs
September 1994

*In oneself lies the whole world and if you
know how to look and learn, then the
door is there and the key is in your hand.
Nobody on earth can give you either the
key or the door to open, except yourself.*
J. Krishnamuri

Introduction

This book is designed to cover the principles and concepts of creativity and their application to the field of business. It concentrates on the model of Creative Problem Solving (CPS) and provides a number of techniques for improving one's creativity, in each of the five steps in creative problem solving. Unfortunately, the name *CPS* implies that the emphasis is exclusively on solving problems. A number of the techniques subsumed within the CPS concept are useful for opportunity finding, as well. Opportunity finding will be illustrated in this book along with problem solving.

The Four-Ps Model of Creativity

Albert Rothenberg believes that creativity consists "of the capacity for, or state of, bringing something into being" and that bringing something into being involves at least three separable components: an agent, a process, and a product. The literature on creativity, according to Rothenberg, can be categorized into these three different areas: the creative person, the creative process, and the creative product. It may be considered "from the standpoint of the person who creates, that is in terms of physiology and temperament, including personal attitudes, habits, and values. It may also be explained by way of the mental process—motivation, perception, learning, thinking, and communication—that the act calls into play. Finally, creativity may be understood in terms of its products, such as theories, inventions, paintings, carvings, and poems."[1]

However, the person-process-product model of creativity is incomplete because it does not address the factor of environment and its effect on creative efforts. The climate for creativity is comprised of those factors that foster or retard creative behavior.[2] Rosabeth Moss Kanter says that managers can induce new styles of thinking by introducing a climate that encourages "kaleidoscope thinking." The colored glass fragments inside a kaleidoscope form a certain pattern. But when the kaleidoscope is twisted, shaken, or approached from a new angle, the exact same fragments form an entirely different pattern. Kaleidoscope thinking, then, involves taking an existing array of data, phenomena, or assumptions and twisting, shaking, or looking at them from another angle, thus permitting an entirely new pattern and consequent set of actions to take place.[3]

George Geis speaks of an organizational psychology of creativity, in which the culture of the organization must make it attractive and easy for people to discover and solve problems.[4] Abraham Zaleznick suggests a psychodynamic of creativity and innovation. "Innovation inertia in institutions is an endemic problem, sometimes called 'the bureaucratic malaise.' Bureaucracy tends to produce power struggles, displacement of goals, and 'trained incompetency,' along with equity, due process, and practical rationality. These bureaucratic problems cause the skills and energy of the bricoleur (innovator) to become repressed and suppressed, when just the opposite should be occurring to stimulate innovation in organizations.... Innovation calls for rediscovery of intuition, judgment, and fruitful trial and error."[5]

The importance of the work environment for encouraging or discouraging creativity is well supported in creativity research. Surprisingly, I've been able to locate only one model of creativity that gives proper emphasis to the environment for creativity. Mel Rhodes added a fourth ingredient to the traditional model of person-process-product: "press."[6] At first, I thought he was working a little too hard on achieving alliteration but later found that *press* is a term from the field of education that refers to the relationship between human beings and their environment. Figure 1 shows that the three Ps, person-process-product, operate within the environment, press.

The Four-Ps model of creativity has several advantages over other models for addressing creativity. The model clearly shows that creativity is a dynamic phenomenon comprised of four highly interactive components. The model's simplicity allows for the individual measurement and assessment of each component as well as evaluation of the interaction of the components. Another strength of the model is that it can be analyzed for a specific functional organization, like marketing or production or information systems, as well as the organization as a whole.

A Pedagogical Approach

The spiral method of instruction is used in this book. An overview of CPS and creativity concepts/techniques is provided in the first five chapters, Part One. The remaining chapters will "spiral" more deeply into each of the major topics introduced in Part One.

Figure 1   Four-Ps Model of Creativity

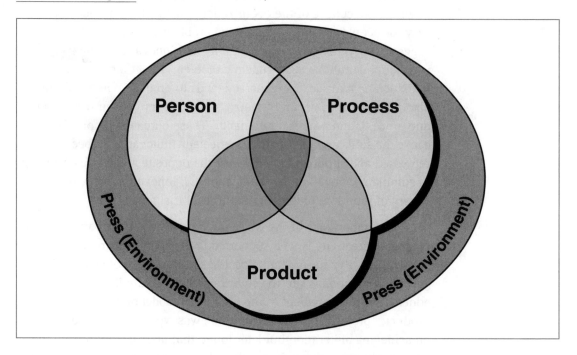

Part One has as its principal objective an explanation of the person and process components of the Four-Ps model of creativity. Creativity is discussed in its relationship to the individual in Chapters 1, 3, and 5. The process of facilitating creativity is discussed in Chapters 2 and 4.

Part Two of the book concentrates primarily on process. The Creative Problem Solving model was derived to assist individuals and teams to more easily apply their creativity. A chapter is devoted to each step in the CPS process, giving both an explanation of how to conduct the step and examples of creativity techniques useful for that step. However, Chapter 9 also provides an in-depth look at the creative product and how to evaluate the creativity of products.

Part Three contains only three chapters. Two of them, 12 and 13, are oriented almost entirely toward the "person" component of the Four-Ps model of creativity. Chapter 12 discusses personal attributes and actions that facilitate creativity; Chapter 13 explains how a person can improve his or her intuitive ability. Chapter 11 is devoted to the remaining component of creativity, environment. Managers have the greatest influence on the environment or climate for creativity. The chapter discusses factors that detract from a climate of creativity and those that enhance it.

The objective of this book is to help individuals and teams improve their creativity. By concentrating on all four components of creativity, there is a higher probability of attaining a holistic effect. Certainly a more synergistic effect results from the attempt to integrate the four components. Plutarch said that "the mind is not a vessel to be filled but a fire to be kindled." It is hoped that this book will help you kindle a fire from that innate spark of creativity that we all possess.

> Man's mind once stretched by a new idea, never regains its original dimension.
>
> *Oliver Wendell Holmes*

Source: Reprinted with permission of DuPont.

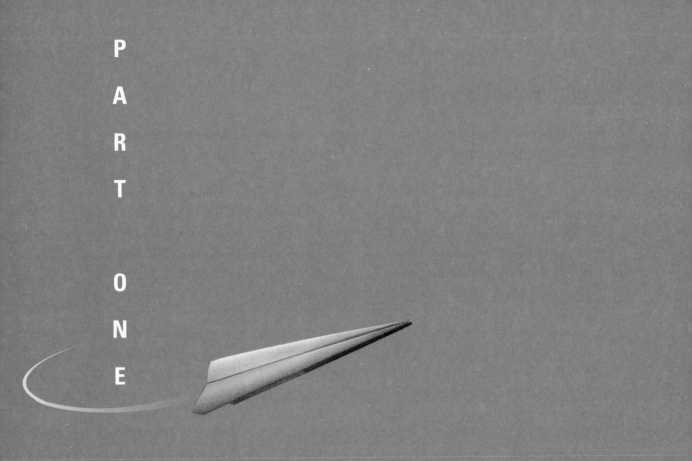

Synopsis of Creativity

Objectives of Part One

You may be tempted to skip this introduction to Part I and dive immediately into the first chapter. I understand the temptation. However, I encourage you to read this short section to better understand why I organized the material the way it is presented. Understanding the objectives and approach to presentation will help you assimilate the material more easily.

The first five chapters of the book explain the application of creativity to the field of business. Chapter 1 provides a foundation for that study. Surprisingly, there are widely differing views of what comprises creativity. For some, defining it is much like Justice Potter Stewart's characterization of pornography: "I know it when I see it." Each of us can give examples of creativity and can identify creative people. Many of us, however, have difficulty explaining creativity precisely. Chapter 1 defines and explains creativity and its concepts. It also gives examples of the cost-effectiveness of creativity. I'm often contacted by persons who would like to attend my two-day workshop on creativity but cannot convince their boss that they can afford the two days away from the job. There is clear-cut evidence of the benefits of creativity. As I show throughout the book, every job in an organization can be creatively improved and everyone can become more creative. A very high return on investment results from introducing a creativity improvement program. Examples of the benefits of improving one's creativity are provided in Chapter 1 as an incentive to reading the entire book.

In Chapter 2, these examples are expanded. Also in this chapter is a discussion of 6 of the 20 techniques for facilitating creativity that are covered in this book: progressive abstraction, interrogatories, force field analysis, associations/images, analogy/ metaphor, and wishful thinking. Three are analytical techniques; three are intuitive. These techniques have been proven effective in a number of studies. (Surprisingly, the one technique that almost everyone has used—brainstorming—is the least effective. Research shows that other techniques are much more productive.)

Five major barriers, or blocks, to creativity are explained in Chapter 3. Knowing these blocks paves the way to diminishing them.

In their preschool years, children have a natural questioning process that becomes blocked as they grow older. Formal education pushes this native creativity below the surface, progressively more so with additional education. The majority of the U.S. workforce needs specific techniques to help resurface that natural creativity. Approaches to restoring that questioning process are provided in Chapter 3. The final third of the chapter discusses the four styles of creativity used by most of today's workers. Understanding your own preferred style helps you utilize your creative abilities more effectively. Also, understanding all four styles helps you work better in teams with persons whose style may be different from yours.

Chapter 4 introduces the five-step creative problem solving (CPS) model, which evolved from the scientific method taught in high school. CPS has some special characteristics that ensure that we not only solve problems but produce creative solutions as well. I use the term *CPS* because it is widely known and accepted. It is important to note, however, that while the term implies that the five-step approach is used only for problem solving, it is equally useful for opportunity finding. A unique feature of CPS is its emphasis on divergence/convergence actions for each step. Each step begins with a divergence activity and ends with a convergence activity. Most people assume that creativity techniques are used only in Step 3, idea generation. They are wrong. Creativity techniques are used in each of the five steps, changing the model to a methodology.

In some respects, Chapter 5, which covers the distinction between creative and critical thinking, could have been the first chapter of this book. From a teaching perspective, however, it's important to cover the other material first. Most people need to see actual examples of the use of CPS and creativity techniques before they are motivated to study mental processes. Understanding thinking and the thought process is essential to improving one's creative and critical thinking ability. Improving one's memory is also important, because creative results that are non-trivial need a solid foundation of knowledge. Being able to store the requisite facts and to recall them upon demand is essential to significant creative results. Chapter 5 provides ways to improve your memory and shows how creative thinking relates to divergent activities and critical thinking relates to convergent activities in the CPS process. The objective is holistic thinking, wherein a person uses both sides of his or her brain in the problem-solving/opportunity-finding process.

The foundation of the first five chapters gives you the proper perspective to delve into the details of the CPS process in Part Two. As mentioned earlier, this book is designed in a spiral fashion. It covers the field of creativity in the chapters of Part One, then spirals into greater depth in later chapters. This approach has been proven quite effective from an educational perspective. Just as we need a domain of knowledge in the field of the problem to be able to derive solutions that are meaningful and non-trivial, we need a domain of knowledge about creativity to be accomplished CPS users. Thus, despite the temptation of going directly to Chapter 6 and a detailed discussion of CPS, you will produce more creative results if you take the longer route of first mastering Part One.

Source: Reprinted with permission of DuPont.

1

An idea is a method of evading,
circumventing, or surmounting through
reflection, obstacles that otherwise
would have to be attacked by brute force.
John Dewey

Concepts and Cost-Effectiveness of Creativity

Although few references on the Creative Problem Solving model note the fact, problem-solving techniques predate CPS by thousands of years. Even before Socrates broached the subject, the Bible records examples of special problem-solving approaches, such as Moses' technique for dealing with the many problems arising from guiding more than 500,000 Israelites across the Sinai desert in search of the Promised Land. He was continually besieged by people wanting counsel, seeking judgment in disputes, or meeting the day-to-day requirements for survival. On advice from his father-in-law, Jethro, Moses appointed twelve judges to subdivide the problem-solving task. Only those problems that could not be handled by the 12 judges were passed on to Moses. This approach was also the introduction of the principle of management-by-exception!

We will return to the discussion of CPS in Chapter 3. Before that, it is important to have a strong foundation on the concepts, principles and definitions about creativity. Some of the techniques for improving creativity will then be illustrated. It is also important to understand some of the blocks to creativity that are common for most persons and to recognize our individual style of creativity. With that background a study of the CPS process will be more fruitful. In this chapter, we will review the concepts, definitions, and models of creativity. First, let's explore the notion that people can be taught to be more creative.

What the educational experience almost completely excludes is the exercise and development of the students' creativity.

Ray Bolz and Robert Dean

Can Creativity Be Taught?

Business Week recently devoted its cover story to creativity. One of the key points made: "The latest research suggests that people can be taught to be more creative. Many companies are applying the new techniques—with surprisingly good results." For many years, James Adams has taught a course on creativity in the engineering school at Stanford University. "Can creativity be taught?" he asks. "Obviously I think it can be...." I am convinced that our efforts at Stanford result in an improvement in the quality of conceptual output from our students."[1] According to Adams, a related question often arises: "Can't conscious efforts to be creative interfere with the creative process?" Adams replies: "If a da Vinci happens to be reading this book, he is probably wasting his time. However, most of us are not da Vincis!" Adams comments that one of the earliest theories about creativity considers it to be a divine spark. He cites Plato, in *III, Ion,* speaking of poets:

> And for this reason God takes away the minds of these men and uses them as his ministers, just as he does soothsayers and goodly seers in order that we who hear them may know that it is not they who utter these words of great price when they are out of their wits, but that it is God himself who speaks and addresses us through them.[2]

Adams concludes, "However, for most of us, creativity is more of a dull glow than a divine spark. And the more fanning it receives, the brighter it will burn."[3]

Many other authors have shown that creativity can be taught. Here are some of the findings:

1. It is a fallacy that we do not need to do anything specific to help intelligent individuals learn to be more creative. Even the literature on gifted education is replete with suggestions for teaching creative problem-solving skills to gifted children. One is led to the conclusion that both average and highly intelligent persons can benefit from instruction in CPS.[4]

2. Five major studies demonstrate the validity of teaching creativity: "Overwhelmingly, these show significant positive results."[5]

3. An analysis of 142 studies shows that schools can help students recapture the natural creativity they had as preschoolers.[6]

4. Virtually everyone's personal creativity can be increased beyond its present level. University and professional level creativity courses regularly try to:

   - Raise creative consciousness, which increases the likelihood of becoming involved in creative ventures.

   - Reach people about the topic of creativity itself, which helps them understand and further appreciate creative thinking.

   - Teach creative thinking techniques and help people realize that creative thinkers consciously use idea-finding strategies.[7]

Definitions of Creativity

Over 100 definitions of creativity have been published. I will provide a range of definitions, from simple to complex, then suggest an approach for classification of the definitions. Bruner provides the simplest definition of creativity: "effective surprise."[8] Miller defines it as the birth of imaginative new ideas.[9] According to Ciardi, "creativity is the imaginatively gifted recombination of known elements into something new."[10]

The French mathematician Poincare provided an elegant description of the creative process as a "fruitful combining which reveals to us unsuspected kinship between facts, long known but wrongly believed to be strangers to one another."[11] Freud's definition contains a delightful mixture of the abstract and the earthy: "a means of expressing inner conflict that otherwise would issue in neuroses...a mental purgative that keeps men sane."[12]

The most comprehensive definition is provided in the landmark paper on "The Process of Creative Thinking," by Newell, Simon, and Shaw.[13] They believe, to be creative, a solution must satisfy one or more of the following conditions:

1. The product of the thinking has novelty or value (either for the thinker or for his culture).
2. The thinking is unconventional in the sense that it requires modification or rejection of previously accepted ideas.
3. The thinking requires high motivation and persistence, taking place either over a considerable span of time (continuously or intermittently) or at high intensity.
4. The problem as initially posed was vague and ill-defined, so that part of the task was to formulate the problem itself.

Although Newell-Simon-Shaw state that only one "or more" of the conditions must be met, they indicate that all four conditions are important. Two characteristics that most often appear in the more than 30 definitions of creativity are "newness or uniqueness" and "value or utility." If the business profession uses a creative approach that includes those outcomes, substantive results can be expected. Therefore, the remaining discussion is based on a concept of creativity

Figure 1–1 Creativity Is a Complex Process

characterized by uniqueness and utility. As Figure 1–1 indicates, creativity is not a simple concept.

Since creativity applies to all areas of life, not just to the business profession, most definitions tend to be somewhat abstract. For the definition to be helpful in business career fields, it must be pragmatized.

Analysis of the definitions identifies several categories of attributes. One relates to the attribute of the fresh idea—something new, unique, or different. Another relates to utility—the result of creative activity must be something of value. Therefore, to be classified as creative, an improvement must:

1. be new or unique
2. have utility or value

Distinguishing Creativity from Innovation and Invention

The *American Heritage Dictionary* defines *innovation* as "that which is newly introduced." The term *innovate* derives from the Latin word, *innovare,* "to renew." The Latin word for create is *creare,* "to bring into existence, to originate." To be creative is to have the ability to create things characterized by originality.

One of the best ways to clarify the distinction between creativity and innovation is to show that they have the same relationship as the concepts of discovery and invention. The article by Hall and Smith in the *Encyclopedia Americana* provides a clear differentiation:

Invention requires a purpose. The inventor must know what it is that he wishes to achieve, and however uncertain his progress is at any moment, he usually has a pretty clear idea of the paths he should explore. It is impossible for him to work successfully without being familiar with the existing state of knowledge in his field of interest or with the variety of techniques he may redirect to his purpose. An accidental invention is almost a contradiction in terms.

Discovery, on the other hand, requires no clear purpose of object, though most successful discoverers have proceeded systematically in their research. Discovery is concerned with the perception of some new property, phenomenon, or truth about things. It is abstract and often quite useless. Whereas the making of some inventions is virtually predictable, many discoveries contain an element of the accidental, though to profit from an accident requires a prepared mind. Invention, involving a deliberate attempt to utilize some particular phenomenon to achieve a given result, depends upon conscious matching of means with ends. Discovery is less controlled; the end is often unknown and the basic event may lead the scientist into a very long course of investigation, that in the end, causes his discovery to appear in a very different light.

Yet, that discovery and invention are interdependent is easily shown by many examples. The discovery of electromagnetic effects permitted the invention of engineering devices such as telegraph instruments, lamps, motors and generators. The development of electrical engineering led men to study large currents and high voltages; the result was the discovery of new knowledge about the properties of materials, about the flow of electricity, and so forth. This knowledge was not only fed back into the engineering industry by way of new invention, but yielded new discoveries in pure physics also.[14]

The discovery/invention relationship can be used to distinguish creativity from innovation. Where invention is concerned with implementation of discovery, innovation is concerned with implementation of inventive ideas. Innovation is pragmatic: the conversion of an invention into a business or other useful application. The appropriate view of innovation is exemplified by the following definitions: "Innovation is a process whereby new ideas are put into practice."[15] "To invent is to find a new thing; to innovate is to get the new thing done."[16] and "Innovation is the process by which inventions are...transformed into a profitable product or system."[17]

Invention results in totally new products, services, or processes.[18] Examples are the airplane (Wright brothers), the light bulb (Thomas Edison), and the telephone (Alexander Graham Bell). In general, discovery precedes invention, which is then exploited for a useful product or service. The exploitation process is often referred to as innovation, but there are inconsistencies in the literature. Sometimes the term *innovation* is used to denote both invention and exploitation.

How does creativity fit into these activities? As shown in Figure 1–2, creativity must be present in each of these steps. For an

Figure 1–2   Differentiation of Discovery/Invention/Innovation
(Creativity Should Be Involved in Each Activity.)

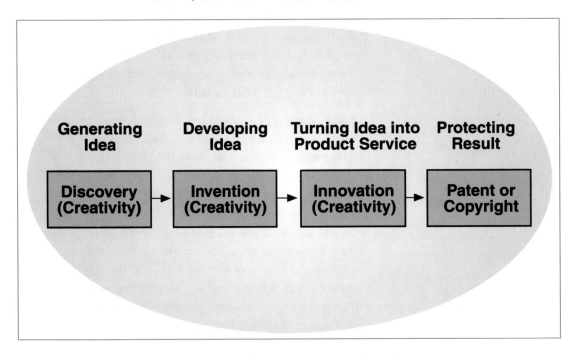

idea to be recognized as a discovery, it must be unique. Invention converts an idea into something useful. Innovation derives a specific product or service.

Although the terms *creativity* and *innovation* are often used interchangeably, they should not be. Creativity is a much broader concept. Innovation is the more restricted process of turning an idea into a product or service. Figure 1–2 shows that creativity is involved in all three stages of the birth of an idea to maturation in practical use: discovery, invention, and innovation. For example, the Japanese have been especially effective at innovation—taking an invention such as the microchip and innovating a variety of ways to improve microchip technology.

Another example is Federal Express' Supertracker. Federal Express founder Fred Smith conceived that wholly reliable service depended upon the firm's ability to track a package at every change of hands or direction. Innovation was the means of moving from Smith's creative insight to Supertracker, a hand-held computer with 392K bytes of memory that can accept data from key entry, bar-code scanning, or electronic coupling.

IBM's development of the Josephson circuit is an example of creativity, while its 4-megabit chip development is an example of innovation. The latter is an extension of silicon chip base technology, while the former uses an entirely new approach—superconductivity—to gain a factor of 10 speed improvement over semiconductor circuitry.

Myths about Creativity

We've heard so many stories of accidental discovery that we've come to believe that it happens frequently. Yet in my research on creativity, I have found few cases of discovery being accidental. Most inventions result from a careful, methodical process.

For example, consider the widely circulated yet erroneous stories about 3M Post-it notes. While many accounts claim that this product was discovered accidentally, it was not accidental and resulted from traditional research methodology in a search for a new glue. One of the glues produced was weaker than desired and the researcher thought of a way to use it for his own notes, marking places in a songbook for his church choir. He then recognized the glue's commercial benefits. The researcher worked for five years, on and off, to get to a point where he could convince management of the viability of his discovery. Writers who chalk this product up to accidental discovery overlook the fact that the researcher followed a planned experimental procedure, a procedure that produced several products, including the Post-it note. This is the key to creativity: a structured approach through which an investigator considers a wide range of alternatives.

Granted, the result was serendipitous; nevertheless, it evolved from a careful, methodical process. The recognition of serendipity does not destroy the rationality of discovery, nor does it sustain the belief that a different mode of explanation is required for revolutionary discoveries. This fact is illustrated quite well in a recent book by David Lamb:

> Scientists are not simple mechanisms tuned only to the recognition of one solution to one problem at a time. Seeking one thing (a sock) and finding another thing (a shirt) is a familiar event in all walks of life,

and it should not be surprising to discover that science, too, develops in this manner. Attention to one problem will rarely block off solutions to other problems. Taking advantage of lucky finds is perfectly compatible with rational methods of hypothesis generation, even with regard to revolutionary hypotheses. The new is created by paying close attention to the old, taking advantage of serendipitous results derived from, and structured by, problems in normal science. Columbus, who was one of the most serendipitous discoverers of all time, did not conjecture without regulative heuristics.[19]

Closely linked to heroic myths about creativity are two philosophical traditions that stress that nothing informative can be said about creativity. The first tradition goes back to the writer of Ecclesiastes in the Bible, who held that there was nothing new under the sun; the second is the romantic tradition stressing the mysterious and inexplicable nature of idea generation.

Robert Weisberg, in *Creativity: Genius and Other Myths,* states that much of what we believe about creativity is not based on hard data but is "more or less folklore, passed down from one generation to the next as if it were the truth." He says that our society holds a very romantic view about the origins of creative achievements in the arts and sciences. This is the genius view, and at its core is the belief that creative achievements come about through great leaps of imagination, which occur because creative individuals are capable of extraordinary thought processes. In addition to their intellectual capacities, creative individuals are assumed to possess extraordinary personality characteristics that also play a role in bringing about creative leaps. These intellectual and personality characteristics are what is called "genius," and they are brought forth as the explanation for great creative achievements. A second assumption of the genius view is that creative individuals possess some indefinable quality that accounts for how they do the great things they do.[20]

To the contrary, in Weisberg's view, creativity is an activity resulting from the ordinary thought processes of ordinary individuals. In a given case the work an individual produces may be extraordinary, but extraordinary work is not necessarily the result of extraordinary personal characteristics.

According to Plato, there was no such thing as having a new concept or a new idea. What appeared as a new idea was merely the recognition of an old one or the new application of a concept. The "newness" of an idea, on these terms, would be the experience of novelty felt by the person who was fortunate enough to receive it.

A modern view is that a new idea "happens" when someone discovers a new combination, arrangement, or adaptation of existing ideas. Things, people, or ideas become connected as no one has connected them before. The connection may already exist in nature, and the "new idea" is only a matter of seeing a pattern for the first time.[21]

Thus, Pasteur saw a relationship between microbes and spoiled wine. He later recognized a connection between different microbes and the anthrax that was killing sheep. Once he discovered the pattern, others saw new applications. Later, a Glasgow surgeon made the connection that microbes in the air caused putrefaction and death after surgery—a discovery that led to the development of aseptic surgery.

Romantic myths about the mystery of creativity have survived long into the 20th century. They appear in scientific biographies, science textbooks, and verbal anecdotes. They are embedded in the philosophy of science, which maintains that the processes by means of which new ideas are generated defy rational analysis and simulation. According to Herbert Simon:

> The subject of scientific discovery (and creativity generally) has always been surrounded by dense mists of romanticism and downright know nothingism. Even well-informed persons, who do not believe the stork brings new babies, and are prepared to accept an empirical account of biological creation, sometimes balk at natural explanations of the creation of new ideas. It appears that the human mind is the last citadel of vitalism.[22]

The Newell-Shaw-Simon contention that the "aha" or "eureka" experience occurs only after a "considerable span of time" is supported by other researchers on creativity. On the other hand, the research differs significantly from the lay literature view of creativity. The latter often views the idea originating in a "flash of lightning," "moment of inspiration," or by "blundering on an idea." Nor does research support the notion of accidental invention.

Rarely is it a flash of inspiration, or an accident. The ultimate idea results from a careful, methodical generation of alternatives. Pasteur said that "inspiration is the impact of a fact on a well prepared mind." One wonders how many accidental discoveries actually occurred. The rumor that polyethylene was made while researchers searched for nylon has no substance. Another example of the gap between discovery and use was demonstrated by the Swiss chemist, George Andeman, who discovered cellulosic materials. Almost a half century elapsed before its practical use as artificial silk, under the name of rayon, by Comte Hilaire de Chardonnet.[23]

William Greatbatch, inventor of the implantable cardiac pacemaker, says, "One of the big differences between other people and me is stick-to-it-iveness; I think it's true of many inventors and entrepreneurs. The most important factor is whether you look at something and wonder, 'What makes it work? Could I make it better?' Inventing takes curiosity; it takes drive; it takes an inability to be discouraged. An inventor is the kind of person who really doesn't get interested in a problem until it looks impossible."[24]

Koestler, in *The Act of Creation*, describes the "bisociative thinker": Once presented with the problem, the person compartmentalizes the problem while doing other things, then comes up with a solution by the very act of thinking of the relationship. Koestler defines bisociation as "an escape from boredom, stagnation, intellectual predicaments and emotional frustration…signalled by the spontaneous flash of insight which shows a familiar situation or event in a new light, and elicits a new response to it. The bisociative act connects previously unconnected matrices of experience; it makes us understand what it is…'to be living on several planes at once.'" Koestler cites the example of Archimedes, who was told to weigh the gold in a king's crown without first melting the crown and separating the different metals. Archimedes fretted constantly with his problem and found it most intrusive in times of repose—as when he was taking a bath. Unable to let go of his mental picture of Hiero's crown, Archimedes noticed his own physical volume displacing the water in his tub and shouted "Eureka!" He had discovered the law of displacement of solids literally surrounding him: "There was for Archimedes that flash of insight, but one that had been arduously cultivated by incessant, obsessive contemplation of the problem."[25] Again, this is not accidental or instantaneous discovery. It is an example of the Newell-Shaw-Simon condition of "high motivation and persistence."

Godfrey Hounsfield, who invented the CT scanning machine, got it together virtually whole in his mind before he set to work on his prototype. "He did not see the concept in a flash of inspiration...living perpetually with his incomplete image of the scanner, Hounsfield finally saw it, built it and it worked."

Another one of the myths in the field is that of "genius-dominated discovery." Many believe that most of the great discoveries were produced by a few geniuses—Leonardo da Vinci, Thomas Edison, Louis Pasteur. Not true. A quick review of the patents issued each year reveal that many persons, not just a select few, are responsible. "Genius, in truth, means a little more than a faculty of perceiving in an unhabitual way," according to William James.

Creative Breakthroughs

P. R. Nayak and J. M. Ketteringham, in their book *Breakthroughs*, document 13 cases of creativity and innovation, including Hounsfield's invention: "In every case...it was the curiosity within the originating person that lit the fire. Neither financial need nor market intelligence played a major role in these exceptional beginnings...it always was a problem to be solved, not a fortune to be made, not a market to be exploited."[26]

I'll summarize three of their examples, then discuss the factors in common for all 13 cases. While all the products/services are familiar, their creative origin may not be. Each illustrates the use of a process or methodology for evolving a creative idea.

Nautilus: The Machine That Stretches As It Strengthens

Arthur Jones, the creator of the Nautilus exercise machine, became interested in body building because of his own slight build. His first attempt was a pullover machine he assembled at a YMCA in Tulsa, Oklahoma, in 1948. He built the machine after achieving what he regarded as inadequate results lifting free weights. "As soon as I picked one [barbell] up, I began to suspect that there was something wrong with the tool," recalls Jones, "because it produced very good results in some portions of your anatomy and much lesser results in other areas."

He worked on and off on the machine for 20 years. "One night, about two-fifteen in the morning, I had an idea for a component to be added to the existing machine." He called an employee out of bed and gave him directions for building the component. "Then, it didn't work at all. It failed. But it failed in such a dramatic fashion that I knew why it failed and I also knew what it would take to redesign the entire machine so it would not fail. Because I suddenly understood the problem."

The problem Jones had understood was a matter of physics. When a person lifts a weight, the combination of gravity and the variations in leverage in the human body create wide disparities in the weight's resistance, and thus in its benefits to the weightlifter. Jones forced the resistance to rotate on the axis of the human body. Jones freed the body and made captive both the weights and the forces of gravity. The result is dramatic. The body (a rotating machine) encounters measured, almost intelligent, resistance from the Nautilus (another rotating machine) and draws from that resistance the maximum benefit to achieve growth. Jones also designed a device that increases the body's flexibility by extending resistance through the complete range of each physical movement. His machine stretches as it strengthens, which free weights do not do.

Nautilus users can train for 30 minutes, three times per week, and get very good results in a short time. This potential was shown by a test at the U.S. Military Academy. In comparisons of two groups of Army football players—one using Nautilus and the other free weights—the differences in strength and flexibility were extraordinary. The Nautilus group, in six weeks, increased physical strength by an average of 60 percent, while the non-Nautilus users improved less than 20 percent. The Nautilus group experienced an 11 percent improvement in the two-mile run, while the other group improved only 2.55 percent. The Nautilus group improved its vertical jumping by 6.5 percent, compared to the other group's 1.4 percent improvement. While the control group did not improve its flexibility measurements by more than 1.3 percent in any of three categories, the Nautilus group showed improvements ranging from 5.6 to 11.6 percent.

But the most significant breakthrough in the Nautilus story is one that has yet to happen. The Nautilus machine is an invention whose potential benefits barely have been touched. Today, in the vast majority of its installations, it is a misused and misunderstood machine. Besides inventing the machine, Jones developed a series of routines for its use—one for building muscle, another for increasing cardiovascular fitness.

The Microwave Oven

Raytheon gave birth to the microwave oven in 1946, but within a few years nearly orphaned it. Based on a marvelous device called the magnetron, the microwave oven was a consumer product trapped within a company whose business was not consumer products. Raytheon's lifeblood was government contracts. Placed next to Raytheon's two proudest offspring, the Hawk and Sparrow guided missiles, the Radarange oven—which warmed up chicken soup and thawed frozen cakes—was a comic oddity. The only way it got to market was through Raytheon's purchase of Amana. After almost 20 years of muddling around with microwave ovens at Raytheon, Chairman Charles F. Adams laid out an ultimatum: "We'd give it one shot," he said, "and if it didn't work, then we'd forget it—put an end to it once and for all."

Microwave technology came to the United States originally from Great Britain. A group of British scientists, led by H.A.H. Boot and J.R. Randall, devised the pulse-type microwave magnetron for radar use in 1939, and it was radar that eventually turned the Battle of Britain against Germany. Raytheon was one of the firms to obtain government contracts to produce radar units.

But with the end of the war, suddenly the magnetron industry ceased to exist. Palmer Derby worked in the plant that made radar units for Raytheon: "The day the war ended, the factory closed down. Down! Boom! That was it. Everybody went home and the next day I went in and there was just nobody there."

The overnight disappearance of their industry meant that the few remaining personnel finally had time to tinker with this cooking notion that had haunted them for almost five years. "In those days we weren't concerned about microwave radiation," recalled Derby. "Those tubes radiated into space. The result was if you tested a magnetron, you tested it by holding a neon tube next to it to see how bright the bulb would get. The brighter it got, the more power it had.... In the process of holding the bulb this way, it was quite obvious that your hands got hot…Percy [Spencer] mentioned and talked frequently that this would be a good device for cooking." They set up a fairly strong power tube (300-500 watts) and one day Leslie Vandt had an idea. "Les went out and bought some popcorn, brought the bag back and held it in front of the wave guide," Derby said. "And it began to jump all over hell." Percy Spencer and his engineers next tried hanging a pork chop in front of the wave guide. Not only did it cook, but someone had the courage to eat it. After a few dozen more trips to the corner grocery, it was time to show off the device to the board of directors. Spencer could have chosen any number of demonstration foods, but he opted for one that would leave an indelible impression—an egg.

"Percy asked the operator to put an egg on the pedestal in front of the wave guide," Derby recalled. "Then the wave guide pumped not 300 or 500 watts, but a kilowatt of energy into the egg. There's only one thing that could have happened. All over everybody." Percy Spencer had won his point. After they cleaned the egg off their faces, suits, and ties, the board of directors agreed to put some money into microwave cooking. The rest is history.

The CT (CAT) Scanner

The scene at the Rochester, Minnesota, airport one warm day in 1971 might have been staged by film director Mel Brooks as part of a sequel to *Young Frankenstein*. At the routine security checkpoint, guards halted a man carrying a suspicious-looking container. When the container passed through the security X-ray machine, the unmistakable contents of a human skull were visible on the display screen.

When the security staff opened the container, they saw that this really *was* someone's head. It was not just a skull, nor was it a preserved head; it was a recently severed head. The removal of the head from the container, before a growing crowd of curious passengers, was a memorable event in Rochester airport history. Women blanched. Children gaped.

The man said he was on his way to London. He said he wanted the head for scanning. They let him make an international call to somebody in England named Godfrey Hounsfield. The negotiations that followed were touchy. The man, with some help from Mr. Hounsfield, explained that he had obtained the head legitimately from the Mayo Clinic in Rochester. (A call to Mayo confirmed this; clinic spokesmen assured the people at the airport that the head's original owner was finished with it.) The head was intended for medical research, to be subjected to a new type of X-ray at the laboratories of EMI, Ltd., in Hayes, Middlesex, England. Airport officials eventually released *both* prisoners.

Godfrey Hounsfield is the inventor who, in 1972, presented to a skeptical medical community, and then to the world at large, the CT scanner (also referred to as the CAT scanner). Hounsfield's computerized tomographic (CT) scanning technology has allowed radiologists to take pictures of much greater clarity inside the human body than was possible through traditional X-ray photography. Hounsfield devised a way to look inside people to see tissues that are too soft for an X-ray to show, and to overcome the obscuring effect of dense materials—like bone—that in conventional X-ray pictures mask system tissues lying behind them. Hounsfield's concept meant that exploratory brain surgery often could be replaced by a swift, painless, and safe computerized probe.

In light of the fact that Hounsfield did indeed launch a revolution in radiology, surgery, and computer technology, one would expect that vast resources and legions of well-trained technicians were the arsenal of his breakthroughs. But Hounsfield invented the CT scanner with a grant of less that $15,000 from the British Department of Health and Social Security. His staff consisted of two research assistants still completing their training. He built the prototype himself.

"We made the observation that if you were to take readings which could detect the presence of materials from all angles through a box, in three dimensions, then you would have enough information, without opening the box, to tell what was inside.... How could you identify the object without opening the box?...If the object were reduced to 'picture points' (the tiny dots that comprise the elements of a photograph), then all picture points could be assigned a mathematical value. Each view through the box could be regarded as the result of a mathematical equation. If you could collect all the individual equations outside the box and teach a computer how to put them back together just as they had been arranged inside the box, you could display the reconstructed object on a computer screen and see what's inside."[27]

The idea was pure science fiction. Hounsfield was proposing a real-life application of the phenomenon called "beaming" in the popular television series, "Star Trek." In the television series, a person stood under a "transporter beam," which reduced all the matter in his body to a stream of molecules, directed the stream to a distant point, then reassembled the molecules at the desired destination. In essence, Hounsfield's notion was to take a picture of each molecule, transport those pictures on an X-ray into computer memory, then have the computer reassemble all the little pictures on a monitor screen in exactly their original order.

Things in Common for All 13 Breakthroughs

There are three things in common for all 13 of Nayak and Ketteringham's breakthroughs, and for many of the other inventions and discoveries researched for this book. **First**, the investigators expected a creative idea to occur—they went into the experiment with a confident attitude. **Second**, they utilized a methodical process to reach the result—it was not a product of chance or inspiration but of systematic investigation. **Third**, all the breakthroughs were cost-effective. They disproved the myth that creativity is expensive.

These three factors are important to remember when we attempt to solve problems and identify opportunities in our areas of responsibility and interest.

Cost-Effectiveness of Creativity

Often when I am talking to managerial groups on the subject of creativity and innovation, a manager holds up his hand and comments: "I'm not sure I want my people to be more creative; they have trouble getting their work done on time and within budget as it is." This manager's view is shared by many others. It assumes that encouraging employees to be more creative will give them license to sit around and "blue sky"—trying to come up with an elegant solution when a workable solution can be derived in much shorter time. What these managers are really asking is: "How cost-effective is a creativity improvement program?"

To illustrate the cost-effectiveness of creativity, I'll give a one-paragraph description of cost-effective results of three uses of one creative process. The first, a financial services firm, wanted to go after more small private investors (with portfolios of about $25,000). The firm introduced a flexible financial instrument that gave investors immediate on-line ability to move their funds among stocks or out of stocks, and it provided money market rates on idle funds as well as liquidity equal to that of a checking account. The first to introduce this service, the company captured a huge initial market share. Continued product enhancement ensures that investors have no incentive to switch services. In the first two years, this original provider achieved six times the volume of its nearest competitor. Five years later, it retains a 70 percent share of the market.

A large pharmaceutical company offers on-line order-entry services to pharmacies for itself and a consortium of allied but not competing companies. Not only has it increased market share, it has also derived sizable added revenues from its consortium partners. Some companies excluded from the bundle threatened legal action because of the damage to their market shares.

On its new line of elevators, an elevator company installed flight recording devices such as airlines use. It did so because customers often place service calls without indicating how the elevators have malfunctioned. The recording device permits the service representative to connect it to the elevator company's computer, discover the cause of the malfunction, and do the necessary repairs on the spot, reducing repair costs and increasing customer satisfaction by correcting problems accurately the first time.

A large manufacturer of industrial machinery has installed an expert maintenance system on its home office computer. When a machine failure occurs on the customer's premises, the machine is connected over a telephone line to the manufacturer's computer, which does the fault analysis and issues instructions to the machine operator. Not only are direct service visits down by 90 percent, customer satisfaction is also up markedly.

However, I am not minimizing the importance of the question of cost-effectiveness brought up in my seminars. The question is legitimate. Many of us are led to believe that creativity is costly. For example, we hear about the costs of some projects such as Gillette's 21-part razor. It was introduced during the 1989 Super Bowl (one I prefer to forget, since my Denver Bronco team was demolished by the New York Giants). Super Bowl advertising is the most expensive in television, so Gillette spared no expense to introduce their new product. The company spent more than $100 million in developing the product and over $150 million to advertise it. Nor is the 21-part razor a very profound invention! The implication is that most products require this kind of investment, causing managers to question the viability of embarking on a creativity improvement program. Yet, a profound invention—the CAT scanner—cost less than $15,000 to develop. Creativity need not be expensive. Creativity is highly cost-effective.

Let's review some hard data to demonstrate that point. Two of the companies in which the author helped introduce creativity programs, United Technology and Federal Express, realized a high return on investment (ROI) from their creativity programs. Federal Express achieved a factor of two ROI, or 200 percent. The ROI for United Technology was even higher, a factor of six. You see, when we are dealing with mental capability there are few limitations. Management in most companies would be excited about a procedure simplification that cut purchasing costs 20 percent, or a manufacturing machine that enables an increase of productivity of 50 percent. These kinds of improvements are limited by manual dexterity or metal fatigue or even the speed of light in a computer microchip. Mental dexterity has none of these limitations. By changing the pathway of neural connections, humans can short-cut thought patterns faster even than nanoseconds. A creative idea can change an entire process, perhaps even eliminate it. A creativity program is the most cost-effective of all programs, even more than a quality improvement program or a new marketing program. A creativity improvement program can provide the approaches to make these other programs more effective. It can enable employees to derive entirely new ways of providing quality or developing unique marketing approaches. The creativity improvement program can be the foundation that enables all other company programs to be effective.

Back to the question of the manager in my presentation. Yes, it may take more time to reach a solution to a problem when we allow

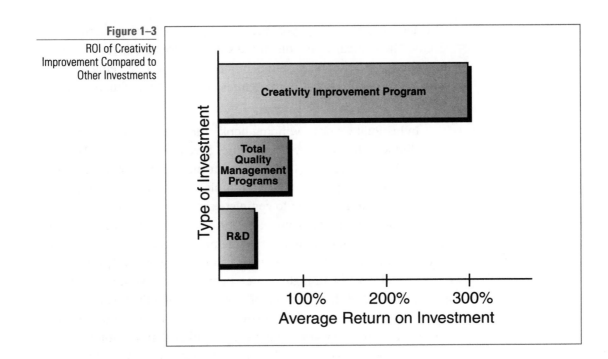

employees the time to consider more alternatives. For example, I encourage designers of computer applications to pause at four points in the system development process and use a creativity technique to ensure that they have considered a variety of solution possibilities before moving on to the next stage of development. I find that the four additional steps lengthen the development process by one-half of 1 percent. The additional time, however, enables the design team to consider richer solutions. Companies using this approach have produced systems that are much more effective than the original design. The ROI is substantial. So, for relatively small increases in development time—of a computer system or product design or a marketing program or a financial plan—huge ROI is possible. Even more important, such improvements can provide a company the competitive edge it needs to retain a marketing niche or acquire a new niche in the market. Figure 1–3 shows how the ROI on creativity in the typical company far exceeds that for research and development and for programs like Total Quality Management (TQM).

Let's depart from the discussion of programs and concentrate on the individual, the person who is enabled to be more creative and hence more productive. By providing persons (the first "P" in the Four-Ps model of creativity) the time and the techniques they need to consider a larger realm of possibilities, we produce two important results. The company benefits in the ways described above. But the individual also benefits—in terms of job satisfaction, of being able to more nearly realize his or her potential. It's a win-win situation for the individual and the company.

In his Pulitzer-prize winning book, *The Soul of a New Machine,* Tracy Kidder tells the story of a product development team at Data General, brought together by a talented team leader to create a state-of-the-art new computer.[28] Like most projects of this type, they underestimated the time required to complete the project. They were under great pressure from management because another team was working on a competing project; the least viable project would be canceled on a specific cut-off date. Three engineers came in to work early one evening and worked all night. When they left the next morning, they had accomplished three months of work. Although they had difficulty explaining how they were able to accomplish this prodigious task, it was obvious that they applied a creative, rather than brute-force, approach. People can accomplish quantum-leap types of thinking if they use their innate creative ability. There are constraints on the amount of work that can be accomplished when we get to the routine part of the job, like writing computer codes or detailing engineering drawings or developing a procedure for sales personnel. That's because we are following a traditional pattern of thinking to complete a project. In the earlier stages of a project, the planning or design part, some order of magnitude improvements can be made through creative thinking. The human mind is unlimited in its possibilities. Too seldom, however, do we fully utilize our capacities. We need processes that help us release this creative potential.

At the turn of the century, the philosopher William James observed that normal, healthy people function at 10 percent or less of their capacity. In 1966 anthropologist Margaret Mead placed it at 6 percent and the most recent estimate by psychologist Herbert Otta is closer to 4 percent. It is clear that we all use only a fraction of our potential.[29]

Conclusion

In the Introduction, I discussed the Four-Ps model of creativity and provided a graphic depiction of the relationship of the three Ps of person, process, and product. The use of a Venn diagram for this figure showed how the three Ps were contained

Figure 1–4

Three-Dimension
Representation of
Four-Ps Model
(The Plane Representing
Press Slices through
(Intersects) the
Other Three Ps.)

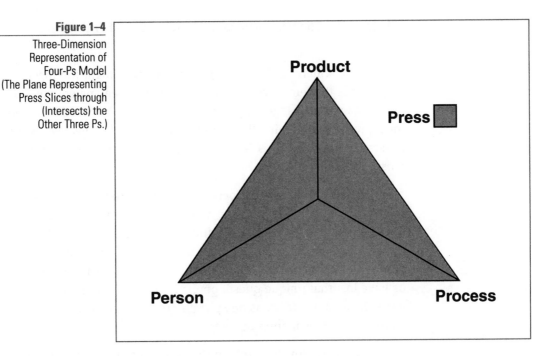

within the fourth P, environment. While the illustration accomplished
my objective, its depiction was somewhat misleading because it
implied that creativity occurred only where the three circles over-
lapped. The three-dimensional diagram, Figure 1–4, more accurately
depicts the relationships by showing that the three dimensions of creativity merge to a common point of connection, that they do not operate in isolation. The fourth P, press, is depicted as a plane that cuts
through the other dimensions. This is an accurate portrayal, because
in actuality press impacts each of the other three dimensions. The
majority of this chapter dealt with the first P, person. It also discussed
product by explaining the cost-effectiveness of creativity. Process was
illustrated through the description of the development of three breakthroughs from the Nayak-Ketteringham book.

Let's spend a few minutes thinking about the fourth P, because
this book has its primary emphasis upon improving creativity in business and industry. If we are working for a business organization, we
cannot avoid being impacted by the business climate or environment.
Hopefully, the climate will be supportive of our creative efforts.
Unfortunately, in many cases it is not. In these cases, we are more
inclined to be innovative rather than creative. The problem is common
to many organizations, necessitating a full chapter on that topic

(Chapter 11). The book will concentrate on the other three Ps until that point.

In the widely read *Changing Times*, editor Knight Kiplinger emphasizes that employers in the 1990s will be seeking employees with "imagination, ingenuity and creativity."[30] To be creative, a person must produce something that is unique and useful. However, everyone possesses creativity. This God-given talent needs to be resurfaced for most persons.

For the 1990s, businesspeople must be more inventive and innovative to enable their companies to gain a competitive advantage. Management can concentrate on hiring and selection to employ persons with proven creativity. However, it is more important to enable the existing workforce to become more creative. By adulthood, most of us have lost that unique questioning attitude we had in our preschool years. Instead, we tend, as one person put it, "to have a diarrhea of words and a constipation of ideas."

The Center for Research on Creativity and Innovation at the University of Colorado, Colorado Springs, investigated a number of disciplines to determine if creativity-generating techniques were in use. A number of successful techniques were identified, and the appropriate ones have been transported to the business field. Therefore, high potential exists for creatively undergirding the activities of U.S. firms to enable them to compete more effectively in the 1990s than they did in the 1980s.

This book will not only change how you perceive your own creativity, but will also strip creativity of its mystique. You will, perhaps for the first time, see endless possibilities stretching before you.

Vincent Ruggiero sums up this view eloquently: "As a child you probably enjoyed throwing pebbles in a still pond and watching the ripples reach out farther and farther until they touched the shore. Through those ripples the tiniest pebble exerts an influence out of all proportion to its size. So it is with ideas. Every discovery, every invention, every new perspective or interpretation makes an impact whose extent is seldom fully realized at first."[31]

This book utilizes the spiral approach to pedagogy. The first five chapters cover the principles, definitions, concepts, and models of creativity, with examples to provide understanding. The remaining chapters provide more depth in each of the topics covered in Chapters 1 through 5.

The primary objective of this book is to enable you, the individual, to better utilize your natural, God-given creativity. A secondary, but also very important, objective is to enable you to work more creatively in groups of two or more persons.

Summary

Research has shown that individuals can be taught to be more creative, that creativity is not some ephemeral, illusive quality but a capability that clearly exists and can be improved through better understanding and practice. Although there are many definitions of creativity, the most common premise is that creativity consists of two elements, uniqueness and utility. There are also a variety of models of creativity. The Four-Ps model (person, process, product, and press) is used in this book because it provides the best framework from which to both analyze and improve creativity.

There are many myths about creativity, most of which cause a person to underestimate his or her creative potential. For example, the myth of accidental discovery, indicating that many inventions are accidents, overlooks the reality that most inventions result from a methodological, systematic process. Breakthroughs have other things in common; first, the investigators expected a creative result. They went into the project with the realization that they were creative individuals and that they could generate unusual and useful ideas.

Most people use the terms *creativity* and *innovation* interchangeably. However, innovation is much narrower in scope. It is the process by which new ideas are put into practice. Creativity is much broader in scope. Creativity is involved in each step of the process of discovery, invention, and innovation.

Although it may take longer to achieve a solution when an individual or group utilizes creativity techniques, they will produce more ideas and analyze more alternatives. The result is a more cost-effective solution, one that is more likely to provide the company with a competitive advantage. The process is also more satisfying to the individuals because it enables them to better utilize their innate potential.

Creativity is quite cost-effective.

Dunagin penned a cartoon that shows a boss standing in an office talking to his subordinates, saying "We've been ordered to cut back on paperwork—write smaller." Our creativity need not be limited to incremental improvements; the examples in this chapter show that we have the potential to make major improvements.

The next chapter demonstrates the use of creativity techniques in facilitating personal and group creativity. It provides the incentive to delve more deeply into the process of exploiting one's creative capacity.

What on earth would a man do with himself if something did not stand in his way?

H.G. Wells

Dreams, not desperation, move organizations to the highest levels of performance.

Robert Waterman

Exercises

1. Identify the four conditions for creativity as identified by Newell, Simon, and Shaw.

2. For the business environment, the definition of creativity consists of two elements. What are they?

3. Explain the components of the Four-Ps model of creativity.

4. How many studies have shown that creativity can be taught?

5. What are the myths about creativity?

6. The book *Breakthroughs* describes 13 examples of major improvements through creative efforts. What three things were in common with all 13 breakthroughs?

7. What is bisociative thinking?

8. The Introduction describes the principal objective of this book. What is it? How is the objective to be met?

9. How cost-effective is creativity compared to other kinds of improvements in organizations?

10. The section on Objectives to Part I explains the spiral approach to the book. How is the book arranged to accomplish that effect?

11. Start a notebook that you'll use all term. It will be useful not only in organizing and reinforcing the material you've studied, it will also help stimulate ideas to make you a more creative thinker. Frederick Holmes, a historian of science, studied the notebooks of Claude Bernard, Hans Krebs, and Antoine Lavoisier. Keeping notes on his own thinking made him aware of what he described as an "activated state—a rapid flow of ideas which were provoked by the sustained immersion in a work."[32] Note-taking is an important aspect of creative endeavor.

Fig. 1.   *Fig. 2.*

Zipper

Patent No. 504,038 (1893)
Whitcomb L. Judson of Chicago, Illinois

"My invention relates to clasp lockers or unlockers for automatically engaging or disengaging an entire series of clasps by a single continuous movement.

The invention was especially designed for use as a shoefastener; but is capable of general application wherever clasps consisting of interlocking parts may be applied, as for example, to mail-bags, belts, and the closing of seams uniting flexible bodies ....By moving the guide, so that the separate parts of the clasp enter the respective channels or cam-ways at the front of the guide, the entire series of clasps will be delivered from the other or rear end of the guide properly engaged together."

2

> *Inspiration is the impact of a fact on a well prepared mind.*
> Pasteur

Techniques for Facilitating Creativity

Chapter 1 concentrated on ways of understanding creativity: concepts, definitions, and models as well as illustrations. This chapter concentrates on structured techniques for facilitating creativity. First, we review the idea of structured creativity. Then, six examples of structured techniques to facilitate creativity are explained and illustrated.

Structured versus Unstructured Creativity

The idea of structure in creativity is abhorrent to some, who believe the best way to generate more creative approaches is to reduce the structure in an individual's thinking process. In literature, for example, one school of writers (including Rousseau and Benet) stresses "spontaneity and inspiration," belying any methodical process that brings a creative work into being. Poetic writings would appear to be the epitome of such a view. The French poet Alfred de Musset described his writing of *La nuit de mai* where, after a whole month of unproductiveness, he was suddenly overwhelmed by inspiration and completed, with astonishing speed, the poem about the muse of the May night. He claimed such occurrences were common in the composition of his poems. This claim was disputed when, after his death, researchers found portions of his manuscripts. For example, in one manuscript was a version of *La nuit de mai* that "differed substantially from the one finally printed."[1]

Carl Fehrman's book *Poetic Creation: Inspiration or Craft* documents the views of several writers who emphasize the importance of inspiration in their work. Samuel Taylor Coleridge went even further than de Musset, reporting that his famous poem *Kubla Khan* came to him in a dream induced by opium. Several years after his death, an early manuscript of the poem was found. Like the de Musset manuscripts, this one showed differences from the published version, leading Elisabeth Schneider in her book *Coleridge, Opium and Kubla Khan* to express considerable skepticism about Coleridge's account of composition in his dream. She comments that "a poem of four or five lines can conceivably be verbalized automatically in a dream but that a composition of the length of *Kubla Khan*—over 50 lines—and with such a stable structure and intricate rhyme—can scarcely be entirely the product of a spontaneous dream improvisation."[2]

Writers who do not hold with the claims of the "inspirationists" include William Morris, who said, "Talk of inspiration is sheer nonsense; there is no such thing. It is a mere matter of craftsmanship."[3] Even more vitriolic was Ezra Pound, who said "Any damn fool can be spontaneous."[4] Edgar Allan Poe had similar views. In discussing the origin of *The Raven,* he said, "It is my design to render it manifest that no one point in its composition is referable either to accident or intuition—that the work proceeded, step by step, to its completion with the precision and rigid consequence of a mathematical problem."[5] French poet Paul Valery "frequently expressed doubts about the fruits of spontaneity and...suspects that all sudden ideas can be improved upon." Poets like Pound, T.S. Eliot, and Robert Lowell shared this opinion and were united in Pound's view that "technique and not spontaneity is the test of sincerity."[6] Stephen Spender, in his book *The Making of a Poem,* explains his method was to write down as many ideas as possible in his notebook. A notebook of a hundred closely written pages might result in six completed poems.[7]

One might think that composers of music would be even more inclined to inspiration. Julius Bahle, in his study of the creative psychology of modern musicians, summarizes the attitude of the interviewed composers: "The...fact that the ideas arise suddenly does not tell us anything about their value."[8] Richard Strauss said that it is exceptional for an absolute melody to arise spontaneously. "I file them away," said Strauss about his musical ideas.[9] Tchaikovsky had similar views: "Inspiration is a guest that does not willingly visit the lazy."[10] The composer Gnecchi reported, "I often write down four or five ideas before I decide on one of them."[11]

Fehrman concludes, "The precondition for such phenomena of inspiration...is the training, practice and preparation the artist has acquired through years of contact with his/her medium—be it language, music or color.... A generation of intellectualist writers who regard writing as work or even as a service to society are far more attracted to an aesthetics of work than to the myth of inspiration."[12]

So, even in a field where one might expect little structure (like written or musical composition), inspiration occurs only after substantial effort. Yet, in a field such as business, with considerable emphasis on structured approaches, it is useful to try to *un*structure the thought process in order to produce some new ideas and perspectives. Just as in the fields of written and musical composition, there are structured approaches to ensuring the unstructuring of the typical thought process to produce some unique and valuable results. Several techniques for idea generation—structured techniques for unstructuring the thought process—will be introduced and illustrated in this chapter. A number of additional techniques will be introduced in the remaining chapters of the book.

Structured Techniques for Facilitating Creativity

Some believe that structuring the creative problem-solving process inhibits creativity. Others, like Herbert Simon, believe the process can be facilitated:

> Science does not demean phenomena by explaining them. Creativity is no less challenging or exciting when the mystery is stripped from the creative process. The most beautiful flowers grow under careful cultivation from common soil. The most admirable products of human effort flourish when ordinary knowledge is nurtured by the solid process of problem solving. Creativity is understandable, but no less admirable for that.[13]

In the past 30 years, a number of techniques have been developed to facilitate unlocking an individual's innate creativity to stimulate creative ideas. The objective is to force persons to move out of their normal problem-solving mode to enable them to consider a wider range of alternatives. Creativity techniques, "when applied conscientiously and repeatedly, will help awaken and strengthen...creative potential."[14] The use of creativity techniques "demystifies creativity and helps convince new innovators that they can build upon, modify and combine existing ideas..."[15]

Some persons well known for their creativity resorted to rather bizarre approaches to stimulate those creative impulses. Most of the following examples are cited in *Stimulating Creativity* by Morris Stein.

> Emile Zola pulled the shades at midday to work in artificial light.
>
> Loménie worked in a room of shadowy darkness.
>
> Kipling wrote only with the blackest ink he could find.

Ben Jonson performed best drinking great quantities of tea, while stimulated by the purring of a cat and the strong odor of orange peel.

Schiller kept rotten apples in his desk and immersed his feet in ice-cold water.

Shelley and Rousseau remained bareheaded in the sunshine.

Bossuet worked in a cold room with his head wrapped in furs.

Milton, Descartes, Leibnitz, and Rossini lay stretched out.

Tycho Brahe and Leibnitz worked secluded for very long periods.

Thoreau built his hermitage to be alone.

Proust worked in a cork-lined room, Carlyle in a noise-proof chamber.

Balzac wore monkish working garb and liked to work at night with strong black coffee.

D'Annunzio, Farnol, Churchill, and Frost also worked only at night.

Picasso could not paint well unless someone was in the studio with him.

Guido Reni could paint and de Musset could write poetry only when dressed in magnificent style.

Mozart worked best following exercise.

Wagner composed music best while stroking velvet.

Fortunately, most of us do not have to resort to unique and unusual approaches to find ways to stimulate our creativity. A number of methods and techniques have been developed to facilitate the creative process.

Edward de Bono is one of many individuals who developed methods to help thinkers produce novel ideas in response to a problem, and thereby generate a fresh way of looking at it that results in a creative solution. These methods are designed to help an individual break away from old habits of thinking and produce ideas in response to a problem that one would ordinarily not produce. This in turn is intended to present the thinker with new combinations of ideas or fresh ways of viewing the problem. To use de Bono's analogy: vertical thinking involves making an old hole deeper, while lateral thinking involves digging a new hole. Sometimes, according to de Bono, to find treasure, you may have to dig a new hole.[16]

As described in Chapter 1, five major studies have demonstrated that creativity can be improved through use of creativity techniques. These techniques have been classified several ways. Harvey Brightman classified them according to Simon's three-stage process of problem solving: intelligence, design, and choice.[17] Arthur VanGundy classified them by individual and group techniques.[18]

Neither classification is adequate because a number of the techniques fit into several categories of either of these two classifications. For example, a technique may be useful in each of the three stages of problem solving, so the Brightman classification does not delineate the techniques. The VanGundy classification is insufficient because a technique useful for helping an individual generate ideas might also be useful for group idea generation. I prefer a two-scale classification of analytical versus intuitive. It is even more useful to think of a continuum where analytically oriented techniques are at one end and the intuitively oriented techniques are at the other end. The analytically oriented techniques use a structure to generate a logical pattern of thought. William Miller explains that analytically oriented techniques "take advantage of different ways of organizing known information to help you approach problems from new angles...and tend to follow a linear pattern or sequence of steps." Intuitive techniques, according to Miller, tend to skip steps in a sequence, that "rely on a single image or symbol to provide a whole answer all at once...to arrive at solutions by a leap."[19]

The intuitive approach was illustrated in a creative analogy by Vargiu, when he described the behavior of a thin layer of iron filing in the presence of a magnet:

> At first the field is too weak to set the iron particles in motion. They are held in position by friction. As the intensity of the magnetic field increases, some of the iron particles overcome friction and begin to move, interacting with the nearby granules in a way that increases the overall magnetization. This in turn sets other particles in motion, accelerating the process and

starting an 'avalanche effect' or 'chain reaction' which causes the pattern to suddenly form itself, independently of any further approach of the magnet.[20]

It is not surprising that technical people are predisposed toward the use of analytical techniques and behaviorally oriented people toward the intuitive techniques. Nevertheless, a wider range of solution possibilities can be derived if both types of techniques are applied. Both help us keep our options open, forcing divergence to consider many alternatives before convergence on an acceptable solution. Even Albert Einstein, generally believed to be the ultimate analytical thinker, used what he called "mental experiments" to stimulate new perspectives and ideas. For example, he once imagined himself as a tiny being riding through space on a ray of light—which helped him develop his general theory of relativity.[21]

Illustrating the Use of Creativity Techniques

Over the course of the book, some 20 creativity techniques will be explained and illustrated. Appendix I provides a description of each technique, with an example of its use. In this chapter, six of these techniques will be explained and illustrated:

Analytical	Intuitive
1 Progressive abstraction	4 Associations/images
2 Interrogatories (5Ws/H)	5 Wishful thinking
3 Force field analysis	6 Analogy/metaphor

Analytical and intuitive techniques will be illustrated for a variety of activities. The objective is to show how the use of these techniques help produce ideas that would not have occurred through traditional problem-solving approaches. Each technique is described, then illustrated. First, I need to provide some background on the approach to providing illustrations.

My objective is to demonstrate the value of creativity techniques on real problems for a variety of activities. Creativity improvement studies were conducted in the following application areas: 1) shortage of qualified employees for a fast-growing, internationally based commercial software development firm, 2) evaluating pilot tests for a new system in a leading express mail company, 3) determining key implementation factors for a creativity improvement program in an electronics firm, 4) reducing programmer/analyst turnover in an insurance company, 5) developing an enterprise model for a microelectronics manufacturing firm, and 6) improving receptivity to CASE (computer-aided software engineering) tools for a firm in the petroleum industry. For each example, I describe the application background, the use of the creativity technique and the results.

Progressive Abstraction Technique

Developed by Greschka and others, the progressive abstraction technique generates alternative problem definitions by moving through progressively higher levels of problem abstraction until a satisfactory definition is achieved.[22] When a problem is systematically enlarged in this way, new definitions emerge that can be evaluated for their usefulness and feasibility. Once an appropriate level of abstraction is reached, possible solutions then can be more easily identified. The major advantage of the technique is the degree of structure provided the problem solver for systematically examining problem substructures and connections.

Using Progressive Abstraction

A commercial software development firm was growing at a rate that dictated the need to plan more explicitly for hiring. A long-term and successful approach had been to hire recent college graduates in computer science or information systems. This source appears questionable for the future. The baby boom era is past; U.S. population growth is on the decline. Fewer persons will enter the workforce beginning in the 1990s. A second factor affecting the entry-level pool is a reduction in the number of persons entering degree programs in computer science or information systems. This trend has existed since the late 1980s. The combination of these factors is expected to produce a serious shortage of entry-level personnel. Using a traditional problem-solving approach, the problem would be broken down (abstracted) into subproblems: identifying new sources for hiring, improving recruiting effectiveness, and improving the selection process. The traditional problem-solving approach would then break these three subareas into lower levels of detail (lower levels of abstraction). However, use of the progressive abstraction technique led the employee acquisition planners through higher levels of abstraction as well.

Figure 2–1   Use of Progressive Abstraction Technique for Identifying Solution Space

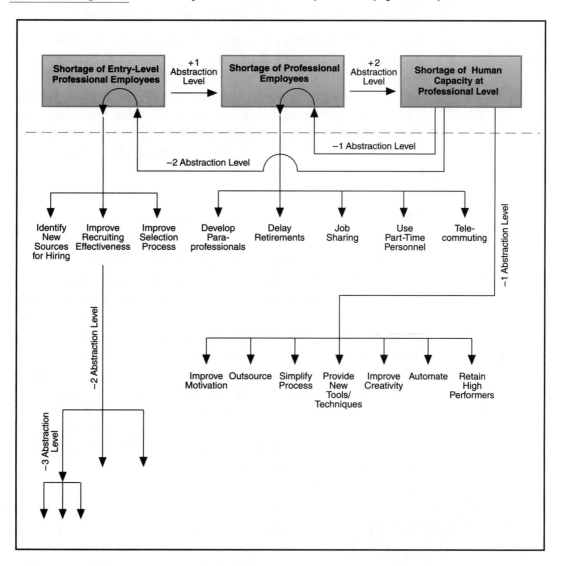

Figure 2–1 shows the next higher level of abstraction (plus-one level) to be the shortage of all professional employees, not just entry-level personnel.

Next, that broadened problem definition was also broken to the minus-one level of abstraction. The planning team began to identify many other approaches to resolving the problem. Five subareas delineated for further abstraction were 1) developing paraprofessionals, 2) delaying retirements, 3) job sharing, 4) use of part-time personnel, and 5) telecommuting. This step illustrates how the progressive abstraction technique utilizes abstraction in both directions.

Next, the problem was abstracted upward to the plus-two level of abstraction, broadening it to one of a shortage of human capacity, not just one of headcount. The shortage can also be counteracted by increasing productivity. The downward (minus-one) abstraction at this level produces seven additional solution possibilities: improving motivation, outsourcing, simplifying processes, providing new tools/techniques, improving creativity, automating, and avoiding turnover of high performers.

Results

By using all 3 levels of problem definition, 15 approaches were identified to reduce the effect of the smaller pool for entry-level employees. Stated another way, by moving to the higher levels of abstraction, solution space was increased from 3 to 15 subareas. The plus-one level of abstraction expanded the solution set from three to eight. The plus-two level of abstraction resulted in a problem definition that identified seven additional areas for analysis. Even though solution of problems defined for the first and second levels of abstraction was outside the area of responsibility of the planners, they produced a solution set useful for the entire firm. Organizations responsible for solving the problems defined at abstraction levels one and two could then use other creativity techniques to generate ideas for resolving their respective employee resource problems.

Interrogatories (5Ws/H) Technique

Asking who-what-where-when-why-how questions aids in expanding an individual's view of a problem or opportunity. The objective is to ensure that all related aspects have been considered. The technique dates back to a poem by Rudyard Kipling:

> I had six honest serving-men,
> They taught me all I knew.
> Their names were What and How and Why
> and When and Where and Who.[23]

The 5Ws/H technique provides a framework for systematically gathering data relevant to identifying and solving the problem. By going through several cycles of the 5Ws/H, alternatives related to the problem/opportunity can be explored exhaustively.

Using Interrogatories (5Ws/H)

An express mail company was considering piloting a new software program. The program could improve service levels significantly; however, if implemented poorly, it could produce the opposite result. On the other hand, a pilot test would delay implementation of the application in a tightly competitive industry. Some team members believed that a pilot was unnecessary. After an hour of discussion, the project leader remarked, "We've been arguing for an hour but don't seem to be anywhere near an agreement. I suggest we use the 5Ws/H technique to make sure we have thoroughly considered all aspects of the problem. The technique will help us better organize our evaluation so we can reach an agreement."

In Round One, the group used the questions associated with the 5Ws/H to identify the reasons for conducting a pilot test.

Round One: Reasons for Conducting a Pilot Test

1. Why would the pilot test be useful?
2. How would we evaluate the results of the test?
3. When should the test be conducted?
4. Where would the test be conducted?
5. Who are the key persons to be involved in the test?
6. What specific things would be included in the test?

Next, the group answered the questions and determined that the test would be beneficial. They then considered whether the benefits of the pilot test would offset the disadvantages of delaying implementation of the software. They developed a second round of questions to provide a comprehensive analysis of the disadvantages.

Round Two: Disadvantages in Conducting the Pilot Test

1. What loss in competitive advantage would occur through the delay in implementation?
2. Who in the marketing department could best provide information on the advantages of early implementation?

3. How might we enhance the unit and integration tests to provide assurance of system integrity?

4. Where could we get a proven list of factors to ensure effective implementation without having to conduct a pilot test?

5. When would be the ideal time to implement the system to reduce the probability of problems?

6. Why are we assuming that this activity is any more complicated than others that have been implemented satisfactorily without a pilot test?

After answering the questions developed in Round Two, the team had the basis for a complete and accurate evaluation of the pros and cons of the pilot test.

Results

In answering the two rounds of questions, the team recognized the need for additional questions, or subrounds. The author's experience is that three rounds can provide a framework for analyzing the typical problem or issue. The group believed that the forced question set caused them to take a more complete and comprehensive approach to both problem identification and resolution.

Using the 5Ws/H technique facilitates a questioning process similar to that of preschool-age children. The education field has documented the loss of creativity in school children, culminating in the "4th grade slump" [Torrance, 1968]. (This phenomenon will be explained in more detail in a later chapter.) The conformity required in school gradually sublimates the natural curiosity so obvious in 5-year-olds. With the help of the 5Ws/H technique, business professionals have greater assurance that they have fully explored an issue.

Force Field Analysis Technique

The force field analysis technique was developed by Kurt Lewin.[24] Its name is derived from the ability to identify forces contributing to a problem or hindering its solution. The technique stimulates creative thinking in three ways: 1) defines direction (vision), 2) identifies strengths to be maximized, and 3) identifies weaknesses to be minimized. The following steps are used:

1. Write a brief statement of the problem to be solved.

2. Describe what the situation would be like if everything fell apart—absolute catastrophe.

3. Describe what the situation would be like if it were ideal.

4. With catastrophic at the left of the continuum and ideal at the right, draw a center line.

5. On the continuum, list the forces that are contributing to make the situation more ideal and those contributing to make it more catastrophic.

The primary function of force field analysis in idea generation is to present three different stimuli for thinking of new options or solutions. Because the field represents a kind of tug-of-war, there are three ways to move the center line in the direction of the more desirable future:

1. Strengthen an already present positive force.

2. Weaken an already present negative force.

3. Add a new positive force.

Force field analysis provides focus for exploring possible solutions.

Using Force Field Analysis

An electronics firm decided to implement a creativity improvement program. As a pilot program, a workshop on creative problem solving was conducted for two of the firm's work units. One month later, the units met with the workshop facilitator to discuss progress. The discussion revealed that the climate for creativity needed improvement. The force field analysis technique was selected as a framework for determining how to enhance the environment for creativity.

The discussion led to the following definition of the problem: "How to ensure that creativity techniques are utilized." Accordingly, the facilitator asked the group to describe a catastrophe situation related to the problem, which the group identified as "minimal use of creativity techniques despite training in the techniques and availability of creativity resource materials." The group then formulated a statement for the ideal situation, selecting "use of creativity techniques in everyday activities, for all employees."

Next, the group discussed the forces "tugging" toward the catastrophic result and those "tugging" toward the ideal result. Figure 2–2

Problem: How to ensure creativity techniques are utilized

Catastrophe:	Optimum:
Minimal use of creativity techniques despite training and availability of published materials	Use of creativity techniques in every-day activities, for all employees

Forces

(–)	(+)
Incorporated in standards manual but not enforced.	Used for all functions.
Managers do not use creativity techniques themselves.	Managers demonstrate value by use of creativity techniques in their own activities.
No change in ways department runs its meetings.	Meeting procedures changed to include creativity approaches.
Training not reinforced.	Follow-up sessions held regularly.
Little recognition given to employees for creative ideas.	Management gives high visibility and recognition to creative employees.
Creativity skills not stressed for advancement.	Skill list for promotion includes knowledge of creativity techniques.
Creativity not rewarded.	Bonuses and salary increases provided to demonstrated creativity.

shows the results of the force field analysis. Each of the factors identified were placed on the organization's agenda for determining ways to strengthen the present positive force and weakening the negative force.

Results

Every factor under the "ideal forces" category was implemented. Creativity techniques were added to the standards manual and were among the factors evaluated in system reviews. Managers worked diligently to demonstrate the value of creativity techniques in their own activities. Meeting procedures included creativity approaches. For follow-up, employees read an assigned article on creativity each month. A discussion leader's role was rotated each month, with emphasis upon how the content might apply to the department's situation. Recognition for creative accomplishment was given within the department and also at higher management levels. The knowledge and use of creativity techniques became one of the skills required for advancement in the organization. Annual performance reviews included an evaluation of creative accomplishment.

The firm's employees had a number of positive comments about their first year with the creativity program. One said it had been the most exciting period of his career. Another said, "We find ourselves less constrained in our thinking." Use of the techniques was not confined to internal operations, as illustrated by the comment of one employee: "When I've scheduled a meeting with our clients, I try to think of one of the creativity techniques that might be appropriate for some portion of the agenda." The success of the organization's creativity improvement program led the Vice President of Operations to ask this department to conduct similar programs for other areas of the company. Unquestionably, the best indicator of success was the improvement in the department's client ratings at the end of the first year of the creativity improvement program. Six of the seven factors rated showed improvement; the overall rating improved by 20 percent, mid-way between "excellent" and "outstanding" on the rating scale.

Associations/ Images Technique

The associations/images technique builds on our natural inclination to associate things. The linking or combining process is another way of expanding solution space. A classic example is George de Mestral, a Swiss inventor who went hunting one day in the late 1940s. He and his dog accidentally brushed up against a bush that left them both covered with burrs. When de Mestral tried to remove the burrs, they clung stubbornly to his clothes.

This would be a minor annoyance to most of us, but de Mestral was curious about why the burrs were so hard to remove. After he got home, he studied a burr under his microscope and discovered that hundreds of tiny hooks on the burr had snagged to the threads of his pants. Burrs, he thought, would make great fasteners. After several years of work, he finally succeeded in replicating this concept. The result: Velcro fasteners, now used on items as diverse as blood pressure cuffs and tennis shoes.[25]

The procedure for using the associations/images technique is as follows, based on an approach used by Gordon:[26]

1. The leader assists the group in identifying the problem or opportunity to be examined (if required).
2. The leader asks the participants to select a solution to the problem, phrased in the form of a goal or wish.
3. The leader picks a key concept central to the goal/wish statements.

4. The leader asks the group to think of a world that is remote from the world of the problem. (The leader chooses the remote world.)

5. The leader requests the group to lay aside both the problem and the goal/wish developed in Steps 1 and 2 and to list associations and images that characterize the remote world.

6. The leader directs the group to relate the list of associations and images of the remote world to the world of the problem.

7. The leader directs the group to develop second-generation associations and images from any one of those listed in Step 6, extracting key principles and applying them in a more realistic way without diluting the innovation.

8. The group selects and implements appealing ideas developed in Step 5.

Using Associations/Images

Most companies experience the highest level of turnover among professional employees during the second and third year after college graduation. Exit interviews identify three principal reasons: 1) employees begin to realize their value—they are on the downward slope of the learning/orientation curve and recognize that they are making substantive contributions; 2) annual salary increases for good performers rarely exceed 15 percent, whereas it is not unusual to be able to attain a 20 to 30 percent increase by changing companies; 3) a variety of other factors, such as lack of recognition, politics, poor feedback, and unrealistic work demands.

One department of an insurance company established a task force to try to reduce turnover in general, and specifically in the 2-to-3-year category for their professional employees. The group was not excited about the assignment. They felt that the turnover problem had been worked on many times previously and that little new light could be shed on the problem. One commented, "Here, in a city where many organizations are located within a two-mile radius, you can change jobs without changing your carpool. You're never going to be able to reduce turnover significantly."

Because of the seeming creativity blockage, a facilitator suggested that the group try the associations/images creativity technique. He suggested that the approach would take them far afield from their normal problem-solving modes and might provide a fresh outlook on the problem. However, prior to initiating the creativity procedure, the group decided that item two under reasons for turnover was outside the control of the company; it couldn't give salary increases to match the increases normal for changing to another company. They concentrated on factors to help in items one and three.

Use of the association/image procedure went as follows:

1. **Problem**: High turnover of personnel.

2. **Select a goal/wish**: Reduce the turnover of professional employees (PEs) between their 2nd and 3rd year to the level for other points in their career.

3. **Pick a key concept from the goal/wish**: Reduce turnover.

4. **Think of an example from a world that is remote from the world of the problem**: Hollywood.

5. **Forget about the problem and the goal/wish and focus associations or images that describe the remote world**:

big dollars	Oscars	critics
acting	rich	parties
Beautiful People	drugs	commercialism
divorces	big dreams	silicone
agents	casting couch	lack of fulfillment
powerful people	*National Enquirer*	

6. **Use these examples to develop related ideas for PEs**:

   Oscars: Statues, plaques for high performance.

   Parties: Social activities to improve rapport.

   Divorces: Keep work demands realistic, provide counseling.

   Agents: Provide mentors to help PEs plan careers, give encouragement.

   Acting: Try to diminish politics, shelter PEs from these effects. Concentrate on the politics essential to their progress.

   Critics: Ensure positive feedback to temper necessary negatives in performance review. Make sure mistakes made do not remain on the employee's permanent record; some people leave because they think they could never change people's minds.

   Big dreams: Develop fast-track programs for exceptional performers, help others determine realistic goals.

   Casting couch: Work to ensure performance evaluation.

Drugs: Help PEs lessen their addiction to reading help-wanted ads by doing a better job of publishing career paths available in the firm.

National Enquirer: Counteract help-wanted ad lure of "greener pastures" by better delineating the strengths of career paths in our firm vs. other principal competitors for employees.

Big dollars: Help PEs understand the true cost of job change: learning/orientation curve, loss of work friends, loss of seniority, relocation costs, need to re-prove oneself.

7. **Develop second-generation ideas from any one of the above ideas, extracting key principles and applying them in a more realistic fashion without diluting the innovation**. The group chose to develop ideas from each of the associations/images it derived. Space limitations prevent recording all their ideas. Ideas generated from one of the above, Awarding Oscars, will be illustrated.

Awarding Oscars: Behavioral research on professional employees shows that managers provide insufficient recognition. The group identified 12 forms of low-cost yet quite effective recognition: verbal commendation at monthly staff meeting, bulletin board announcements, E-mail announcements, letter for permanent employee file, dinner for two, "attaboy and attagirl" awards, plaques, certificates, show tickets, lunch with your boss, $50 gift certificates.

8. **Pick ideas that have appeal from the second-generation ideas**. The task force decided that all of the ideas were useful and that the full set should be provided to management to enable recognition to occur in a variety of ways. They produced recommendations for the remaining 17 items on the associations/images list, as they had done on the one for Awarding Oscars. Two to three suggestions were made for each of the 17 items.

Results

Using the associations/images technique helped the task force overcome their belief that the turnover problem had been analyzed so often that few new ideas were possible. A report on the results was provided to the executive who approved the task force recommendations. Meetings were held with managers to review the recommendations and to demonstrate top management's concern in implementing them. Turnover was significantly reduced, both in the 2nd-3rd year category and for other categories. However, because other factors also had impact on turnover (such as the national recession), it was not possible to determine precisely the impact of the task force recommendations.

Wishful Thinking Technique

The wishful thinking technique is particularly useful for people who typically take a very analytical approach to problem solving. It enables them to loosen their analytical parameters to consider a larger set of alternatives than they might ordinarily consider. It is designed to permit a degree of fantasy in the solution process, and this loosening-up may result in some unique approaches. By taking unusual positions to start the problem-solving process, a perspective might arise that would not ordinarily be brought forth. VanGundy developed a procedure for use of the technique:[27]

1. Develop a problem statement.

2. Open up the solution space to all possibilities—*i.e.,* assume *anything* is possible.

3. State the alternatives in terms of a wish or a fantasy. Examples: "I wish that I could be able to…," "What would happen if we tried…," or "What really needs to be done is…"

4. Convert each wishful statement to a more practical one. Examples: "How about our…," "Assuming that we could get around the starting constraint, what might be the advantages…," "It may be possible to meet our wish, but first we would have to…," or "Perhaps our wish is not as farfetched as we first thought; what if we tried…"

5. Move on to the normal analytical problem-solving approach to developing a solution.

Using the Wishful Thinking Technique

The systems department of a microelectronics firm was examining approaches to developing an enterprise model for the company. While the department was in the midst of discussions with vendors and consultants about different approaches, the company's CEO attended a seminar on the Hoshin planning technique. This technique is comprised of seven planning techniques for solving business problems. He conveyed his enthusiasm about these techniques to his senior managers.

Picking up on the CEO's interest, the systems department manager pulled together a group of professionals to explore how they might respond. They decided to use the wishful thinking technique to combine the two needs of developing an enterprise model and a new business planning technique. In Step 1, they chose to deviate from modeling the present business and, instead, to concentrate on modeling the "ideal" business. From Step 2 of the wishful thinking procedure came the additional "wish" to identify opportunities to re-engineer the company's business process flow. They developed a series of "what if" questions related to these wishes (Step 3). Then, following Step 4 in the procedure, they converted each "wishful" statement to a practical one. Finally, they formulated an approach for integrating the techniques of Hoshin planning, enterprise modeling, and re-engineering processes (Step 5).

Results

After receiving senior management's enthusiastic approval of their recommendation, the systems department organized a working session with the operations group, resulting in the identification of 16 major business processes. Next, senior management approved their request to organize 16 working groups of 6 to 10 people with the task of further analysis of subprocesses. The groups consisted of personnel from different organizational areas of the firm. Each group met for four intensive sessions to carry out the assigned tasks. In the first meeting, subprocesses were identified and grouped according to natural relationships between these processes. In the second meeting, the subprocesses were further refined and organized into a hierarchy. The third meeting identified the data flows between the major subprocesses and the 16 processes. The fourth meeting developed a matrix, mapping the subprocess groupings and the systems needed to support them.

Based on this foundation, the systems department was able to develop an enterprise model. This model helped identify re-engineering opportunities. The manager was directed by the CEO to reconvene each of the 16 groups and identify differences between the model and the current company environment. The groups each selected a representative to participate in the final companywide prioritization. The results were given to senior management who put into place action plans to reconfigure company processes and systems to the target model.

Another important outcome resulted. The integrated techniques, now referred to as the enterprise model, support management's "wish" to develop a culture consistent with the specifications of the Malcolm Baldrige National Quality award.

Analogy/Metaphor Technique

The development of the analogy/metaphor creativity technique is generally credited to de Bono.[28] However, Aristotle spoke of the value of metaphor almost 2,200 years ago: "Ordinary words convey only what we know already; it is from metaphors that we can best get hold of something fresh."[29] An analogy is a similarity between two things otherwise dissimilar. Analogies serve to "make the familiar strange and the strange familiar." By the use of analogies, an individual or group can often find a new insight and approach to the nature of a problem and thus its resolution. Many analogies are taken from nature. Gordon and Poze give the analogy of a person long ago, who has trouble keeping his pants up, seeing a snake wrapped around a rock, suggesting the first belt.[30] (For a problem "lower" on the clothing chain, think of how the garter snake gets its name!) Gordon was leading a problem-solving session where the problem was to package potato chips compactly without breaking them. The analogy of wet leaves—how they pack snugly together without breaking—led to the innovation of Pringles Potato Chips. Magnesium-impregnated bandages that accelerate healing came from the analogy of a broken electrical wire.[31]

It is not as easy to develop an analogy for the creative problem-solving process as it is for some other creativity approaches. VanGundy facilitated the process by originating a procedure, which follows:[32]

1. Withholding all evaluation, generate a list of objects, persons, situations, or actions that are similar but unrelated to the problem. An example is the use of the resistance or reluctance aspect as the focus for building the list. Some of the possibilities are:

   Reluctance to believe politicians

   Aversion to change

   Dislike of (resistance to) certain vegetables

   Children's resistance to parental control

   Resistance to taking medicine

   Hesitancy to learn a new VCR procedure

   Faulty resistance to adopt a new textbook

   Management resistance to conduct performance reviews

   Consumer resistance to try a new product when the old one still meets their need

2. Select one of the analogies and describe it in detail. Try to accomplish this step without relating to the original problem.

3. Examine the items generated and translate them into statements that apply to the problem or opportunity being analyzed.

4. Examine each statement and discuss its application to the problem or opportunity.

The procedure typically produces a broadened perspective on the issue at hand, and typically leads to an expanded solutions set.

Using Analogy/Metaphor

The Information Systems department of a firm in the petroleum industry was experiencing difficulty in motivating employees to adopt a new technology, Computer Aided Software Engineering (CASEtools). CASEtools simplify the development of computer applications. The department had a long-standing policy of including a selected set of system development techniques in the standards manual and permitting development teams to utilize the technique they preferred. Management wanted more employees to utilize CASEtools to improve the consistency of system development and to move toward the integration provided by the Information Engineering approach.

The department manager made members of the technology assessment group responsible for encouraging increased use of CASEtools. A group of managers and subordinates from several units together with a facilitator met to attack the problem. They included CASEtool users and others.

Since other approaches had not been successful in motivating personnel to use CASEtools, the facilitator recommended the use of the analogy/metaphor creativity technique to provide a different perspective. Based on his use of the technique in other companies, he believed that some factors would emerge that would have been overlooked in traditional problem-solving methodology.

Step 1.   The facilitator suggested that the group use the list of analogies described above, on resistance or reluctance aspects.

Step 2.   From the list of suggested analogies, the facilitator suggested "Dislike of certain vegetables." He told the group, "We could concentrate on the dislike of brussels sprouts, which has larger numbers in the opposition ranks. However I suggest we use canned spinach because of the long-standing tradition of resistance."

The group identified the following factors related to the dislike of spinach:

> taste—subdued compared to green beans
>
> appearance—dull compared to carrots, squash
>
> aftertaste—slightly sour, compared to baked potatoes or carrots
>
> texture—Chinese enjoy foods that provide texture to "tickle the palate," such as squid or sea cucumber; this culinary ability must be cultivated.
>
> capacity—steals space away from favorite foods
>
> aftereffects—causes flatulence in some persons
>
> cost—higher than some foods, such as rice and beans
>
> time-consuming to chew—compared to mashed potatoes
>
> not elegant—"Popeye" image compared to "beautiful people" image of those who eat caviar
>
> no tradition—compared to grits for southerners, corn on the cob in summer, fried chicken for picnics
>
> aphrodisiac—overrated compared to eggs
>
> healthful—get more iron from breakfast cereal

Step 3.   The group examined each item listed and translated it into a statement that applied to the problem of resistance. The following translation applied to the reluctance to use CASEtools.

1. taste—Some of the pleasurable activities of CASEtools are subdued, less enjoyable than those of the existing methodology.

2. appearance—The thought of using CASEtools is not as attractive as our favorite, proven approach.

3. aftertaste—Results are not as visible, hidden within storage devices compared to the previous system development approach where lots of visible results occurred after each step in the development cycle.

4. texture—Problem of assimilation, cultivating a "taste" or preference for the new methodology of CASEtools.

5. capacity—Prefer some aspect of prior methodology, such as coding or programming logic chart development to tasks imposed by CASEtools.

6. **aftereffects**—Less pride of authorship in the results, less sense of being creative because driven by the system.

7. **cost**—Learning curve is high: manual reading, procedures learning, working out bugs in the CASEtool software.

8. **time consuming**—Lengthy time required to develop data flow diagrams and data dictionary.

9. **elegance**—Less art, more science—loss of elegance in developing unique coding logic or algorithms because the CASEtool translates everything into common logic.

10. **lack of tradition**—Could go to professional meeting and spend hours with peers discussing coding approaches and debugging episodes—with CASEtools, personnel feel more like draftsmen than engineers.

11. **aphrodisiac qualities**—Most persons are not turned on by the opportunity to use CASEtools; considered more like a cold shower than an aphrodisiac.

12. **healthful**—Conversion to CASEtool use is not necessarily seen as improving one's health, that is, one's security within the department.

Step 4. The group examined each item in the list of problems and suggested an approach to counter or lower the resistance. For improved CASEtool acceptance the following approaches were suggested.

1. Emphasize the ability to experience other pleasurable activities, such as more time to spend on designing the system, to build a more sophisticated system, with the saving in time over the traditional development cycle. Incentives could be provided for persons who make the conversion to CASEtool use.

2. With the acquisition of state-of-the-art development knowledge, personnel are more mobile, have higher job security.

3. A loss of visibility in the final product, such as documents produced by the life cycle method, is offset by graphs of the user surveys showing improved user satisfaction, graphs of development schedule compliance, and graphs of improved cost-effectiveness.

4. Trade-off from the comfort level of long experience in the use of the prior methodology to a higher comfort level through knowledge that the design is better, with the assurance of a more valuable result for the company.

5. Despite the prior preference for certain tasks in the life cycle development methodology, the higher performance ratings on design accomplishments enable faster career progression.

6. A pride in accomplishment occurs because some weak areas are strengthened, such as improved accuracy in cost/schedule estimating due to standardization of activities in development. The improved effect on the company bottom line (through more cost-effective applications) is visible to many people compared to the mere self-satisfaction acquired through writing an elegant subroutine.

7. Once the learning curve is overcome, the process of development is speeded considerably. Applications are not only implemented sooner and revised more easily, the risks of not meeting specifications are reduced. The ease in making revisions because everything is now stored saves the boring time in manually revising data flow diagrams, programming revised procedures.

8. Data flow diagram/data dictionary development time is offset by reducing the time-consuming tasks of documentation and coding under the prior life cycle development methodology.

9. Rather than reduce a feeling of professionalism, the revision in time allocation to the development activities allows personnel to be primarily designers rather than programmer/analysts.

10. Designers will feel more at home in management-oriented professional society meetings than in programmer-oriented meetings, talking about the "effect on the company of my systems," comparing design approaches, acquiring a management perspective. There is a de-emphasis on loyalty to the profession and new emphasis upon loyalty to the company that expands one's circle of relationships from a few "coding techies" to many persons within the company.

Results

The group normally would have resorted to brainstorming as a means to accomplish its assigned task. While brainstorming assures production of a large number of ideas, it does not ensure that all facets of the problem have been addressed. The group believed that the forced question-set caused them to take a more complete and comprehensive approach to both problem identification and resolution.

Conclusion
The preceding section concentrated on the "how" in use of creativity techniques. Implicit in those descriptions were the "when" and "where" of use of these techniques. "When" becomes more explicit by taking a vertical slice through the organizational functions. The "where" question becomes explicit by taking a horizontal swath across organizational activities. All functions (vertical slice) can be improved with the use of creativity techniques. It is also my experience that all phases of an activity (horizontal swath) can utilize creative techniques. I've had the opportunity to use these techniques in a variety of organizations and have not yet found any company activity immune to their use.

When to Use Creativity Techniques

At the top of the vertical cut are the macro-level strategic activities. At the bottom are the micro-level operational activities. The example of developing an enterprise model represents the strategic area. The wishful thinking technique facilitated the team's modeling of the ideal business. An analytic technique, such as the interrogatories (5Ws/H) is then useful in fleshing out the characteristics of the ideal business.

The example of using analogies/metaphors to improve receptivity to CASEtools is an illustration for intermediate, tactical functions. A second example was the use of 5Ws/H for determining the feasibility of a pilot test. To illustrate further, we apply associations/images to help analysts better understand client needs. In addition to the "remote world" of Hollywood described above, I use the "remote world" of "Star Trek."

Participants are asked to identify all the characters in the cast of "Star Trek," to discuss their characteristics and assignments, then to project how this framework causes one to look differently at user needs. I ask participants to think of the difference in approach to user responsiveness by a Commander Data or Spock versus a Counselor Troy or Guinan. Most technical personnel take the analytical approach of Data or Spock. The intuitive approach of Troy or Guinan enables a very different view of clients and their needs.

Although creativity techniques are often thought of as more appropriate for broad-scope activities, perhaps their most important use is in daily activities that tend to become routine. Frequent use helps practitioners obtain a fresh perspective on frequently performed functions. For example, a metaphor could be used to force an individual to view his/her job with a "fresh eye." We use the nursery story of the Three Little Pigs to help employees look at client relationships from a different viewpoint. We ask them to place themselves and clients in the roles of the pigs and wolf, then evaluate present ways and generate new ways to interact with users. We ask them to think of the relationship of the construction of the three pigs' houses and the way they build solutions to meet client needs.

Where to Use Creativity Techniques

Are the techniques most useful at the start of an activity or do they apply to all phases? The latter is true—techniques add value not only in "kick-starting" a project or activity but also in providing breakthrough thinking when an impasse occurs in the midst of a project. Using the development of computer applications as an illustration, a variety of creativity techniques can be used at four key points in the system development cycle (requirements definition, logical design, physical design, and program design), to ensure that a full range of alternatives is considered at each stage. The earlier examples illustrate this point. Creativity techniques are useful in the initial stages of a project, as the example of the use progressive abstraction in problem definition demonstrates. Another example described above was the use of the associations/images technique to resolve the problem of high turnover of personnel in the second to third year of employment. Creativity techniques are also useful in later stages of a project, as illustrated by the description of the use of force field analysis in planning implementation of a creativity improvement program.

Figure 2–3   Matrix of Solution Approaches: Six Creativity Techniques to Flesh Out 15 Solution Approaches for Shortage of I.S. Professionals in the 1990s

Solution Approaches	Progressive Abstraction	5Ws/H	Force Field Analysis	Wishful Thinking	Associations and Images	Analogy and Metaphor
Improve recruiting effectiveness	X	X	X	X	X	X
Identify new sources for hiring	X	X	X	X	X	X
Improve the selection process	X	X	X	X	X	X
Develop paraprofessionals		X	X	X	X	X
Delay retirements		X	X	X	X	X
Job sharing		X	X	X	X	X
Use part-time personnel		X	X	X	X	X
Telecommuting		X	X	X	X	X
Improve motivation		X	X	X	X	X
Outsource functions	X	X	X	X	X	X
Simplify processes		X	X	X	X	X
Provide new tools and techniques		X	X	X	X	X
Improve creativity	X	X	X	X	X	X
Automate		X	X	X	X	X
Retain high performers		X	X	X	X	X

Creativity techniques are commonly used in the midst of problem solving or opportunity delineation. After definition and fact finding, the techniques are used to help generate ideas.

This chapter illustrates that a rich array of techniques is available to facilitate the creativity process. Figure 2–3 shows how versatile the creativity techniques can be. Although some techniques, such as progressive abstraction, are somewhat specialized, the others could be used to generate creative ideas to exploit all 15 solution approaches for the problem of shortages of professionals in the 1990s. For example, the first solution area, improving recruiting effectiveness, could use any of the six different creativity techniques to assist in fleshing out the solution.

Figure 2–4 pictures the Swiss army knife, a graphic reminder of the intent of this chapter. Like the variety of functions served by the Swiss army knife, a wide variety of techniques can facilitate and enhance our native creativity.

Figure 2–4

The "Creativity Tool Kit"
Has a Variety of
Techniques to Handle a
Multitude of Problems
and Opportunities, as Does
the Swiss Army Knife

Source: Joyce Faust/The Bettmann Archive.

Summary

Chapter 2 concentrated on the second "P" of the Four-Ps model of creativity: process. Creativity techniques provide a structure to help individuals resurface their innate creative potential. I've identified 20 techniques useful in other disciplines and have transported them over to the business field. The techniques have been classified as either analytical or intuitive in their orientation. The analytical process tends to be linear while the intuitive process enables leaps, bypassing blocks of linear steps. The analytically oriented techniques described and illustrated were progressive abstraction, interrogatories (5Ws/H), and force field analysis. The intuitively oriented techniques were associations/images, wishful thinking, and analogy/metaphor. Although the intuitively oriented techniques help us better use our intuition and imagination, they utilize a procedure to do so. In other words, both types of techniques use structured approaches to help us unstructure our thought processes.

It is enigmatic that some pre-20th century writers and composers felt obligated to demonstrate to both peers and public that their works came primarily from "inspiration and spontaneity." Many 20th-century writers, composers and artists seem more disposed to demonstrate that their creativity requires considerable "suffering" to reach fruition. Although persistence and fortitude are often required for successful creative results, fortunately those of us in the field of business rarely need to "suffer" to achieve creative solutions. We have proven techniques to help us reactivate the creative abilities that we all demonstrated naturally in our preschool years.

> Keep on going and the chances are you will stumble on something, perhaps when you are least expecting it. I have never heard of anyone stumbling on something sitting down.
>
> *Charles Kettering*

> Other people see things and say 'Why?'...But I dream things and say, 'Why not?'
>
> *George Bernard Shaw*

Exercises

1. Explain the distinction between analytical versus intuitive creativity techniques.
2. What was the negative consequence of placing so much emphasis upon the need for inspiration in the fields of art and literature?
3. Develop one-sentence descriptions of the six creativity techniques described in this chapter.
4. Explain when and where to use the various creativity techniques.
5. The author's wife, who is a musician and artist, said she felt like throwing up when she saw him using the term *structured creativity*. She says that creativity requires spontaneity and inspiration. What is the justification for using the concept of structured creativity?
6. There are some similarities in the approaches of force field analysis and the interrogatories techniques. What are they?
7. Explain how one of the six techniques applies to an assignment you had in one of the courses you took in college.

Polaroid Camera

Patent No. 2,435,720 (1948)
Edwin H. Land of Cambridge, Massachusetts

"This invention relates to photography, and more particularly to apparatus for bringing photographically exposed photosensitive film material and individual sheets of another preferably nonphotosensitive material into operative assembly and for spreading a processing liquid within the assembly of materials by providing a predetermined compression thereof."

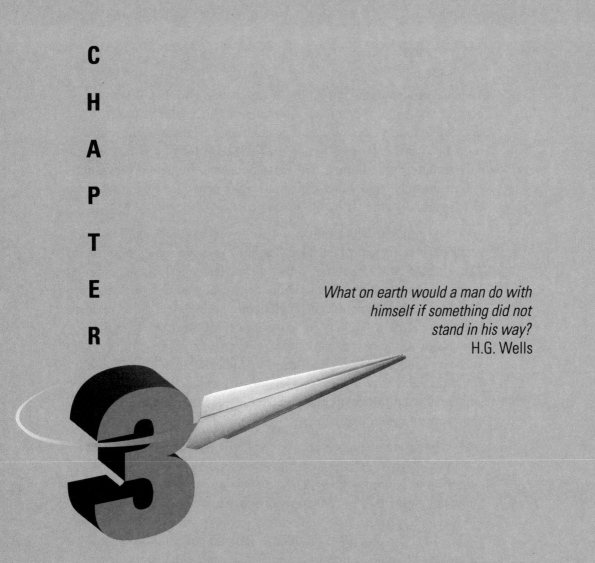

What on earth would a man do with himself if something did not stand in his way?
H.G. Wells

Removing the Barriers to Creativity

The goal of identifying opportunities and defining problems is to become completely open to all alternatives. This goal is virtually impossible to meet because all humans build up blocks in the maturation/socialization process. Some of those blocks have external causes, such as family environment, the educational system, and organizational bureaucracy. Other blocks were internally generated by our responses to external factors or by physical factors.

A key to improving ability to identify opportunities and to solve problems is to recognize our blocks so we can begin to demolish them. These blocks have been studied by several researchers in the field of creativity. Parnes summarized them under two headings: anxiety about our ideas and conformity/habit-bound thinking.[1] Shallcross identified five categories of barriers to creativity: historical, biological, physiological, sociological, and psychological.[2] The most complete analysis of the blocks was developed by James Adams. In his book *Conceptual Blockbusting,* Adams identifies the blocks as perceptual, emotional, cultural, environmental, and intellectual, and describes approaches to eliminating them.[3]

While everyone has blocks to creativity, blocks vary in quantity and intensity from individual to individual. Most of us are not even aware of our conceptual blocks. Awareness not only allows us to know our strengths and weaknesses better but gives us the necessary motivation and knowledge to modify or break down these blocks (see Figure 3–1). The objective is to help us expand our solution space. Following are some examples of conceptual blocks that served as blinders for thinking:

Flight by machines heavier than air is unpractical and insignificant, if not utterly impossible.

Simon Newcomb, an astronomer of some note, 1902

It is an idle dream to imagine that...automobiles will take the place of railways in the long distance movement of...passengers.

American Railroad Congress, 1913

There is no likelihood man can ever tap the power of the atom.

Robert Millikan, Nobel prize winner in physics, 1920

Figure 3–1 It Is Necessary to Break Down Common Blocks to Creativity to Reach One's Creative Potential

There is no reason for any individual to have a computer in their home.

Ken Olson, President of Digital Equipment
Corporation, 1977

Min Basadur has identified other perceptual blocks. So have Eugene Raudseep and Morris Stein. I built on the factors cited in the work of Adams, Basadur, Raudseep, Shallcross, and Stein to explain the blocks of creativity under the following categories of perceptual, emotional, cultural, environmental, and intellectual.[4]

Blocks to Creativity

Perceptual Blocks

Perceptual blocks are obstacles that prevent us from clearly perceiving either the problem itself or the information needed to see the problem. Most of us have seen graphic evidence that we do not always perceive things accurately. For example, answer these questions about the symbols below.

Figure A – Which of the lines is longer? ____

Figure B – Are the two vertical lines parallel? ____

Figure C – Are the vertical lines parallel? ____

Figure D – Are the circles in the center of the two groups the same size? ____

Answers

Figure A: Both lines are the same length.

Figures B, C, and D: The answers are all "yes."

Our eyes deceive us in observing these figures. Our perceptions are not accurate. We need to be aware of the following perceptual blocks in order to begin the unblocking process.

1. Accepting as "facts" data that are really unsubstantiated assumptions.
2. Difficulty in isolating the problem—inability to separate the basic problem from apparent or related problems or cause from effect.
3. Narrowing the problem too much—missing the "big picture."
4. Broadening the problem too much—the inability to break large, complex problems into small, component problems.
5. Failing to use all the senses in observing—overreliance on sight.
6. Difficulty in seeing remote relationships.
7. Prematurely assuming the nature of the problem—the inability to understand that the same situation may give rise to diverse goals, motives, and problem definitions for different people and circumstances.
8. Overemphasizing solutions rather than defining the problem—the unsupported belief that "I know what the problem is."
9. Failing to observe and consider "trivia" and failing to investigate the "obvious."
10. Working with false data—using concepts derived from one field in another where they don't apply.

Emotional Blocks

Emotional blocks interfere with our freedom to explore and manipulate ideas. They prevent communicating our ideas in such a way that others will accept them. Shallcross called these blocks the psychological barriers. She believes them to be the most significant and prevalent barriers, "if we define a barrier as a factor that impedes progress or restricts free movement."[5] Examples of emotional/psychological blocks are:

1. Fear of making a mistake, of failing, of risk-taking; inordinate desire for security.
2. Inability to tolerate ambiguity.
3. Preference for judging ideas rather than generating them. If we judge too early, we will reject many ideas. This is detrimental for two reasons: 1) newly formed ideas are fragile and imperfect and 2) ideas lead to other ideas.
4. Inability to relax, incubate, and sleep on it.
5. Lack of challenge—the problem fails to engage interest.
6. Fear and distrust of supervisors, associates, and subordinates.

7. Difficulty in changing our mind-set (inflexibility and dependence upon biased opinion).

8. Excessive zeal—overmotivation to succeed quickly.

9. Overly strong desire for "closure"; inability to use "deferment," to reject one workable solution or viewpoint and continue searching for a better one.

10. Unwillingness to take detours to reach goals.

11. Lack of drive in carrying problems through to solution and test.

12. Negative attitudes toward new ideas.

13. Premature assumption that "it can't be done" or "I'm not a creative person."

Cultural Blocks

Cultural blocks are acquired by exposure to a given set of cultural patterns. Adams believes that "our culture trains mental playfulness, fantasy and reflectiveness *out* of people by placing stress on the value of channeled mental activities… A four-year-old who amuses himself with an imaginary friend, with whom he shares his experiences and communicates, is cute. A 30-year-old with an imaginary friend is something else again!"[6] Examples of cultural blocks are the following:

1. Taboos

   Ellen J. Langer, in her book, *Mindfulness,* illustrates a taboo:[7] Start by moistening your mouth with your saliva, from the back of your teeth to the tip of your tongue. It should be very wet, smooth, and comfortable. It should feel pleasant because a moist mouth is a natural and healthy condition. Next, take a little paper cup or glass and spit some of that saliva into the container. Now, sip it back in. What is your response? Disgust? Why? It is your own body fluid. You just had it in your mouth two seconds ago. And yet, we learn cultural rules when we are young (spitting is nasty and unhealthy, and to be spat upon is an insult) that bound our behaviors and set our actions such that even thinking about sipping our own saliva revolts us.

2. Belief that indulging in "fantasy" (imagining) is a waste of time or immature

3. Reason, logic, numbers, utility, and practicality are *good;* feeling, intuition, qualitative judgments, and pleasure are *bad.*

4. Any problem can be solved by scientific thinking and lots of money.

5. Overly strong desire to conform to accepted patterns, to "belong." Tradition is preferable to change.

6. Desire to be "practical" and "economical" above all things, so that judgment comes into play too quickly and ideas with some merit are discarded because they are imperfect rather than built upon

7. Feeling that it is "not polite" to be too inquisitive, or, worse, to express doubts or to express ignorance or ask "Why?" about matters that seem to be accepted or "known" by everyone else

8. Desire for the safety of the known, the familiar

9. Too much or too little knowledge of the field of work involved

10. Tendency to follow the "all-or-nothing" attitude. Inability to compromise ideas.

11. Stereotyping—assuming facts about situations and people based on preconceived notions from categorizing from previous experience and hearsay.

12. Fear of asking questions that show ignorance

13. Belief that problem solving is serious business and humor is out of place. Playfulness is for children only. An environment of playfulness and humor has been proven to be very creative. Recent research has shown that laughter releases natural endorphins that give a person more energy and lead to increases in creative ideas.

Environmental Blocks

Environmental blocks are imposed by our immediate social and physical environment. Organizational climate or culture can be a barrier or a stimulus to creativity. The organization can provide a nurturing environment or one that represses creativity. However, the organization involves many elements, such as managers, teammates, subordinates, clients, and competitors. All need to be considered to measure environmental blockage to our creativity. Some of the blockage elements are these:

1. Lack of cooperation and trust among colleagues

2. Autocratic bosses who values only their own ideas and do not reward others

3. Distractions—phone, easy intrusions

4. Lack of support to bring ideas into action

5. Overemphasis on cooperation or on competition

6. Punishment for risk-taking that doesn't work out

Intellectual Blocks

Intellectual blocks are caused by an inefficient choice of mental tactics or an unwillingness to use new solution approaches. Through these blocks our identification of alternatives and choices of strategy are limited significantly. Examples of intellectual blocks are the following:

1. Strong tendency to use only those solution methodologies that worked previously

2. Reliance on logical thinking. Many people in the business world are primarily left-brain, logical thinkers.

3. Hesitancy to use intuitive thinking approaches. Left-brain thinkers can train themselves to use the right hemisphere of their brain more effectively and produce a wider range of solutions to a problem.

4. Too much faith in "statistics" and "past experience" so that new ideas are prematurely "mentally tested" in the abstract rather than tried out

5. Superficiality—shallowness, incompleteness, and haste in thinking and problem solving

6. Inability to abandon an unworkable approach

7. Fear of exploring the unknown

8. Mind-sets

9. Functional fixation, where a single function becomes firmly fixed in our minds so that we remain mentally blind to other possible uses, extension, or modification possibilities

10. Rigidity and uniformity, where habitual actions result in convergent rather than divergent thinking

11. Paradigm fixation, where we have difficulty viewing things outside our normal view of the world

12. Betriebsblind—what the Germans call "company blind": how a person who has worked in a particular company for some time fails to see problems in new ways

Once we are aware of our conceptual blocks, we can begin to tear them down. Doing so will enable us to identify a myriad of alternatives and possibilities that were hidden to us previously. We are reminded of human shortcomings in this respect by a poem by Emily Dickinson:

We Never Know How High

We never know how high we are
Till we are called to rise
And then, if we are true to form,
Our statures touch the skies.
The heroism we'd recite
Would be a daily thing,
Did not ourselves the cubits warp
For fear to be a king.[8]

Paradigm Trap

Paradigm is a Greek word meaning "a pattern or set of rules that defines boundaries." Adam Smith defined a paradigm, in his *Powers of the Mind,* as a shared set of assumptions. He explained: our paradigm is "the way we perceive the world; water to the fish. The paradigm explains the world to us and helps us to predict its behavior...." He concludes: "When we are in the middle of the paradigm, it is hard to imagine any other paradigm."[9]

The concept of the paradigm was introduced to the scientific world by the scientific historian Thomas Kuhn. Kuhn wrote that scientific paradigms are "accepted examples of actual scientific practice, examples which include law, theory, application, and instrumentation together—[that] provide models from which spring particular coherent traditions of scientific research." He adds: "Men whose research is based on shared paradigms are committed to the same rules and standards for scientific practice."[10]

Kuhn's objective was to help scientists be open to new paradigms, to remove their conceptual blocks. He spoke of how difficult this task is:

> The man who embraces a new paradigm at an early stage must often do so in defiance of the evidence provided by the problem solving. He must, that is, have faith that the new paradigm will succeed with the many large problems that confront it knowing only that the older paradigm has failed with a few. A decision of that kind can only be made on faith.[11]

Kuhn's work is difficult reading, even for experienced scientists. Fortunately, Kuhn's work was translated into layperson language by Joel Barker. In the rest of this section, we summarize Barker's explanation and, where appropriate, quote him.

"A paradigm, in a sense, tells you that there is a game, what the game is, and how to play it successfully. The idea of a game is a very appropriate metaphor for paradigms because it reflects the need for borders and directions on how to perform correctly. A paradigm tells you how to play the game according to the rules."[12]

All of us are urged to be "paradigm shifters." The paradigm shifter plays the role of catalyst, of change agent, and stirs up a lot of thinking in the prevailing paradigm community. "The community acknowledges that the problems on their shelf should be solved. They know they are not solving them. They also know that the paradigm shifter has offered an alternative way of thinking about these difficult and important problems. Yet the community continues to defend the prevailing paradigm, because it is still very successful."[13]

Barker goes on to say that: "In the midst of this ambiguity, a few members of the prevailing paradigm community begin to assess the suggested *new* paradigm in an unusual way. You hear phrases like:

> "You know, the more I examine these rules, rudimentary though they are, the more interesting they seem."

> "There is something clever about the way these rules approach these intractable problems."

> "I like the elegance of this approach."

> "I don't know what it is, but there is something special going on here."

These musings reflect a kind of judgment being made about the new paradigm that is "not quantitative but qualitative." An even better word to use is *intuitive*. "There are many phrases for this kind of decision making: gut-level; seat-of-the-pants, from the heart, a gestalt."[14] He thinks the most appropriate description, however, is "intuitive." Intuitive judgment is the ability to make good decisions with incomplete data.

Figure 3–2 shows a list of words that represent subsets of the paradigm concept. They form a spectrum from the "challengeable to the unchallengeable." Look at the words and think about the boundaries and rules and regulations for success that are implicit in them.[15]

Our paradigms act as *physiological filters*—we see the world through our paradigms. This means that any data that exists in the real world that does not fit our paradigm will have a difficult time getting through our filters. The data that does fit our paradigm not only makes it through the filter, but is concentrated by the filtering process. Thus, we create an illusion of even greater support for the paradigm.

Figure 3–2 Concepts as Paradigms and Relative Difficulty in Changing Those Paradigms

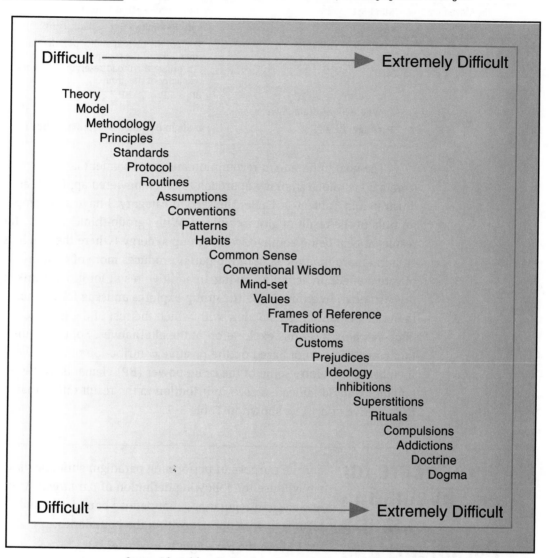

Difficult ⟶ Extremely Difficult

Theory
Model
Methodology
Principles
Standards
Protocol
Routines
Assumptions
Conventions
Patterns
Habits
Common Sense
Conventional Wisdom
Mind-set
Values
Frames of Reference
Traditions
Customs
Prejudices
Ideology
Inhibitions
Superstitions
Rituals
Compulsions
Addictions
Doctrine
Dogma

Difficult ⟶ Extremely Difficult

Source: Adapted from Barker, J. A., *Future Edge* (New York: William Morrow and Co., 1992), p. 72.

Therefore, what we actually perceive is dramatically determined by our paradigms. What may be perfectly visible, perfectly obvious, to persons with one paradigm, may be quite literally invisible to persons with a different paradigm. Barker call this the "Paradigm Effect."

The result of the paradigm effect is illustrated when people say, "That's impossible." Those two words can be translated to, "Based on the paradigm we are practicing right now, we don't know how to do it."

Table 3–1	**Constrained Thinking**	**Empowered Thinking**
The Move from Constrained to Empowered Thinking	"Mind-Set"	Mind-Reset → Mind Unlock
	"Group-Think"	Group-Rethink → Synergistic Thinking
	Delimited Thinking	To pool the mental ability of individual members of the group. To utilize the broad reservoir of mental capacity of the group.
	$BP_1 + BP_2 + \ldots BP_n$ (Where BP = Brain Power)	$BP_1 \times BP_2 \times \ldots BP_n$
	"Paradigm Paralysis"	Paradigm Breaking → Paradigm Shift

The goal in paradigm recognition and improvement is to move from a constrained thinking approach to an empowered approach as illustrated in Table 3–1. Under the second category, I have an example formula of the result of group thinking. With "group-think" I show the results at best being additive, while group synergy (where the whole is equal to more than the sum of the parts) produces more of a multiplicative effect. In actuality, giving an additive result for group-think is unwarranted. In group-think, the group explores an issue for a time, then one person presents a view with which the rest of the group concurs—without a serious exploration of the alternatives. So, the resultant conclusion is not based on the positive contribution of all members. Therefore, some of the brain power (BP) elements in the equation should indicate a zero contribution to the result rather than the additive effect I've shown in Table 3–1.

Procedure for Evaluating Existing Paradigms and Developing New Paradigms

For the purpose of performing paradigm shift analysis, we will use the following definition of *paradigm*: A set of rules and regulations that defines boundaries and tells us how to operate within the boundaries.

1. **Choose the paradigm to evaluate**.

   Criteria:

   a) Where problems exist

   b) Where competitors have performance advantages

   c) Where new efficiencies are needed

   d) Where the paradigm has not been evaluated recently

2. **Examine the purpose of the paradigm**.

   What does it accomplish, in what circumstances does it apply, to whom does it apply?

3. **Delineate the parameters related to the paradigm being examined**.

   Assumptions, explicit rules/implicit rules, procedures, resources utilized, constraints

4. **Examine the rationale for the parameters**.

   Validity of the assumptions, reasons for the rules and procedures, validity of perceived constraints

5. **Question the paradigm: is it still appropriate**?

   Have changes in related factors invalidated the paradigm?

   New technology available

   Improved skills and qualifications of personnel

   Different business conditions

   Revised organizational structure

   Improved management practices

6. **Develop an improved paradigm**.

   Utilize approaches from the reservoir of 22 creativity techniques (Appendix) to enable paradigm-shift thinking, concentrating on the question: "If we had never done this process (activity, task) before, how would we accomplish it most effectively and efficiently?"

Resurfacing the Questioning Process We Had as 5-Year-Olds

Recently on a flight to Phoenix, I sat in front of a five-year-old. He was seated next to a window and the minute he took his seat, he began a barrage of questions to his parents. He continued as we took off and never let up (except during the snack!). I noticed his parents switched seats halfway through—to take turns handling the questions. I was especially intrigued by one of his questions. We had reached an altitude where we were above the clouds and he soon exhausted his questions about the clouds. He couldn't find much interesting out the plane window and after a few minutes said, "Why don't they have little TV sets in the back of the seat in front of me so I have something to do until we get back below the clouds?" A great product idea—not original but excellent! United Air Lines experimented with that idea in the early 1970s. I remember being on a flight where my set was working and the one next to me was not. I was irritated when the person next to me wanted me to turn on my set so he could view it, while I wanted to read. He was in a center seat so I was not very interested in giving up my window seat so he could watch TV in my preferred seat. Because of the difficulty of keeping the sets operational, the airline removed them. However, because of the improved reliability of today's TV sets, individual sets are becoming available in first class.

Even though the idea was not original, the five-year-old had come up with a viable product idea, thanks to the questioning attitude normal for that age. Oh! To be able to return to the creativeness of our fifth year in life.

That natural inquisitive quality has been socialized out of most people by the time they become adults. Research in the field of education shows that the education acquired before age six enormously exceeds what we are taught in school. In other words, the questioning attitude of the child causes him or her to assimilate an enormous amount of information in just a few years.

The educational and developmental processes most people go through, while ostensibly preparing them for the responsibilities of adulthood, nevertheless manage to conventionalize them to a point where lively curiosity and wonder almost cease to exist. In addition (or perhaps as a consequence), many adults have a deep distrust of curiosity, imagination, and fantasy making. They often show this dislike by a trigger-ready tendency to criticize or dismiss thoughts that cannot be defended by facts or logic. This closed-mindedness conditions much of our social environment with a timid cautiousness, preventing many valuable ideas from taking root.[16]

Educational research shows that children begin to lose that natural curiosity and inquisitiveness as soon as they enter school. As mentioned earlier, research shows that creativity is normally distributed, as is IQ. However, the educational process changes that distribution. The results of studies conducted by Dacey and Ripple at Cornell University are reflected in Figure 3-3. The researchers label the normal curve as the scores "unaffected by schooling." The curve with lighter lines reflects the results of their studies. They concluded that there is a "suppressing affect of schooling" powerful enough to affect some of the students: the bottom three-fourths. They hypothesize that the top quarter of students are impervious to the effect; they go on being creative no matter how they are treated in the school system. The Cornell group saw the results as clearly supporting the hypothesis that teachers, especially elementary school teachers, are guilty of suppressing

Figure 3–3

Comparison of Creativity
Test Scores versus IQ Test
Scores for Schoolchildren

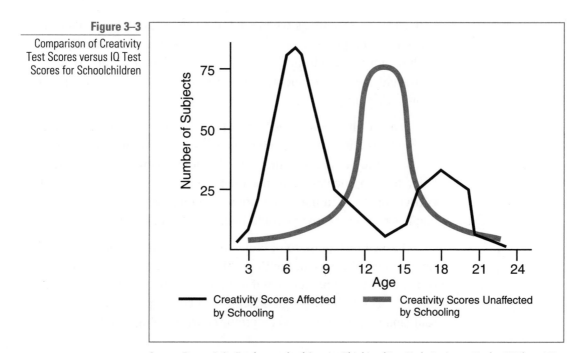

Source: Dacey, J. S., *Fundamentals of Creative Thinking* (New York: Lexington Books, 1989), p. 203.

creativity. Furthermore, the evidence of the problem was demonstrated through tests of creativity, which showed the effects of education on functional fixity.[17]

The principal causes of the loss of creativity:

1. Students are discouraged from inquiry, by the educational process and by parents who are not as patient with questions after a child reaches school age.

2. The educational process concentrates on imparting knowledge, not on continuing the natural process of questioning things.

3. There are pressures to conform, to think in conventional ways.

4. Parents delegate to the school the nurturing behavior used in the home. They think it better to direct the child to other sources: "Look it up yourself." Or, they lose patience and give signals that the questioning process is no longer appropriate, saying things like: "Curiosity killed the cat!"

The creative thinking process continues to diminish throughout school age and into adulthood. It is not surprising that most persons above the age of 18 do not perceive themselves as creative. Most are inclined to believe that creativity is inherited and that we either do or do not possess it. It is documented that we utilize less and less of our native creative ability as we mature and age. Nationwide studies of schoolchildren produce progressively lower scores on creativity tests as they move through the school system. The loss of creativity in school children is documented by test results that show a precipitous "4th-grade slump".[18]

This decline continues into college. A national study of engineering students showed that seniors were less creative than first-year students. A study of architectural schools showed similar results. The latter study particularly surprised me. You would think that one of the curriculum areas in the university where there would be particular emphasis upon creativity would be the school of architecture.

I asked this question of Professor Joseph Juhaz of the College of Environmental Design at the University of Colorado, Boulder. He responded that he hadn't seen the study but believed that it is "bound to be true." Through the program, students become professionalized, he said, and their creativity is compromised by learning about constraints:

> building codes
>
> materials
>
> methods of construction
>
> customer taste

Thus their range of creativity diminishes. "As a person becomes socialized to the profession and absorbs its norms, creativity is bound to be reduced," Juhaz said. "On the other hand," he commented, "creativity still may be increased within this narrow range."

The Cornell research group found the more education a person has, the less proficient he or she is in problem-solving skill. They conducted tests on problem solving, finding that about 90 percent of sixth graders studied could solve the typical problem within the 15 minutes allowed. "Eighty percent of ninth graders could do so, 50 percent of college students were successful, and only about 20 percent of graduate students achieved a solution." They conclude that "schools generally do not reinforce creative thinking."[19]

As adults, we need some special prodders, some tools to help us move from the judgmental to the questioning mode. I'll provide some, but also ask you to try to overcome your conceptual blocks and your educational process to try to regain the inquisitiveness you had at age five. I like to use the analogy of volcanic activity to discuss this creative power. That innate power was most noticeable (erupted) in childhood. We went off to school and began to confront things that caused the power to begin to subside; none of the power was lost, it was just pushed below the surface. As when volcanic activity subsides, there is no reduction in power. It remains just as powerful, but is below the surface, unseen by the human eye. Circumstances can cause the volcano to again erupt, releasing fully its strength and power. Although some people can individually find ways to resurface their innate creativity, most of us can benefit by a process that provides techniques to help us resurface and rechannel our creativity.

An example of a person who found a way to channel his creativity occurred in 1845. A man needed money quickly to pay a debt. "What can I invent to raise some money?" he thought. Three hours later, he had invented the safety pin. He later sold the idea for $400. Many of the products we use every day have similar, though perhaps less dramatic, stories. The hammer, the fork, the alarm clock, the electric blanket, the toothpaste tube, the matchbook—these and thousands of other products first occurred as ideas in a creative mind. And new ideas are occurring every day. Two relatively recent ones you may not have heard of are Graffiti Gobbler, a chemical compound that can remove ink or paint from wood, brick, or steel, and the Moto-Stand, a three-wheeled, upholstered, motorized truck invented by a man paralyzed from the chest down. The vehicle permits him to maneuver around the house in a standing position.[20]

Preschoolers are especially good at asking "Why?" They ask it to the point that we often become exasperated! The "why" question is the most important question in creativity. If we continue to ask why, we can get to the root of any problem and identify any opportunity. "What if" questions are also quite valuable. They are the adult counterpart of the child's "Let's play like...."

Reading the data about continuous decline in creativity in the education process is a "bummer," isn't it? Yet, if we diligently concentrate on resurfacing creativity, most of us are able to regain our natural curiosity and inventiveness. Use of a creative process facilitates this restoration of our natural creativity. The good news is that research shows that school children can not only retain their creative ability but enhance it. An approach like the CPS method is one way educators have demonstrated that creative thinking ability can be improved. We'll discuss that proven method at length throughout the remainder of this book.

At this point I want to concentrate on a simple yet profound approach to prepare you to better use your creative potential. This approach is to focus on regaining the natural questioning process that you exhibited at age five—to be curious about everything around you—to quit taking things for granted.

Restoring Our Natural Inquisitiveness

One of the goals of divergence is somehow to restore that natural inquisitiveness we had as preschoolers. We need to regain the questioning attitude that was so spontaneous at that age. I'll provide some examples that demonstrate the fact that most of us do not question things that are commonplace. In the following exercises, try to logically deduce an answer before looking at the answers. Record your answers on the line below the question.

1. Ever wonder why manholes are always round?

   _____

2. Ever wonder why riders mount horses from the left side?

   _____

3. Ever wonder why the racing bike has such an uncomfortable seat?

   _____

4. Ever wonder why the stripes on men's ties almost always slant downward and toward the wearer's left?

   _____

5. Ever wonder how doughnuts got their name?

   _____

Answers

1. If they were any other shape—rectangular, oval, triangular—the cover could be turned so it would fall through the hole. Round covers never do.

2. Centuries ago, most men carried their swords on the left hip, which was easily accessible to the right hand. With a long sword dangling from a rider's left hip, it was easier to mount a horse by putting

one's left foot into the stirrup and throwing one's right leg across the horse's back.

3. It comes from a saddle—it's even called a saddle. Instead of something that has two parts to place our duality on!

4. The reason is largely practical. The four-in-hand knot forces the cloth through tremendous contortions, and cutting the material diagonally across the weave makes the tie more supple. Since the fabric is cut uniformly, the stripes always fall in the same direction.

5. The original doughnut had a nut in the center instead of a hole.

Before discussing some helpful approaches for stimulating curiosity, let's look at what various writers have said about the topic. Michael Ray and Rochelle Myers, in their book *Creativity in Business,* say: "Implicitly or explicitly, creativity always begins with a question. And in both your business and personal lives, the quality of your creativity is determined by the quality of your questions—by the way you frame your approach to circumstances, problems, needs, and opportunities. Preschool children ask dumb questions about everything. We wrote down some questions a four-and-a-half-year-old named Scott asked in less than an hour:[21]

> What's behind a rainbow?
>
> What color is the inside of my brain?
>
> What's inside of a rock? A tree? A sausage? Bones? My throat? A spider?
>
> Does the sky have an end to it? If it doesn't, how come you can see it?
>
> Why are my toes in front of my feet?

You once asked questions like that, too. That's how you learned about the world. But sooner or later your authorities—parents, teachers—gave you the message that such questions were not welcome. You became more careful. Ray and Myers say we internalize adult laughter, scorn, and irritation, and learn to avoid the questioning creative process. Pretty soon the questions stop coming; perhaps cynicism sets in instead.

Ray and Myers advocate asking "dumb" questions! They cite the case of R. Buckminster Fuller, famous architect and inventor of the geodesic dome. "In 1927, 32 years old, he was on the edge of Lake Michigan, reviewing his life with despair: a daughter dead at four; five factories failed. He was facing bankruptcy, with a brand-new baby. Before he did what he came to do—end it all in the water—he entered into a dialogue with himself. He first asked if there was a greater intelligence operating in the universe. Yes, he decided, on the basis of the exquisite design of everything, from the microcosm of atoms to the macromagnitudes of the galaxies. He then asked, 'Do I know best or does God know best whether I may be of any value to the universe?'? In view of the answer he had just forged, he decided that the very fact of his existence meant that he had some purpose, some value. But what? In answer, he found within himself this next, very personal question: 'What does my experience tell me needs to be attended to, which if attended to completely will bring advantage to all humanity, and which if left unattended can very readily have all of humanity in great trouble?'? He turned from Lake Michigan, and spent the next 56 years answering that question, eventually earning the description of 'a twentieth-century daVinci.'"[22]

Czech novelist Milan Kundera believes that "the stupidity of people comes from having an answer for everything. The wisdom of the novel comes from having a question for everything."[23] Mark Steurer, Syntex Corporation, firmly believes that "Creativity has to do with the ability to question," and elaborates in this way:

> How many people in business school get graded highly for keeping questions open, rather than for finding the answers? We're real quick to jump at the answer. Notice how the answer closes out a domain of questioning. Take the guy who invented McDonald's: If he said, "Hey, they already have hamburgers in the world, I don't need to do that," he wouldn't have invented McDonald's. But he questioned, "Where can I get a consistent hamburger on the road?" So that's how he invented McDonald's. Not by having the answer, but by keeping the question open.[24]

Raudseep thinks that creativity is contingent upon the "preservation of the curiosity and sense of wonder that is so apparent in youth, and so conspicuously absent in many grownups." Children have a keen and intense awareness of their environment.

They have a ready feeling of curiosity toward everything they touch or experience. They have a precious
propulsion toward seeking understanding, toward
piercing the mystery they sense in everything they
perceive. The rapt sense of children's wonder and
their avid interest in the minutest details of their surroundings disappears sooner than all the other characteristics of childhood. Only the truly creative
individual manages to retain his pristine sense of
curiosity. And it is this lively attitude of curiosity and
inquiry that enables the creative person to constantly
enrich and add to the store of information and experience that he draws upon when creatively engaged.[25]

The TV show "Why Didn't I Think of That?" is about ordinary people
solving everyday problems with ingenuity and humor. Sample stories
are about the kid who came up with a motorized spaghetti fork and the
smoker who designed a hat to use in non-smoking restaurants (it
covers his head and keeps the smoke inside the hat as he puffs away).
The host, Wink Martindale, says that the "show is more about problem
solvers and their solutions than being about inventors and creators."

According to psychologist Abraham H. Maslow, the really creative person is one who accepts his essentially androgynous character:

This is the person who can live with his unconscious; live with, let's say, his childishness, his fantasy, his imagination, his wish fulfillment, his
femininity, his poetic quality, his crazy quality.[26]

Helpful Approaches for Stimulating Curiosity

Curiosity, useful in every CPS phase of thinking, is
indispensable in the first phase, problem identification—searching for challenges and opportunities.
Curiosity is not confined to the gifted few; all of us
demonstrated boundless curiosity as children.

How can we resurface our natural curiosity?
There's the story of the father and his young son who were walking
down the street one day. The boy asked how electricity went through
the wires overhead. "Don't know," said the father. "Never knew much

about electricity." A little later the son asked why some flowers are red and others are blue. "I'm not sure," said the father. "I always wondered about that myself." After similar responses on the remainder of their walk, the little boy remarked: "I'm sorry I bothered you with all those questions, dad." "That's o.k.," the father responded. "If you don't ask questions, how are you going to learn about everything?"

Yes, we can depend on other persons for curiosity stimulation. Perhaps the results will be beneficial, perhaps more like those of the son in the above story. A better approach is to find ways for self-renewal.

Ruggiero's book, *The Art of Thinking,* suggests some approaches you can use to help regain the questioning attitude:[27]

1. Be observant.
2. Look for imperfections in things.
3. Note your own and other's dissatisfactions.
4. Search for causes.
5. Be sensitive to implications.
6. Recognize the opportunity in controversy.

Another approach is to pay less attention to how others assess your abilities. Winston Churchill was branded a slow learner. Thomas Edison was urged to quit school because he was considered hopelessly stupid. Later, on his first job, working for the railroad, he set a train on fire with one of his experiments and was fired. Albert Einstein's early record was even worse. Here are some of the details:[28]

- He was not only an unimpressive student; he was told flatly by one teacher, "You will never amount to anything."

- At age 15 he was asked to leave school.

- When he took his first entrance exam to Zurich Polytechnic School, he failed it and was required to spend a year in a Swiss high school before he could be admitted.

- At Zurich he did mediocre work and was so unimpressive to his professors that he was rejected as a postgraduate assistant and denied a recommendation for employment.

- He eventually obtained a job as a tutor at a boarding school but was soon fired.

Figure 3–4

The Incongruity of Einstein
as a Football Player Is the
Type of Paradigm-
Questioning Thinking We
Need to Stimulate
Breakthrough-Type
Thinking

Source: Courtesy of Wang.

- He submitted a thesis on thermodynamics for a doctoral degree at Zurich; the thesis was rejected.

- Four years later, he submitted his special theory of relativity for a doctoral dissertation at the university at Bern; it was rejected.

Figure 3–4, picturing Einstein as a football quarterback, produces instantaneous surprise. Few people would think of Einstein in this context. As such, the illustration is a perfect example of the kind of thinking representative of Einstein. He often worked with others, and when their thinking became too confined or they began to use "tunnel vision," he would do something to jolt the thinking. It would have been in character for him to put on a football uniform to shock the group, to stimulate different thought patterns.

Ruggiero comments: "Unlike most people, creative people do not allow their minds to become passive, accepting, unquestioning. They manage to keep their curiosity burning, or at least to rekindle it. One aspect of this intellectual dynamism is playfulness. Like little children with building blocks, creative people love to toy with ideas, arranging them in new combinations, looking at them from different perspectives."[29]

Isaac Newton had the same outlook: "I do not know what I may appear to the world; but to myself I seem to have been only like a boy playing on the seashore, and diverting myself in now and then find-ing…a smoother pebble or a prettier shell than ordinary whilst the great ocean of truth lay all undiscovered before me."[30] Einstein's view was even stronger. He believed playfulness as "the essential feature in productive thought."[31]

But whatever the place of playfulness among the characteristics of creative people, Ruggiero says, one thing is certain: "It, and the dynamism it is a part of, provide those people a richer and more varied assortment of ideas than the average person enjoys."[32]

Clark, whom we talked about in Chapter 1, gives some sugges-tions for "moving out of ruts." He believes that unthinking habitual behavior is ingenuity's worst enemy. "Everyone gets into ruts without realizing it: the coffee break comes at the same time every morning; day after day the same forms are used for letters or for answering the phone. Before long, approaches to people, problems, and opportunities become predictable. The mystery, the sense of discovery, and the awareness that a person had when the job was 'new' give way to safe routines. Variety spurs ingenuity—new hobbies, different forms of recreation, simple rearrangements of home or office furniture, lunch with different persons from the office, a new route to the train station. Playtime with puzzles and challenging games activates the mind. Intense exercise jogs out the cobwebs."[33]

Sometimes an imaginative step outside of your cultural boundaries helps. Clark suggests, as problems are approached, that you ask how an American Indian would deal with the same situation. "Put yourself in the place of an ancient Egyptian or Greek, or use any contemporary cul-ture with which you have some familiarity. Or imagine that the objects associated with a particular problem were 100 times larger than in real life. How would the change in size necessitate a change in tools? What would happen if these objects were microscopic?"[34]

Despite the evidence that we tend to lose touch with our natural creativity, starting in elementary school and continuing throughout life, the trend can be reversed (see the Torrance and Parnes studies cited in Chapter 1). People can learn to rekindle the creativity of their childhood years by using CPS, to be discussed in the next chapter. The key process is to restore our natural inclination to question things—everything around us. While there are specific techniques, such as those described in Chapter 2, to facilitate the surfacing and application of our creativity, there is one simple but very powerful aid to the questioning process. It is called the "WHY" technique. Simply ask "why" continually throughout our daily activities.

Why do we begin the day by reading the morning newspaper or listening to news broadcasts or telecasts? I quit doing that 10 years ago when I realized that my freshest, more alert period of the day was five minutes after awakening, when I was halfway through my first cup of coffee. I began mentally attacking my toughest problems at that time. The process has proved to be highly beneficial for me. A colleague finds his most creative period to be the period just before he goes to sleep. He is relaxed and believes that the ideas flow more easily at that time. He finds himself highly productive. He just records his ideas on a notepad next to his bed lamp and goes to work to flesh them out the next day at work. To realize these truths for ourselves, my colleague and I asked "why" in regard to our daily routines.

If you can get in the habit of asking "why" about all things related to your daily life, you begin to recover the questioning process that was natural and normal as a five-year-old. You didn't have to prod yourself to ask "why" at that age—we need that self-prodding in later years. In my years of study of creativity I've learned that this simple practice of asking "why" is the most important thing we can do to reactivate our innate, God-given creative potential.

There are some other positive activities underway to help young people resurface and channel their creative potential. It is a national program called "Odyssey of the Mind" (OM). Conceived in a New Jersey basement by Samuel Micklus, OM is run by his wife, Carole. Micklus, a Glassboro State University professor, started OM to stimulate children's creativity. "I've been in higher education for more than 20 years," he explains, "and we do practically zero for creative kids." Odyssey of the Mind is one man's attempt to bring fun to learning—where it belongs. The contest is open to students from kindergarten through college.

Some examples of the projects are writing and performing a new ending to *Moby Dick* and one called "Humor from Homer." Micklus admits it's a way of tricking the kids into reading the classics. "When something stands for 2,000 years," he says, "it's a pity when it's not studied anymore." Another example of kids' ingenuity: The McFly, an invention that earned a high school team a place in the world finals.

Created for businessmen, this device beeps if your zipper is down. Micklus also cites a team that had a production line called "Teeth Are Us," which churned out tiny, cotton-lined boxes for the Tooth Fairy. By its tenth anniversary in 1985, OM was an international competition involving more than 350,000 kids.[35]

Before you get the idea that the projects are trivial, look over some of the required projects for the international competition:

Problem: Design and build a structure from balsa wood and glue. It must stand between eight and eight and a half inches high, weigh no more than 15 grams, and support close to 1,000 pounds.

Can you imagine loading dense, bulky weights onto such a tiny, open-weave structure without it collapsing? Some very imaginative structures are built by these kids. OM is an example of the ways to motivate children to continue their natural creativity.

Perhaps you've wondered about the effect of age on creativity. Research shows that great inventors tend to be young. Their performance peaks at mid-career and then drops. But for many innovators, their greatest achievements come in life's prime years. It seems to be a fact that fewer patentable inventions are made in the older years. On the other hand, there is abundant evidence that creativity may actually increase in our older years. One example is Alexanderson. He received 350 patents in his life, getting two-thirds of them beyond age 40. His last patent issued when he was 95![36]

"Creativity is not the direct result of intelligence, talent or skills," says Denise Shekerjian in her book *Uncommon Genius: How Great Ideas Are Born*. "Instead it comes from having an open, 'beginner's mind'; from curiosity, close observation, divergent thinking, bissociation (seeing relationships between apparently unrelated factors), and intuition; from an absence of negative judgment, where 'failure' is learning; and from a tolerance for the 'long dance of uncertainty' that precedes most breakthroughs."[37]

Implicitly or explicitly, creativity always begins with a question. And in both your business and personal lives, the quality of your creativity is determined by the quality of your questions.

Michael Ray/Rochelle Myers

> I ask questions. The stupidity of people comes from having an answer for everything. The wisdom of the novel comes from having a question for everything.
>
> *Milan Kundera*

Understanding Your Style of Creativity

Although each of us can improve his or her creative thinking ability, we have exhibited various degrees of creativity throughout our lifetime. Typically, we have settled into a pattern or style of creative thinking. Just as it is valuable to understand our blocks to creativity, it is useful to understand our style of creativity. Each of us has different habits, ways of expressing ourselves, talents, knowledge, values, and interests. Although we all have the ability to be creative, individual differences cause us to approach creative problem solving in different ways. Because we often work with others to explore opportunities and to solve problems, it is important that we recognize these basic differences in individuals. Each person has a contribution to make due to his or her unique set of qualifications. However, the very different styles of other persons sometimes cause us to hesitate to accept their ideas and approaches. We tend to favor the approach of persons whose style is similar to ours. Yet, one of the major objectives in identifying opportunities and solving problems is to consider a variety of alternatives. It is advantageous to have team members with different styles of creativity, to stimulate our thinking in different directions and to cause us to re-think our usual approaches.

A questionnaire developed by William Miller helps people identify their style of creativity.[38] Although titled the Innovation Styles®* Profile, the questionnaire is not confined to innovation. In the context of this book, it would be more aptly called Creativity Style Profile. Therefore, I'll use the abbreviation ISP for the questionnaire, instead of spelling out the name of the questionnaire, because I want to emphasize that the instrument is not limited to helping us identify our style of innovation but relates to our style of creativity. Remember in Chapter 1 I explained that creativity is the more inclusive concept, covering discovery, invention, and innovation.

*Innovation Styles® is a federally registered trademark of the Global Creativity Corporation.

The ISP will help you understand how you prefer to promote creativity and change. It is based on three premises:

- Each of us has the ability to think creatively—so the main issue is not "Am I creative?" but "How am I creative?"

- As individuals, we have equal potential for being creative, yet have different approaches to fostering change where we work.

- We do not have a single style, but a basic mixture of styles. Each style is like a language; we can speak many, yet still have a favorite "mother tongue."

By knowing how you and others use different creativity styles, you will:

- Be more open and flexible.

- Invite a wider variety of ideas and input into your life.

- Present your ideas more effectively.

- Build a harmonious work team.

Your creativity style is based on how you like to use information to stimulate your creativity. Each creativity style prefers a different methodology for generating and evaluating ideas. Miller's research shows that preferences for styles fall in four categories (Figure 3–5). The preference is illustrated by the basic question posed when faced with a creative challenge.

- The **modifying style** likes to ask:
  What can we adapt to improve upon what has worked before?

- The **visioning style** likes to ask:
  What can we realistically imagine as the ideal solution over the long term?

- The **experimenting style** likes to ask:
  What ideas can we combine and test?

- The **exploring style** likes to ask:
  What metaphors can we use to challenge our assumptions?

Each style is like a point on a compass. By putting a problem in the middle of the compass, we can approach ideas for solving the problem from all four directions. There are many different idea-generation techniques based on the methodologies of the four different styles. Each

Figure 3–5   Model for Distinguishing Style of Creativity

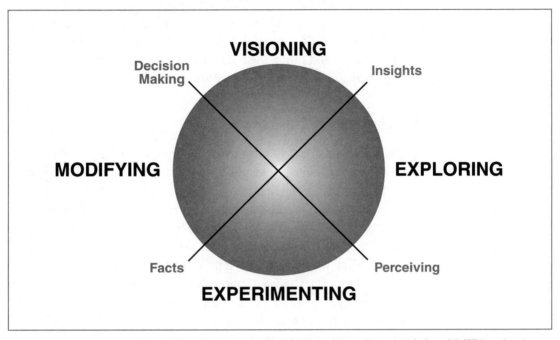

Source: Miller, W., *Creativity: The Eight Master Keys to Discover, Unlock, and Fulfill Your Creative Potential* (Pleasanton, CA: SyberVision Systems, Inc., 1989). The Innovation Styles® Profile can be purchased from Global Creativity Corp., 4210 Spicewood Springs, Room 205, Austin, TX 78759.

creativity style is based on an understanding of how we like to use information to stimulate our creativity, including:

- the information we look for—some people like to look for facts first; others search for insights.

- what we do with information—some people like to gather as much information as possible, others like to concentrate on making decisions and taking action with the information they've already gathered.

Miller provides descriptive comparisons of the various styles, as follows.[39]

Modifying Style of Creativity

People who take a modifying approach to creativity are most comfortable working with facts and making decisions. They like to solve problems. They seek solutions by applying methods that have worked in the past. These people tend to be precise, reliable, efficient, and disciplined. They would approach a project with a comment such as "Let's build on what we already have and make improvements where necessary." An example of modifying style of creativity would be Gutenberg and his printing press. Before 1440, books were printed by hand using inked woodblock letters. Gutenberg modified this process by developing movable metal ones and fitting them into an adapted wine press. The result was the availability of books in quantity for the first time in history.

Visioning Style of Creativity

People who favor the visioning style trust their instincts and like to make decisions. They seek solutions that focus on maximizing potential rather than focusing on what has gone on in the past. Driven by their long-term goals and their organization's mission, they solve problems by relying on their vision of the future to guide them. This style is characterized by people who are persistent, determined, hard-working, and visionary. They would approach a project with a comment such as "Let's develop a clear sense of purpose and goals to focus and drive our creative energy." An example of visioning style of creativity would be John F. Kennedy and his vision of space exploration. When he set this goal for the United States (to put a man on the moon in ten years), he gave all Americans something to work for. Millions of people aligned their personal visions with the dream of the nation and the result was not only Neil Armstrong's famous step for mankind, but the inventions of thousands of new products, from Tang to Mylar.

Experimenting Style of Creativity

When people use the experimenting style, they emphasize fact-finding and information gathering. They seek solutions by applying pre-established processes and experimental trial and error. As problem solvers, they like to gather as many facts and opinions as possible before they make their decision. They are curious, practical, and good team players. They approach a project with a comment such as: "Let's combine different elements in new ways and assess the result—let's get people involved to ensure an implementable plan of action." An example of the experimenting style of creativity would be Benjamin Franklin. One summer's eve in 1752, Ben Franklin decided to prove that lightning was a manifestation of electricity. So he got out his kite,

Table 3–2 Typical Questions for Each Style of Creativity	**Questions the Modifying Style Loves to Ask**	**Questions the Visioning Style Loves to Ask**	**Questions the Experimenting Style Loves to Ask**	**Questions the Exploring Style Loves to Ask**
	How can we build on what we already have?	In a perfect world, what would this be?	How can we test it out?	Why not?
	Can we adapt this idea?	Let's imagine that…	What if we combined…?	Have you thought about starting from scratch?
	Do we have all the facts?	How does this all fit together?	Who's on board?	What is this like?
	What's a short-term solution?	What is your long-term goal?	What's the process?	What have we assumed here?

tied a key to one end of it, and conducted his famous experiment. He proved his point by trial and error.

Exploring Style of Creativity

People who take an exploring approach to being creative like using their insights to guide them. They gather lots of information in the hope that it will help them approach problems from new angles. They tend to question assumptions and often will try to implement their ideas despite resistance from others. They are adventurous, dislike routine, and like to be challenged. They would approach a project with a comment such as "Let's explore in new directions and see where we end up." An example of the exploring style of creativity is Wayne Silby, founder of the Calvert Group, which manages billions of dollars in assets. Silby's business card reads "Chief Daydreamer." He spends a large amount of his time exploring a variety of possibilities, keeping his company at the forefront of its industry.

Analyzing Your Style of Creativity

Your own emphasis and blend of these four creativity styles is simply a way of describing how you feel most comfortable and capable in bringing about creativity and managing change in your life. Table 3–2 aids us in better understanding our individual creativity style.[40] Figure 3–6 shows a plot of one person's responses to the ISP questionnaire. Although the modifying style is dominant, the individual has

Figure 3–6   Example of an Individual's Style of Creativity

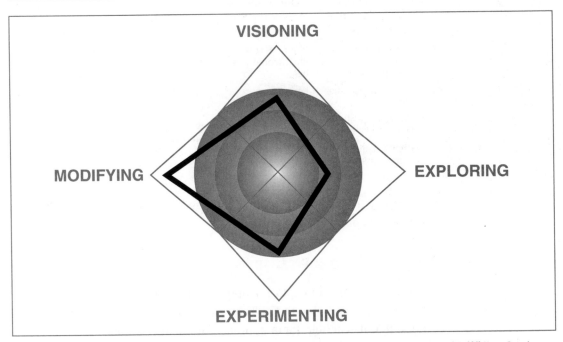

Source: Miller, W., *Creativity: The Eight Master Keys to Discover, Unlock, and Fulfill Your Creative Potential* (Pleasanton, CA: SyberVision Systems, Inc., 1989). The Innovation Styles® Profile can be purchased from Global Creativity Corp., 4210 Spicewood Springs, Room 205, Austin, TX 78759.

secondary styles of visioning and experimenting. This individual has very little interest in using an exploring style of creativity.

Relative Value of the Four Styles

When I ask groups to complete the ISP questionnaire, some are disappointed to find that their dominant style is not visioning or exploring. They implicitly conclude that these styles are the truly creative styles and that the modifying and experimenting styles are less valuable.

All we have to do is look at the track record of the Japanese industry to recognize the value of the modifying and experimenting styles. They did not invent the videocassette recorder, the personal computer, the hard disk drive, photocopiers, stereo, flat screen technology, integrated circuits, and ceramic superconductors. Those inventions occurred in the United States. Japanese industry took these inventions and made them commercially marketable. Joel Barker says that the Japanese are outstanding "at taking someone else's paradigm shift and...making it commercial, marketable.... The Japanese have harvested paradigm shift ideas from around the world: from VCRs (United States) to electronic watches (Switzerland) to diamond coating (USSR), each of which spawned a revolution in its field."[41]

The Japanese have been willing to do the work to complete the rules of the new paradigm so that it can be used effectively. They've gained world dominance through the modifying and experimenting styles of creativity. On the other hand, U.S. inventions have followed a similar pattern. Fully 80 percent of the patents issued by the U.S. Patent Office are not for new inventions but for improvements in existing ones.[42]

All creativity styles are valuable. Every company needs individuals with each style. Ideally, every team would have each style represented. An ancient story illustrates the radical difference such cooperation makes. A man who led a basically good life died, and was assigned to hell for a short time. He discovered that the main torture in hell was that everyone was forced to eat with spoons that were longer than their arms. The condemned spent eternity in the midst of excellent food they couldn't eat. When he was finally transferred up to heaven, he found that the blessed were given the same spoons. In heaven, however, no one went hungry because they fed each other.[43]

We can all be more creative if we "feed" each other's creativity by supporting the need for individuality in our creativity styles. Through this harmonizing process the shared contributions produce a synergistic result.

We have finally abandoned the myth of the melting pot and learned to celebrate ethnic diversity. The new languages, ethnic food and restaurants, and the additional layer of foreign cultures all around us seem to fit the multiple-option mood. This new openness enriches us all.

John Naisbitt

The chief test of civilization is the amount of "difference" it can tolerate and absorb; the one characteristic of all primitive societies is a horror of diversity.

Sydney J. Harris

Conclusion

The following parable helps illustrate the problem of functional fixity, a typical block to creativity.

Once upon a time a disciple traveled thousands of miles to meet a master. Having finally arrived, he slept, washed himself, and carefully prepared himself for the long-awaited encounter. When the appointed time came, he was anxious to ask as many questions as possible.

Upon meeting with the disciple, the master quietly prepared some hot tea. He offered the refreshment to the disciple, who accepted by extending his cup. The master began to pour and continued until the boiling tea began to overflow onto the disciple's lap. In great consternation, the disciple waved his other hand and cried out, "Master, you must stop pouring!"

The master looked up and said, "Your mind is like your cup. It is so full of questions that there is no room for answers. You must first empty your mind if we are to start our discourse."

This parable teaches, according to John Dacey, that life is a process of growing functional fixity—the more we learn how things work, the more we tend to accept the patterns as unalterable.

It is important to recognize our blocks to creativity so we can begin breaking them down. Likewise, it is important to recognize that we have individual styles of creativity and to encourage rather than disparage differences in other people.

By understanding that people use different styles to approach problem solving and opportunity finding, we become more tolerant to different views. Equally important, we recognize that the ideas generated will be more comprehensive, more likely to span the full scope of opportunities than those of a group of persons possessing identical creativity styles. If your style is radical, people who favor the exploring style will probably immediately agree with you. Visioning-oriented persons will want to see exactly how your idea will help achieve goals, before they show their support. People with an experimentation orientation will examine how your idea provides new choices and options—they might also take a consensus of everyone concerned before committing to the idea. Modifying-oriented people will ask you many questions to make you prove that your idea will work, but once committed, they will cooperate fully.

Bear Bryant, former football coach at Alabama, emphasized the importance of diversity: "Don't make them (your employees) in your image. Don't even try. My assistants don't look alike, think alike, or have the same personalities. And I sure don't want them all thinking like I do. You don't strive for sameness, you strive for balance."[44]

In a group where one of the creativity styles is not represented, you might play that role, to help the group get the full range of ideas. And, in working individually, after our natural approach to problem solving/opportunity finding, we might play the roles of the other styles to ensure that all sides of the issue have been exhausted.

Even though you may have one primary creativity style, you have the seeds for all four styles as part of your makeup. Miller says that each creativity style is like a language. "While you probably feel comfortable speaking one or two languages well, you can benefit from learning to use all four."

The Japanese have been especially effective in teamwork. Sheridan Tatsuno in his book *Created in Japan* explains that "the goal of Japanese creativity is not just to create new products and ideas, but to also build teamwork and a sense of harmony. Japanese creativity thrives on group interaction and brainstorming."[45]

On the other hand, one place America might gain a competitive advantage over Japan is by better blending our different styles of creativity. The Japanese have sacrificed individuality for harmony. Tatsuno comments on the negative aspects of Japan's approach to teamwork in its overemphasis upon conformity: "Individuals are encouraged to contribute ideas for the benefit of the team, not to be overly spontaneous or different. People who refuse to cooperate or continue to advocate unique ideas are distrusted, laughed at, or ignored by their peers in Japan. The Japanese prefer to hide their ideas behind a facade of conformity to avoid being embarrassed in public."[46] If we recognize the advantage of individual styles, but develop a creative fusion of ideas, we may make a quantum leap in the creative output of our teams.

One study of creativity revealed that only about two percent of adults are using their creative ability. This contrasted with 10 percent of 7-year-olds and 90 percent of 5-year-olds![47]

A capacity for childlike wonder, carried into adult life, typifies the creative person.

Don Fabun

Summary

This chapter has focused on introspection—examining your approach to creative problem solving/opportunity finding to try to: 1) recognize blocks that might prevent your exploring the full solution set and 2) recognize your style of creativity as well as those of your colleagues, so you can be a more effective team member. In recognizing our perceptual, emotional, cultural, environmental and intellectual blocks, we can concentrate on circumventing those blocks to open new avenues to view and solve problems.

By understanding the four styles of creativity (modifying, experimenting, visioning, and exploring), we can approach problems and opportunities more completely. We can work better as a team when all styles are represented and better as individuals when we role play each style in the process of examining a problem and its solution possibilities.

Research with the ISP questionnaire reveals that all persons possess some characteristics of each style of creativity. When we are on teams where some styles are missing, we can role play the missing styles to ensure that a variety of alternatives are generated.

Research also shows that most people have difficulty changing their paradigms. Most of us need to avail ourselves of the procedure for evaluating paradigms and generating new paradigms.

It is said that necessity is the mother of invention, but there had been a curious lack of interest in discovering the father. Could it be that the father is curiosity?

Raudseep

Exercises

1. Distinguish the five blocks to creativity: perceptual, emotional, cultural, environmental, and intellectual.

2. Explain paradigm. What is the paradigm trap?

3. What are the reasons for the loss of our natural curiosity/inquisitiveness?

4. What is the function of a paradigm shifter?

5. What approaches are useful in regaining the questioning attitude you had as a child?

6. Is there proof that school children can regain their natural creativity? Explain your answer.

7. Distinguish the four styles of creativity (innovation): modifying, visioning, experimenting, and exploring.

8. What is functional fixity? How can one overcome it?

9. What are the reasons for knowing the ISP of teammates?

10. How does knowledge of the four styles of creativity relate to the knowledge about the common blocks to creativity?

Submarine Vessel

The *Nautilus* by Robert Fulton was a two-man submarine, driven by a hand-crank when submerged and by sail while surfaced. It was successfully submerged on June 13, 1800 in Paris but was deemed not fit for battle against the British navy. Napoleon financed the project, much to his regret. He turned down Fulton's steam-powered ship proposals.

4

*What is now proved was
once only imagined.*
Proverb

*Scientists with superior heuristics and
better problem solving techniques are
more likely to make significant
discoveries and take advantage
of lucky breaks.*
David Lamb

The Creative Problem-Solving Methodology

In his *Rules for the Conduct of Understanding,* the famous philosopher René Descartes advised would-be problem solvers to "reduce involved and obscure presuppositions step by step to those that are simpler, and then starting with the intuitive apprehension of all those that are absolutely simple, attempt to ascend the knowledge of all the others by precisely similar steps."[1]

This chapter discusses an approach to problem solving that has evolved from centuries of theorizing and testing. David Lamb tells us that "for a logic of discovery," to reject the emphasis frequently placed on "great moments" in the discovery process. He offers as an alternative the suggestion that "discovery and creative thinking in general can be seen as a mode of problem solving."[2]

Herbert Simon elaborates on the need for process: "Does science depend, for its major progress upon heroes who have faculties not possessed by journeymen scientists? Or are the men whose names we associate with the great discoveries just the lucky ones—those who had their hands on the lever at the precise moment when the jackpot showered its rewards?"[3]

Two very different models of problem solving were proposed by Wallas and Dewey. In 1926 Graham Wallas proposed four steps in the problem-solving process: preparation, incubation, inspiration, and verification. A few years later, John Dewey suggested that problem solving was comprised of defining the problem, identifying the alternatives, and selecting the best alternatives. The latter approach is more closely related to scientific analysis. The Wallas approach was the first of the "creative" problem-solving approaches. We will attempt to merge the two approaches into an integrated approach that provides not just a reconciled approach but a synergistic one.

CPS also owes credit to the scientific method for part of its origin. The scientific method included rules for concept formulation, conduct of observations and experiments, and validation of hypotheses by observations and experiments. In this century the most widely used framework for problem solving was developed by Simon, who proposed a three-stage approach: intelligence, design, and choice.[4] **Intelligence** involves recognizing the problem and analyzing problem information to develop a useful problem definition; **design** is the generation of solutions; and **choice** involves the selection and implementation of a solution. Several persons have derived their own version of the problem-solving process. Problem-solving models continue to evolve. For example, Kingsley and Garry observe that these stages are characteristic of the process:[5]

1. A difficulty is felt.
2. The problem is clarified and defined.
3. A search for clues is made.
4. Various suggestions appear and are evaluated.
5. A suggested solution is accepted or the thinker gives up in defeat.
6. The solution is tested.

These authors join problem solving and learning in a dual fashion: "we learn by thinking and we improve our ability to think by means of learning."

There are dozens of models for problem solving. It is not necessary to review all of them, but McPherson provides a good way of comparing a sample of these models to the Simon model.[6] In Table 4–1, McPherson maps the Simon framework to the variants of Von Fange, Gregory, Bailey, and Rossman.

The CPS concept might appear to be just another variant. It isn't, however. It has several important differences. The most widely used model was developed by Alex Osborn and Sidney Parnes. Osborn wrote extensively on the importance of imagination and creativity in solving problems. His *Applied Imagination* is probably the most frequently cited publication in the field of creativity.[7] It was in this book that he introduced the technique of brainstorming. His model of CPS contained three stages: fact finding, idea finding, and solution finding. Sidney Parnes expanded the three-phase model to five phases.[8] He stressed the importance of solving the right problem by adding a problem-finding stage between fact finding and idea finding. Parnes also felt the need to highlight the importance of implementation, so he added the fifth stage, acceptance finding. The five-stage CPS model of Osborn-Parnes is shown in Figure 4–1. It is appropriate to add other stages for certain problem/opportunity situations. Examples will be provided later.

A unique feature of CPS is the addition of the divergence-convergence activities to the problem-solving process. J.P. Guilford was the first to add this feature to the CPS model. He did so in his 1950 presidential address to the American Psychological Association, in which he

Table 4–1

Mapping Four Alternative
Approaches to Simon's
Framework for
Problem Solving

Von Fange (G.E. Creative Engineering Program)

1. Investigate direction
2. Establish measures } **Intelligence**

3. Develop methods
4. Optimize a structure } **Design**

5. Accomplish this structure
6. Convince others } **Choice**

Gregory (The Scientific Problem Solving Method)

1. Deciding on objective
2. Analyzing problems
3. Gathering data
4. Organizing data } **Intelligence**

5. Inducting
6. Planning } **Design**

7. Prechecking
8. Activating plans
9. Evaluating } **Choice**

Bailey (Disciplined Creativity)

1. Problem inquiry
2. Specifying goals
3. Determining means } **Intelligence**

4. Solution optimization } **Design**

5. Construction and verification
6. Convince others } **Choice**

Rossman

1. Need or difficulty is observed
2. Problem formulated
3. Available information surveyed } **Intelligence**

4. Solutions formulated
5. Solutions critically examined } **Design**

6. New ideas formulated
7. New ideas tested } **Choice**

Source: Evans, J. R., *Creative Thinking: In the Decision and Management Sciences* (Cincinnati: South-Western Publishing Co., 1991), p. 91. Reprinted with permission of South-Western College Publishing. Copyright © 1991 by South-Western College Publishing. All rights reserved.

scolded his fellow psychologists for neglecting needed research on creativity. Through the use of a statistical technique known as factor analysis, Guilford and his colleagues have attempted to map the intellectual operations of the human mind, with a special interest in its creative functioning. The result has been the creation of a theory he calls the **structure of the intellect**.[9]

Figure 4–1   Osborn-Parnes Creative Problem Solving Model

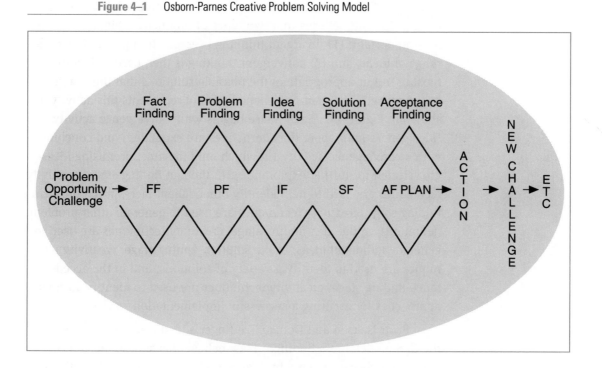

In building this theory, Guilford and his associates gave a large variety of mental tests to a large number of people. Some were standard IQ tests; others were more unusual, such as tests of spatial relations and social knowledge. He wanted to see how ability on one type of test interrelates with ability on the other types of tests. From this, he believed he could identify the basic cognitive abilities. His most significant finding is that the intellect is made up of five types of mental operation, his structure of intellect. They are as follows:

1. **Cognition**—discovery, rediscovery, or recognition
2. **Memory**—retention of what is cognized
3. **Convergent thinking**—thinking that results in the right or wrong answer to a question that can have only one right answer ("How much is 2 + 2?")
4. **Divergent thinking**—thinking in different directions, or searching for a variety of answers to questions that may have many right answers ("What is the cause of our environmental problem?")
5. **Evaluation**—reaching decisions about the accuracy, goodness, or suitability of information

Although all five operations are involved in creative thinking to some extent, Guilford believes that two types of productive thinking are most important: (1) divergent thinking is essential in generating a wide range of ideas, and (2) convergent thinking is then used to identify the most useful or appropriate of the possible solutions that the thinker has produced. The diamond-shaped symbol represents this activity as shown in Figure 4–2. Each phase begins with a divergence activity (idea generation, where the alternatives are expanded) and concludes with a convergence activity (in which only the most promising ideas are selected for further exploration). In the fact-finding stage, creativity techniques are used to help identify other salient facts; in the problem-finding stage, creativity techniques are used to generate other problem definitions; in the idea-finding stage, creativity techniques are used to generate additional ideas; in the solution-finding stage, creativity techniques are used to identify a variety of solutions; and in the acceptance-finding stage, creativity techniques are used to identify various approaches for assuring a successful implementation.

Scott Isaksen and Donald Treffinger added a step at the start of the CPS model: mess finding.[10] They believe this additional step is appropriate because many problems are "fuzzy" and poorly defined. Figure 4–2 depicts their model and is useful because it describes the divergence/convergence activities of each step.

I have developed a variant to the CPS model that I feel more appropriate for the business world. Before explaining this variant, I want to review a very culturally different approach: the Japanese Mandala approach.

Mandala Approach

Sheridan Tatsuno, in his book *Created in Japan*, says that the Western approach to creativity is more of a linear process, based on individual effort. "By contrast," Tatsuno says, "the more cyclical form of Japanese creativity can be viewed as a 'mandala of creativity' divided into five related phases," as shown in Figure 4–3:[11]

- Idea recycling (new uses for old and existing ideas)

- Idea search (the search for new ideas when existing ideas are inadequate)

- Idea nurturing (the seeding and incubation of new ideas)

Figure 4–2 Isaksen/Treffinger CPS Model Showing Divergence/Convergence Activities in Each Phase

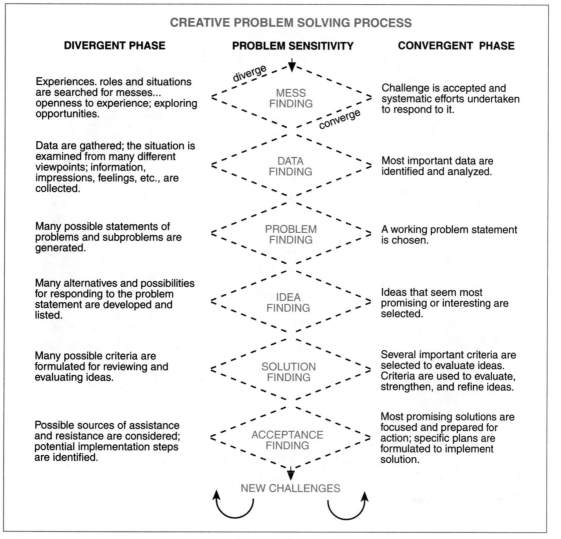

Source: Isaksen, S. G., and D. J. Treffinger, *Creative Problem Solving: The Basic Course* (Buffalo, NY: Bearley Ltd., 1985), p. 16.

- Idea breakthroughs (new breakthrough ideas)
- Idea refinement (improving and adapting new ideas to the changing environment)

"In this view, old ideas never die," Tatsuno says, "but, like energy, are transformed into new ideas as they race around the mandala. Although they may lie quietly for years or even centuries, a new development may trigger their reappearance in the world—a form of cre-

Figure 4–3   The Mandala of Creativity

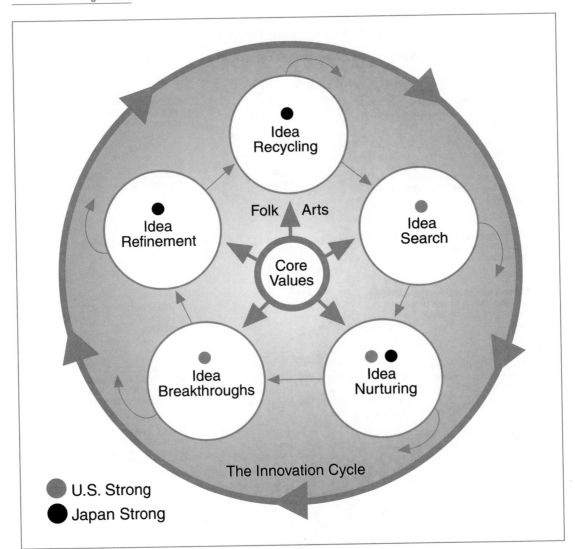

Source: Tatsuno, S., *Created in Japan* (New York: HarperBusiness, 1990), p. 50.

ative reincarnation. For example, many of Leonardo da Vinci's ideas and the science fiction of H.G. Wells could not be realized in their times because of limitations in existing technologies; now these ideas are technically possible. Their ideas about the helicopter and the submarine were far ahead of their times. As the Japanese have long known, it is worth reviewing and recycling old ideas from time to time because of their renewed potential."[12]

According to Tatsuno, Japanese companies find that exploring creativity using the mandala structure is a "dynamic, whirling process." These companies set up traditional *gonin-gumi* (five-person teams), which work together to develop and refine new ideas. These groups resemble planets revolving around the sun; they go through all five phases of the mandala. Although group creativity predominates, individual creativity gradually emerges in this process. "It resembles moons orbiting around each group, however, in contrast to the lone genius notion of Western creativity, which is more like meteors shooting through space. From this swirling flow of ideas comes innovation, which is a concept very distinct from creativity. While creativity refers to pure ideas, innovation is the translation of ideas into tangible products and intangible services. Thus, the Japanese are very good at refinement (such as refining existing theories about video technology), as well as innovation (translating these theories into innovative new products). The distinction is subtle and often confused by Westerners. Not all creative ideas are innovative (or turned into tangible products and intangible services), nor are all innovative ideas necessarily creative—they may simply be well executed."[13]

Parnes provides an example of distinguishing between creativity and innovation. He uses the illustration of the common screwdriver. Innovation might put rubber grips on the handle for greater efficiency in turning; creativity might view the problem not necessarily as turning the handle but as getting the screw into the wood, and might invent the "push-pull" type of screwdriver or even the power-driven model. Another example is the continual improvement, refinement, and correcting of deficiencies in buttons and zippers as compared with the Velcro "transformation."[14]

Thus, the Japanese notion of creativity can be visualized as a helix, according to Tatsuno, "in which each revolution through the cycle leads one to higher and higher levels of creativity. The ultimate level of creativity, if it can be achieved, is *satori,* or spiritual enlightenment, in which the creator and idea become one. On a more philosophical level, the mandala of creativity is analogous to one strand in the double helix of DNA—the basic chain of life—or to the yin and yang of creation. Western creativity is clearly stronger in three phases of the mandala process: idea exploration, idea cultivation, and idea generation. Westerners have traditionally excelled in pursuing basic research and exploring new scientific frontiers, activities that require maximum intellectual curiosity and adventurousness.[15]

Couger Variant of CPS

Roger von Oech, author of *A Kick in the Seat of the Pants*, articulates his view of creativity:

> I've found that the hallmark of creative people is their mental flexibility. Like race-car drivers who shift in and out of different gears depending on where they are on the course, creative people are able to shift in and out of different types of thinking depending on the needs of the situation.[16]

Von Oech notes that people play four different roles in the creative process: the explorer (when searching for new information), the artist (when turning the information into new ideas), the judge (when evaluating the merits of an idea), and the warrior (when carrying the idea into action). Using Tatsuno's analogy, von Oech could have added a fifth role, often overlooked by Americans, but at which the Japanese excel: the antique dealer (when recycling old ideas for new applications).

The description by Tatsuno gives additional credence to my emphasis in earlier chapters on the distinction between creativity and innovation. If America is to regain its position of leadership in the development of new products and processes, we must rejuvenate our previous abilities in phases one through three of the CPS process.

Figure 4–4 is the model that I believe is most appropriate for the present-day business environment. The fact-finding phase is indicated as the second phase for most problems/opportunities. Unquestionably, there are situations where a problem exists but has not been specifically identified. Some facts will need to be acquired and assessed before the problem definition can be developed. There are also situations where not all of the phases are necessary and the solution begins beyond phase one of the model. An example is the situation where the problem is clear to everyone, so phase one is unnecessary. On the other hand, the literature is replete with cases where the problem solvers assumed they understood the problem and wasted effort on solving the wrong problem.

Figure 4–4   Couger Variant of the Creative Problem-Solving Model

AA - Attribute Association
AM - Analogies/Metaphors
BE - Boundary Examination
BL - Bug List
BS - Brainstorming
BW - Brainwriting
CBS - Crawford Blue Slip

DI - Disjointed Incrementalism
DM - Decomposable Matrices
5Ws/H - Interrogatories
FFA - Force-Field Analysis
GW - Goal/Wish
LB - Lotus Blossom
L/R - L/R Brain Alternations

MC - Morphological Connections
MV - Manipulative Verbs
NGT - Nominal Group Technique
PA - Progressive Abstraction
PR - Problem Reversal
PS - Peaceful Setting
WI - Wild Idea
WT - Wishful Thinking

Note in Figure 4–4 the names of various techniques listed under each problem-solving phase. Note also that some techniques are useful in more than one phase. This is not a exhaustive list of techniques, but a representative one. These are the 22 techniques covered in this book, proven in other disciplines and transported over to the business field. The addition of these techniques changes this variant from a model to a methodology for problem-solving and opportunity delineation. Remember, even though I use the term CPS, because of its wide-spread use, the method is not limited to problem solving. There is equal emphasis upon opportunity identification. Simon referred to this activity as opportunity surveillance. Although we have been discussing ways to more clearly define a problem, many of these same techniques are useful in clearly describing an opportunity. The main difference is that we often identify opportunities in the idea-generation phase, then move on to define them.

Remember the example in Chapter 2 of George de Mestral turning a problem into an opportunity? The Swiss mountaineer could have continued to be frustrated and complain, as most us have been in picking burrs from our clothes. Instead he turned the problem into an opportunity: Velcro.

How do we identify opportunities? Parnes emphasizes the use of both analytical and intuitive approaches. He advocates "concentration on imagery, analogy, and metaphor." In the early phases we should be "sensing, discovering and defining visions, dreams, wishes, goals, opportunities for the future."[17] Parnes describes diverging for new perceptions and ideas "like opening a faucet to allow the flow,... procedures will serve as pumps to *increase* the flow. If these pumps are used without assistance from deferred judgment, it may be like trying to pump water through an unopened, or partially opened, tap. Fully opening the tap or the mind provides a surge of flow. But, if you are already deferring judgment, and then add procedures...you feel the added surge of the 'pump' to whatever has been coming." These outside excursions are generally applied by inventors and creative people in general, according to Parnes. When they "apply these processes *deliberately,* they speed up their creative processes and experience greater creative productivity." He gives the example of Fran Striker, creator of "The Lone Ranger" character and his popular escapades in radio, TV, books, and comic strips that lasted for decades. Striker found he could apply the CPS procedures to his already productive creative writing to reach new levels of productivity. He then successfully introduced the concepts into courses he was teaching in creative writing, culminating in publication of a creative-writing workbook.[18]

Tatsuno mentions the linearity of Western creativity. However, the graphic representation of the CPS process implies a linearity that is not actually there. As stated by VanGundy, it is actually more nonlinear and recursive.[19] We may not be able to define the problem until the second phase, after reviewing all the relevant data. Or, in the idea gen-

Figure 4–5 Alternate Portrayal of the CPS Model Showing That Stages
Do Not Necessarily Occur in Sequence

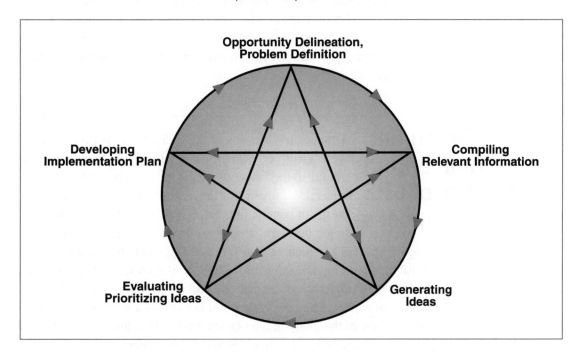

eration phase we may recognize that we need more data to be able to fully attack the problem or opportunity. VanGundy also reminds us that the activities within each stage are rarely mutually exclusive, that is, the activities in one phase will likely have an effect on those in other phases. The first three phases are more *inter*dependent than the last two. Evaluating, prioritizing the ideas, and developing an implementation plan are more independent. However, in the evaluation phase, we may decide that the ideas generated thus far are not an optimal solution, therefore must recurse back through phase three, the idea generation phase.

A more graphically accurate model of the CPS process, therefore, would be one which is star-shaped, as shown in Figure 4–5. It clearly shows how one often moves to and from the various phases in a typical problem-solving or opportunity identification situation. Again, I have changed the names of the phases to reflect the situation more common to the business arena. I've not found this five-point model in any of Parnes' publications, but according to Gary Davis, Parnes deserves credit for it. In *Creativity Is Forever,* Davis describes Parnes' "napkin-origination" of the model. "While chatting with Parnes over 1½ hot fudge sundaes (yes, Parnes ordered 1½ hot fudge sundaes), he mentioned that people tend to use the five stages too rigidly. On a sticky napkin he diagrammed a star-shaped model and enclosed it in a circle, emphasizing that one may flexibly move directly from any one step to any other."[20]

Divergent/ Convergent Quality of CPS Process

One of the strengths of the CPS process is the divergent versus convergent emphasis. That is the reason the diamond shaped symbol was selected to represent each phase. We diverge at the start of each phase and converge in concluding the phase. In creatively approaching a problem or opportunity, we want to expand our range of choices as much as possible. Specific creativity techniques are useful in expanding the range of choices. In the example in Chapter 2, by the use of progressive abstraction I expanded the solution set from 3 to 15 categories. The important point is to be in a mind-set of divergence. Many of the analytic type courses taken in a business school place the emphasis upon convergence—the management science tools and techniques taught in these courses help us converge on the best solution. For example, linear programming provides us with the capability of examining a very large data set. We can simultaneously evaluate a large number of variables, many more than we could evaluate without a specific methodology, to converge on the optimal solution. We can set up the methodology to converge to the lowest-cost solution, or the highest-profit solution or a variety of other objectives. In a problem where we do not have access to all the data we need, such as projecting future economic conditions in which our company will operate, we can use the simulation technique to help us identify a large number of possible scenarios. We can alter the data associated with each variable, or alter the types of variables we want to consider, in order to simulate many different economic circumstances to help our company be better prepared and more responsive to whichever economic circumstances occur. The simulation technique helps us narrow the possibilities and to choose most appropriate planning scenarios.

It is helpful in avoiding overconcentration on convergence to formally separate each step in the CPS process into a divergence phase and a convergence phase. In examining challenges and opportunities, the divergence phase has the identical purpose, to identify as many options as possible. In the convergence phase, the options are narrowed to a select few.

Just as there are specific techniques to aid in divergence, specific techniques have been developed to facilitate convergence. Two mentioned above are linear programming and simulation. Another is statistical analysis. Special methods have been developed to analyze a mass of data to determine which are significant in relation to the problem or opportunity at hand. For a manufacturing problem, statistical analysis of data related to equipment, material and personnel would help identify the variables which have most impact on the problem, and hence, its solution. For a marketing opportunity, statistical analysis of all the variables related to customer demand and satisfaction would determine which are most influential in the decision to buy our product or service. It is inappropriate in this book to try to review all of the analytical techniques for facilitating convergence on the optimal solution. In Chapter 9, I'll explain general techniques for evaluating and prioritizing ideas. Those same techniques are appropriate for use after each phase in the CPS process. For example, one of the techniques is the Battelle method, where all the alternatives are listed, then weighted according to a scheme that provides culling criteria. The alternatives are then ranked according to the computed weight score. Some of the criteria for evaluating would be cost, usefulness, quality, length of time to implement, and acceptability.

It is not surprising that the intuitive techniques are more useful for facilitating divergence and the analytical techniques are more useful for convergence. However, most of the analytical techniques are also useful for divergence. For example, the 5Ws/H technique helps us in terms of quantity in divergence and quality in convergence. In divergence it aids in expanding solution possibilities, by forcing us to consider the broad range of questions. It also is useful in convergence by forcing us to consider another set of questions related to the quality of the idea. Intuitive approaches are more broadly applicable in divergence, but intuition is also useful in convergence. Several examples will be provided shortly. Another useful way to compare the divergence/convergence activities is to use the analogy of brainstorming. Brainstorming will be explained in more detail in the chapter on idea generation. However, because it is the most widely used creativity technique you probably have an understanding of the process. The key rule in brainstorming is to separate the idea generation activity from the evaluation activity. People feel more free to verbalize ideas if they know someone won't be immediately criticizing their idea. To make sure there is an environment of receptivity of ideas—an atmosphere conducive for building on ideas rather than tearing them apart—the evaluation of the ideas is done in an entirely separate session. The divergence/convergence activities in CPS are performed in a similar manner. For example, in Phase Two where we are reviewing the relevant information about the problem or opportunity, we want to diverge to consider a wide range of data before converging, that is, deciding which data are most relevant.

There are general guidelines for divergence and convergence that apply to all five phases of the CPS process, as follows:

Guidelines for Divergence

1. **Defer judgment**. Because of the fear of social disapproval or authority hierarchy, people need assurance that their ideas will be given a fair hearing. Formal deferring of judgment helps provide the atmosphere of receptivity, of idea building, and encourages people to share their ideas. Criticism is ruled out in the brainstorming session. The expectation is a free-wheeling session where people feel at ease in suggesting any idea that comes to mind, the wilder the better. We want an atmosphere of idea spurring instead of idea spurning.

2. **Quantity breeds quality**. Research on the results of brainstorming proves that when many ideas are generated, the higher the probability of some good ideas coming out of the session. Stated another way, some ideas will not solve the problem or meet the opportunity at hand. The goal is to identify as many ideas as possible from which to choose the most appropriate. Linus Pauling said, "The best way to have a good idea is to have lots of ideas." Parnes says that "spontaneous associations...may trigger important connections with knowledge and experience that we may have forgotten or repressed."[21] Parnes gives an example of this associative type of thinking. A brainstorming session was held to work on the problem of wasted time by the people packing parts in an auto parts company. The company used old newspapers as packing material and the packers were wasting time reading the papers. Four ideas emerged: 1) hire illiterate packers, 2) use foreign-language papers, 3) blindfold the packers, and 4) hire blind packers. The fourth solution was adopted by the parts manufacturer. Note the interesting associative

process that led to the adopted solution. Of course, today it is cheaper to use plastic "peanuts" than newspaper.

3. **Hitchhiking is not against the law, it is encouraged**. Orally presenting ideas in a brainstorming session stimulates other ideas. "Hitchhiking," or piggybacking on another person's idea, are also useful in generating additional ideas. For example, in attacking a product quality problem, one person may suggest that purchased components need closer inspection. A "hitchhiker" might then produce the idea that the company place inspectors on the supplier's premises so the problem can be detected sooner. A third "hitchhiker" may come up with the idea that rather than send inspectors, designers might be sent to work with suppliers' design teams to design quality into the components.

4. **Combine and modify ideas**. Sometimes the combining of ideas occurs naturally, such as an idea to combine designers and inspectors for the above problem. Other times, we need conscious effort to consider the possibility of combining or modifying ideas. Each brainstorming session should include a period after the initial idea generation where the group purposefully seeks to combine ideas, to make new connections, to build on previous ideas. It is normal for the idea flow to diminish after a while, and at this point the facilitator can ask participants to begin to think about ways to combine ideas.

5. **Think in pictures**. Min Basadur recommends that we use all five senses to make these pictures.[22] Imagination comes from the Greek word "image." Smell, feel, hear, taste, and see your ideas.

6. **Stretch for ideas**. Some interesting research by Basadur and Morrison shows that stretching the brainstorming session, after the inevitable lull in the flow of ideas, can produce still more quality ideas. At this point the session may become more dependent upon the facilitator to suggest different ways to think about the problem to rekindle ideation. Basadur found, in evaluating the quality of ideas produced by a brainstorming session, that one-third of the quality ideas were produced in the early rounds of the session, one-third in the middle, and one-third in the latter part of the session. In other words, quality ideas are produced equally throughout the session. If participants can be encouraged to stretch the ideation session, they will continue to produce quality ideas.[23]

Guidelines for Convergence

1. **Be systematic**. Try to identify all the factors that are appropriate for evaluating the alternatives.

2. **Develop evaluative measures**. Rating and ranking are examples of evaluative measures.

3. **Use intuition**. Although the convergence activity by nature deals more with facts, it is important to try to be open to feelings and hunches as well. It is possible to evaluate intuitive data as well as facts. For example, if a team member says "This solution doesn't feel right to me," it is a clue that we may not have taken the analysis far enough. We can also explore the reasons for those hunches. By delving more deeply into our feelings or hunches, we may identify factors that have not yet been surfaced.

4. **Avoid quickly ruling out an area for consideration**. Although convergence involves judgment, it should avoid the use of "pat" answers or company/department policies that have not been questioned lately.

5. **Avoid idea-killer views**. The tendency in convergence is to quickly move to what at the outset appears to be the best idea, killing the remainder of the ideas. Further evaluation may prove that other ideas are equally good.

6. **"Satisfice."** In using a satisficing strategy, one quits searching when an acceptable solution has been identified, rather than spending a great deal of additional time to find an optimal solution. Satisficing is a perfectly good approach when time and budget do not permit further analysis.

7. **Use optimizing techniques when possible**. An example is linear programming, as explained earlier.

8. **Use heuristics**. A heuristic is a rule of thumb. Such rules help simplify evaluation. An example is the critical success factor approach, which forces the group to determine the five or seven factors critical to the success of a project.

9. **Don't avoid but assess risk**. Risk is often necessary for new approaches. Risk can be assessed, however, to facilitate the ranking of alternative solutions.

Techniques to Help Us in the Divergence Process

Isaksen and Treffinger suggest that one of the most common obstacles in divergence activities is being habit-bound in our thinking.[24] There are good habits and bad habits. Good habits prevent us from having to stop and think about everything we do each day (such as tying shoes, brushing teeth, watching both ways before we cross the street). Isaksen and Treffinger refer to these habits as "friendly little routines" to help us get things done efficiently and quickly. Unfortunately, they often become so routine that they cause us not to think. Sometimes habits are even dangerous. When I travel to England, I have near misses as a pedestrian in traffic because I am so used to looking for cars driving on the right side of the street. I have to constantly remind myself to watch for cars coming down the opposite side of the street.

We can become habit-bound in our thinking. When we don't question things, our creativity is stifled. Teaching a course in creativity has helped me question the way I normally teach. After a number of years of teaching, I have found an approach that is apparently successful—gauged by end-of-term student evaluations and by how well my students are prepared for a career. With the additional goal of trying to ensure that students will be creative in applying their knowledge, I find that I should alter my normative approach. Graduates need to be more creative than their predecessors to help their companies in an increasingly competitive environment. I have been forced to rethink each session in terms of pedagogical approach. Having found a successful teaching approach, I previously only had to rethink content of the session.

Chapter 1 referred to the Nayak and Ketteringham book, *Breakthroughs,* which documented thirteen cases of creativity and innovation. "In every case," they say, "...it was the curiosity within the originating person that lit the fire. Neither financial need nor market intelligence played a major role in these exceptional beginnings...it always was a problem to be solved, not a fortune to be made, not a market to be exploited."[25]

However, because the questioning process is no longer natural for most of us, we have to use some techniques to assist our questioning process, to diverge. John Arnold reminds us that:

> ...the creative potential can be realized through training and exercises, just as the development of our full capabilities along analytical lines can be obtained.[26]

Several excellent approaches have already been illustrated. Others are to come. The following is an example for use of the interrogatories (5Ws/H) technique described in Chapter 2.

Interrogatories Technique Applied to System Development

The Who-What-Where-When-Why-How questions aid in expanding our view of a problem or opportunity, to try to make sure that all related aspects have been considered. By going through several cycles of the 5Ws/H, alternatives related to the problem or opportunity can be explored exhaustively. For example, the 5Ws/H technique can be used at key points in the system development cycle to ensure that creative approaches have been utilized.

The divergence activity would be useful in each phase of the development of a computer application.[27] For brevity's sake, we will illustrate the following responses to just one of the 5Ws/H questions, the Why question, posed during each phase of system development.

1. **Specification Development**: Why does the organization need this system? Why have you limited the system to this particular set of functions? Why have you selected the specified procedures for accomplishing the tasks of this system?

2. **Logical Design**: Why is this set of logic the most appropriate for the system? Why have you selected this specific methodology for portraying the system specifications? Why are you dividing the logic among modules in the manner you have chosen?

3. **Physical Design**: Why are you using traditional system life-cycle development methodology instead of prototyping? Why have you chosen to use on-line processing (or batch) instead of batch processing (or on-line)? Why are you using the database access methodology you have chosen instead of (relational, direct, etc.)?

4. **Program Design**: Why have you chosen to partition system functions into this particular set of modules? Why not use other optimization techniques for data processing? Why have you selected this programming language?

The same approach would be used for other development processes in a firm, not just the development of computer systems. For example, in product development, there would be the phases of product requirement determination, product design, product manufacturing, product evaluation and testing, and product distribution. A creativity divergence activity could be used in each of those steps in product development. The same approach would apply to the process of developing a marketing plan, an employee compensation program, or a strategy for acquiring new products or facilities.

Conclusion

The Total Quality Management (TQM) program will be used to illustrate how CPS can facilitate almost any program/activity in a company. TQM has taken on huge importance in the past ten years, to make U.S. products and services more competitive. Our quality levels were unsatisfactory compared to those of our major international competitors, Germany and Japan. The TQM program was developed to provide an approach to improving quality. It consists of setting quality objectives, training work teams in use of special techniques to analyze products/services for quality improvement, and developing approaches to implement quality improvement.

TQM's sequence of activities is similar to that of CPS. While TQM provided some excellent techniques for detecting and analyzing quality problems, it is deficient in techniques to develop improved solutions. Only one technique was taught to quality improvement teams: brainstorming. Yet it is the least effective of the 20 proven techniques that I transported over to the business field from other disciplines. I'll explain more about the deficiencies of brainstorming in Chapter 8.

By overlaying the CPS process onto the TQM process, enrichment occurs. A richer set of techniques is available for both analysis of problems and generation of improved solutions. The full set of 20 techniques can be used to generate ways to improve quality in products and services. Also, by concentrating on the divergence/convergence approach at each stage of the quality improvement process, a more comprehensive and complete solution is possible. For example, the techniques taught for TQM are introduced in the quality problem detection/analysis stage. CPS provides for its set of techniques to be used in every stage, so they would be used in the TQM objective setting stage and in the implementation-planning stage as well as the problem detection-analysis stage.

By training all employees in the CPS methodology, they are prepared to use a more systematic and creative approach to solving any company problem, whether in marketing, production, finance, or any other function within the company.

> Daring ideas are like chessmen moved forward; they
> may be beaten, but they may start a winning game.
>
> *Goethe*

All of us are born with a natural facility for creative thinking and problem solving. And, like many other human facilities, it has to be developed.

Michael LeBoeuf

Summary

Although the Creative Problem-Solving model is a latter 20th century development, it evolved from an ancient concept, the scientific method. The CPS model consists of five steps in the process of identifying problems and determining a satisfactory approach to resolution. The diamond-shaped symbols in the model represent the divergence-convergence activities necessary to fully explore a variety of alternatives before converging on the best alternative. The Couger variant of the model consists of three refinements: 1) adding opportunity finding as well as problem definition to Step One, 2) moving fact finding to Step Two because it represents the most common sequence of problem solving/opportunity delineation in the business world, and 3) identifying creativity techniques useful in each phase of CPS, changing it from a model to a methodology. A fourth but relatively minor improvement is the use of a solid line in the diamond to represent divergence and a dotted line to represent convergence. This change reminds us that there are special techniques to facilitate convergence as well as creativity techniques to facilitate divergence. There are guidelines for divergence and for convergence that help us conduct a more comprehensive and optimal CPS process.

The problem of the model is its linear representation. A more appropriate representation is the mandala, which represents the circular or continuous improvement aspect of creativity. The five-star representation also shows graphically the characteristic of variation in the sequence in some problem-solving/opportunity delineation situations.

Often we need to use some special techniques to help us unearth our innate creativity. The CPS methodology comprises a rich set of tools and techniques to facilitate our creative restoration process. It is highly appropriate in almost any business situation where problem solving and opportunity finding are desired.

Efficiency is concerned with doing things right. Effectiveness is doing the right things.

Peter F. Drucker

Exercises

1. Differentiate Simon's three-stage approach to problem solving.

2. Creative Problem Solving evolved from the scientific method. What is the scientific method?

3. What are the differences between the Osborn-Parnes creative problem-solving model and the Simon three-stage model?

4. How does the concept of the mandala differ from CPS?

5. The Couger variant of the CPS model contains three enhancements to the Osborn-Parnes model. What are they?

6. Is the CPS methodology always linear? Explain.

7. Explain the divergent/convergent aspects of the CPS methodology.

8. Tatsuno says that the Japanese are best at innovation while the Western world is best at creativity. Explain.

9. What are the guidelines for divergence?

10. What are the guidelines for convergence?

Nose Shaper

Patent No. 850,978 (1907)

Ignatius Nathaniel Soares of Framingham, Massachusetts

"The noses of a great many persons are slightly deformed, and therefore because of the prominence of this feature the appearance of the face is more or less disfigured. Such deformity can frequently be remedied by a gentle but continuous pressure, and it is the object of this invention to bring about this result in a way that shall be painless to the individual..."

Any notion that better thinking is intrinsically unlearnable and unteachable is nothing but a lazy fallacy, entertained only by those who have never taken the trouble to consider just how a practical job of thinking is really done.
James Mursell

Creative versus Critical Thinking

Although titled "Creative versus Critical Thinking," this chapter covers a much broader perspective than the distinction between those two categories of thinking. We'll begin with an intellectual analysis of the thought process, then look at the physiological aspects of thinking: functions of each brain hemisphere and the characteristics of short-term versus long-term memory. Then we'll distinguish creative from critical thinking. Both are essential in creative problem solving. The objective is to merge and unify the two types of thinking into holistic thinking patterns.

Thinking and the Thought Process

Thinking is a general term covering numerous activities from daydreaming to reflection and analysis. Here are just some of the verbs *Roget's Thesaurus* includes for the word *think:*

appreciate	consult	fancy	reason
believe	contemplate	imagine	reflect
cerebrate	deliberate	mediate	ruminate
cogitate	digest	muse	speculate
conceive	discuss	ponder	suppose
consider	dream	realize	weigh

Edward de Bono likes to start his lectures on creativity by asking members of his audience to define thinking. He allows only a minute; therefore, the responses are not polished. Here are some of the definitions of thinking that emerge from his audience:[1]

- Mental process of rationalizing. Attempt to come to some conclusion about certain things.

- The process of using one's brain to attempt to solve some problem or to arrive at some conclusion on some particular topic.

- Creative process concerned with problem solving.

- Working something out by the intellectual use of reason.

- Pursuing an idea to some purpose.

- Using cognitive faculties to work things out as opposed to being guided by emotions.

De Bono uses this definition session to prove to the group that there is consistency among participant answers, that thinking is a matter of problem solving, the attempted achievement of some end. Daniel Jay broadens the concept of thinking to include "purposeful mental activity that helps formulate or solve a problem, make a decision, or fulfill a desire to understand. It is searching for answers, reaching for meaning."[2]

De Bono would agree that, in the short time members of his audiences are allowed to develop their definitions, they have derived too narrow a concept of thinking. He believes that thinking must be viewed within the "educational trinity of knowledge, intelligence, and thinking." He says that intelligence is an innate quality that may depend on genes, early environment or a mixture of the two. "Thinking," in his view, "is the operating skill through which intelligence acts upon experience.... At one extreme thinking is impossible without some information on the subject. At the other extreme perfect information would make thinking unnecessary. In between these two extremes both thinking and information are required."[3]

Intelligence vs Thinking Ability

Most of the authorities in the field of thought and reasoning agree that intelligence and thinking ability are not necessarily mutually dependent. An analogy developed by de Bono is useful in considering the relationship of intelligence to thinking ability.

> The engine power of a car, the effectiveness of its brakes, its road-holding ability, the sensitivity of its steering are all part of its innate characteristics. But the skill with which a car is driven is something apart. A powerful car may be driven with little skill. A humble car may be driven with great skill. There is of course a connection between driving skill and the power of a car inasmuch as a *skilled* driver would do better in the powerful car than in the humble car. Innate intelligence or IQ can be compared to the intrinsic power of the car. The skill with which this power is used is the skill of thinking. Thinking is the operating skill through which innate intelligence is put into action. A high intelligence may be allied to a high degree of thinking skill, but

this is not necessarily so. Conversely, a more modest intelligence may be accompanied by a high degree of thinking skill.[4]

Some persons claim that a person with a very low IQ could not exhibit thinking skill. The same type of reasoning assumes that people with a very high IQ are effective thinkers. Such argument has little validity. High IQ is not necessarily associated with skill in thinking. Often persons with high IQ are narrowly focused and have a limited perspective in their thought process.

There are also mistaken perceptions about the comparison of feelings and thought. They are not mutually exclusive. Feeling and thought are perfectly complementary. According to Vincent Ruggiero, "Feeling, being more spontaneous, is an excellent beginning to the development of conclusions. And thought, being more deliberate, provides a way to identify the best and most appropriate feeling. Both are natural."[5]

Ruggiero warns us, however, that thinking is less automatic than feeling. "To do it well demands a systematic approach and guided practice."[6] I'll suggest approaches to help you be more systematic in your cognitive process. However, as a background for those suggestions, it is necessary first to examine the physiological aspects of thinking.

Physiological Aspects of Thinking

We have sparse knowledge about the workings of our brain. Kubie cites a phenomenon about hypnosis that dramatizes this fact. A subject is brought into a strange room for a few minutes. When subsequently asked to list every item seen, the subject will reproduce 20 or 30 items. Under hypnosis, the subject will reproduce about 200 more. There are ways to surface our unconscious. To be able to utilize such methods, it is useful to examine our brain physiology.[7]

Brain function research has revealed the importance of the corpus callosum, a small bundle of nerves found between the left and right sides of the brain. Until recently, the corpus callosum was thought to have no significant function. Now, however, scientists know that the brain is not one center of thought and learning but two. Each side has control over certain skills. When the corpus callosum is intact, the two sides work in harmony, although one may dominate.

But when the corpus is cut or damaged, the left side of the brain is no longer aware of what the right side is doing and vice versa.[8]

The study of the functions of our brain hemispheres began in 1836. Marc Dax, an obscure country doctor, presented a short paper at a medical society meeting in Montpellier, France. Like most of his contemporaries, Dax was not a frequent contributor to medical conferences. In fact, this paper was to be his first and only scientific presentation. During his long career as a general practitioner, Dax had seen many patients suffering from loss of speech (known technically as *aphasia*) following damage to the brain. This observation was not new. Cases of sudden, permanent disruption in the ability to speak coherently had been reported by the ancient Greeks. Dax, however, was struck by what appeared to be an association between the loss of speech and the side of the brain where the damage had occurred. In more than 40 patients with aphasia, Dax noticed signs of damage to the left hemisphere of the brain. He was unable to find a single case that involved damage to the right hemisphere alone. In his paper to the medical society, he summarized these observations and presented his conclusions: each half of the brain controls different functions; speech is controlled by the left half.[9]

Although clinical data pointing to brain asymmetries have been available for over 100 years, current interest in the left brain and right brain is traceable to recent work involving so-called split-brain patients. For medical reasons, these patients have undergone surgery to cut the cortical pathways that normally connect the cerebral hemispheres. After recovering from the initial shock of major brain surgery, most patients report an improved feeling of well-being. Springer and Deutsch report that less than two days after surgery, one young patient was well enough to quip that he had a "splitting headache"![10]

Special techniques make it possible to confine detailed sensory information to just one hemisphere. The limiting of stimuli to one hemisphere is often called *lateralization*. One way to accomplish lateralization is to let a blindfolded patient feel an object with one hand only. A split-brain patient who does this with the right hand (which is controlled principally by the left hemisphere) will have no difficulty naming the object (Figure 5–1). But if the procedure is repeated, this time using the left hand, the patient will be unable to name the object. Apparently, information about the object does not get through to the

Figure 5–1 Crossed Functions between Brain and Rest of the Body

Source: Springer, S. P., and G. Deutsch, *Left Brain, Right Brain* (New York: W.H. Freeman and Co., 1981).

speech centers located in the left hemisphere. Nevertheless, the patient can easily use his or her left hand to retrieve the object from a number of other objects hidden from sight. A casual onlooker might conclude that the left hand knew and remembered what it held even though the patient did not.

Taking advantage of other techniques that confine visual and auditory information to one hemisphere at a time, researchers have demonstrated significant differences in the capabilities of the two hemispheres in split-brain patients. The left hemisphere has been found to be predominantly involved with analytic processes, especially the production and understanding of language, and it appears to process input in a sequential manner. The right hemisphere appears to be responsible for certain spatial skills and musical abilities and to process information simultaneously and holistically.[11]

The preeminent *split-brain* research studies were conducted by Dr. Roger W. Sperry and his associates at the California Institute of Technology. Sperry, along with Joseph E. Bogen, Michael S. Grazzaniga, Jerre Levy, and other members of his group, worked with end-state epileptics in whom the corpus callosum had been severed in an effort to relieve severe seizures. Remarkably, the split-brain patients showed virtually no obvious changes in personality, capacities, or behavior. But if severing this massive neural connection had no influence on temperament or behavior, why did it exist at all? And what was the function of the mute right brain? To find out, Sperry and his colleagues designed a set of subtle tests to isolate and reveal the functioning of each hemisphere. The findings of these tests revolutionized our understanding of the human brain—and earned Dr. Sperry a Nobel Prize in 1981.[12]

We now know, too, that each half of the brain has its own memories and its own train of thought. The left half deals mainly in words and is associated with analysis and logical thinking. The right half deals mainly in sensory images and is associated with intuition and creative thinking. Despite the separateness of the hemispheres, however, the brain's functions are profoundly integrated.[13]

Some researchers regard the brain as synonymous with the mind. Western philosophy, however, has traditionally held that there is an important difference. According to this view, the brain is a physical reality whereas the mind is metaphysical—that is, nonmaterial.[14]

Rational and Arational Modes

John Fabian refers to the two modes of thinking not as creative/ critical but as the rational and the arational (see Table 5–1).[15] In actual working, however, there is much interaction, much blending between these modes. As with psychological types, however, people

Table 5–1		Rational	Arational
Rational and Arational Modes Contrasted	**How you think**	Reduce	Expand
		Step by step	Simultaneous
		Analyze	Intuit
		Use verbal	Use nonverbal
	What you do	Search for correct way	Search for variety of ways
	What this requires	Precision	Approximation
		Control	Letting go
	How you respond	For arational thinkers this seems confining, slow, narrow, detailed, unnecessary, too linear	For rational thinkers this seems chaotic, diverting, scary, obscure, untested, too random or risky

Source: Fabian, J., *Creative Thinking and Problem Solving* (Chelsea, MI: Lewis Publishers, Inc., 1990), p. 39.

often prefer one style. An individual, therefore, tends to use one mode more than the other.

If your *rational mode* is predominant, you try to reduce or squeeze data down to their essential elements. You sift through a variety of information in a step-by-step fashion, looking for logical connections. Time is taken to weigh bits and pieces of information. Through analysis of the data you arrive at a conclusion. Your primary vehicle of analysis and expression is verbal—using known symbols of language and mathematical and scientific equations that are familiar to you and to others with whom you want to communicate....[16]

If your *arational mode* is predominant, you allow the data to grow, to expand into whatever patterns emerge. You take in information from a variety of sources or directions simultaneously, using a soft approach rather than a hard, rational one. Intuition is a key mechanism that helps you see a bigger picture from pieces of information, from clues and cues that give you an image, an impression, or sense of the answer or direction to be taken. Conclusions may come in the form of images, sounds or feelings.

Properties of Memory

Memory has an important function in thinking, both creative and critical thinking. We not only need to be able to store and catalog the ideas we generate, we need to rely on our domain of knowledge for both processing and generation of ideas. Our memory is comprised of several

Figure 5–2   Human Memory System Showing Flow of Input to Storage

Source: Adam, J. L., *Care and Feeding of Ideas* (Reading, MA: Addison-Wesley, 1986), pp. 31–32.

components with different storage functions. Figure 5–2 shows how
we receive the input to memory, through the five senses. Transactions
or messages are input to memory primarily through visual or auditory
sensors, recording what we see and what we hear. Messages also are
input to a less extent through the other senses of touch, taste, and
smell. Each of these five inputs has its own sensory memory area and
is retained there only a few seconds before being transferred for processing in short-term memory (STM). The message is scanned for pattern recognition, then passed on the STM. The message will be
retained in STM only by repeating it, that is, rehearsal. If not
rehearsed, the message will be retained for less than 30 seconds.
Through repeating it, such as you do in a telephone booth when
you've looked up a number and are about to dial it, you can retain the
item for more than 30 seconds. Most of us have had the experience of
driving through a metropolitan area looking for a street address that
we've marked on our city map. We memorize the street address by
repeating it to ourselves several times. We frequently check the streets
we're passing against the map to see how close we're getting to our
destination. Sometimes we must pull over to the side of the street to

make that check. It would be much more convenient, and safer, to memorize all the streets surrounding the destination. Unfortunately, only small amounts of information can be retained in short-term memory. George Miller's research showed that 7 ± 2 chunks of information could be retained in STM at any one point in time.[17] A chunk is a configuration that is familiar to an individual and can be manipulated as a unit—a cognitive structure that can grow as information is integrated into it.

In other words, if we concentrate on it, we can store more data in each chunk. For example, the telephone number of seven digits is fairly easy to remember. However, what if we need to remember an area code as well, or worse yet, the international code too? In such a situation, we need to devise a chunking approach to simplify retention. We "beat" the 7 ± 2 constraint by grouping of digits into 4 segments: country code, area code, city code, and the four digit individual number, *e.g.,* 011–800–555–3403. We can better remember because we have converted the 13 numbers into 4 numbers or chunks.

Yet, the limitation of STM is further complicated. The capacity of STM is lowered if other processing demands are made. The normal capacity of seven chunks or so may be reduced to a capacity of two or three chunks if other tasks are taken on simultaneously, such as search processes or counting. The objective is to get the message into long term memory (LTM), where there is unlimited capacity. "Elaborative" rehearsal allows us to link the incoming message with a related item in LTM, in order to retain the input indefinitely. There is one other aspect to consider: transfer time. The amount of time to transfer an item from STM to LTM (if the type of coding needed to allow retention in LTM is performed) is from 5 to 10 seconds to fixate one chunk in LTM, if one must later recall the information. To illustrate, can you recall an input which triggered memory of an event from long ago—an event you thought you'd forgotten? An example is having a near-miss on an automobile collision, triggering your recollection of a similar event that happened when you were a child riding in your parents' car. The input was temporarily stored in sensory memory and transferred to STM, then may have been linked to LTM if it was a meaningful event. No rehearsal was required in this transaction. The message was automatically processed because of the link. Most incoming data is not meaningful and therefore is not linked automatically. To make sure the data we want remembered is stored in LTM, we must make a conscious effort to move it from STM.

In critical thinking, we want to be able to extract important, related information from LTM in order to more effectively evaluate an idea. For example, if we see a wasp nest next to an entrance we must use, we try to recall all that we know about wasp behavior to create several possible strategies for safe bypass of the nest. Before we choose an entrance strategy, we want to evaluate the risks of the various strategies we've created.

With that brief overview of the functions of memory, we will next examine each component of the cognitive process more thoroughly. Before starting that, it is important to review the purpose for exploring the neurological process to this level of depth. How can it make us more creative? First, anything we can learn to make us better understand the brain anatomy and our own cognitive process is useful. However, a more direct objective is to help us in two ways: 1) improving our memory capability and 2) helping us move to a more holistic use of our abilities. The research on creativity has revealed that knowledge domain is an essential element for producing ideas that are substantive, not just simplistic solutions. We need to have a firm knowledge foundation in the subject area where the problem or opportunity exists. A better understanding of our memory processes helps us acquire and retain knowledge more effectively. If we read some material or hear a lecture and retain only a small amount of the content, we have very inefficient mental processes. Full understanding of the cognitive process helps us better retain and retrieve the information that our sensors pick up. Understanding the process can also help us achieve a holistic perspective, to be able to combine and relate data and information to the problem/opportunity at hand. We can become more creative and critical thinkers.

Sensory Memory

It is helpful to think of sensory memory as VSTM, very short-term memory. It is believed that each sensory memory area contains only simple information, such as color, but not complex characteristics that require reference to learned patterns in LTM, *e.g.,* "this is the color of the sun."[18]

Note in Figure 5–2 that there is a "scanner" that interprets information exiting sensory memory. Scanners operate at a frequency of about 10 cycles per second. They also control the rate at which humans search or scan LTM for specific items of information.[19] Another factor involved in transfer of information is channel capacity. A.C. Walker's research shows that the magnitude of this human limitation can best be appreciated by comparing typical channel capacities for various types of electronic equipment to human sense organs. Electronic channels have capacities of hundreds to billions of bits (binary digits) per second, while the eye can process about a million and the ear 10,000 bits per second.[20] The practical consequence is the inability to apprehend or catch more than a few simultaneous events (chunks).

Cognitive psychologists such as John Hayes hold that the primary purpose of sensory memory is to retain raw information just long enough for appropriate processing. For example, visual patterns must be held long enough so that they can be recognized as belonging to a category, *e.g.,* a letter, a word, a face.[21]

Studies by Sperling and Darwin, Turvey, and Crowder reveal that visual sensory memory can store nine to ten symbols for less than one second and that auditory sensory memory can hold about five symbols for less than four seconds.[22]

If we do not pay attention to the information in sensory memory ("attend" to it, in the parlance of cognitive psychology), the memory decays in seconds. Therefore, attention is key to transferring of a message from VSTM to STM, then linking it to information in LTM. Take the example familiar to each of us: we are carrying on a conversation with a classmate during a class where the instructor is lecturing. We are aware of the words of the lecturer, but our attention is on the words of our classmate. If the instructor sees our inattention and calls out our name, he or she gets our immediate attention. The research shows that we can be aware of several conversations simultaneously, but can attend to only one at a time. Attention is a limited resource.

Short-Term Memory

In the computer field, the term *working memory* represents the intermediate storage area (STM) used to process data before sending it to permanent storage (LTM). The concept derives from the workings of human memory. The computing field also uses the concept of temporary storage "registers," where small units of data are retained before being accessed by working memory. The term register is also used in cognitive psychology for sensory storage (VSTM). STM is working memory—where the majority of the action occurs. Klatzky describes STM as a workbench where information recognized in the sensory registers and information retrieved from LTM may be processed and put to work. As stated above, STM holds only a limited amount of data and will retain the data only for a limited amount of time.[23]

Although we may not have heard of STM previously, most have heard the term *memory span.* Some of us have been involved in tests to determine how many numbers we can remember from a list or a table. Memory span is less for words than for letters. According to Hayes, the memory span for familiar words averages 5.86 compared to 7.2 for letters.[24] However, the span is large when we recognize that many letters are contained in the 5.86 words. This is another example of the concept of chunking. Using chunking, we can remember larger amounts of information for longer periods of time, hopefully until we can get the information into LTM. As our skills develop, the amount of information contained in each chunk becomes larger so that we are able to hold larger amounts of data in STM.

Chunking helps not only in storing but in retrieving information from LTM. In the field of computing, data and information are differentiated. Data has limited usefulness until combined with other data to produce information. The term *chunking* is not used in the computer field but is similar to converting data to information. For example, the grades of each student on an exam are useful information. But when we compute mean and standard deviation from those data, the information produced from the original data is much more useful.

Cognitive research shows that continuous rehearsal permits us to keep information in STM long enough to set up the link to LTM. Nevertheless, the limited capacity of STM may result in that chunk being lost if another message is entered that causes the capacity of STM to be exceeded.

While some chunking is automatic, the ability to improve memory (move items on the LTM) can be enhanced by explicitly coding data. The following exercise was developed by James Adams to provide a better understanding of the workings of STM.[25]

STM Exercise

To better understand the workings of STM, complete the following exercise. Read each of the following sequences of numbers to yourself evenly and carefully. Then, *immediately after each sequence,* close your eyes and repeat the numbers to yourself.

7   4   9   5   2   8

5   8   3   6   1   4   9   0   2

8   3   9   4   1   6   0   2   5   7   3   0

You probably noticed several things. If you read the numbers evenly, the initial sequence (six digits) was relatively easy to recall. The next sequence was more difficult, and the last was impossible for most of us. After a mere doubling of information, from a paltry six digits to a mere twelve, most of us reached our limit of short-term memory.

Example: You are in a phone booth with no directory, no pencil and no credit card. You insert coins, dial the information operator and are given the area code and the number—a sequence of ten digits. You repeat the sequence to yourself (rehearsal) while hanging up, retrieving the coins, and dialing it. Before the ringing begins, you stop repeating the sequence. If you get a busy signal instead, where are you? Probably with an overstretched STM and the need to return to the operator!

The problem is working with uncoded nine-digit numbers. When the telephone system included an alpha prefix (such as Riverside 9-3403), the partial coding enabled us to more easily remember the number in order to move it into LTM.

This exercise illustrated the capacity limitation of STM. It also illustrated the time limitation of STM. Unless you have a photographic memory, you cannot now recall the nine-digit number in the second line of the list you read a few moments ago.

During the exercise you may have noticed that you tended to read the digits to yourself in groups rather than evenly. That is another example of the process of chunking.

Coding helps STM capacity a great deal. We use this technique constantly and automatically (because we derived the strategy earlier in life). There was massive resistance to the change from the word prefix in telephone numbers because the word prefix conveniently coded the first two symbols, making the number easier to remember.

If you performed a similar exercise with letters rather than numbers, you would probably notice that, even though you were dealing with vision, you held the information in STM as sounds. You silently speak the names of the letters to yourself as you read them and you recall them as sounds rather than as visual images of the printed characters. In STM we tend to confuse letters such as *B* and *V*, which have similar sounds.

Long-Term Memory

Similar to the use of the term *permanent memory* in the computer field, something stored in LTM can last a lifetime. However, the computer analogy breaks down, because in computer memory new information can be written over previous information, effectively erasing it. A human's LTM capacity is virtually unlimited. Although we may use the more recent information more frequently, the old information still exists. Each of us is occasionally surprised by our own LTM retentive ability, as in remembering the face of a childhood playmate.

To summarize, LTM is a permanent and essentially unlimited store, characterized by the following properties:

1) Semantic concepts, associations among concepts, visual images, and auditory events may be stored.

2) The form of storage for the semantic concepts can be viewed as a network, with nodes representing concepts and links representing the associations between concepts.

Memory Strategies

Through rehearsal we can retain something long enough in STM to transfer it to LTM. However, in order to fix something in LTM, more elaborate processes are required. They are referred to as *memory control processes*—strategies used by individuals for controlling the flow of information into and out of memory. There are six basic processes:[26]

1. **Rehearsal**—the process of further analysis made up of maintenance of information and transfer to LTM. Rehearsal can be mere repetition (less retention) or more detailed analysis of the information (more retention).

2. **Coding**—the way individuals structure information for rehearsal, such as mnemonics, associations, and images.

3. **Transfer**—the decision of what to store in memory and the form in which to store it. Information that is important for attaining goals and information that is easily stored are likely to be given highest priority.

4. **Placement**—determining where an item is to be stored in memory. Depends on the existing organization of memory and the particular associations utilized in coding the item. "Where" does not refer to a physical location but the association structure developed when the item was processed.

5. **Retrieval**—extraction of information from LTM. Retrieval processes can range from almost immediate access for familiar items to involved problem-solving search processes for other items. Forgetting is a failure of the retrieval process rather than a decay or loss of items.

6. **Response generation**—items are not merely revived or reactivated in recall; instead, the stored fragments are used as information to support a new construction.

Relationship of Memory to Creativity

Creative thinking consists of three major steps, which John Clemmons calls "The New Three Rs." Each step depends on the success of the previous one. Together they act synergistically to produce whatever is new. The steps are:[27]

1. Recording information (committing it to memory)
2. Retrieving information (recalling, reconstructing it)
3. Recombining information (putting it together in a different way)

Recording

Highly creative people are also highly curious and knowledgeable about many subjects. They mentally file vast amounts of information that might be used for recombining (Step 3). The more we know, the more we can recombine.

Retrieving

This is the most difficult, unreliable step. It's entirely dependent on what has been recorded. If we've never experienced college, we'll have fewer images associated with it than if we had been there. And even if we have gone to college, at any given moment we can recall—or reconstruct—only a tiny percentage of our college memories.

Recombining

Some hold, like the writer of Ecclesiastes, that "there is no new thing under the sun." It is evident that most ideas come from associations with previous information. In *The Art of Clear Thinking*, Rudolph Flesch observes that a new idea is the reassociation of existing ideas—or parts of ideas—to form a new combination. This step is entirely dependent on the success of Step 1 (recording) and Step 2 (recall/retrieval). If there's not much information in memory, not much can be recalled. If little can be recalled, the chances of recombination are slim.

I believe this discussion of the neurological processes is useful to better understand the thinking process. However, I agree with Bettman when he says descriptions of storage, retrieval, processing seem to imply that a person is an information processor, like a computer "with skin." It is true that a person is an information processor. Computers and people both possess certain basic organizational similarities. However, there are important differences. As Hunt and Mackous point out, the specific components differ greatly. A person has great input capability, an unlimited and efficient permanent memory, and a slow, inefficient short-term memory. A digital computer is essentially the opposite.

> A great many people think they are thinking when they are merely rearranging their prejudices.
>
> *William James*

Ways to Improve Memory and Thinking Ability

The number memory exercise earlier in this chapter showed ways we can encode data to enhance our ability to process and retain information in memory. I'll now review a number of other approaches to improve thinking and memory ability.

Improving Concentration

We often tend to attribute special endowments to creative persons, like a unique ability for concentration. More often these abilities are acquired. We all are confronted with things that can distract us; we cannot avoid them. However, we can learn ways to better cope with these distractions, to more quickly regain our concentration.

Ruggiero says that concentrating is much like steering a car. When experienced drivers steer, they don't lock their hands on the wheel in one fixed position; they turn it slightly to the right and to the left to keep the car on course. Even on a straight road, the car stays on course only a small percentage of the time. They must make constant adjustments, many of them almost imperceptible. Experienced drivers are not more talented than inexperienced ones; they have simply learned to make subtle corrections at the right time. Similarly, the secret of efficient thinkers is not that they experience fewer distractions but that they have learned to deal with them more quickly and more effectively than inefficient thinkers do. There is no magic in what effective thinkers do. You can learn it as they did, by practicing.[28]

John Dewey observed that more of our time than most of us care to admit is spent "trifling with mental pictures, random recollections, pleasant but unfounded hopes, flitting, half-developed impressions." Dewey believed that mental discipline was possible:

> If a man's actions are not guided by thoughtful conclusions, then they are guided by inconsiderate impulse, unbalanced appetite, caprice, or the circumstances of the moment. To cultivate unhindered, unreflective external activity is to foster enslavement, for it leaves the person at the mercy of appetite, sense, and circumstance.[29]

Primacy/Recency Effects

The following exercise by Adams helps understand primacy/recency effects in storing and retrieval of items in memory.[30] Read the following list of words just once. Do not study it. Simply read each word to yourself in order. As soon as you have finishing reading the list, turn the page and write down as many of the words you recall in whatever order they occur to you.

can   church   house   orange   table   sky   rock   quick

brown   fox   coronary   chin   knob   year   cancer   field

cat   Beethoven   flower   hill   wine   dog   president   car

nose   harassment   divorce   apple   sheep   mouse   tree

_____

_____

_____

_____

_____

Since there are more than seven words you probably did not remember them all. However, primacy and recency effects determine which you did recall. You were more likely to remember the word at the beginning of the list and at the end. The explanation for the primacy effect is that you had a clean slate when you began. The reason for the recency effect is that there was less interference between the words at the end of the list and the recall time than between the ones in the middle of the list and the recall time. The same thing applies to listening to a lecture. A study by E.J. Thomas revealed that students best recall material at the beginning and end of the lecture.[31]

Adams provides an example of applying knowledge of the primacy/recency effect to running a meeting more effectively. If you are trying to make a point that people remember, make it either early or late. Try not to run the meeting continuously for several hours. Breaks are essential. As an attendee of meetings, make sure you take good notes in the middle of the meeting.[32]

Returning to the results of the exercise: you might also have remembered words that stood out from the rest of the list (such as *Beethoven*). This is called the Von Restorff effect, after a psychologist who experimented with various types of lists and found that words or numbers were remembered better if surrounded with symbols of a different type. You might have recalled words from the list that were personally important to you—that were accompanied with some sort of emotion when you read them, such as harassment. Finally, you might have remembered *quick brown fox,* since the three words were presented in a structure with which you were familiar.

These effects should make you knowledgeable about the information in your memory and the way to store it. They should also give you clues about how to make better use of your memory capability.

Mnemonics as a Memory Aid

Mnemonics are devices (structures) such as jingles, formulas, or rhymes used as an aid to remembering.

> ***Example:***   Medical students use the following mnemonic aid to remember branches of the abdominal aorta:
>
> "Please, Can Soft Soap Remove Tint in Ladies' Stockings?"
>
> Phrenics, Coeliac Artery, middle Suprarenal, Superior mesenteric, Renal, Testicular, Inferior mesenteric, Lumbar, middle Sacral

Assume you are preparing to take a test on this book and I asked you to remember key people in your preparation. In the test I ask, "Who has been most frequently quoted so far in this book?" You might have used a mnemonic from a children's game to help you remember this name. _____

> ***Hint:***   He is one of the developers of the four-component definition of creativity and is the person who derived the best known three-element approach to problem solving.
>
> ***Answer:***   Herbert Simon. For most persons, the name would be more easily recalled by thinking of the game "Simon says!"

Another memory aid is referred to as the method of locus of attention. In order to remember a list of disparate items, you can mentally place each of the items in one of the loci. You could do that with the rooms of a house or building. That technique was first described by Quintillian about 50 A.D.

Or you could think of a familiar walk and "place" items at points you remember on the path. I use a variation of this approach the second class of each semester. Our university is in a beautiful setting where I can take students on a walk up the wooded hill behind the building where I teach. Within ten minutes we can be over the hill, in a valley where we cannot hear any traffic or campus noises, just the sounds of the countryside. I ask students to use both loci and their five senses to aid memory. The instructions given at the outset are as follows:

"I provided you a mnemonic for data gathering, when I gave instructions for our walk up the hill behind the university. I asked you to observe unusual things from the fauna and flora as well as the views from progressively higher heights. That is called the locus of attention approach. You can easily remember seven loci as initial chunks. Under the locus (chunk) of Cragmor Hall, some of you recall the building's cupolas. Under the locus (chunk) of fauna, some of you recall deer track and raccoon track. On the other side of the hill, under the locus of the sense of sight, you recall the red-tailed hawks. Under the locus of sense of smell, you recall cedar sprigs and cedar berries. Under the locus of sound, you recall the unique shriek of the red-tailed hawk, or my voice (somewhat less of a shriek) as I read the background material. Under the locus of sense of taste, you recall the bitter, acrid taste of the berries. Under the locus of sense of feel, you recall the smooth surface of berries as contrasted to the rough texture of the rocks where you were seated."

Characteristics of Critical Thinking

For many people, the word *critical* has a negative connotation; it implies excessive faultfinding. Some people have that connotation in mind when they hear or see the term *critical thinking*. The major problem in discussing critical thinking arises from the lack of a common definition. The variety of ways critical thinking is defined range from reasoning, to high-order thinking, to intelligent behavior.[33] Also, some view critical thinking as the comprehensive thought process that includes creative thinking as a subcategory, while others have the opposite view: that critical thinking is an activity within the process of creative thinking which refers to the process of evaluating ideas.[34] Grant provides a comprehensive analysis of the process of critical thinking: "When we think critically, we judge the accuracy of statements and the soundness of the reasoning that leads to conclusions. Critical thinking helps us interpret complex ideas, appraise the evidence offered in support of arguments, and distinguish between reasonableness and unreasonableness. Both problem solving and decision making depend on critical thinking, as does the meaningful discussion of controversial issues."[35]

Clear thinking is essential to facilitate two principal business needs: problem solving and opportunity finding. For this purpose, two categories of thinking are useful: creative thinking and critical thinking, in that order. Creative thinking gives us new ideas; this kind of thinking is an exercise of imagination. Critical thinking "comes into play after we have an idea to try out, a theory to test, a proposition that someone wants to prove or refute."[36]

The distinction is still not as clean as I'd prefer. For example, another category of thinking, reflective thinking, has some useful components for producing creative ideas. But also included under the heading of reflective thinking are daydreaming and fantasizing. Some would consider the latter activities as relatively unproductive compared to creative thinking. Yet, appropriate behavior when one is in the midst of problem solving and has reached an impasse, is to shift one's mind into neutral, to daydream or to fantasize. Although such activity rarely "blows away the cobwebs," it often permits us to find a path through the cobwebs, or to circumvent the cobwebs to arrive at new alternatives for resolution of the problem.

Jay distinguishes creative thinking and critical thinking as follows.[37]

1. **Creative Thinking: the Production Phase**

   In this phase the mind produces various conceptions of the problem or issue, various ways of dealing with it, and possible solutions or responses to it. Good thinkers produce more and better ideas than do poor thinkers. They become more adept in using a variety of techniques, enabling them to discover ideas. More specifically, good thinkers tend to see the problem from many perspectives before choosing any one, to consider many different investigative approaches and to produce many ideas before turning to judgment. In addition, they are more willing to take intellectual risks, to be adventurous and consider outrageous or zany ideas, and to use their imaginations and aim for originality.

   In contrast, poor thinkers tend to see the problem from a limited number of perspectives (often just a single narrow one), to take the first approach that occurs to them to judge each idea immediately, and to settle for only a few ideas. Moreover, they are overly cautious in their thinking, unconsciously making their ideas conform to the common, the familiar, and the expected.

2. **Critical Thinking: The Judgment Phase**

   In this phase the mind examines and evaluates what it has produced, makes its judgments and, where appropriate, adds refinements. Good thinkers handle this phase with care. They test their first impressions, make important distinctions, and base their conclusion on evidence rather than on their own feelings. Sensitive to their own limitation and predispositions, they double-check the logic of their thinking and the workability of their solutions, identifying imperfections and complications, anticipating negative responses, and generally redefining their ideas.

In contrast, poor thinkers judge too quickly and uncritically, ignoring the need for evidence and letting their feelings have disproportionate effect on their conclusions. Blind to their limitations and predispositions, poor thinkers trust their judgment implicitly, ignoring the possibility of imperfections, complications, or negative responses.

De Bono believes that logical thinking is not helpful in creative thinking (in generating new ideas), because it "follows the most obvious line." That is, we try to solve problems using our past experience, our "tried and true" methods. According to de Bono, many problems, including presumably the most important ones, require a fresh viewpoint that is not provided by ordinary "tried and true" logical thinking.[38]

Creative versus critical thinking is represented in the CPS model as the opposite sides of the diamond symbol used to denote each of the five CPS phases (Figure 5–3). The left side of the diamond, giving the visual representation of an opening-up process, is the creative activity of each phase. Two other ways to express this activity are divergent thinking and generative thinking. Critical thinking (the right side of the diamond) is also referred to as evaluative thinking or converging thinking.

Figure 5–3

Creative versus Critical Thinking Applied to Each Phase on CPS Process

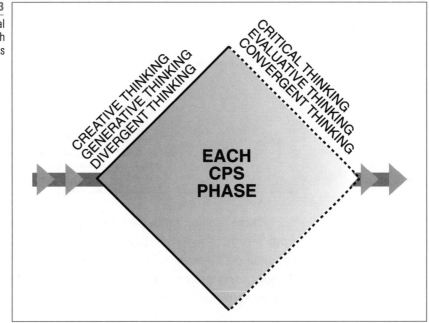

Table 5–2 How to Overcome the Problem and Become More Proficient Thinkers	"Mine is better"	Preferring your own ideas for no other reason than that they are yours. Remind yourself that all people tend to regard their ideas that way, but critical thinking demands that you examine your ideas as you would other people's.
	Resistance to change	Preferring familiar to unfamiliar ideas. Expect your first reaction to new ideas to be negative. Set that reaction aside and judge the idea on the basis of your critical appraisal.
	Conformity	Thinking the way others do because of the group or your desire to belong. (Or, conversely, thinking the way others do *not,* simply because they do not.) Base your thinking on the evidence and not on how others do or don't think.
	Face-saving	Attempting to preserve your self-image or the image you project to others when some unpleasant reality threatens it. Distinguish between what you wish were so and what is so. Be honest with yourself.
	Stereotyping	Making fixed, unbending generalizations about people, places, or things. Remind yourself that most things do not fit into neat categories. In addition, resist the feeling that you *know* what the correct judgment is when that feeling arises early in the information-gathering process.
	Oversimplification	Simplifying that does not merely scale down complex matters to more manageable proportions but twists and distorts them. Be sure your views are an accurate representation of reality.
	Hasty conclusions	Judgments made before sufficient evidence is obtained. Withhold judgment until you have answered all important questions pertaining to the issue. If you must answer without sufficient evidence, use the "If...then" approach. If the evidence will support probability but not certainty, limit your conclusion to one that is merely probable.
	Unwarranted assumptions	Ideas that you have in mind and that influence your reasoning without your being conscious of it; ideas you take for granted. Develop the habit of reading (and listening) between the lines for ideas that are unexpressed but nevertheless clearly implied.
	Logical fallacies	Specific errors that occur in your reasoning about issues. Monitor your thinking for signs of these errors, especially when you are planning an oral or written presentation of your views.

There are several behaviors/attitudes which prevent some of us from becoming more proficient critical thinkers. Recognizing these common deficiencies enables us to work on eliminating them. Ruggiero defines each problem and how to recognize and deal with each as shown in Table 5–2:[39]

Learning to think critically is one of the most significant activities of adult life. When we become critical thinkers we develop an awareness of the assumptions under which we, and others, think and act.

Brookfield

Functional Fixedness

Let's contrast critical/creative thinking from a different perspective. K. Duncker investigated how past experience could limit problem-solving productivity.[40] He defined the problem as one of "functional fixedness"—a mental block against using an object in a new way that is required to solve a problem. To investigate this phenomenon more carefully, he devised a series of problems that he thought might involve functional fixedness and presented them to subjects in his laboratory. For example, the subjects were given three cardboard boxes, matches, thumbtacks, and candles. The goal was to mount a candle vertically on a nearby screen to serve as a lamp. Some subjects were given a box containing matches, a second box holding candles, and a third one containing tacks—preutilization of the boxes—while other subjects received the same supplies but with the matches, tacks, and candles outside the boxes—no preutilization. The solution—to mount a candle on the top of a box by melting wax onto the box and sticking the candle to it, and then tacking the box to the screen—was much harder to discover when the provided boxes were filled rather than empty. Duncker's explanation was that the placement of objects inside a box helped to fix its function as a container, thus making it more difficult for subjects to reformulate the function of the box and think of it as a support.

Adamson reran several of Duncker's experiments, including the box problem. Fifty-seven subjects were divided into two groups, preutilization and no preutilization, and each subject received three different problems for a maximum of 20 minutes each. The results were similar to those in Duncker's original study. For example, with the box problem, 86 percent of the subjects solved the problem within 20 minutes when the boxes were presented empty, but only 41 percent solved the problem when the boxes were presented as containers.[41]

A series of problems was developed by Paul Torrance as a part of his well-known *Torrance Tests of Creative Thinking.* According to Torrance, "The basic battery of the Torrance Test of Creative Thinking has been used in over 1,000 published research studies…and about 150,000 children and adults are being tested with these instruments each year."[42] These problems measure an intellectual skill that Guilford has called *divergent thinking*—thinking that moves outward from a problem in many possible directions, such as required in "List all the uses for a brick."[43] In contrast, many problems focus on *convergent thinking*—thinking that proceeds toward a single answer, such as $33 \times 14 =$ ____.

I'm going to use one of the Torrance exercises to help you improve your functional fixedness. We all have the problem, to various degrees. We all can improve our creativity by concentrating on reducing our functional fixedness. The exercise is a fun one.

> ***Exercise:*** Suppose all humans were born with six fingers on each hand instead of five. List all the consequences or implications that you can think of. (Give yourself three minutes.)

_____

_____

_____

_____

_____

_____

_____

_____

_____

How would Torrance derive a creativity measurement from your responses? Solutions to divergent thinking problems are most often scored for two factors:[44]

1. **Fluency**—the number of solutions that fit the requirements of the problem, and

2. **Originality**—the number of unusual or unique solutions, that is, solutions generated by very few other people.

For example, suppose your answers for the six-fingers problem were: 1) we would need to make gloves with six fingers, 2) we would need to redesign handgrips on bicycle handlebars, 3) we would be able to invent new obscene gestures, 4) we would be able to give a new secret handshake, 5) we would say "Give me six" instead of "Give me five" when giving a hand slap, and 6) we would use a base 12 number system instead of base 10.

To measure fluency, we simply can count the number of answers, which is six. To measure originality, we can see that when we give this test to many individuals, answer one is given by almost all of them, so it is low in originality; however, answer four is given by only a few people, so it is high in originality. By comparing the above six answers to the answers most commonly given, we could find that only two of the answers are rarely generated, so the originality score is two. Other possible measures are importance (*i.e.,* the usefulness of each solution as rated by a panel of judges), flexibility (*i.e.,* the number of different categories or approaches to the problem), and elaboration (*i.e.,* the number of embellishments to an idea).[45]

Let's take another look at the answers. Go back and underline the three most important answers you generated.

This task, which requires that you evaluate the possible solutions you have generated, is a central aspect of what has been called *critical thinking*. Thus, two skills needed for solving creative problems are the ability to generate alternatives (as measured by tests of divergent thinking) and to evaluate alternatives (as required in critical thinking).

Mayer comments, "It strikes many observers as strange that we expect students to be effective problem solvers yet we seldom provide direct instruction in how to solve problems."[46] At the same time, the consensus is growing that "thinking is a skill and can be taught."[47] Polya insists: "Solving problems is a practical art, like swimming, or skiing, or playing the piano: you can learn it only by imitation and practice."[48]

Holistic Thinking

Although it is useful to separate brain functions to better understand our own thought processes, it is important to have a holistic approach to thinking. The following observation by Vera John-Steiner is a valuable starting point in trying to think more holistically.

Traditionally the study of thought has been the domain of men; women were considered to be too subjective and lacking in the sustained commitment necessary for distinguished achievements, to be taken seriously as thinkers. These beliefs were unwittingly symbolized by the great French sculptor, Auguste Rodin. His well-known *Le Penseur* (The Thinker) is a seated, male figure. In the larger-than-life model exhibited in the garden of the Rodin museum in Paris, one sees the heavy head resting on a fist; the statue reveals taut and compact energy. In one of the rooms inside the Rodin museum there is another statue. It is a small head which bears the title *La Pensee* (Thought): the face is soft, the eyes are luminous, the brow is clear. The difference in the scale and the power of these two figures captures well the relative importance assigned to men and women in the traditional literature of the intellect, and the odd separation of "The Thinker" and the "Thought."[49]

Janusian Thinking

One group of psychologists holds that we simultaneously approach problems with our conscious and our subconscious. But since we have no control over our subconscious, this knowledge is not helpful to us in improving creativity. The more practical Janusian theory helps us think of our duality of creativity as a right brain/left brain process. Rothenberg originated the term *Janusian thinking* to symbolize and describe the mind processes which simultaneously realize the natural unity and harmony in apparent opposites.[50]

The Roman god Janus was a mythical figure depicted with two faces looking simultaneously in opposite directions (Figure 5–4). In Janusian thinking, creative insight and its ultimate expression—a creative product—involve simultaneous resolution of contradictory concepts.

In his discussion of innovative problem-solving strategies, Roger von Oech, founder and president of Creative Think, divides all types of thinking into two contrasting groups: "soft" and "hard." His "soft" thinking list includes metaphorical thinking, paradoxical thinking,

Figure 5–4

Janus, Roman God with Two Faces, Who Looked and Apprehended in the Opposite Directions Simultaneously

Rothenberg chose the term Janusian thinking to refer to the capacity to conceive and utilize two or more opposite or contradictory ideas, concepts or images simultaneously.

ambiguous thinking, and fantasy thinking. His "hard" list includes thinking that is exact, analytical, logical, and focused.

There are dozens of everyday examples of the duality in thinking:

yin and yang in the philosophy of Tai Chi

right versus left brain thinking

hard versus soft thinking

unconscious versus conscious thought

arts versus science

analytical versus intuitive creativity techniques

One group refers to the dual classification approach as structured versus unstructured techniques. But that thinking is entirely fallacious. You got an inkling in Chapter 2 but you'll have substantive proof of structure in intuitive techniques when we get to Chapter 8—idea generation. We'll use intuitive techniques that employ a high degree of structure to force us to better use our right brain so we can be more intuitive. We need to let ourselves go emotionally in order to tap our own subconscious creative reserve and make it work for us.

Wasserman believes it is the kind of mythic, primitive, symbolic process that most of us are trained to avoid!

We produce suboptimal results if we rely primarily on one of the two hemispheres of our brain. We need, as in Janusian thinking, to be trying to use both hemispheres simultaneously. Springer and Deutsch conclude their book, *Left Brain, Right Brain,* with the statement: "We have seen evidence that, after the surgical division of the two hemispheres, learning and memory can continue separately in the left brain and right brain. Each half of the brain of a split-brain patient is able to sense, perceive, and perhaps even conceptualize independently of the other. Furthermore, in virtually every approach to the study of hemispheric processes, including approaches using normal individuals, findings support the existence of hemispheric differences.... Since the first split-brain operations, a progression of labels has been used to describe the processes of the left brain and right brain. The most widely cited characteristics may be divided into five main groups, which form a kind of hierarchy. Each designation usually includes and goes beyond the characteristics above it."[51]

Left Hemisphere	Right Hemisphere
Verbal	Nonverbal, visuo-spatial
Sequential, temporal, digital	Simultaneous, spatial, analogic
Logical, analytic	Gestalt, synthetic
Rational	Intuitive
Western thought	Eastern thought

Latting has developed a schematic to show how the hemispheres of the brain should work in union in problem solving (Figure 5–5).[52] The steps on the left, although not identical to the ones used in the CPS model in this book, are quite similar. They reveal that the CPS model primarily depicts left brain or analytical activities. The right side of the schematic shows how the intuitive abilities can be invoked at each stage of the CPS process to produce a more holistic result.

Other investigators have emphasized the significance of the differences between the hemispheres. It has been claimed that these differences clearly show the traditional dualism of intellect versus intuition, science versus art, and the logical versus the mysterious. Psychologist Robert Ornstein believes brain research shows that these distinctions are not simply a reflection of culture or philosophy. What used to be a belief in an Eastern versus a Western form of conscious-

Figure 5–5

Analytic versus Intuitive Actions/Reactions

Analytic Thought and Action (Left Hemisphere)	Intuitive Conceptualization and Reaction (Right Hemisphere)
1. Description and reformulation of the problem	1. Intuitive understanding of the problem incorporating emotional and "irrational" aspects
2. Development of criteria for problem resolution	2. Brainstorming to check that all criteria—rational, emotional, and value-based—are included
3. Development of alternative actions	3. Brainstorming to search for new arrangements to produce previously overlooked alternatives
4. Evaluation of alternatives against criteria	4. Growing awareness of intuitively preferred choice
5. Tentative decision	5. Visualization, insight, or other checks to see if the tentative decision is intuitively sound
6. Identification of negative consequences of decision	6. Awareness of a sense of ill- or well-being
7. Retention or change of choice	7. Emotional satisfaction with new or previous choice
8. Monitoring to diminish impact of negative effects	8. Monitoring to see if decision continues to feel right

Source: Latting, J. E., "Creative Problem-Solving Technique," *The 1985 Annual: Developing Human Resources* (Los Angeles, CA: University Associates, 1985), pp. 163–168.

Table 5–3

The Yin and Yang of Creativity

The Western Approach	The Eastern Approach
Breakthrough creativity	Adaptive creativity
Spontaneous creativity	Cultivated creativity
Creative fission	Creative fusion
Cartesian logic	Fuzzy logic
Uni-functional creativity	Multi-functional creativity

Source: Tatsuno, S., *Created in Japan* (New York: Harper Business, 1990), p. 16.

ness, he argues, now has a physiological basis in the differences between the two brain hemispheres.[53]

Sheridan Tatsuno, in *Created in Japan,* provides a table that represents this view of the yin and yang of creativity (Table 5–3). However, rather than accept that the left column (Western Approach) accurately represents our sole pattern of creativity, we should take the holistic perspective that we can utilize the Eastern approaches too. We can expand our creative abilities if we attempt to approach all our problems and opportunities holistically.

Conclusion

A major effort to improve the problem-solving performance of college students was carried out at the University of Chicago by B.S. Bloom and L.J. Broder. They wanted to boost the problem-solving performance of students. They addressed two issues: what to teach and how to teach. In determining what to teach, Bloom and Broder made the following distinction:

> Products of problem solving—whether the student arrives at the correct final answer or not

> Process of problem solving—the strategy people use on their way to getting the answer

Bloom and Broder argue that the present teaching mode places too much emphasis on the products of problem solving, instead of emphasizing the processes involved in creative problem solving. The two researchers decided that instruction in problem solving should not focus on reinforcing students for getting the right final answers but rather on teaching the problem-solving strategies useful in generating answers. They asserted that the "habits of problem solving, like other habits, could be altered by appropriate training and practice."[54]

The results of the study were significant. Students who participated in the process-oriented training tended to score an average of 0.49 to 0.68 grade points higher on the exam than matched groups who did not take the training. In addition, students who took the training expressed high levels of confidence and optimism concerning their newly acquired problem-solving abilities.

I've concentrated on process in this book. In this chapter, we've looked in depth at the thinking process. Mayer provides a nice start to our wrap-up for this chapter: "If we want to teach people to be more creative and critical problem solvers, we must first define what we mean by *creative thinking* and *critical thinking*. In the narrow sense, we can define creative thinking as a cognitive activity that results in one or more novel solutions for a problem. Thus creativity training involves teaching people how to generate new ideas or hypotheses regarding a given problem. Critical thinking can be viewed as cognitive activity that results in the selection of an appropriate solution or hypothesis. In the narrow sense, training in critical thinking involves teaching people how to evaluate and test ideas or hypotheses regarding a problem."[55]

In the broad sense, however, people are most creative when they are thinking holistically. While it is good practice to separate our generative (creative thinking) and evaluative (critical thinking) activities, we need to be using both hemispheres of the brain simultaneously in attacking the problems that face us. Fortunately, because the two hemispheres are linked, it is a natural thing to be using them in union. However, we tend to rely more on one than the other in the way we approach problems. We can consciously choose to utilize the other hemispheric approach at will so we can apply both in a more holistic fashion.

Bob Samples explained at a Whole Brain conference that it is biologically impossible not to use the whole brain when thinking, but it is possible not to pay attention to part of it. We can deliberately pay attention to each hemisphere and gain "whole-brained" response to our challenges.

However broadening dual hemispheric thinking might be, we need to be even more expansive, to try to achieve a holistic approach to life—unifying body, mind, and spirit. It is more natural than you might think. British neurosurgeon Penfield demonstrated by means of electrodes attached to a patient's brain that internal stimulus of the imagination could cause neuronal pathways to fire in a similar way that an external stimulus to the retina or other sense organ causes an image to occur in the brain. The mind and body are closely related. Note how we blush when embarrassed or yawn when bored.[56]

Including the other element of holistic existence, spirit or soul, can be just as natural. We need only to accept the reasoning of the value of the spiritual in the creative process—then utilize it.

This synergistic, holistic perspective is well explained by Dr. Sperry. "Consciousness, ideas, feelings, values, intentions, hunches, gut feelings, and beliefs can be considered emergent properties of the physical brain. When the brain is whole, the unified consciousness of the left and right hemispheres adds up to more than the composite properties of the separate hemispheres."[57]

Creative thinkers make many false starts, and continually waver between unmanageable fantasies and systematic attack.

Harry Hepner

All thinkers have their share of frustration: Confusion, mental blocks, false starts, and failures happen to everyone. Good thinkers, however, have learned strategies for dealing with their frustration, while poor thinkers merely lament it—thus allowing themselves to be defeated by it.

Henry Hazlitt

Summary

The study of right/left brain orientation and of memory in general is in full sway. It shows us that our memory contains key information for creativity and for response to change. It also reveals that we are heavily programmed in our problem solving. Adams reminds us that, "Traditional priorities, structures, and access programs are not always likely to give us the desired combinations. We once again should suspect that conscious effort is necessary to overcome the business-as-usual nature of the mechanisms of memory and that knowledge of memory (functions) is necessary in order to be effective in this effort."[58]

Understanding how memory works was a major objective of the chapter. If we know how to better capture important data, to process and store it as information, we are more qualified to produce substantive creative ideas. Knowledge domain is essential to creativity productivity.

Our cognitive process involves both creative and critical thinking. Divergent and convergent thinking is another way of expressing these characteristics. Generative and evaluative thinking are the third pair of terms that express this important contrast in productive thought process in problem solving and opportunity finding. Even though we need to separate these two mental activities to achieve a more effective CPS process, we need to keep a holistic frame of reference throughout the process. By consciously forcing ourselves to employ both hemispheres of our brain, aided by use of analytical and intuitive techniques, the holistic result is more easily achieved.

Gates found that individuals learn best when they test themselves during the learning process. He found that they can recall up to 80 percent of the study material if they spend an equal percent of time in self-recitation.[59] We can improve our ability to store key information and to be able to recall it.

A Chinese proverb

I hear; I forget
I see: I remember
I do: I understand

Exercises

 1. Differentiate creative from critical thinking.

 2. The result of split-brain research is knowledge about the different functions of each hemisphere of the brain. What are these functions?

 3. Differentiate intelligence from thinking.

 4. Distinguish the rational from the arational modes of thinking.

 5. Explain the differences in the three principal components of memory: VSTM, STM, and LTM.

 6. Explain the concept of chunking. What does George Miller's "7 ± 2" theory mean?

 7. Differentiate the memory strategies of rehearsal, coding, placement, retrieval, and response generation.

 8. List the behaviors that prevent some of us from becoming more proficient critical thinkers.

 9. Explain the ways to improve memory and thinking ability: improving concentration, awareness of primacy/recency effects, and mnemonics.

10. What is the concept of Janusian thinking? How does it relate to the earlier material of the chapter?

11. Explain holistic thinking.

12. Michalko refers to a popular children's puzzle that shows six fishermen whose lines are tangled together to form a sort of maze.[60] One of the lines has caught a fish; the problem is to

find which fisherman it belongs to. You are supposed to do this by following each line down through the maze, which may take up to six tries, depending on your luck. It is obviously easier to start at the other end and trace the line from the fish to the fisherman, as you have only one possible starting place, not six. That is an analytic, left-brain solution. Try to think of a right-brain approach to solving the problem.

13. An excerpt from a book by Edward Hanna, *The Whitechapel Horrors,* provides an interesting exercise in logical deduction.[61] Hanna has written this modern fiction about Sherlock Holmes and describes an example of his deductive ability. After you have read the excerpt, I'll point out a factor that was missing and ask you to use your own deductive ability.

"Really, Holmes, you exaggerate," Watson replied defensively. He was both hurt by Holmes's sarcastic rebuke and just a little annoyed.

"Do I? Do I indeed? Well, let us try a little test, shall we? Take, for example, the couple sitting at the table to my left and slightly behind me. You've been eyeing the young lady avidly enough during our meal. I deduce that it is the low cut of her gown that interests you, for her facial beauty is of the kind that comes mostly from the paint pot and is not of the good, simple English variety that usually attracts your attention. What can you tell me about the couple in general?"

Watson glanced over Holmes's shoulder. "Oh, that pretty little thing with the auburn hair—the one with the stoutish, balding chap, eh?"

"Yaas," Holmes drawled, the single word heavy with sarcasm. He examined his fingernails. "The wealthy American couple, just come over from Paris on the boat-train without their servants. He's in railroads, in the western regions of the United States, I believe, but has spent no little time in England. They are waiting—he, rather impatiently, anxiously—for a third party to join them, a business acquaintance, no doubt—one who is beneath their station but of no small importance to them in any event."

Watson put down his cup with a clatter. "Really, Holmes! *Really!*" he sputtered. "There is no possible way you could know all that. Not even you! This time you have gone too far."

"Have I indeed? Your problem, dear chap, as I have had occasion to remind you, is that you see but do not observe; you hear but do not listen. For a literary man, Watson—and note that I do not comment on the merit of your latest account of my little problems—for a man with the pretenses of being a writer, you are singularly unobservant. Honestly, sometimes I am close to despair."

He removed a cigarette from his case with a flourish and paused for the waiter to light it, a mischievous glint in his eye.

Watson gave him a sidelong look. "Very well, Holmes, I will nibble at your lure. Pray explain yourself!"

Holmes threw back his head and laughed. "But it is so very simple. As I have told you often enough, one has only to take note of the basic facts. For example, a mere glance will tell you that this particular couple is not only wealthy, but extremely wealthy. Their haughty demeanor, the quality of their clothes, the young lady's jewelry, and the gentleman's rather large diamond ring on the little finger of his left hand would suffice to tell you that. The ring also identifies our man as American: A 'pinky ring,' I believe it is called. What Englishman of breeding would ever think of wearing one of those?"

Holmes drew on his cigarette and continued, the exhalation of smoke intermingling with his dissertation. "That they are recently come from Paris is equally apparent: The lady is wearing the very latest in Parisian fashion—the low décolletage is, I believe, as decidedly French as it is delightfully revealing—and the fabric of the gown is obviously quite new, stiff with newness, probably never worn before. That they arrived this very evening is not terribly difficult to ascertain. Their clothes are somewhat creased, you see. Fresh out of the steamer trunk. Obviously, their appointment at Simpson's is of an urgent nature, otherwise they would have taken the time to have the hotel valet remove the creases before changing into the garments. That they are traveling without personal servants can be deduced by the simple fact that the gentleman's sleeve links, while similar, are mismatched, and the lady's hair, while freshly brushed, is not so carefully coiffed as one might expect it to be. No self-respecting manservant or lady's maid would permit their master or mistress to go out of an evening in such a state, not if they value their positions and take pride in their calling."

Watson sighed, a resigned expression on his face. He smoothed his mustache with his hand, a gesture of exasperation. "And the rest? How did you deduce all of that, dare I ask?"

"Oh, no great mystery, really. The man's suit of clothes is obviously Savile Row from the cut; custom made from good English cloth. It is not new. Ergo, he has visited our blessed plot before, at least once and for a long enough stay to have at least one suit, probably three or four, made to measure."

"Three or four? You know that with certainty, do you?"

Holmes, who was fastidious in his dress and surprisingly fashion conscious, and the possessor of an extensive wardrobe now that his success permitted it, allowed a slightly patronizing tone to color his reply.

"Formal attire would usually be a last selection; an everyday frock coat or 'Prince Albert' and more casual garments for traveling and for weekend country wear would customarily be the first, second, and third choices."

Watson looked pained, but he bravely, perhaps foolishly, continued: "You said he was a railroad man. How do you come by that, eh? And your conjecture that he is waiting for an urgent appoint, a business engagement, you said—and with someone beneath his station? How do you arrive at those conclusions?" He snorted. "Admit it, Holmes: pure guesswork, plain and simple!"

"You know me better than that," Holmes said, casually dabbing at his lips with a napkin. "I never guess." His lips puckered in a prim smile.

"Well then?" said Watson impatiently, drumming his fingers on the table.

"It is manifestly clear that the gentlemen is waiting for another individual because of his repeated glances toward the door—anxious glances which suggest that the other party is not only eagerly awaited, but of no small importance to the gentleman in question. That it is one individual and not more is supported by the obvious fact (so obvious, Watson) that the gentleman and lady are seated at a table for four, and there is only one other place setting in evidence. These conclusions are all supported by the additional observations that the man and his charming companion—his wife, I daresay, from his inattentive manner—have yet to order from the menu despite being at table for some considerable time, and the wretched fellow is well into at least his third whiskey and soda—with ice, I might add," he said with a slight curl to the lip, "further evidence he is an American, should any be needed."

"As for the rest—" Holmes stubbed his cigarette out and continued: "That the man has a well-stuffed leather briefcase on the chair beside him suggests an engagement of a business nature. Why else would anyone bring such an encumbrance to a late evening supper? As for the engagement being with someone beneath his station..." Holmes sighed and gave Watson a somewhat patronizing look. "Really, Watson, this is getting tiresome. Obviously, our friends over there are wealthy enough to dine at the Ritz or the Cafe Monico. Why Simpson's, as good as it is, with its simple English fare? Hardly what a wealthy American tourist or business magnate would choose unless he had good and sufficient reason to do so—such as not wishing to appear in a highly fashionable restaurant that caters to the *créme* of society with someone unsuitably dressed or of a lower station."

Watson raised his hands in a gesture of surrender. "Enough, enough; I should have known better than to doubt you. You have my most abject apologies. Now, for God's sake let us get the bill and find our way home. I am suddenly very weary and want only my bed."

Task: Despite his excellent replication of the style of Arthur Conan Doyle in describing Holmes's deductive ability, Hanna left out the rationale for deducing that the man was a railroad man. Can you think of a way Holmes might have known this fact?

Horse Taillight

Patent No. 2,079,053 (1937)
John E. Torbert, Jr., of National City, Calif.

"...to provide a device of this character adapted to be supported and held in place by engagement with the tail of the animal and carrying safety reflectors disposed at opposite sides of the animals' tail so that when a person is riding a horse along a road at night and an automobile approaches the horse from the rear, the signals will be illuminated by reflecting light..."

P A R T T W O

Creative Problem Solving (CPS)
and Opportunity Finding

Objectives of Part Two

The five phases of the creative problem-solving process are explained and illustrated in Part Two of this book. With the solid foundation gained through reading Part One, you are ready to delve deeply into the CPS methodology. Careful study of Part Two provides a foundation to apply your domain of knowledge about creativity, acquired in Part One.

Each of the five steps, or phases, of CPS has a divergence and convergence activity. The graphic representation of the CPS process uses the diamond symbol for each of the five steps, not just the third step, idea generation. We need creativity in problem definition and in data gathering as well as in solution finding. We also need creativity in evaluation of alternatives generated in Step 3. Finally, creativity is required for effective implementation planning. Many great ideas never become operational because of ineffective implementation plans. So, for each step, we diverge to produce a variety of alternatives and converge to reach the set of acceptable alternatives.

Chapter 6 covers problem definition, CPS Phase One. Elements of a good problem definition are explained. However, first we need to gain a good grasp of what the problem really is. Sometimes we have a "mess" to analyze, to determine the real problem. There are search processes to ferret out the problem from the mess. And, there are special creativity techniques to help us derive alternative problem definitions. As mentioned earlier, I have added "opportunity finding" to the first step of the CPS process. The traditional CPS model concentrates on problem solving. I've found that the same techniques can be used to identify opportunities. Again, this sounds like Step 3, idea generation, but it isn't. We identify opportunities in Step 1 and generate ideas about how to capitalize on those opportunities in Step 3.

CPS Phase Two is covered in Chapter 7: compiling relevant information about the problem or opportunity. This activity may precede problem definition, for example, in a "mess" situation. We may have to sift through a lot of data and information to separate problems from their symptoms. Not all problem solving follows the same sequence; however, all five steps are normally required to determine an optimal solution to a problem or to fully identify opportunities. There are special approaches and techniques that facilitate the activity of compiling relevant information.

CPS Phase Three, idea generation, is the exciting step in problem solving (Chapter 8). Few people need special motivation to participate in this activity. All 20 of the techniques described in the Appendix are appropriate for this phase of CPS. However, sometimes we need to combine the use of intuitive with analytical techniques, to generate a wide range of alternatives. Also, there are special approaches to use when we reach an impasse in problem solving or opportunity identification.

The evaluation and prioritization of ideas is the objective of Phase Four of CPS. Chapter 9 covers a variety of techniques for accomplishing this objective. First, however, we need to develop evaluation criteria. Risk analysis is another important activity in this step of CPS. The chapter covers criteria for evaluation of creative products and services as well as creative ideas.

The final step in the CPS process is development of an implementation plan, Phase Five. Chapter 10 describes the two components of this activity: acceptance planning and action planning. Both are essential and both require creative approaches. Some spe-

cial creativity techniques are useful for this phase of the CPS process as well.

One needs to consciously and continuously proceed through all five phases of problem solving and opportunity finding until the process becomes a demonstrable skill. Once the process is mastered, it becomes automatic. One of the managers of an organization where we helped introduce a creativity improvement program told us he was most pleased when he saw his employees using the CPS process on daily activities, not just special projects. In my university course on creativity, one of the assigned projects is to use CPS on a personal problem. Some of the topics selected by my students are: selecting a spouse, planning a wedding, deciding whether to enter graduate school, enabling their children to be more creative, planning an optimal vacation, purchasing a car or a house, time management, and dozens of other activities. Recognizing the usefulness of CPS in both job and non-job activities is "the proof of the pudding" in teaching a course on creativity.

Source: Reprinted with permission of DuPont.

C H A P T E R

6

A problem well stated is half solved.
John Dewey

STIMULUS → Opportunity Delineation, Problem Definition

Problem Definition/Opportunity Delineation

The previous chapters provided the overview of our study of creativity. We now begin the spiral approach of providing more depth on the material covered previously. This the first of five chapters, one devoted to each of the five phases of the Creative Problem Solving process. This chapter concentrates on the first step in the CPS process, problem definition.

Unfortunately, this phase of CPS is often given less attention than is needed. People tend to come to a rather quick conclusion on the nature of the problem and are more motivated to delve into its resolution than its definition. Yet, because so many problems are poorly defined, this phase of the CPS process is a lot more challenging than many people recognize.

Dewey believed that a problem well stated was half solved. Albert Einstein was even more emphatic about the importance of the definition of the problem. He was once asked: "If you have one hour to save the world, how would you spend that hour?" He replied, "I would spend 55 minutes defining the problem and then five minutes solving it." Einstein highlighted the importance of problem formulation in another way:

> The formulation of a problem is often more essential than its solution which may be merely a matter of mathematical or experimental skill. To raise new questions from a new angle, requires creative imagination and marks real advance in science.[1]

According to Lyles and Mitroff, problem formulation involves three primary steps: 1) sensing the existence of the problem, 2) identifying the contributing factors, and 3) reaching a problem definition.[2] This chapter will provide the details for each of those steps.

Peter Senge talks about the excitement of developing a clear definition of a problem. He characterizes it as a mystery to be solved. "Unfortunately," he says, "the way knowledge is organized and structured in contemporary society destroys this sense of mystery." The "compartmentalization of knowledge" creates a false sense of confidence in sizing up the problem, according to Senge. For example, the traditional disciplines that influence management—such disciplines as economics, accounting, marketing, and psychology—divide the world into neat subdivisions within which one can often say, "This is the problem and here is its solution." "But the boundaries that make the subdivisions are fundamentally arbitrary," says Senge, "as any manager finds out who attempts to treat an important problem as if it is purely an economic problem, or an accounting problem, or a personnel problem. Life comes to us whole. It is only the analytic lens we impose that makes it seem as if problems can be isolated and solved. When we forget that it is only a lens, we lose the spirit of mystery."[3]

John Naisbitt and Patricia Aburdene, in their book *Reinventing the Corporation* discuss MBWA (*Management By Walking Around*). In this approach, managers walk through the company to look for problems to tackle. This approach may be more difficult than it first appears, however. David Hubler characterizes this kind of problem-searching activity: "So natural a challenge to creative problem-solvers, but so frightening to those not accustomed to this kind of ambiguous challenge." Sidney Parnes comments on this apprehension about "walking around" to observe potential problems: "A personnel executive at one of our Institutes reported that only ten new junior executives out of 200 responded well to an opening assignment to 'look around for a few months and then tell me what you want to do.' The other 190 found this too unstructured and insecure a situation."[4]

While the task of problem definition should be perceived as challenging and mystery-solving, a too-unstructured approach may be unsettling to most persons. Therefore, we will look at several approaches to provide structure to ensure that the task is done effectively. At the same time, we want to maintain an "unstructured" view of the problem and all its circumstances, in order not to confine its definition so narrowly as to suboptimize.

> The secret to solving problems is to find the bridge between the way things are and the way you want them to become. That bridge is your definition; the link between the situation as already solved and its resolution as you envision it to be.
>
> *Dave Kolberg*

Gap Analysis

In Herb Simon's three-stage approach to problem solving (described in Chapter 4), the first stage is intelligence. The objective of this phase is recognition of the problem and analysis of problem information to design a useful problem definition. In addition to Simon's approach,

we will view several other researchers' approach to problem definition. Brightman divides the problem definition into two categories: disturbance problems and entrepreneurial problems.[5] The goal in solving
disturbance problems is to remove the disturbing influences by returning to where we were (or should be) before the disturbance.
Brightman refers to the gap as representing the difference between the
normal state of affairs and the state resulting from the disturbance.
Therefore, eliminating the gap is the goal in problem solving. An
example would be a system failing to meet its design objectives. The
gap may be the result of many things, such as poor design or due to
people not operating the system properly. In the second category of
problems, entrepreneurial problems, the goal is to close the gap
between the present level of performance and a desired higher level.
The gap can result from a variety of causes, such as a change in the
environment or a change in the goals. An example is the different
goals in today's business environment related to quality. Customers
are not willing to accept merchandise or service at the quality level of
five years previously—they've experienced a major quality improvement in some products and services and now expect a similar level of
quality from all companies. Figure 6–1 provides a graphic representation of the components of gap analysis. The figure also relates gap
analysis to CPS Phase One. The problem defining activity identifies
what is necessary to move from the disturbed state to the normal state.
The opportunity definition identifies what is necessary to move from
the normal to the desired state.

It might be helpful to view gap in a different way. Newell and
Simon suggest the use of means-ends analysis, which compares differences between initial and goal states, then determines if a discrepancy
exists.[6] Then the task is to apply some means to resolve the discrepancy.

Problems may be real or perceived. In either case, we would
have to gather the facts to prove or disprove the existence of a problem. Also, in both cases we would need to clearly define the problem
to be certain that we gather the appropriate facts. Parnes did not use
the term *problem definition* in his CPS model. He substituted a step he
called *mess finding.* It was derived from the work of Russell Ackoff,
who defined a mess as "a system of external conditions that produces
dissatisfaction; alternatively, a mess can be conceptualized as a system
of problems."[7] Colin Eden says that the interaction among problems
generally is complicated and not clearly understood.[8] James Evans

Figure 6–1   Relating CPS Phase I to Gap Analysis

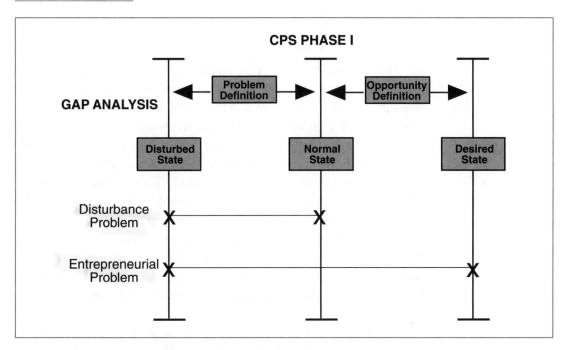

expands the mess-finding phase, indicating that it is concerned with sensing an awareness of the challenges, concerns, and opportunities within the system and involves the selection of important objectives.[9] He goes on to say that messes will become messier as one deals more with organizational and human response concerns, compared to problems of a technical nature. David Cowan developed a model of mess recognition that expands the problem definition activity when a complicated problem is being attacked. He proposes that mess recognition consists of the following stages:[10]

1. **Gestation/latency**—the period before the problem is recognized. Gestation refers to situations where conditions in the environment are changing and building toward recognition. For example, an employee may become more and more frustrated with work but the supervisor is not aware of the trouble. The problem begins to move out of its latency stage when an event or situation triggers some actions that cause the supervisor to become aware that a problem might exist.

2. **Categorization**—the individual becomes aware that the problem exists but cannot fully identify or define it. In the above example, the frustrated employee begins to exhibit some behavior that makes

it clear to his or her supervisor that a problem exists but the cause is far from clear.

3. **Diagnosis**—required to determine the relevant factors and to produce a clear problem definition.

Once the cause of the gap can be identified, work can be begun on closing the gap. However, there needs to be some measure of the gap to know if the problem is solved and the degree to which it is solved. In technical problem solving, a measure of effectiveness (MOE) is more easily determined. For example, it may be response time after a manager enters an inquiry to the computer system. We may know that the response time is unacceptable but may not be certain about the causes for the delay in response. In the frustrated employee example, the MOE might be performance, such as meeting assigned goals. Other measures might be absenteeism and tardiness, prolonged lunches or break periods, or time spent in non-productive activities, such as discussing sports or TV shows. Note that the ability to measure diminishes as the factors expand. Behaviors even less measurable would include non-business phone calls, working on personal business, and daydreaming. All these behaviors would result in a lowering of performance against assigned goals but are individually measurable to a varying degree. Another, but quite different, measure of gap in the behavioral area would be the periodic employee attitude survey. The disturbance gap would be represented by a survey that showed a reduction in morale or satisfaction. The entrepreneurial gap would be represented by the difference between the present level of satisfaction and what management believes would be the realistic level of satisfaction.

Nevertheless, it is important to have some clear indication of the amount of the gap in order to determine if the problem has been solved or the degree to which it has been solved. In the entrepreneurial gap, the measurement is less tangible. For example, I was working as a consultant to Wal-Mart during the time that they moved into the top position in the retailing industry. Previously, the entrepreneurial gap had been clear: the amount of sales necessary to reach the top position. Management, after reaching the number-1 position, still perceived a gap to exist, not just the level of sales necessary to maintain their top position but the gap between the top position and their sales potential.

We will not use the term *mess finding* although we want the first step in the CPS process to be clearly understood to be more than definition of simple problems. A concise definition of a problem is necessary to make sure everyone concerned has a common understanding of the problem before any effort at solution is begun. However, it may take considerable effort to determine the real problem. Also, sometimes our "problem" is determining how we can be better when things appear to be working satisfactorily. Therefore, we will use the phrase *opportunity delineation/problem definition* as the first step in the CPS process. This approach relates directly to the Brightman classification of disturbance problems and entrepreneurial problems. Opportunity delineation is examination of potential: for a system, an organization, or an individual, for a product or a service. We want to identify new and unusual possibilities, to explore wishes, dreams, and aspirations.

Problem Statement

Arthur VanGundy recommends use of the Why method to explore a variety of abstraction levels of the problem, to ensure we are working on the problem or opportunity of most importance to our organization. He gives an example of the combined use of Why and IWWMW (In What Ways Might We) techniques to try to reduce employee accidents:[11]

Question: Why do we want to reduce employee accidents?

Answer: To protect employees from physical harm.

Redefine: IWWMW protect employees from physical harm?

Question: Why do we want to protect employees from physical harm?

Answer: So that they will be able to perform their jobs.

Redefine: IWWMW help workers perform their jobs?

Question: Why do we want to help workers perform their jobs?

Answer: To increase company profits.

Redefine: IWWMW increase company profits?

Question: Why do we want to increase company profits?

Answer: To do our part in making the United States more competitive.

Redefine: IWWMW make the United States more competitive?

The focus of the problem has moved from reducing employee accidents to helping the United States be more competitive. The last round moved the problem beyond the scope of the company's resources and objectives. Therefore, the best redefinition will be found as one of the lower levels of abstraction.

Another good approach is to use the "what if" technique, asking "What if...?" about all aspects of the problem. Figure 6–2 depicts the approach as championed at Hewlett-Packard where management wants its employees to be asking "What if" in every aspect of their jobs. The "What if" question is important in each phase of CPS, beginning with Phase One in defining the problem or opportunity.

Elements of a Good Problem Statement

Evans suggests that a good problem statement for CPS has four major elements: 1) an invitational stem, 2) an ownership component, 3) an action component, and 4) a goal component. He uses the invitational stem of: "In what ways might we...?" This approach encourages a divergent response, rather than using the more narrow "How...?" The example below provides the invitational stem, an indication of who owns the problem, and an action verb in conjunction with the goal statement to specify what is to be done.[12]

In what ways might we improve the information provided the finance manager to enhance the quality of his decision making?

The problem components are as follows:

- In what ways might (stem)
- we (owner of problem)
- improve (action)
- information provided to the finance manager to enhance the quality of his decision making? (goal)

Other examples of problem statements containing the four components are as follows:

- In what ways can we improve system response time to prevent marketing analysts from waiting for an answer to an inquiry?
- In what ways can management improve feedback to employees?

Figure 6–2

"What If" Thinking Is a Key Part of the Divergent Thinking Process Useful in All Phases of CPS, Starting with Problem Definition and Opportunity Finding.

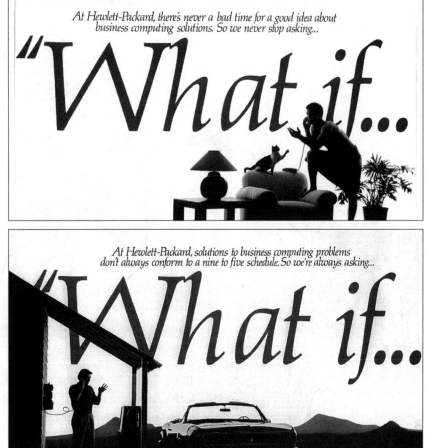

At Hewlett-Packard, there's never a bad time for a good idea about business computing solutions. So we never stop asking...

"What if...

At Hewlett-Packard, solutions to business computing problems don't always conform to a nine to five schedule. So we're always asking...

"What if...

Source: Reprinted by permission of Hewlett-Packard.

Use of Creativity Techniques to Facilitate Problem Definition

Figure 6–3 shows how we must overcome the blocks to creativity that we've acquired as we've matured. They are a handicap that prevents our realizing our creative potential. It is obvious that creativity techniques are useful in idea generation, Phase Three of the CPS process. They are also useful in Phase One.

VanGundy's example of the use of the IWWMW method is a variation of the progressive abstractions technique, used in Chapter 2 to illustrate definition of the problem of fewer persons entering the workforce in the 1990s. The initial problem definition

Figure 6–3   We Can Break Loose from the "Cinder Blocks" to Creativity by Using Creativity Techniques

was "Shortage of Entry-Level Professional Employees." The progressive abstractions technique generates alternative problem definitions by moving through progressively higher levels of problem abstraction until a satisfactory definition is achieved. When a problem is systematically enlarged in this way, new definitions emerge that can be evaluated for their usefulness and feasibility. Once an appropriate level of abstraction is reached, possible solutions then can be more easily identified. The major advantage of the technique is the degree of structure provided the problem solver for systematically examining problem substructures and connections.

Progressive Abstraction Technique

The progressive abstraction technique starts with a basic problem description, then moves progressively through higher levels of abstraction. The example in Chapter 2 illustrated that the second level of abstraction (Figure 2–1) broadens the problem to one of a shortage of professional employees, resulting from the shortage of entry-level employees. The next higher level of abstraction broadens the problem as one of shortage of human resources at the professional level. By expanding the scope of the problem, by moving to the higher levels of abstraction, solution space was increased from three to 15 subareas. The plus-one level of abstraction expanded the solution set from three to eight. The plus-two level of abstraction resulted in a problem definition that opened seven additional areas for resolution. Figure 2–1 shows that 15 approaches can be called on to reduce the effect of the smaller pool for entry-level employees.

Boundary Examination Technique

Another technique for problem/opportunity definition is *boundary examination.* The objective is to restructure assumptions (boundaries to our thinking) and provide new ways of looking at the problem. Another way of thinking about this situation is to try to suspend assumptions. Senge says that "suspending assumptions is a lot like seeing leaps of abstraction and inquiring into the reasoning behind the abstraction."[13] Sometimes suspending assumptions must be done collectively, by a team. The team's discipline of holding assumptions "suspended" allows team members to see their own assumptions more clearly because they can be held up and contrasted with each others' assumptions.

Boundary expansion is used primarily to question various frames of reference in defining a problem. The act of defining a problem involves certain assumptions about problem boundaries. The technique is also useful for other phases of the CPS process, such as expanding boundaries for idea generation. Boundaries determine how information is gathered, organized, and processed. Boundary rigidity will affect problem-solving success. Boundary examinations are based on the assumption that a problem's boundaries are neither correct nor incorrect. The objective is to restructure the assumptions of a problem to provide a new way for looking at it. The major strengths of the technique are its potential for: 1) producing more provocative problem definitions, 2) clarifying often indistinguishable problem boundaries, 3) demonstrating the importance of formulating flexible problem definitions, and 4) coping with management teams that are overly precise in their problem definitions.

> ***Problem:***   Smaller pool of candidates for entry level positions during the next decade.
>
> ***Objective:***   Expand the boundaries for the traditional candidate pool.

Traditional Boundaries of Candidate Pool:

1. A select set of colleges and universities
2. Only selected degree candidates
3. Heavy reliance on help-wanted ads
4. Heavy reliance on employment agencies
5. Heavy reliance on college placement centers
6. Minimum grade-point average (GPA) of 3.2 or so

Expanded Boundaries for the Candidate Pool:

1. **Broaden the set of colleges and universities**. Although there may be a smaller percent of students who meet our company requirements, some outstanding people are available. Use professors to assist in identifying the exceptional students in the less recognized schools.

   - Some academic programs are excellent in colleges and universities not normally recognized as top-tier schools. Use recognized professors to help identify good students in smaller schools.

   - Consider hiring liberal arts degree holders. Provide on-the-job training through company training department and/or provide tuition reimbursement for liberal arts students to go over to academic programs where shortages exist.

   - In the next decade there will be more emphasis upon effective user interaction. Consider hiring graduates of communications degree programs and training them in the areas of shortages.

2. **Reduce dependence on employment agencies**. Use the money saved to fund tuition for entry-level persons to take courses wherever deficiencies might have occurred in their educational program.

3. **Consider technical schools and junior colleges**. Hire part-time students with the agreement that they will complete degree programs in the areas of shortages. Provide on-the-job counseling regarding the courses needed for this career path.

4. **Introduce the Rebound Program**. Many accounting degree holders become disenchanted with the field after one or two years and are willing to move into another field. Identify these potential "rebounders" and work on motivating them to change fields.

5. **Place less reliance on GPA**. Many students must work their way through college. Their GPA realistically reflects the knowledge acquired but not their motivation and work habits. Use professors and employers as sources to check on these characteristics.

6. **Use other college sources than placement center**. Contact faculty and staff to recommend students to help identify promising candidates instead of depending so much on the placement center.

7. **Emulate successful recruiters**. Companies like EDS and IBM have hugely successful recruiting programs with unique features.

8. **Consider niche recruiting**. Find some colleges on the less-traveled circuit whose graduates meet company requirements, and put a large share of the recruiting dollars in those efforts.

> Suspending assumptions is difficult...because of the very nature of thought. Thought continually deludes us into a view that "this is the way it is." The discipline of suspending assumptions is an antidote to that delusion.
>
> *Peter Senge*

Example of Ill-Defined Problem

An author of a recent book provides an example of the use of a variation of the 5Ws/H for problem definition. He points out that in the past decade almost 7,000 public schools closed because of declining enrollments, budget cuts, and inflation. Further enrollment declines are expected to cause additional closings. Here are the various ways the problem was expressed:

1. How can school enrollments be increased?

2. What economies can be made to reduce school budgets?

3. How can inflation's impact on education be lessened?

4. How can school buildings best be used after schools are closed?

5. How can the unused space in school buildings be used to generate income so schools will not have to be closed?

6. How can school buildings be used in evenings and on weekends to generate income?

7. How can the empty buildings be used after the schools are closed?

8. How can unemployed teachers be reassigned after the schools are closed?

Do you agree that these are problem statements? I don't. They are questions relating to resolution of the problem. They would arise in Phase Three of the CPS process, idea generation. The data cited are part of Phase Two, identification of relevant information: "In the past decade or so almost 7,000 public schools around the country have closed their doors because of declining enrollments, budget cuts, and inflation. With further enrollment declines expected in some areas, school budgets increasingly under attack and inflation continuing to rise, additional closing can be expected."

Looking at these eight "problem expressions," you see that points 1–3, 5, and 6 deal with ways to keep the buildings open for school purposes. Points 4 and 7 should be combined; they say the same thing. Both deal with ways to use the buildings after they have been closed. Point 8 deals with finding ways to help teachers when schools are closed. This reanalysis not only simplifies the problem expressions, it leads to redefinition of the problem.

The approach may first appear to be a matter of semantics. You might ask, "Other than the nicety of more formal organization, what do you gain by rearranging the author's statements as you have done?" The answer is that we need to decide what the principal problem is, in order to generate more effective solutions. Is the problem one of keeping buildings open for educational purposes, finding employment for teachers released when building are closed, or finding a way to use the buildings once the schools are closed? In this case, it appears that the real problem must be derived from "reading between the lines." From the limited data available to us, we might deduce that a school board and school district have the problem of continuing to pay for a building that is no longer needed for education. They also have a problem (whether contractual or ethical) of trying to provide employment for the teachers who teach in these buildings. By more careful definition of the problem, the problem solvers can explore more specific solutions. They can also more easily develop cost/benefit analysis for their solution alternatives since the resolution objectives are now clear: we need to obtain enough revenue to pay for the buildings and to pay the remainder of the teacher contract obligations. This example is helpful in illustrating the difficulties of problem definition.

Wishful Thinking Technique

The CPS methodology (Figure 4–4) identified another technique, wishful thinking, as useful for this phase of the process. Wishful thinking was illustrated in Chapter 2. The example was developing an enterprise model for a firm, where the management team sought to visualize what the firm might become. While the wishful thinking technique is useful for problem definition, it is especially helpful in opportunity delineation. The objective is to expand your horizons in viewing the situation, to not be confined by your understanding of constraints. Rather than define an opportunity as the most effective way to accomplish a goal within the resource constraints of the firm, we would approach it by saying, "What would be the best possible outcome that we could hope for?" For example, in the problem of the shortage of entry-level employees, we could restate the problem as an opportunity: "How do we show college students that ours is one of the best companies to work for in the entire country?" Another example would be defining the requirements for a computer application. It could be defined as "the set of requirements necessary to meet the operational needs of the personnel in the application area." Reformulated as an opportunity delineation, in wishful thinking terms the statement might be "How can we provide employees in this area with information to enable the company to gain a major competitive edge?"

Another example occurred in our College of Business recently. Enrollments are declining across the country because of population demographics; smaller numbers of persons are reaching college age than in prior years. One administrator suggested that the problem is "How to maintain our fair share of the pool of high-school graduates?" A faculty group redefined the problem as "How do we produce graduates who will have a significant impact on the profession and community?" Their "wish" was a restructured educational program that would benefit the individual, employers, and the community.

The 5Ws/H technique can also be used for problem definition/opportunity identification. This approach is especially helpful in a "mess" where we are uncertain what the problem really is. We could record separate lists for questions relevant to the problem: Who, What, Where, When, and Why. This comprehensive approach helps ensure that a complete analysis of the problem/opportunity has been undertaken.

Conclusion

John Fabian describes the differences between people who are analytical or intuitive in their approach to problem solving. "People who have a practical, sensing, quick-closure bent often like to have the constraints up front. They want to detail criteria before they come up with ideas. They don't like to generate options that might be wasted or not meet the requirements. Intuitive types often chafe at this early detailing of the boundaries. Many times they believe that setting the criteria before searching for ideas is putting a noose around their thinking. The challenge to them often comes from generating ideas that can get around or obliterate what seems to them like unreasonable or unrealistic constraints."[14]

Elements of both these approaches are important for valid definition of a problem or opportunity. We need to push back the boundaries and thoroughly examine the characteristics of the problem or opportunity. On the other hand, we must stay within the time and resource constraints available to us. Use of proven approaches helps us produce valid problem definitions within practical constraints.

In their landmark book, *Introduction to Operations Research,* authors Churchman, Ackoff, and Arnoff discuss a common and perplexing behavior of problem solvers: the "anxiety" to get the solution underway frequently leads to reduction of the time and effort that should be devoted to formulation of the problem. Even though the problem is common to all disciplines, so is the result of lack of proper definition: costly rework due to inadequate solutions. A little additional time at the beginning of the CPS process can save multiples of time at the end, if the problem or the opportunity are properly assessed and delineated.

Getzels believes that "education at all levels by and large ignores problem finding to concentrate on the solving of presented problems." He says that "after years of such training one result is seen in graduate students who are well enough equipped to execute a dissertation study in every respect save formulating a problem at the start. Understandably little emphasis is placed on problem finding, for it is processes involved in this kind of thought that we know least about from the point of view of either learning or teaching."[15] The validity of this observation is demonstrated by inspection of laboratory manuals in the "new" science curricula. According to Herron, "Not a single exercise in biology, chemistry and physics failed to state explicitly the problem to be solved—and in most cases the method and solution as well."[16] Thus, schools, as Thelen remarked, "collapse inquiry to mere problem solving," and he conceives education as "a process that only begins with someone else's statement of the problem."[17]

As mentioned earlier, in the 40th-anniversary issue of *Changing Times,* Knight Kiplinger emphasized that employers of the 1990s are seeking employees with imagination, ingenuity, and creativity. Those characteristics are not confined to the idea-generation phase of the CPS

Figure 6–4 Guilford Model for Problem Solving

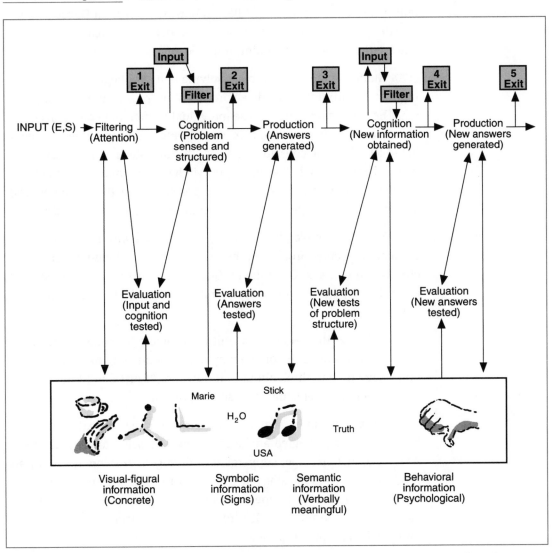

Source: Guilford, J. P., *The Nature of Human Intelligence* (New York: McGraw-Hill, 1967).

process. They need to be exhibited in each of the phases for creative problem solving and opportunity delineation.

A very different CPS model was devised by J.P. Guilford in 1967.[18] Figure 6–4 is a schematic drawing of his model, based on his theory of the structure of the intellect. I provided a brief description of this theory in Chapter 4, where I explained that Guilford was responsible for adding the convergent/divergent features to the CPS model. I want to briefly review Guilford's model in order to bring out an important point about the steps of CPS. I'll borrow from John Dacey's concise description of Guilford's model, then discuss the reason for placing the model at this point in the book.[19]

Guilford states that problem-solving behavior begins with some input, either from the outside environment or from within the body: what he calls *somatic input*. The individual is often not consciously aware that new information is being presented and sometimes is unwilling to let it become conscious. Thus at this first stage a filter exists, which determines whether the input will have any influence on behavior. Exit 1 represents avoidance of the problem altogether. If the process aborts at Exit 1, the person is not even aware that a problem exists.

Memory storage affects all steps, beginning with the filter. Evaluation occurs throughout the process as the individual constantly checks and corrects. Once the problem is recognized (a cognitive operation that depends upon memory and evaluation), the search for answers starts.

At Exit 2, the person may quit the problem for some conscious reason. For example, he or she may decide something like, "I just don't have time to think about that now," or "I just don't know enough about it. Let someone else deal with it."

If the problem is recognized as one that must be dealt with, Exits 1 and 2 are avoided and specific answers begin to be generated. At the production stage, convergent or divergent answers (or both) are produced. Exit 3 is the stage at which most people give up. They accept any answer that appears to suffice, because problem solving is viewed as an onerous task. It is often a difficult struggle, one that calls for tenacity and perseverance.

If an individual can withstand the temptation to "cop out" at Exit 3, new structuring of the problem through higher-level cognition of its nature is likely to happen. New and richer inputs add to the deeper understanding of the situation, and if the thinker does not give up at Exit 4, the production of uniquely valuable ideas may occur at the second production phase. The problem solver who makes it to Exit 5 is clearly the one most likely to offer a truly creative solution.

Note the symbols provided in the rectangular box at the bottom of the model. They represent the variety of information that people typically process in creative problem solving: visual-figural, symbolic, semantic, and behavioral. They assist in the evaluative process going on after each step in the CPS process; they can be considered convergent activity. They also assist in the divergent process for each CPS step. An individual needs a wide variety of information to assist in problem solving/opportunity delineation. Because much of this information acquisition-processing activity occurs continuously, we don't tend to think of the step identified as "compiling relevant information" as a distinct step in the CPS process. Although this activity is involved in each step, it needs to be considered separately to ensure that we are acquiring the right data and processing it properly. Guidelines and techniques for this step are explained in the next chapter. In testing the book I found that readers tend to skip Chapter 7, because the task of compiling relevant information is not nearly as exciting as the task of idea generation (covered in Chapter 8). I've included an introduction to the information-processing step in this chapter in hopes that you will be motivated to read Chapter 7 and not skip directly to Chapter 8!

Summary

Careful problem definition ensures that we are working on the right problem. There are a variety of ways to ensure that the problem is properly defined. Sometimes the problem is unclear; we just have data on the symptoms and need to delve more deeply into the circumstances surrounding the problem in order to derive a definition. Such a problem is referred to as a "mess."

A good problem statement contains an invitational stem, an ownership component, an action component, and a goal component. This first phase of the CPS process also covers opportunity delineation. This is not just declaring that every problem should be looked at as an opportunity, moving from a negative to a positive approach to resolution. Creative persons should be looking for opportunities for their organization, not just concentrating on problems. They should be proactive as well as reactive.

A good facilitation device for this process is gap analysis.

The *gap* represents the difference between the normal state of affairs and the state resulting from the disturbance. Therefore, eliminating the gap is the goal in problem solving. Opportunity delineation (sometimes referred to as *entrepreneurial problems*) involves removing the gap between the present level of performance and a desired higher level. In both cases, gap analysis helps to establish an objective. It aids in the determination of where we would like to be compared to where we are now. It is not unusual to have to plow through a "mess" to come up with a good opportunity delineation or problem definition. Special techniques, such as boundary examination, Why, IWWMW, and wishful thinking, are important aids in proper problem/opportunity definition.

With the clear problem statement, we are ready to conduct the second phase of CPS: compiling relevant information about the problem or opportunity to lead to resolution.

Exercises

1. What is the goal in solving disturbance problems?
2. Summarize the concluding paragraph from the section on Objectives of Part Two.
3. What is the goal in solving entrepreneurial problems?
4. Why is problem definition so important?
5. Explain the "mess" concept.
6. Why could the MBWA approach be classified as opportunity finding?
7. Explain the three stages in mess recognition.
8. Where does mess finding occur in the author's version of the CPS model?
9. What are the four elements of a good problem statement?
10. Opportunity delineation is synonymous with what concept described in this chapter? Why?
11. Prepare one-sentence descriptions of the following creativity techniques: IWWMW, boundary examination.
12. Give an example of how the Boundary Examination technique would apply to an assignment you've had in one of the courses you took in college.

Balloon Birds

Patent No. 363,037 (1887)

Charles Richard Edouard Wolfe of Paris, France

"By this present invention the mechanical motor...is replaced by a living motor...taken from the flying classes of birds...

The corsets or harnesses have forms and dimensions appropriate to the bodies of the birds chosen, such as eagles, vultures, condors,...

As the balloon floats in the air the man placed on the floor can easily cause the cross to turn by means of the hand-wheel, and, with the cross, the birds, so as to utilize their flight in the direction of the axis of the balloon, or in any other direction he desires. On the other hand, by working the rollers, he can direct the flight of the birds upward of downward. The result of these arrangements is that the flight of the harnessed birds must produce the motion and direction of the balloon desired by the conductor.

It may be observed that the birds have only to fly, the direction of their flight being changed by the conductor quite independently of their own will."

*Reason can answer questions, but
imagination has to ask them!*
Ralph W. Gerard

Compiling
Relevant
Information

**Compiling Relevant Information about
the Problem/Opportunity**

In Colorado we have many gold and silver mines. They were an important source of revenue for people in this region even before Colorado became a state. Everyone has seen pictures of a person prospecting for gold. The prototypical view is an old timer in tattered clothes leading his heavily burdened burro up a rough mountainside, hunting for previously unexplored areas. This analogy closely fits the search for data to begin the solution of a problem. Trying to find an unseen gold vein in mass of rock is not unlike the search for relevant data in the midst of a mountain of data. The prospector depended upon his experience to recognize "color" when chipping away at rock. He also looked for evidence on the ground or in nearby streams, bits and flakes of gold that may have been washed away from the vein by erosion. We can also find salient facts that are some distance from the problem and do not in themselves provide enough information to help solve the problem, merely to point a way to a potential solution area. Modern prospectors have some additional help in locating gold, such as chemicals to analyze the rock. Likewise, business professionals have techniques available that were not available to early-day business problem solvers, such as statistical analysis to separate unimportant from significant data.

The old-timer also relied on intuition: hunches about where gold might be found. The thousands of "glory holes" throughout the Colorado mountains are evidence of how many of these hunches were wrong. Nevertheless, we have a number of examples of gold million-aires whose intuition was correct. Intuition is not as important in the data location phase as it is in the idea-generation phase. However, feelings and impressions are important data to gather concerning many business-related problems. In the entry-level employee shortage problem, obtaining information about college students' feelings and impressions is important in learning about what motivates or demotivates them concerning taking a job with our company.

For the majority of prospectors who struck it rich, hard work was the principal cause. They stuck at the job day after day, week after week, and year after year, trudging over the hills to a new site, pickaxing, digging, chipping, and sorting. The same applies to data gathering on most complex business problems. Finding all the relevant information requires conscientious, careful work.

Another part of the gold production process is refining. The prospectors located and sold the raw ore. The processing companies refined the gold out from the other materials. Likewise, the data-gathering phase consists of subparts or subactivities:

1. the search for data

2. the analysis of the data

3. the extraction of salient information related to the problem/opportunity at hand.

Reasons for the Data-Gathering Activities

At first appearance, this phase of the CPS might appear to be the least interesting. Defining the problem and diving into solution generation would appear to be much more interesting. To the contrary, this phase can be just as interesting if one approaches it as the kind of task that confronts a thoughtful and creative detective. A Sherlock Holmes approach to investigation is challenging. Gathering the right set of facts is essential to generating a creative solution to a company problem, just as it is to a criminal investigation.

Isaksen and Treffinger have developed a list of reasons for the importance of data gathering.[1] The activity helps:

1. Break away from stereotyped or habit-bound thinking.

2. Uncover key pieces of information about the problem that might be obscured, overlooked, or so obvious that they were unnoticed.

3. Take stock of the situation by sorting out just what we really do and don't know about the problem, thereby helping us avoid premature closure.

4. Determine our primary priorities: the parts of the problem that stand out and really demand attention and action.

5. Look at the problem as broadly as possible, stretching ourselves to consider data in many ways.

6. Unlock hidden patterns or relationships among data in the generation situation: patterns that we may not have considered previously.

7. Create a reasonable basis for prioritizing and making decisions about how to structure and analyze the problem.

8. Establish and maintain a focus on the process that we are employing.

9. Examine and test the relative strength or value of various components of a problem so we can clarify our viewpoints and establish priorities for dealing effectively with the components.

10. Remove blinders caused by assumptions.

Before we review the three steps for compiling relevant information about the problem/opportunity, let's look at some of the other characteristics of a successful investigation.

Ensuring a Complete Fact-Finding Process

In the CPS process we gather information that is not often sought in some other business problem-solving areas. For example, in developing computer applications, the client is interviewed to obtain a variety of information (*e.g.,* about his or her requirements and about the present procedure to conduct the business activity in question). Rarely does the question set include questions about the feelings and impressions of individuals who work in the area where the application will be in operation. The questions concentrate on the information needed and the procedure to acquire the data and prepare the output to meet the client's information needs. The same thing would apply to problem solving in the finance or manufacturing area. On the other hand, in the marketing area, feelings/impressions data are important to obtain when dealing with customer reaction to products and services. This type of information is also essential for computer applications being developed for the human resources department of the company.

According to Eugene Raudseep, data analysis is "frequently thought of as being diametrically opposed to creativity, but it is part and parcel of the ability to synthesize.... The creative person is able to analyze and break down a problem into parts and to perceive the relationships that exist between the parts and the whole."[2] Raudseep claims that prolonged searching and analysis almost always precede creative synthesis; they are complementary aspects of a single process in creative problem solving. Analysis is necessary because it helps the creative person break the problem down into manageable elements. Synthesizing creatively means combining or rearranging many elements in a way that results in the formation of a new whole: "Thus, the creative person has strong dual abilities, both to abstract the details and to synthesize or orchestrate a new configuration."[3]

The fact that creative people tend to spend more time than do less-creative people in the analytical phases of problem solving has been documented by several experiments. For example, psychologist Gary A. Steiner maintains that data gathering separates "high" productivity creative individuals from "low":

> Experiments have indicated that highly creative individuals often spend more time in the initial stages of problem formulation, in broad scanning of alternatives. Less creative individuals are more apt to "get on with it." For example, in problems divisible into analytic and synthetic stages, highs spend more time on the former—in absolute as well as relative terms. As a result, they may leapfrog lows in the later stages of the solutions process. Having disposed of more blind alleys, they are able to make more comprehensive integrations.[4]

Researchers S.I. Blatt and M.I. Stein reached a similar conclusion with their experiments:

> Our more creative individuals spent more time and asked more questions that were oriented to analyzing the problem.... Our observations suggest that the more creative...were "feeling out" the problem, attempting to understand it, to become one with it; and, after they understood what they were about, they then integrated what they had learned. Consequently, they spent more time analyzing the problem and less time synthesizing the information they had. Our less creative individuals looked as if they were going to wrench the solution from the problem, to dominate it; they "went after" the answer even before they knew the structure of the problem.[5]

We need ingenuity in seeking out the appropriate data to understand and solve problems. We need to question things. Sizing a problem is another need: gaining perspective on the problem. Creative firms such as Microsoft use questions in the employee selection process that illustrate how a person can "size up" the problem before delving into possible solutions. A "perceptual sweep" is another way of phrasing the task of gaining perspective. According to Edward de Bono, the "deliberate directing of attention to as broad a field as possible is a very basic part of the skill of thinking.... There are times when we must recognize certain patterns: different ways of being right, different ways of being wrong, types of evidence. At other times we may have to make judgments or decisions: about values, about belief and so on. Then certain operations have to be carried out: organizing; challenging concepts; asking questions. All these take place in the perception area. They are devices and frameworks for directing attention."[6]

Marilyn vos Savant, who has a column in the Sunday newspaper supplement, also illustrates how you get perspective. We are besieged with information on the exploding world population and have great uneasiness about the prospects of overcrowding. Vos Savant provides us with a new perspective by giving us a visual image of the scope of the problem. She calculates that gathering the world population of 5.4 billion people together in one location and allowing each person a two-by-two patch of ground, would require an area less than 800 square miles. That is only about the size of Jacksonville, Fla. That new knowledge immediately narrows the scope of the problem. Space becomes a less important variable to consider in looking for solutions to population growth. If we carefully examine each of the major variables associated with our particular problem/opportunity, we will find that some are relatively unimportant—that we do not really need to try to gather data about that variable and can concentrate on the variables most influential on the result.

James Evans suggests that in data gathering we need to use all our senses: seeing, hearing, touching, smelling, and tasting. He gives the example of Gene Woolsey, who says that every time he walks into a warehouse with pallets two deep, he knows that he is going to make some money (in consulting). He says:

> Look closely at boxes on the second pallet back at the top level. You are looking for dust. Every box found with discernible dust on the side should be recorded.... If the majority of boxes on the second pallet at the top level exhibit dust, then we should proceed...[to] examine the second pallet at the second level.... If the majority of pallets on the second level exhibit dust, then proceed to...examine the second

pallets on the first level. If these show dust on the sides, I start planning a vacation in Bermuda.[7]

Some of Woolsey's fact-finding questions in dealing with inventory are, "How much is this part worth?" "How many of these are in the bin?" "How long has this bin been here?" and "What's your cost of money for this company?"

In Chapter 3, we emphasized the need for recapturing the natural curiosity you possessed at age 5. That curiosity is especially useful in CPS Phase Two. Curiosity keeps your mind alert and contributes to the playfulness Einstein regarded as "the essential feature of productive thought." In his book *The Art of Thinking,* Ruggiero provides an example of the value of curiosity. "A strict creationist, who believes that the earth is only a few thousand years old, will tend to avoid pondering the question: 'Is it likely that scientific techniques for dating rocks and other materials are as inaccurate as my belief would suggest?' Similarly, a strict evolutionist, who attributes all that exists to strictly material causes, will tend to avoid pondering the question: 'Is it possible that a Supreme Being created the evolutionary process by which all things come into existence?' It almost goes without saying that both would be better thinkers for asking the questions they tend to ignore."[8]

Steps in Data Gathering

Step 1. Gathering the Data

VanGundy has developed a checklist of questions to use in data gathering:

1. What do you know about the situation?
2. What would be better if you resolved this situation? What would be worse?
3. What is the major obstacle facing you in dealing with this situation?
4. What parts of the situation are related?
5. When is the situation likely to get worse? Get better?

Our goal in problem solving/opportunity identification is closure of gap—for problems, the gap lies between the expected result and actual performance; for opportunities, the gap lies between present accomplishment and potential. Kepner and Tregoe developed a checklist that uses the term *deviation* where we used the term *gap:*[9]

1. What is the deviation (versus what is it not)?

2. When did the deviation occur (versus when did it not occur)?

3. Where did the deviation occur (versus where did it not occur)?

4. To what extent did the deviation occur (versus to what extent did it not occur)?

5. Who is associated with the deviation (versus who is not associated)?

This illustrates once more the use of the 5Ws/H technique. Note that the "why" question is missing. One writer in the CPS field says that it does not make sense to ask why at this stage of problem analysis, since one does not have enough information. His view is that once these other questions are answered, the "why" will become obvious, that is, "Why did the deviation occur?" I disagree. It seems reasonable to add a "why" question at this stage as well, such as "Why are we interested in the gap (deviation)?" From time to time we need to question our original premise about the situation: "Is it still viable?"

David Morrison begins his fact-finding sessions with the following questions:[10]

1. What do you know (or think you know) about this situation? Consider categories such as:

   - timing
   - people
   - rewards
   - cost
   - equipment
   - tasks
   - systems

2. What do you not know, but wish you knew, about this situation? Examples:

   We don't know what it costs to …

   We don't know how long it will take to …

   We don't know who …

3. Why is this situation a problem for you as

   - an individual?
   - a group?
   - a company?

4. What have you and others already thought or tried?

5. What assumptions have you made about this situation?

6. You know you have been successful in resolving this situation when ...?

7. How much (time, money, people) are you willing to use to resolve this situation?

Morrison stresses the need to set standards on the quality of facts. He gives the following example of poor to satisfactory quality on a statement of fact on cost:

Poor .... Satisfactory

Costs are high

Fork truck costs are high

Fork truck maintenance costs are high

Fork truck maintenance costs are $9370/year

Fork truck tune-up costs are $2290/year

Guidelines for Closure on a Fact-Finding Session:
Morrison suggests the three following guidelines to determine when to end a fact-finding session (this applies only to data gathering through group discussion):[11]

1. How much time is available to gather facts?

2. Observe group energy—when it starts to ebb, the facilitator should start probing to stretch the session. Morrison finds that good questions sometimes restore group energy. We might want to organize it by cost categories or by sequence of activities—whatever approach allows us to focus on the high-priority facts of the problem/opportunity.

3. Sense when the group feels the facts are sufficient to start Step 2.

Step 2. Organization of the Data

An important aspect of data gathering is the organization of the data once obtained. This activity greatly reduces the time required for Step 3.

Step 3. Analysis of the Data

The purpose of the analysis is two-fold: 1) to determine if the problem was correctly defined and 2) to aid in the resolution of the problem. In some cases, the problem is so fuzzy that the data-gathering phase must be undertaken as the first step in the CPS process in order to fully understand and define the problem.

There are a number of approaches and procedures for use in analyzing the data:

1. Mental analysis
2. Statistical analysis
3. Modeling analysis

Sometimes the data set is not complex enough to require the use of statistical or modeling tools; it can be solved by logical, mental analysis. Organizing data into charts, tables, matrices, and graphs are examples of the approaches to facilitate mental analysis. In other cases, the amount of data or complexity of data requires the use of other analytical tools to supplement the mental process. For example, if a group of employees is exhibiting poor morale, a manager's analysis of the data resulting from employee surveys or interviews may be sufficient to determine the causes. If a larger group is involved, some statistical analysis might be beneficial in isolating the groups and individuals for whom the problem is more significant, or for determining the level of significance among the causes. If a manager were trying to determine how employee morale or productivity would be affected by a new building, he or she might resort to the use of a simulation model to project behavior in the new environment.

If you torture the data long enough, it will confess.

Ronald Coase

Sources of Data

Figure 7–1 categorizes sources of data in the CPS process: published materials, interviews, discussions, observations, and impressions. Note the full range of data, gathered by use of all six senses: the five senses plus intuition.

Let's examine the data associated with the problem we've been using throughout the book: the entry-level employee shortage. The relevant data concerned the declining number of college-age persons and the decline in enrollment in computer science and information systems degree programs. However, a more comprehensive review of the data associated with employment levels would show another data set impacting the problem. The third factor occurs at the other end of the employment spectrum: there is an increase in early retirements. These three factors combine to cause a serious shortage of professional

Figure 7–1 Sources of Data

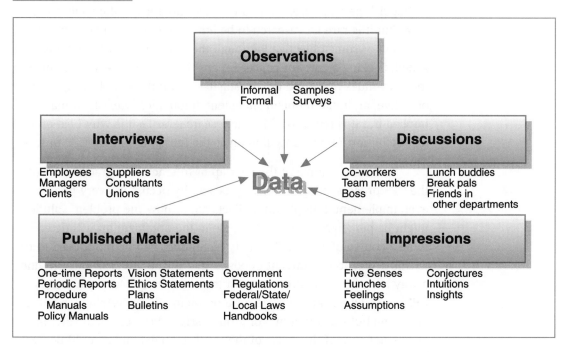

Figure 7–1 Sources of Data

employees for a least the next decade. The third area of information also leads to a revised problem definition, the one shown for the second level of abstraction (Figure 2–1). This situation shows that the phases in the CPS process can be iterative. This example supports the notion that fact finding should be Phase One in the CPS process for this particular problem. A fact (data on the impending shortage of entry-level personnel) led to reformulation or redefinition of the problem. This situation is not uncommon and led one group of researchers to add a preceding phase—mess finding—to the CPS model. For example, Isaksen and Treffinger's model has six phases, beginning with mess finding.[12] The term is misleading, however. We are not looking for a "mess" but for ways to search through a maze or mess to identify the real problem. A more accurate term would be mess analysis.

As mentioned in Chapter 6, Russell Ackoff originated the term *mess,* but for a more narrow scope of activity. He defined a mess as a system of external conditions that produces dissatisfaction. He also suggested that a mess can be conceptualized as a system of problems. Taken as a system, problems do not exist in isolation; each affects the result of the mess of which they are a part.

The term *pure research* (as opposed to *applied research*) is used to distinguish general research in an area without a specific application area. But it is rare for research to be initiated without some notion of direction or some objective, although the objective may be broadly stated. Seeking a cure for cancer is considered pure research because so many avenues remain to be investigated. With the establishing of an objective, an initial problem statement automatically exists. It may be implied but it is recognized by the researchers. That is why I list problem definition/opportunity finding as the first phase in the CPS process.

Another example of the overlap or interactive characteristics of the CPS process is fact finding. This activity occurs in every phase, even implementation planning. Facts about how the problem solution might be perceived by certain people in the organization will determine a course of action. Creativity techniques can be introduced to try to find a way to circumvent opposition to the solution or to try to find a way to reach a compromise with the opposition. Mess analysis as CPS Phase One is appropriate for a problem where certain results are occurring but the individual or group assigned the problem-solving task is not sure of the cause of the results. An example would be overheating of certain areas of the building during the summer. The first thought might be that the air conditioning is set too low. Further investigation might reveal that the problem is lack of insulation or ineffective windowpane treatment. These examples show that it is not unusual for problem definition to be a progressive process.

Critical Thinking in Data Gathering/Analysis

The prior discussion shows that Chapter 5, which concentrated on the use of both critical and creative thinking, has special application to Phase Two of the CPS process. Ray and Myers illustrated how the two approaches are used in combination. After the initial data-gathering activity, they suggest that you "try meditating, exercising, sensing your arms and legs, or any of the approaches…for putting you in touch with your inner creative ability." Then try answering any or all of the following questions.[13]

- *What is it I don't yet understand?* This question or ones like it can penetrate the mind for clarity and understanding.

- *What is it that I'm really feeling?* When there is a problem, there are usually emotions—fear, anger, hurt, or sorrow—and this question can help you become aware of them specifically.

- *What is it that I'm not seeing?* Problems usually come from not seeing clearly. By asking about what you are not seeing specifically, almost as if it consists of material objects, you heighten your perceptual ability.

Chapter 5 also emphasized the importance of holistic thinking—using both sides of your brain in problem solving/opportunity delineation. Ray and Myers suggest that "you ask a question with your left brain and answer it with your right as a demonstration of your unused resources."[14]

Mental Processes of Assuming, Guessing, and Knowing

It is important in data gathering/analysis to use both the left and right brain processes. Three other mental processes need special caution for use in CPS Phase Two: assuming, guessing, and speculating. They might appear to be the same thing, but they are quite different. Vincent Ruggiero gives examples of these three approaches as an aid to helping us know how to use them in the data gathering/analysis task:[15]

1. *Assuming* is taking something for granted—that is, unconsciously holding an idea about something without ever trying to verify it, sometimes being unaware we have the idea.

   Many people, for example, never give much thought to the daily life of fish. They may have their curiosity aroused as they walk through a discount store, stop at the pet section, and stare for a few minutes at the tank of goldfish. They may even spend an occasional half-hour studying the habitat and movements of fish in a fish tank in the dentist's waiting room. But they've never really pondered the social roles and relationships of a community of fish. As a matter of fact, they *assume* that fish have no such roles and relationships. Yet the fact is, in the words of underwater sociologist C. Lavett Smith, "There are fish equivalents of barbers, policemen, and farmers. Some are always on the move and others are sedentary. Some work at night and some by day."[16]

2. *Guessing* is offering a judgment on a hunch or taking a chance on an answer without any confidence that it is correct. It's a common, everyday activity. For students who don't do their studying for

exams, it's a last-ditch survival technique. For an example of guessing, though, let's take a more common student activity—drinking beer. Some time ago, a professor of behavioral science at a California college conducted a beer taste test among his students. The question was whether they could really tell a good beer from a bad one or their favorite from others. Many students would guess they could. A number of participants in the test guessed that way. However, the test showed that when the labels were removed, not one student could identify a single brand.[17]

3. *Speculating* is making an "educated" guess, selecting an answer without any confidence that it is correct but with some evidence for believing it is probably correct. It is commonly used in matters that resist close observation. Science offers numerous examples. The traditional scientific idea of the surface of the planet Venus is one. Because that planet is usually covered with dense clouds, scientists until recently were unable to observe its surface. On the basis of their calculations of erosion rates, they speculated it was quite smooth. But with the development of new radar-mapping techniques, they learned that their speculation was incorrect—Venus is heavily pockmarked with craters.[18]

Ruggiero concludes, "Each of the above examples of assuming, guessing, and speculating concerns ideas that were incorrect. It is possible, of course, for the ideas to be correct. But even when they are, it is wrong to say the people *knew* the truth, for as noted previously, to know means not only to have the correct answer but to be aware that we have it."[19]

Appropriate Questioning and Listening Techniques

There are many possible sources for gathering data related to a problem or opportunity. Figure 7–1 listed five principal categories of information: observations, discussions, impressions, published materials, and interviews. Valuable data can be ferreted out of company and industry reports, library references, and studies you conduct through questionnaires and sampling. Interviewing is another primary source of information.

Although watching well-known interviewers on TV, such as those on "60 Minutes," might lead one to conclude that interviewing is an art, there is a science to the process, enabling even novices to become proficient. Five steps ensure a comprehensive and effective interview.

Steps in Conducting an Effective Interview

Step 1. **Review printed information.**

Read as much background material as possible. In a company setting, preparation would include a review of documents such as organizational charts, annual reports, corporate newsletters, corporate library references, and departmental policies and procedures.

Step 2. **Establish the interview objectives.**

Select a half-dozen key areas to examine. The 5Ws/H technique is helpful for this task.

Step 3. **Determine whom to interview.**

There are obvious persons, such as the person who first reported the problem. But there are others equally important, such as persons impacted by the problem. If the task is to develop some opportunities, such as generating new products or services, then a third category of persons to interview would be customers or clients. To broaden perspective, it is useful to interview both management and non-management personnel in the areas related to the problem/opportunity.

Step 4. **Prepare the interviewee.**

Not only is it important to make an appointment for the interview, it is also important to fully explain the purpose of the interview. That way, the interviewee is better prepared to participate and share information/ideas.

Step 5. **Determine the structure of the interview.**

Interviews may be structured or unstructured, may contain closed or open-ended questions. A combination is usually the optimal approach. Bringing a prepared list of questions not only makes better use of both persons' time, it helps ensure that the interview captures the complete and correct information. However, the interviewer should make sure there is time for the interviewee to elaborate on responses and to pursue related areas.

Approaches to Improving Listening Effectiveness

Most people are inefficient listeners, both in an interview or a presentation. Tests have shown that immediately after listening to a ten-minute oral presentation, the average listener has heard, understood, properly evaluated, and retained approximately half of what was said.

Within 48 hours, that drops off another 50 percent to a final 25 percent level of retention. In other words, unless you work hard at listening, you will probably only retain one-quarter of what you hear.[20] Mike Michalko, in his book *Thinkertoys,* developed a list of ten keys to better listening:[21]

1. **Find areas of interest**. Ask "What's in it for me?"

2. **Judge content, not delivery**. Skip over a speaker's errors.

3. **Hold your fire**. Don't judge until you've heard everything.

4. **Listen for ideas**. Try to discern the central themes.

5. **Be flexible**. Use four or five different systems to help you remember the content.

6. **Work at listening**. Work hard, keep your body alert.

7. **Resist distractions**. Fight or avoid distractions; tolerate bad speaker habits and know how to concentrate.

8. **Exercise your mind**. Use difficult expository material to keep your brain working.

9. **Keep your mind open**. Interpret color words; do not get hung up on them.

10. **Capitalize on the fact that thought is faster than speech**. Challenge, anticipate, mentally summarize, weigh the evidence, and listen between the lines to tone of voice.

You can observe a lot just by watching.

Yogi Berra

Techniques for Facilitating Phase Two of the CPS Process

Asking "Why" is a powerful data-gathering device. It substitutes for that natural curiosity we had as preschoolers, illustrated in Figure 7–2. A number of other techniques are useful in CPS Phase Two. The bug list is one of these and will be illustrated on the problem of shortage of computer professionals; another is the Lotus Blossom technique.

Lotus Blossom Technique

The Japanese have developed several creativity techniques based on cultural or religious traditions. One of these is the Lotus Blossom technique. Using this approach, the petals around the core of the blossom are figuratively "peeled back" one at a time, revealing a key component

Figure 7–2

Curiosity Is an Important
Aid to Data Gathering

Source: Reprinted with special permission of King Features Syndicate.

or subidea. This approach is pursued in ever-widening circles until the problem or opportunity is comprehensively explored. An example of its use is strategic planning. A good way to begin a planning session is to identify the assumptions that may constrain planning.[22]

The core question is "What assumptions tend to constrain our creative view of the future?" The petals represent the categories of assumptions that need to be investigated, such as competition, product trends, legal constraints, production capacity, people skills/capabilities, and policy constraints. Each of these assumption areas forms the next "lotus blossom" to be examined. For example, the core assumption area of "production capacity" might contain six or seven petals, for example: 1) **basic components**—we will continue to acquire raw materials and develop basic components rather than purchase them; 2) **people skills**—we will continue to hire high-school graduates for production tasks and college graduates as supervisors, training both groups in company policies and practices; 3) **facilities**—we will continue to upgrade our existing facilities to maintain industry levels of proficiency; and 4) **quality**—we will continue to upgrade our quality efforts to maintain quality at the level of our competition.

With this powerful technique, the full set of assumptions can usually be identified in less than two hours. The planning team can then begin to question these assumptions to determine if they are appropriate for company needs over the planning horizon. For example, they might question the assumption of maintaining quality at the level of the competition, then decide that it should become the industry leader in product/service quality.

Another example of use of the Lotus Blossom technique is to determine ways to motivate employees to accept a new policy, technology or methodology. It is a highly versatile technique that is useful in any realm of activity, company or personal. Figure 7–3 provides the format of the Lotus Blossom technique.

Bug List Technique

It is unclear who originated the Bug List creativity technique, a simple but powerful device. The technique was developed to facilitate the invention process, but is useful in many other problem/opportunity areas. Ruggiero provides a nice summary of the rationale for use of a technique like the bug list: "Instead of surrendering yourself to your own feelings of dissatisfaction or plunging into other people's laments, pause and remind yourself that viewed positively, every dissatisfaction is a signal that some need is not being met. In other words, regard the situation not merely as an aggravation but also as a challenge to your ingenuity, and consider how the situation can best be improved."[23]

A good example of how dissatisfaction can be used to produce creative ideas is consumer activist Ralph Nader's proposal for a new measure of the state of the economy. Disturbed over the fact that the Gross National Product focuses on things (notably production) instead of on people, Nader proposed recording how many people are being fed rather than how much food is being produced and how many people have shelter rather than how many houses are being constructed.[24]

"Ideas sometimes grow out of irritation, like the pearls that grow when an oyster is irritated by grains of sand inside its shell," in the view of Michael Michalko. One creative soul was bugged by his inability to remember important dates such as anniversaries and birthdays. He was always a day late with presents. He made this bug into a challenge and created a novel product: vacuum-packed roses to be stored and used for emergencies.[25]

Michalko provides "opposite-ends-of-the-continuum" illustrations of how persons used bugs to generate important inventions. The first involved Charles Kettering, General Motors' head of research. The

Figure 7–3   Lotus Blossom Creativity Technique

Petals around the core of the blossom are "peeled back" one at a time, revealing a key component for an idea. Then the component ideas are fleshed out.

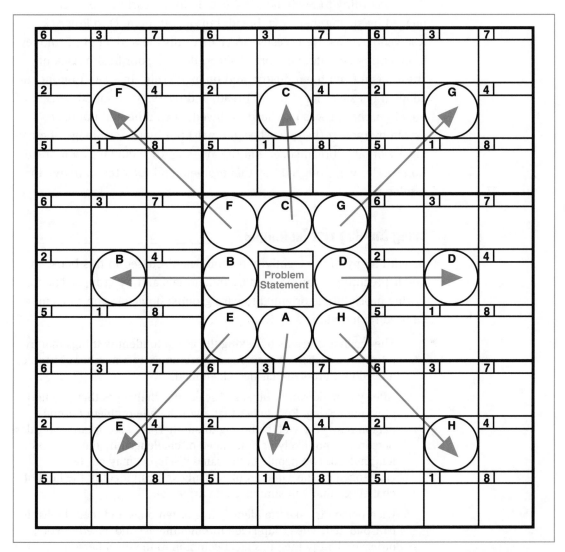

Source: CREATED IN JAPAN by Sheridan M. Tatsuno. Copyright © 1989 by Ballinger Publishing Company. Reprinted by permission of HarperCollins Publishers, Inc.

second featured Otto Frederick Rohwedder, a person with no background in research. According to Michalko, Kettering almost broke his arm cranking his car one morning. A few days later, a friend of his was killed while crank-starting his car. Sad and angry, Kettering sat down and listed ten major obstacles that would have to be overcome before cars could be started automatically. He arranged them from the simplest to the most complex and began to solve them one at a time. The result was his first invention: the Delco self-starter.[26]

According to Michalko, few people in the early 1900s were bugged by slicing their own bread, but one of them, Otto Fredrick Rohwedder, was. He invested 16 years of his life and all of his money in inventing an automatic bread slicer, despite poor health, lack of enthusiasm from the industry, and financial ruin. In 1930, Continental adopted his slicer for Wonder Bread, and by 1933, about 80 percent of bread purchased was presliced. Rohwedder said he had not been driven by money (he never became rich) but by the challenge of creating a workable bread slicer and the aversion to slicing his own bread.[27] Rohwedder was "bugged" by this problem and took the initiative to resolve it.

Using the Bug List Technique

As with many of the creativity techniques discussed in this book, the bug list technique can be used by individuals and by groups. The following procedure is oriented toward groups; however, the steps may be used by individuals as well.

1. The facilitator begins by asking the group to identify things that irritate or "bug" them. When bugs are common to a number of people, a need or a problem has been identified.

2. After you make your "bug list," select the challenges that you find most interesting. Remember that a worthwhile problem for one person may very well be boring to another. An accountant and salesperson will not likely be stimulated or challenged by the same problem; indeed, two people in the same discipline may not be challenged by the same problem. Only you can identify the kind of challenges that will stimulate and drive you.

3. Each person is asked to identify five or ten bugs and then the list is consolidated. The group is led through the list and asked to vote, in order to identify the bugs most common to the most persons.

4. The group brainstorms ways to resolve the bugs. The bug list is a good way to narrow down the pertinent data about the problem.

Example Problem: What things bug highly experienced and proficient employees, causing them to want to retire early, resulting in the company's loss of their valuable expertise and wisdom?

Bugs:

1. Management not fully utilizing our "highly valuable expertise and wisdom."

2. Unwillingness on the part of management to provide flexibility (*e.g.*, four workdays per week so we can play golf one day per week with our buddies who have already retired).

3. Lack of recognition of the needs of older employees (*e.g.*, the changing metabolism). President Reagan's afternoon nap was widely ridiculed, yet a half-hour nap would be all we'd need to be energetic for the remainder of the day.

4. Not having time to:
   - properly train my subordinates
   - counsel my subordinates
   - interview job candidates thoroughly
   - conduct strategic planning

5. Repetitious work. We've done the same thing so many times; we'd like a chance to work on some different kinds of activities.

6. Lack of respect. In Japan, age is revered. Here, the younger employees think they know everything there is to know.

7. Lack of recognition from management that we are more productive than younger people in several ways, because of our acquired experience of knowing what not to do and what to avoid.

8. Stigma attached to being passed over for management. There are only a few management positions available because of the management pyramid. Those of us who are in non-managerial positions have a great deal to contribute—you can't have all chiefs and no Indians.

9. Stigma attached to dropping out of management. Some of us would like to move to a less stressful job where we could still make a significant contribution. We'd be willing to take a salary cut so long as it didn't affect our retirement benefits.

10. Stigma attached to being one of the persons affected by the emphasis upon reducing levels of management. We know we are fortunate to still have employment, but there is a negative aura associated with those of us who were downgraded.

Creative Responses to Bug List Problems:

1. Institute a formal policy statement of respect for the experience and wisdom of older employees.

2. Establish position of Senior Adviser for older, experienced employees to provide more prestige and recognition, enabling them to share their valuable experience and wisdom.

3. Formalize the mentor role, so these persons have time to advise, counsel, and encourage younger employees.

4. Establish a system like that in Germany where every high-level manager has a high-level administrator to handle all but the technical details of a job.

5. Give near-retirement employees "nap time." Women are allowed three months of maternity leave, which is 528 work hours; a half-hour nap per day is 125 hours per year. Giving a near-retirement person "daily recuperation time" during the last four years of employment would be equivalent to the time provided for maternity leave. Providing a "club room" for reading and napping is an essential part of this recommendation.

6. Allow senior employees to teach seminars on Understanding Company Politics. Such a course should be on the skill list for all new employees.

7. Provide senior employees the opportunity to work on special projects to give them more variety in their work.

8. Couger's research on motivation shows a lessening of need for growth/achievement above age 50 for the average employee.[28] Some of these persons would be more satisfied with a more routine assignment. There is important work not considered challenging by younger employees that still must be done. Assign this work to those older employees with less need for growth and achievement.

Conclusion

This chapter has shown that there are some valuable approaches to acquiring the information pertinent to a problem or opportunity.

The objective is to gather facts, impressions, and opinions to describe the forces, factors, causes, and consequences in the current problematic or opportunity-laden situation. As much as possible, determine the elements at the core—conflicts, unwanted features, deviations, and inconsistencies in technical or institutional systems. Then, use an appropriate analysis method.[29]

Too often, this phase of CPS is inhibited by assumptions on the part of the problem solver or team. Some of those assumptions may be hidden or may need to be dug out. Ralph Kilmann, in *Beyond the*

Quick Fix, emphasizes the critical role that hidden assumptions play in corporate culture.

> Assumptions are all the beliefs that have been taken for granted to be true but that may turn out to be false under closer analysis. Underlying any decision or action is a large set of generally unstated and untested assumptions. If some of these assumptions turn out to be false, then the decisions and actions taken are likely to be wrong as well. Assumptions drive the validity of whatever conclusions are reached. We should not let our important decisions be driven out by things that have not been discussed or considered. Assumptions need to be surfaced, monitored and updated regularly.[30]

Some interesting examples of dangerous assumptions are provided by Ruggiero:[31]

- For a long time, surgeons used talc on the rubber gloves they wear while performing surgery. Then they discovered it could be poisonous. So they switched to starch, only to find that it too can have a toxic effect on surgical patients.

- For hundreds of years historians believed that, though the people of Pompeii were trapped by the eruption of Mount Vesuvius in 79 A.D., the people of neighboring Herculaneum escaped. Then the discovery of 80 bodies (and the hint of hundreds more) under the volcanic ash revealed that many from Herculaneum had also been trapped.

- Your grandparents probably learned that there are eight planets in our solar system. Since Pluto was discovered in 1930, your parents and you learned there are nine. But if the observations of Joseph L. Brady of the University of California prove correct, your children will learn there are ten.

"The human mind is such that it cannot absorb pure data," says de Bono. "Data become information only when they are looked at through the spectacles of an idea. Einstein looked at the data that had been seen through the Newtonian idea and by looking at them in a different way came to a different conclusion."[32] De Bono provides an excellent conclusion to this chapter on compiling relevant information about our problem or opportunity.

> The constant interplay between information and ideas cannot be neglected. Ideas are generated by the application of thinking to data. When we collect information we collect data that have been organized by the old ideas. To improve those ideas we need thinking, not just more information. Until recently we thought that dinosaurs had died out. Now it seems that far from disappearing the dinosaurs may have evolved into birds. This illustrates the interplay between information and ideas. So even when it seems possible to fill a field with information this should not exclude the necessity for thinking.... It is best to remember that information is no substitute for thinking and that thinking is no substitute for information. There is a need for both.[33]

Summary

There are many guidelines and checklists to aid in the process of compiling relevant information about the problem or opportunity. There are three basic steps in Phase Two of the CPS process: gathering the data, organizing the data, and analyzing the data. Calling on our preschool inclination for curiosity is very useful for this phase of CPS, as shown in Figure 7–2.

Techniques such as the Bug List help identify the data to be acquired. The 5Ws/H technique is also useful in this phase. By asking the six questions about the data needed, the acquisition of a complete and correct data set is strengthened. The Lotus Blossom technique is also quite useful for CPS Phase Two. Although the example given was identifying assumptions, the technique has much broader use. For example, it can be used for identifying categories of data and information to be gathered.

The lay person visualizes creativity techniques primarily for use in the next phase of the CPS process, generating ideas. However, the checklists, guidelines, and data gathering/organization techniques described in this chapter illustrate that many of the idea-generation techniques are useful in the other phases as well.

Exercises

1. What are the reasons for data gathering?

2. How do we ensure a complete fact-finding process?

3. Explain the steps in data gathering.

4. Some of the material covered in Chapter 3 about the characteristics of five-year-olds applies to Phase Two of the CPS process. Explain.

5. Four of the five categories of data sources shown in Figure 7–1 would be found in the typical systems book. Which category is non-typical? Explain.

6. What are Morrison's guidelines for a fact-finding session?

7. Distinguish the mental processes: assuming, guessing, and knowing.

8. Explain the steps for conducting effective interviews.

9. What are the keys of better listening?

10. Give an example of how the Lotus Blossom technique would apply to an assignment you've had in one of the courses you took in college.

Crashproof Railroad Cars

Patent No. 536,360 (1895)
Henry Latimer Simmons of Wickes, Montana

When one trail overtakes or meets another train, one train will run up the rails carried by the other train. The train will run along the rails and then descend the rails at the end of the lower train.

If the ends of the rails are not exactly the same level then the inclined lower rails can be adjusted at different distances from the other rails. The train having the ends of its rails higher above the rails than those of the train it meets will rise and run up on the rails of the other trail.

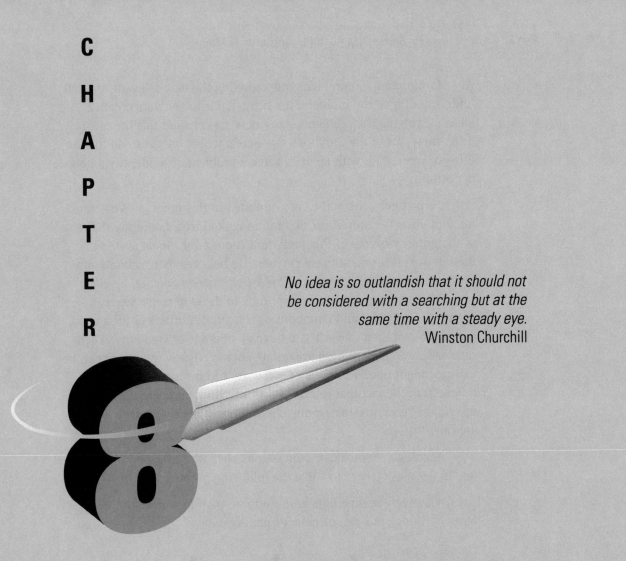

No idea is so outlandish that it should not be considered with a searching but at the same time with a steady eye.
Winston Churchill

Generating
Ideas

Generating Ideas

After formulating the problem and gathering the data relevant to a full understanding of the problem, the next step is to generate creative ideas for solving the problem. Many persons consider this the most interesting part of the CPS process—here's where we get to do the fun thing of coming up with ideas to solve a problem or to identify a new opportunity.

Surprisingly, most of us are inhibited in this process. We come up with ideas but stop short of a full range of ideas. Some say that one of the primary causes of this limitation is our educational system. Russell Ackoff is one of these persons. He believes that "schools suppress creativity in children." In *The Art of Problem Solving,* he elaborates: "Educators generally attempt only to develop competence, communicativeness and (sometimes) concern for others in their students. Most of them never try to develop courage or creativity. Their rationalization is that these are innate characteristics and hence can be neither taught nor learned. That creativity can be acquired seems to follow from the fact that it tends to get lost in the process of growing up. Adults recognize that young children, particularly preschoolers, are full of it."[1]

Ackoff gives the illustration of a teacher who assigned his daughter "in her early teens" to solve the following problem:

"Connect the nine dots with no more than four straight lines without lifting your pen or pencil from the paper."

Ackoff's daughter had tried to solve the problem without success. She then asked him for help. He recalled seeing the problem before. However, he said he wanted to get back to the work she interrupted and told her to forget about the problem, "It's not that important," he

Figure 8–1a

Ackoff's Solution No. 1

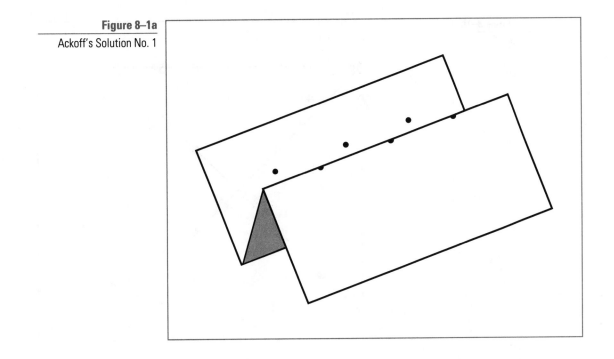

said. A short while later he heard her sobbing in the next room. When he went to see what was wrong, she told him she was ashamed to go to school without a solution to the problem. He invited her back into his study and said that "this time I will make a real try."

He knew that a puzzle is a problem that usually cannot be solved because people make incorrect assumptions that preclude a solution. Therefore, he looked for such an assumption. The first one that occurred was that the paper had to remain flat on the surface where the lines were drawn. "Once this assumption came to mind, and I put it aside, a solution came quickly." He folded the sheet "in across the middle line of dots and out across the bottom line so that the bottom dots fell on top of the dots of the top line (see Figure 8–1a). Then, using a felt-tipped pen, he drew a line through the top line of dots, holding the pen against the folded edge on which the bottom dots were located. Keeping his pen on the last dot, he unfolded the paper and flattened it. There was a line through the top and bottom rows of dots. With the three lines left it was easy to cover the remaining dots.

His daughter was delighted with the solution. However, she was downcast when she returned from school the next day. She told her father that the teacher asked the class who had solved problem. About

Figure 8–1b

Teacher's Solution

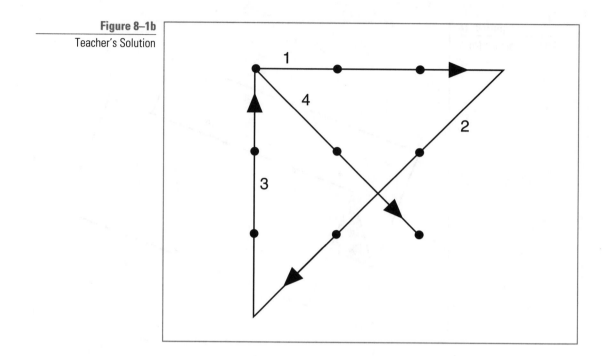

five students raised their hands. The teacher called on another student, who drew the solution shown in Figure 8-1b.

"Then what happened?" Ackoff asked.

"The teacher congratulated the girl, told her to return to her seat, and started to talk about something else. I raised my hand. She stopped and asked what I wanted. I told her I had a different solution to the problem, the one that you had told me. She was annoyed but asked me to go to the board and show it to the class. I told her I couldn't show it on the blackboard and needed to use the large pad on the easel in the corner of the room. She told me to go ahead. I drew the nine dots on a blank sheet and started to fold it when she asked what I was doing. I told her I was folding the paper. She told me I couldn't do that. I told her the instructions didn't say I couldn't. Then she told me she didn't care what the instructions said; that was what she meant. She told me to sit down, so I never got to finish showing the solution."

Ackoff comments, "This is how creativity is suppressed, although not usually so overtly. The teacher made it clear to the class that the objective of the assignment was not to find a solution to the problem,

Figure 8–1c
Ackoff's Solution No. 2

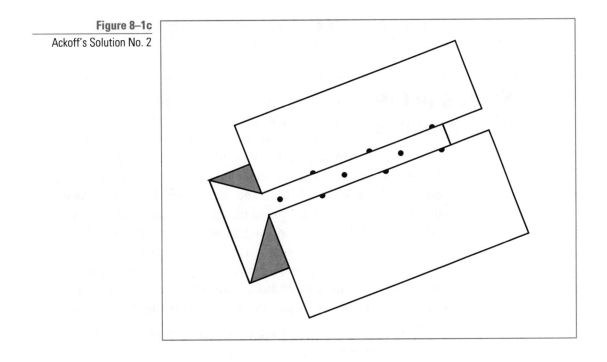

but to find the solution **she knew....** She had no interest in any other solution."

Ackoff concludes, "Imagine what a teacher interested in promoting creativity could have done with the situation involving my daughter. She could have revealed the common property of both solutions: **they broke the assumption that the solution imposed on the problem**. In the teacher's solution, the broken assumption was that the lines drawn had to lie within the perimeter of the square formed by the dots. She could have gone on to encourage the students to find other solutions. Had she done so, one of the students might have discovered how to fold the paper so that one line drawn with a felt-tipped pen can cover all the dots" (Figure 8–1c)."

Ackoff reinforces the conclusions drawn by James Adams in his book, *Conceptual Blockbusting.* Adams defines conceptual blocks as "mental ways that block the problem-solver from correctly perceiving a problem or conceiving its solution." We reviewed in Chapter 3 the conceptual blocks identified by Adams and others, as the ones most common in preventing creative solutions. To unlock our God-given creative talent, we need continuously to be chipping away at our conceptual blocks to creativity.

Stages in the Creative Process

One of the oldest models of creativity was developed by Graham Wallas in 1926.[2] He indicated that there were four phases: preparation, incubation, illumination, and verification. Although the five-phase CPS process used in this book is more appropriate for practical problem solving and opportunity finding, the Wallas model is useful conceptually. His preparation phase would be subsumed under CPS Phases One and Two, while his incubation and illumination phases would fall under CPS Phase Three, idea generation. His verification phase is similar to CPS Phase Four, idea evaluation and prioritization. Wallas doesn't deal with implementation, Phase Five of the CPS model. Figure 8–2 provides a comparison of the Wallas and CPS models.

It is useful for us to rethink the creativity process in terms of Wallas' model in his emphasis upon incubation. This activity is important but often gets overlooked in the pragmatic methodology of CPS. We will review Wallas' four phases before we begin a discussion of creativity techniques for idea generation.

Preparation

The creative act may be motivated by a desire to solve a problem previously identified. Or, it may begin with germ of an idea. In either case, we read, note, discuss, question, collect data, and explore possibilities.

This phase requires disciplined concentration. Philosopher Richard Guggenheimer explains it this way:

> A great disciplinary effort is required for most productive minds before they reach a stage where they are able to swiftly launch themselves into completely spontaneous absorption in the creative business at hand. A thousand and one diverting thoughts must be suppressed; the mind must brush aside myriad temptations to amble here and there along the enticing byways of casual thinking. It must become totally involved in the mounting wave of its deep intent.

Phase	CPS Model	Wallas Model
One	Problem Definition Opportunity Delineation	Preparation
Two	Gathering Pertinent Information	
Three	Generating Ideas	Incubation Illumination
Four	Idea Evaluation and Prioritization	Verification
Five	Implementation Planning	???

Figure 8–2

Comparing the CPS and Wallas Models of the Creative Process

The principal labor is getting the wave started; most of us splash about in our thinking and mistake the ripples of our noisy commotion for real movement.[3]

The preparation phase has a paradox, referred to by George Kneller, that in order to think originally, we must familiarize ourselves with the ideas of others, which may appear to detract from originality.[4] Henle also writes about this paradox:

It seems that creative ideas do not occur to us unless we spend a great deal of time and energy engaged in just the activity that makes their emergence most difficult.... It may be that immersion in our subject matter is a condition of creative thinking not only because it gives us the material with which to think but also because it acquaints us with the difficulties of the problem.[5]

Incubation

Whether or not one concurs with the views of psychological research, that the subconscious is just as important as the conscious in the creative process, there is ample evidence in the sciences that an incubation period is often necessary in the creative process. Michael LeBoeuf comments the incubation period can "take six minutes or six months."[6]

The French mathematician Poincaré said of his discoveries, "Most striking at first is the appearance of sudden illumination, a manifest sign of long, unconscious prior work. The role of this unconscious work in mathematical invention appears to me uncontestable."[7]

Eugene Raudseep explains that "there comes a time, during the creative process, when thinking gets ponderous and clogged, when errors start to pile up and no further new insights occur. This is the time when the creative person ceases his work on the problem and turns to something different and less confining."[8] In other words, we let our subconscious go to work on the problem while our conscious is in neutral!

Approaches to Incubation

We'll spend more time on the incubation process than on the other stages because it is the least well known. It is helpful to study the approaches of others to find ways to make our incubation activity more fruitful. Although creative persons spend a great deal of their conscious effort to solve a problem, they realize the limitations of this effort and often resort to incubation. As psychologist John M. Schlien points out:

> Although he has confidence in his ability, the creative person also has an attitude of respect for the problem and admits the limits of his conscious power in forcing the problem to solution. At some point, called "incubation" by many who have reported the process, he treats the problem "as if it had a life of its own," which will, in its time and in its relation to his subliminal or autonomous thought processes, come to solution. He will consciously work on the problem, but there comes a point when he will "sleep on it."[9]

For example, President Harry S. Truman bore up under the stress and strain of being a wartime president especially well. Despite a multitude of problems, the office of the presidency did not appear to age him or exhaust his vitality. When asked by a reporter how he achieved this result, Truman's answer was, "I have a foxhole in my mind." He explained that, just as a soldier has a foxhole for protection, he would retreat to his own mental foxhole, where he allowed nothing to bother him.[10]

A prominent French scientist observed that practically all of his good ideas came to him when he was not working on a problem or even thinking about a problem, and that many of his contemporaries made their discoveries in the same way. When Einstein was troubled by a problem, he would lie down and take a long nap.[11]

Many people find a welcome change of pace in music, painting, sightseeing, manual tasks, daydreaming, reverie, etc. Raudseep says that "these activities not only provide a refreshing interlude, but allow the unconscious mental processes freedom to operate unrestrained by conscious concentration."[12]

A "change of venue" is another approach that helps when the creative juices seem to diminish. Helmholtz advocated a "walk over wooded hills in sunny weather." Mozart also took exercise. Hart Crane played jazz loudly on a Victrola.

Most of us have had the experience of unconscious, autonomous thought processes during the incubation period taking over and solving the problem. Often, when the conscious forcing of the problem to solution fails, the incubatory process succeeds.

The philosopher Bertrand Russell provides an excellent example of the value of incubation:

> Very gradually I have discovered ways of writing with a minimum of worry and anxiety. When I was young each fresh piece of serious work used to seem to me for a time—perhaps a long time—to be beyond my powers. I would fret myself into a nervous state from fear that it was never going to come right. I would make one unsatisfying attempt after another, and in the end have to discard them all. At last I found that such fumbling attempts were a waste of time. It appeared that after first contemplating a book on some subject, and after giving serious preliminary attention to it, I needed a period of subconscious incubation which would not be hurried and was if anything impeded by deliberate thinking.... Having, by a time of very intense concentration, planted the problem in my sub-consciousness, it would germinate underground until, suddenly, the solution emerged with blinding clarity,

so that it only remained to write down what had appeared as if in a revelation.[13]

Planned Incubation.   The approaches above illustrated how a person sets aside time for incubation, or partakes in some activities that often result in incubation. Research has shown that a person can precipitate the act of incubation. Sidney Parnes describes the objective in "planned incubation":

> In the early days of creativity...the message people received from the literature was basically, work hard, gather and analyze abundant data, then "sleep on it"—get away from it—let it simmer—and hope for illumination—the "aha"—to rise up from the subconscious bombardment and resulting interconnections of memory data and/or new sensory input to the brain.... While this activity is still extremely important to the birth of new ideas, an abundance of evidence—both scientific and anecdotal—now indicates that we can also use deliberate methods and procedures to *stimulate* that incubative activity and thereby increase the *probability* of "ahas" occurring more frequently.[14]

Parnes suggests the following activities in the "planned incubation" process: "Keep pad and pen with you at bedside and wherever you go, being ready to capture an incubated thought, dream or idea. Make *planned* incubation a *habit*...in your total living experience, no matter what you are doing. If you have a dream tonight, describe it on paper, or even draw it upon arising. Look for meanings and interpretations of symbols and images if they are not obvious.[15]

In the experience of Michael Michalko, you can create your own inner sanctuary, and you can create it any way you want. He suggests the following: "Close your eyes and relax as deeply as you can. Visualize yourself in an ideal environment, any place that appeals to you, such as a forest, by the sea, on a mountain, in a meadow, a cave, a foxhole, a desert, or wherever. Create a vivid mental picture of your sanctuary. It might have a house with a fireplace, a grass shack by the ocean, a spaceship orbiting Earth, or just a peaceful place surrounded by a soft light. This is now your special place, where you can go just by closing your eyes and wishing to be there. Retreat to your own inner sanctuary whenever you wish peace and tranquillity."[16]

I've developed a creativity technique that is related to the incubation-type activity. It has broader application than planned incubation; in addition, it is used at points when I've reached an impasse in the solution-generation process. It is called Peaceful Setting and it will be illustrated in Chapter 13.

> The thoughts that come often unsought, and as it were, drop into the mind, are commonly the most valuable of any we have, and therefore should be secured, because they seldom return again.
>
> *John Locke*

> When you have a case of the dooms about a challenge, incubate it. Then, when you least expect it, in perfect silence, the answer will come like a flock of birds breaking out of a tree, but you will feel as if the tree itself is breaking up, sending particles of ideas into the air.
>
> *Michael Michalko*

Illumination

Rosner and Abt refer to the illumination phase as *discovery*.[17] Neither discovery nor illumination are appropriate terms, in my view, because of the connotation of "suddenness." A more appropriate term is *insight*. One of the myths about creativity is the idea of instantaneous revelation. A careful perusal of the literature on invention/discovery shows that moments of inspiration and "eureka" are rare. Instead, as stated by Kneller, "The moment of illumination brings the process of creation to a climax. This is the period when the innovator grasps a solution to his problem—the concept that focuses all his facts, the thought that completes the chain of ideas on which he is working. In the moment of inspiration, everything falls into place."[18] Gardner Murphy speaks of a moment of "illumination" in which "integration" occurs.[19]

The apple falling in the garden of Isaac Newton merely completed the chain of ideas that produced the law of gravity. Einstein said of the process:

> This combinatory play seems to be the essential feature in productive thought—before there is any connection with logical construction in words or other kinds of signs which can be communicated with others.... Conventional works or other signs have to be sought for laboriously only in a secondary stage, when the mentioned associative play is sufficiently established and can be produced at will.[20]

> Ideas, like young wine, should be put in storage and taken up again only after they have been allowed to ferment and to ripen.
>
> *Richard Strauss*

Verification

Rosner and Abt refer to this phase as validation. However, they insert a prior phase, elaboration, "where new ideas may arise or new approaches to existing problems can be found."[21] There appears to be little justification for a separate phase for elaboration; it is more logically contained within the discovery phase. The verification phase, according to Poincare, is the one in "which the results of the inspiration are verified and the consequences deduced."[22]

The phases of the creative process are not an invariant sequence. As explained by Gary Davis, "Some stages may be skipped or the thinker may backtrack to an earlier stage. For example, the process of defining and clarifying the problem (preparation) often leads directly to a good, illuminating idea. Or, if the verification (phase) confirms that the idea won't work or is not acceptable, the thinker may be recycled back to the preparation or incubation stage."[23]

> Keep on going and the chances are you will stumble on something, perhaps when you are least expecting it. I have never heard of anyone stumbling on something sitting down.
>
> *Charles Kettering*

Persistence in Idea Generation

An enormous capacity for taking pains, a dogged persistence in the face of difficulties and frustrations, and a vast amount of sheer arduous work are some of the additional outstanding attributes of creative persons, according to Raudseep.[24] These qualities stand out in their biographies, and are also the ones emphasized most when they counsel others with creative aspirations.

Edison said that inspiration was 2 percent of the job of creativity, and that the other 98 percent was "perspiration." Raudseep tells us that creation is preceded by hard thinking, prolonged reflection, and concentrated hard work. "There is a continuous assimilation of new knowledge and experience, a steady pondering on the causes of the difficulties that are met with regularly, and a sorting out of hunches and ideas that flash across the firmament of consciousness. It's apparent that all this takes time and a willingness to experience and accept many agonies along the route. Occasionally, these conscious efforts may even appear excessive. It is almost proverbial how many creative individuals have threatened—especially when their wastepaper baskets overflow with discarded work sheets—to quit their work for good. But the next day they are back, probing and attacking problems, determined to complete what is unfinished."[25]

Edgar Guest summarizes the need for persistence and for self-confidence in creative work, in his book *The Path to Home:*[26]

It Couldn't Be Done

Somebody said that it couldn't be done,
But he with a chuckle replied
That "maybe it couldn't," he would be one
Who wouldn't say so til he'd tried.
So he buckled right in with the trace of a grin
On his face. If he worried he hid it.
He started to sing as he tackled the thing
That couldn't be done, and he did it.

Somebody scoffed: "Oh, you'll never do that;
At least no one ever has done it";
But he took off his coat and he took off his hat,
And the first thing we knew he'd begun it.

With a lift of his chin and a bit of a grin,
Without any doubting or quiddit.
He started to sing as he tackled the thing
That couldn't be done, and he did it.

There are thousands to tell you it cannot be done,
There are thousands to prophesy failure;
There are thousands to point out to you, one by one,
The dangers that wait to assail you.
But just buckle in with a bit of a grin,
Just take off your coat and go to it;
Just start to sing as you tackle the thing
That "cannot be done," and you'll do it.

The creative process is hard. It's hard to be creative. It's hard work because you have to push yourself into the unknown, to take risks. It's so much easier to do something the way everyone has always done it—and that's why I think that most of the time most people aren't very creative.

Congressman Ed Zschau

Ideas are such funny things; they never work unless you do.

Herbert Prochow

Importance of Humor in Enhancing Creativity

Arthur Koestler, one of the important writers on conceptualization, wrote an essay on the "Three Domains of Creativity." The first is artistic creativity, which he calls the "ah" reaction. The second is scientific creativity, which he calls the "aha!" reaction. The third is comic inspiration, which he calls the "haha" reaction. According to Koestler, humor is the only domain of creative activity where a stimulus on a high level of complexity produces a massive and sharply defined response on the level of physiological reflexes.

Research at the University of Michigan shows that laughter causes the release of endorphins, which in turn provide a burst of energy and an impetus to creativity. The Michigan study reports that, on the average, children laugh about 150 times per day, while adults average only 15 times per day. William Fry, the principal on the study, recommends that adults try to laugh 150 times per day. He reports

I'M JUST AS SURPRISED AS YOU ARE —— I WAS TRYING TO INVENT THE VIOLIN.

Source: Reprinted with permission of DuPont.

three beneficial effects. In addition to the release of endorphins, we will obtain the effect of 15 minutes of exercise on a stationary bike. Laughter also reduces stress.[27]

Koestler's research shows that an environment of playfulness and humor is highly conducive to creativity. In his book, *The Act of Creation*, he devotes a section to humor. He says that the boundaries between discovery and comic invention are fluid, although at first sight this is less obvious to see. "That the Jester should be brother to the Sage may sound like blasphemy, yet our language reflects the close relationship: the word 'witticism' is derived from 'wit' in its original sense of ingenuity, inventiveness. Jester and savant must both 'live on their wits'; and we shall see that the Jester's fiddles provide a useful back-door entry, as it were, into the inner workshop of creative originality."[28]

Spontaneous laughter is produced by the coordinated contraction of 15 facial muscles in a stereotyped pattern and accompanied by altered breathing, according to Koestler. "But what is the survival value of the involuntary, simultaneous contraction of 15 facial muscles associated with certain noises which are often irrepressible? Laughter is a reflex,…one might call it a …utilitarian function, to provide temporary relief from utilitarian pressures. On the evolutionary level where laughter arises, an element of frivolity seems to creep into a humorless universe governed by the laws of thermodynamics and the survival of the fittest."[29]

I use humor continuously in my creativity classes and workshops. It clearly generates an atmosphere of openness, relaxation, and affability which facilitates creativity. For example, in illustrating functional fixedness as a barrier to creativity, I tell the story of the psychiatry patient who had a fixation on death. He believed that he was already dead! His psychiatrist failed to dissuade him of his fixation, despite several sessions. Finally, the doctor came up with an approach he thought might work.

He asked the patient: "Do dead men bleed?"

"Of course not," responded the patient.

The psychiatrist then asked the patient to hold out his finger, took a needle and pricked the finger tip. When a drop of blood popped out, the patient said with astonishment:

"Well, I'll be—dead men *do* bleed!"

In his book, *Laugh Again,* Charles Swindol speaks of the advantages of humor: "A good sense of humor enlivens our discernment and guards us from taking everything that comes down the pike too seriously. By remaining lighthearted, by refusing to allow our intensity to gain the mastery of our minds, we remain much more objective."[30] Swindol cites experts Peter and Dana, who tell us that laughter not only makes our serious lives lighter, but laughter also helps control pain in at least four ways: 1) by distracting our attention, 2) by reducing the tension we are living with, 3) by changing our expectations, and 4) by increasing the production of endorphins, the body's natural painkillers.[31] Swindol says, "Laughter, strange as it may seem, turns our minds from our seriousness and pain and actually creates a degree of anesthesia. By diverting our attention from our situation, laughter enables us to take a brief excursion away from the pain."[32]

Surely God smiles with understanding, Swindol says, "when he hears prayers like the one Erma Bombeck says she has prayed for years: "Lord, if you can't make me thin, then make my friends look fat!"

Humor, as Harvey Mindess says in his book *Laughter and Liberation,* "offers us release from our stabilizing systems, escape from our self-imposed prisons. Every instance of laughter is an instance of liberation from our controls." In his perspective analysis of the process of joke-making, Frank Wicker talks about "stretching" the meanings of old symbols to create new ones or "defrosting" frozen metaphors by reminding us of literal meanings that have nearly disappeared. Consider, he suggests, this example of a defrosted metaphor:

Tarzan came home in the afternoon and asked Jane for a triple bourbon. Jane blurted out:

"Tarzan, I'm worried about your drinking. Every afternoon you come home and get totally sloshed."

"Jane, I can't help it," Tarzan protested. "It's a jungle out there."

Woody Allen provides another favorite story. He tells his audience:

I'd like to say just a word about oral contraception.

I was involved in a very good example of oral contraception.

I asked a girl to go to bed with me and she said, "No."

The bibliography of Greig's *Psychology of Laughter and Comedy,* published in 1923, mentioned 363 titles of works bearing partly or entirely on the subject—from Plato and Aristotle to Kant, Bergson, and Freud.[33]

I'll intersperse some humor in the remaining chapters to help you get an endorphin spurt and keep you upbeat in your reading and reflection about creativity!

Techniques to Facilitate Creativity

John Arnold states that the "creative potential can be realized through training and exercises, just as the development of our full capabilities along analytical lines can be obtained."[34] His belief is verified by the thousands of persons who have become more effective through training in the use of creativity techniques. *Business Week* provided a variety of examples in its lead story in a recent issue.[35]

Appendix I describes 20 techniques useful for idea generation. Some of those techniques have been illustrated in prior chapters. This chapter will illustrate the following techniques: brainstorming, nominal group technique, metaphors/analogies, interrogatories (5Ws/H), problem reversal, wishful thinking, and wildest idea.

Although the experts on approaches to idea generation have preferred techniques, the one guideline that is consistent among the entire group is the need to delay evaluation. Normal practice in business and government is to begin evaluating an idea the instant it is produced. The following is a sample of the evaluative kind of comments that detract from an idea-producing session:

"We tried that before."

"That's too expensive."

"We could never sell that to upper management."

"That's not our responsibility."

These statements are idea-killers. When people respond to your ideas with statements like those above, you are not motivated to continue to share ideas with the group. Evaluation of ideas is an essential part of the CPS process; however, it should take place in a separate session, after the idea-generation session is completed.

Ideas are fragile; they need to be nurtured. Few ideas are mature when first suggested. They are seeds that need to be nourished in order to reach maturity. The expression "half-baked idea" is a term of criticism, when it should be considered a natural step in the progression to produce a "fully baked" idea. If people know that their peers and bosses will greet their ideas with a positive attitude, they will be more inclined to share their ideas. If the climate for creativity is satisfactory, one never hears comments like: "That's the last time I'll bring up an idea before this group—they jumped all over me."

The Brainstorming Technique

Although I've identified more than 20 techniques for generating creativity in other disciplines, the business field primarily uses only one technique: brainstorming. Probably everyone reading this book has participated in brainstorming activities. Few are aware, however, that the psychology literature identifies a number of experiments which show that individuals, working alone, produce a greater number of ideas than the same individuals produce through brainstorming in small face-to-face groups. The principal reasons are group effects that inhibit idea generation for many participants:

1. Fear of social disapproval when expressing true feelings.
2. The effects of authority hierarchy—hesitancy to expose your ideas in a meeting attended by your boss or even your boss's boss.
3. Domination of the session by one or two very vocal persons.

These effects are eliminated by the use of brainwriting, a technique rarely used in business. As the name implies, individuals write down their ideas and submit them to the facilitator anonymously. On the other hand, it has been proven that public idea-sharing stimulates additional ideas. The nominal group technique (NGT), developed by Andre Delbecq Van de Ven and D. H. Gustafson, utilizes the positive features of both brainstorming and brainwriting.[36] This technique uses:

1. Silent generation of ideas in writing,
2. Round-robin recording of ideas,
3. Serial discussion for clarification,
4. Then, subsequent rounds of writing.

Using this approach, the inhibiting factors of both brainstorming and brainwriting are reduced, while retaining public sharing of ideas to stimulate new ideas.

There is no evidence, in either the literature or through observation, that business organizations are utilizing the nominal group technique. If not, their employees would have more productive idea generation by working alone instead of in groups.

Brainstorming can be effective when there is strong reinforcement of the rule of separating evaluation from idea generation. The stimulation of ideas by hearing others' ideas is an important factor. The rationale is explained by Oliver Wendell Holmes and Thomas Carlyle. Holmes said: "Many ideas grow better when transplanted into another mind than the one where they sprang up." Carlyle said: "The lightning spark of thought generated in the solitary mind awakens its likeness in another mind."

Thomas Bouchard, in a series of experiments at the University of Minnesota, found that a group's effectiveness depends very much on the way it is allowed to operate. Bouchard tested the performance of groups where each member had to participate sequentially or say "pass" if he/she had nothing to contribute that round. Comparing the performance of groups conducted in this way with those using normal brainstorming procedure revealed "spectacular" differences. On average, the structured groups generated 87.5 percent more ideas than unsequenced groups.[37]

My own experience supports these differences. I like the sequential response approach because it assures 100 percent participation.

Even when persons pass on one round, they typically contribute on the next round. I find, especially in large groups, that some people do not speak up even though they have ideas. The sequential approach gets everyone involved. Another way to improve the output of brainstorming sessions when they begin to lag is to channel the brainstorming into certain topics. The initial brainstorming session produces, while channeling produces depth—a wealth of ideas in special topical areas.

> A new idea is delicate. It can be killed by a sneer or a yawn; it can be stabbed to death by a quip and worried to death by a frown on the right man's brow.
>
> *Charlie Brower*

Brainstorming, originated by Alex Osborn, was designed to distinctly separate idea generation from idea evaluation.[38] Yet, the term *brainstorming* has come to mean idea generation, rather than just one approach to idea generation. The procedure for brainstorming will be explained next.

Procedure for Brainstorming

Miller suggests the following ground rules for effective brainstorming:[39]

1. Pick a problem/opportunity where each person has the knowledge/ motivation to contribute.
2. Define the problem in neutral terms rather than a preselected solution (*e.g.,* "How do we get this job done?" rather than, "How do we get this person or this group to do this job?").
3. Record the ideas on a flip chart or on large pieces of paper where everyone can see them.
4. Suspend evaluation or judgment until all ideas have been given.
5. Stretch for ideas.
6. When you think you've got all the ideas, go for another round, being even more outrageous in possible solutions.
7. Aim for quantity to help find quality.
8. Accept all ideas, even wild ones.
9. Encourage embellishment and building on ideas.

Osborn emphasized idea production first, evaluation later: imagination, then judgment. At the *Fourth Annual Creative Problem-Solving Institute* in 1958, he stated:

> Time after time we have said that the ideas should
> be regarded as *ore*—ore which has to be refined into
> maximum value. Our average yield is less than 10
> usable ideas per 100 produced. Is that so bad? In
> gold mining, it takes nearly 200,000 ounces of ore to
> produce one ounce of gold. And it takes 6,000,000
> blossoms to produce a pound of honey.[40]

It helps to remember a quote from Mikimoto: "You cannot expect good
ideas from one who cannot even put forth bad ideas."

Additional Brainstorming Guidelines

James Evans suggests that a brainstorming session last 30 to 45 minutes.[41] The recommended length of the session is disputed, however.
Dave Morrison has conducted over 1,500 sessions; he says that groups
can be kept at the task for several hours.[42] Several experts suggest a
warm-up exercise with a whimsical or humorous problem, to loosen
up the group. Davis believes these exercises should include physical
stretching—to get the blood flowing and "to clear the cobwebs out of
the cortex."[43] VanGundy indicates that groups can continue to generate
ideas if they take breaks periodically.[44] My experience is that, ideally,
the group meets for 30 minutes on successive days until the ideas are
exhausted. This approach has two advantages: 1) people are fresh,
having worked on other things during the rest of the day, and 2) there
has been an incubation period, allowing help from the subconscious.

While brainstorming is the most widely used idea generation
technique, a number of other techniques have been developed for idea
generation. "Originality is simply a fresh pair of eyes," according to
Woodrow Wilson. The objective in use of creativity techniques is to
help us restore our "fresh eyes." Frank Kingdom said that "questions
are creative acts of intelligence." We resort to techniques that help us
question things, to quick-start the creative process. Figure 8–3 illustrates the activity of gaining a fresh perspective.

> Nothing is more dangerous than an idea when it is
> the only one you have.
>
> *Emile Chartier*

Figure 8–3   A Fresh Perspective

As you might try on someone else's hat, try on someone else's viewpoint. How would Henry Kissinger have approached this problem? Or Whoopi Goldberg? Or Robin Williams?

The best way to have a good idea is to have lots of ideas.

Linus Pauling

The person who is capable of producing a large number of ideas per unit of time, other things being equal, has a greater chance of having significant ideas.

J.P. Guilford

The Analogies/ Metaphors Technique

The analogies/metaphors technique was introduced and illustrated in Chapter 2. Analogies are very powerful in scientific thought and probably generate and regulate more ideas than any other mode of thinking. They've been used for centuries. Hideki Yukawa, Nobel prize winner in physics, says that analogies are an area where the Chinese have excelled since ancient times. "The oldest form in which it appears is the parable. In a large number of cases, the arguments of the thinkers of old depend upon analogy or parable. A similar tendency was also to be found in ancient Greece."[45]

Metaphors function as bridges between disciplines, according to David Lamb, "extending meanings from an established context to provide clarity in another."[46] Goodman and Elgin provide an interesting description of metaphors: "Although buildings do not blow saxophones and beat drums, they can be described as being 'jazzy,' for the system of musical meanings can overlap with architecture. 'Loud' may be a literal description of a band, but it serves as an adequate metaphorical description of a neck-tie. It works as a metaphor because it brings the notion of excessiveness from one framework to another. Metaphorical references to 'blowing off steam,' 'getting wires crossed' and 'keeping the pressure up,' all reveal the ease with which the human situation can be metaphorically depicted in a technical framework."[47]

Francis Bacon insisted that one of the requisites of scientific ability was "a mind nimble and versatile enough to catch the resemblance of things which is the chief point and yet at the same time steady enough to fix and distinguish their subtler differences."[48]

Robert Boyle went so far as to find evidence for God's existence in the analogy between clockwork regularity and cosmic uniformity when he described the universe as being "like a rare clock...where all things are so skillfully contrived, that the engine being once set a-moving, all things proceed according to the artificer's first design."[49]

We use metaphors frequently in our everyday conversations. Examples are: "You can't offend him; he's really thick-skinned." "I can read her like a book," and "They're like birds of a feather."

Analogies have been especially beneficial in the field of invention. Close scrutiny of the structure and function of the wings of bats and birds have provided useful analogies for aircraft designers. Obviously, there is a limiting factor for analogies. No airplane wing could ever be an exact copy of a bat's wing. The extent and limitation of the analogy is either modified by the researcher's knowledge of scientific laws and accumulated wisdom or is discovered later as the analogy is developed.

Alexander Graham Bell compared the inner workings of the ear and the movement of a stout piece of membrane and conceived of the telephone. Edison invented the phonograph after developing an analogy between a toy funnel and the motions of a paper doll and sound vibrations. Underwater construction was made possible when someone observed how shipworms tunnel into timber by first constructing tubes.[50]

To find radical solutions to old problems, it is essential to take the imaginative leap to produce an image or metaphor that you can grip and mold into a new idea. Michalko gives the following example.[51] Imagine you own a company that manufactures television sets in a country where only the rich can afford to own one. Your sets are out-performed in the city market by every competitor and you lack the resources to advertise nationally. What do you do? Matsushita faced this problem in the early 1950s. They were outranked and outper-formed by just about every competitor, in Japan and elsewhere. The executives knew, as everybody else did, that televisions were too expensive for the Japanese. In 1955, the chairman of Toshiba said, "Japan is too poor to afford such a luxury." Toshiba and Hitachi made better sets at the time, but they displayed them only on the Ginza in Tokyo and in big-city department stores, making it clear to the average Japanese that this product was beyond their reach.

Matsushita's national sales manager said, "What if Japanese farmers were rich and could afford televisions?" and proceeded to devise a sales plan based on this fantasy. His salesmen sold televisions to poor farmers door-to-door, something no one in Japan had ever done with anything more expensive than cloth or aprons. Japanese farmers could not afford the sets, but bought them anyway. They wanted access to the outside world and were willing to make incredi-ble sacrifices to get it.

Michalko suggests the use of analogies and metaphors as "direct-ed imagination," which focuses us on how to solve a problem instead of wondering if the problem can be solved. He cites the Matsushita case as an example: "Once the sales manager imagined the farmers as a market, he set about to make it happen. Today, Matsushita is better known by its brand name—Panasonic. *The lesson:* "In a land of with-ering grapes, imagination can make a raisin a king."[52]

In Chapter 2, an example of the analogy/metaphor technique was provided. A list of objects was used as a starting point to tackle the problem of resistance to the use of a new software package. The "dislike of certain vegetables" was selected as the analogy. The procedure led to identification of 12 different approaches to easing the way to acceptance of the new software. Another example is provided in Appendix I. Rather than provide a third example, I'd like to illustrate the use of several creativity techniques in conjunction. The progressive abstraction technique is also useful in working on the problem of reluctance to adopt new software. We can move the problem orientation up one level of abstraction: reluctance to accept computer technology in general, not just the one package being considered. This approach allows us to relate the problem at hand to the approaches used in the past for motivating people to use various elements among the full spectrum of computer technology—a wide variety of hardware innovations and a wide variety of software innovations. The progressively higher abstraction opens up the solution space. Then we might abstract the problem to the next higher level—the reluctance to change. Doing so makes a wide range of research available to us. We could go to the library and review the background on why people are reluctant to change, and the approaches used over the years to circumvent this reluctance. Abstracting the problem two levels has significantly broadened the scope of solution opportunities.

Most of the creativity techniques can be used in combination. Once one becomes proficient in the use of a technique, it is useful to experiment with combining that technique with others already mastered.

The real act of discovery consists not in finding new lands but in seeing with new eyes.

Marcel Proust

Really we create nothing. We merely plagiarize nature.

Jean Baitaillon

The Interrogatories (5Ws/H) Technique

The Who-What-Where-When-Why-How questions aid in expanding a group's view of a problem or opportunity, to try to make sure that all related aspects have been considered. By going through several cycles of the 5Ws/H, alternatives related to the problem or opportunity can be explored exhaustively. Each person builds upon the responses of other persons in the room to move toward an optimal solution.

In Chapter 2 the interrogatories technique was illustrated using the problem of determining the feasibility of a pilot test. It will now be illustrated for another facet of the problem of the entry-level employee shortage. One of the areas identified to lessen this problem for a specific company was the improvement of recruiting effectiveness on college campuses.

Problem: Improving company image on the campus, to be more effective in recruiting students.

Objective: To increase the number of applicants and the probability of hiring.

First Round of Questions:

Why are students not impressed now?

What activities have the best chance of improving image?

Who are the best persons on the campus to get involved in changing the students' views?

Where are the points (places) that command the most attention of students?

When are the best times of the week (or day) to get their attention?

How are students most impressed by companies?

Second Round of Questions:

Who from our company should be involved?

What kinds of exposure are most effective?

When are the periods during the year that they have time to spend listening to company reps?

Where in the university are natural exposure points?

Why would students want to listen to your pitch?

How can we use our promotion efforts more cost-effectively?

Remainder of the process: Typically, only three rounds of the 5Ws/H are necessary to produce a range of questions to properly scope the problem or opportunity. The next round of questions would be used to generate possible solutions.

The Problem Reversal Technique

Reversing your assumptions about a problem provides new perspectives in thinking. Persons often generate their most original ideas when they challenge and reverse the obvious. Consider two examples provided in Michalko's *Thinkertoys.* The first example involves Henry Ford. Instead of answering the usual question, "How can we get the workers to the material?", Ford asked, "How can we get the work to the people?" With this reversal of a basic assumption, the assembly line was born.

Alfred Sloan took over General Motors when it was on the verge of bankruptcy and turned it around. He often reversed assumptions to derive breakthrough ideas. For instance, it had always been assumed that consumers had to pay for a car before driving it. Sloan reversed this to mean consumers could pay for the car while driving it, pioneering the concept of installment buying. Sloan also changed the American corporate structure by challenging conventional assumptions of how organizations were operated. He realized that GM's haphazard growth was stifling its potential. So he reversed the basic assumption that major companies are run by an all-powerful individual, creating a multi-layered managerial structure that allowed for entrepreneurial decision making while still maintaining ultimate control. Under Sloan, GM grew into one of the world's biggest companies, and this reversal became the blueprint for the modern American corporation.[53]

Procedure for Use

The reversal technique is particularly valuable for defining a problem in more solvable terms and for finding solutions to everyday problems. The following steps are used:

1. Write the problem statement in a question form.
2. Identify the verb, or "action" content, of the statement.
3. Reverse the meaning of the verb or action content and restate the problem in question form.
4. List answers to the reversed problem statement.
5. Reverse the answers stated in Step 4.

For the problem of a shortage of entry-level personnel, one solution area was improving the effectiveness of the interviewing process. Problem reversal would be: "How to turn off prospects in the initial interview." The following responses might be generated:

1. **Be impersonal**—Avoid any indication of interest in the person as anything other than as a human resource.

2. **Be indifferent**—"I was assigned this task of interviewing and I'll get it over as soon as possible to get back to my job assignments."

3. **Be impatient**—Show that you have dozens of interviews ahead of you and a set of questions you must get answered in a prescribed time.

4. **Keep the interview one-sided**—Remember that your prime purpose is to weed out undesirable candidates.

5. **Be rigid**—Don't allow extraneous questions by interviewees to deter you from getting through your assigned list of questions.

6. **Avoid establishing rapport**—Avoid subjects in which the candidate might be interested.

I often use problem reversal to help teams improve their climate for creativity. We begin by brainstorming approaches to improve the climate. Then I ask the team to reverse the problem: "What would ruin the climate for creativity?" Although many good ideas are generated in the brainstorming session, the second exercise with problem reversal always results in some ideas that were not mentioned in the brainstorming session. This also illustrates the value of using creativity techniques in combination.

The Wishful Thinking Technique

The wishful thinking technique was introduced in Chapter 2. It was then illustrated on the problem of developing an enterprise model for an electronics firm. The CEO wanted to model the "ideal" business. The team developed a series of "wishful" statements about what they would like the firm to be. They then converted these wishful statements into practical ones.

Fabian provides another example, which he calls the "Case of Computer Friendliness."[54] He tells about a forward-looking computer development company, Starcom, that knows "to get ahead it has to think ahead." To aid their peering into a crystal ball and to create their own future, they set up a series of meetings with customers. They bring a variety of customers together, from novices fearful of the com-

MAKE A WISH.

puter but forced into using it to highly knowledgeable users who play with every tool and gadget that comes along. Starcom knows that computers require users to "work and wait," that is, users produce commands or type words, then wait for the computer to catch up to their thinking, like a cat-and-mouse game. The company places a mixture of customers in groups of five to ten, believing they will get rich feedback even though the knowledge level among the users varies greatly.

Outcome desired: Since Starcom is after the customer's wish list, the company is willing to take a first cut at computer users' hopes and dreams. Refinement can come later.

Question prompt: If your dreams could come true, what do you wish your computer could do for you?

Wishful Statements:

- Allow for normal communication.

- Respond to my verbal commands.

- Let me make thumbnail sketches on it.

- Accommodate to my specific thinking and working style.

- Automatically fix the words I regularly misspell.

- Get into selected files and prepare a contrast of actual vs. budgeted costs when I verbally tell it to.

- Read my mind.

- Quickly bring me a key paragraph in something I've written.

- Do what those information centers in department stores do: tell me where to find a pink ballerina outfit for my daughter or how to locate a military style men's hairbrush.

- Give me direct access to travel information.

- Let me play "what if" scenarios quickly.

- Move my data from one graphic style to another so I can see which one best conveys my message.

- Set up a conference call just by my telling it to.

Through this approach the company zeroed in on some solution possibilities that it would not have otherwise considered. One might be somewhat reluctant to suggest the wishful thinking technique with a group of sophisticated business professionals or managers. Nevertheless, we can motivate these persons to try the techniques by relating some evidence of its value in use, such as the examples described above and in Chapter 2.

The Wildest Idea Technique

The approach in use of the wildest idea technique is to move people out of their normal problem-solving modes, which are usually quite conservative, by asking them to try to come up with a "wild" idea. An example was the discovery of radar, which was developed from the bizarre suggestion of a radio death-ray for shooting down planes. Instead of rejecting the idea, someone used it as a stepping stone to the concept of radar.

Another example is D.B. Kaplan's, a Chicago delicatessen that approaches menu writing with its tongue well in cheek (and in some cases, in the sandwich). Items include Tongue Fu, The Italian Scallion, Chive Turkey, Ike and Tina Tuna, Dr. Pepperoni, The Breadless Horseman, Annette Spinachello, and Quiche and Tell. The ingredients are as creative as the names.[55]

Even the most bizarre ideas, the ones that absolutely will not work, the ideas that Edward de Bono calls "impossible intermediates," can trigger new and better ideas.

An example was recorded by John Dacey, in his book *Creative Problem Solving.*[56] Telephone-company managers were working on a major problem in Oregon. The state's two major population centers are on opposite sides of the state, separated by the steep Cascade Mountains. In winter, the telephone lines connecting the center become laden with snow and ice and frequently snap. They must be repaired at a high cost in terms of people and equipment.

Conventional approaches to problem solving had been unsuccessful; the problem had persisted for years. Some "wild" ideas led to a feasible solution, but it took a while for the group to get past their normal analytical approach to problem solving. For example, the early suggestions included burying all wires underground, using radio waves (satellites had not yet been invented), and so on. Urged to depart from their normal problem-solving mode, the group began to produce more imaginative ideas: move all the people from one side of the state to the other, cover the state with a giant plastic bowl, wrap the wires in fur, and trap all the pigeons living in San Francisco building eaves and train them to sit on Oregon's wires, thus "killing two birds with one stone." I think you'll agree that the group had finally moved into full-fledged use of the wildest idea approach!

Then someone proposed heating pads (connected to an electrical source by long extension cords) strapped to the bellies of airplanes: the planes would fly low over the wires and melt the ice before it became too heavy. This got a few laughs but also inspired the idea that finally was accepted: instead of planes, use helicopters and instead of heating pads use the vibration of the helicopter blades to shake the lines, causing the ice to fall. The method undoubtedly saved the lives of telephone repair crews and more than $8 million per year.

It takes a while to get a group into the swing of generating wild ideas. Most of the ideas are impractical, but eventually a useful idea emerges. It is usually one that couldn't be produced by one of the more conservative techniques.

Procedure for Use

The facilitator selects (or asks the group to select) a wild idea. With this starting point, the group continues to generate ideas. If no practical ideas emerge, another wild idea is used and the process continues until an acceptable idea is found. This is an important technique because it produces a surge of ideas that are often highly cost-effective.

Glassman uses the following procedure for use of the wildest idea technique:[57]

1. Form four groups and ask the recorder of each group to draw lines with a marker that divide the page of a large flip chart into quarters.

2. Ask each group to generate a very weird idea to solve their Problem Statement and to write it in the first quadrant. (The idea is to be as exotic, absurd, or bizarre as possible; to generate an impossible intermediate; or to come up with an off-the-wall, get-fired idea.) The flip chart is now passed to another group.

3. Ask each group to use the Weird Idea to trigger a Great, Witty Idea and write that in the second quadrant of the flip chart. The flip chart is then passed to another group.

4. Ask each group to use the Great, Witty Idea to trigger a Practical Idea and to write it in the third quadrant of the flip chart. The chart is then passed to another group.

5. Ask each group to use the Practical Idea to trigger a Workable Idea and to write it in the fourth quadrant of the flip chart. Turn the idea into a sensible, practical solution.

In Glassman's experience, the more bizarre and weird the first idea is, the more likely it is that the final workable idea will be different, original, and creative. I find similar results in using the technique in both classroom and industrial situations.

The technique will be illustrated on another facet of our continuing illustrative problem of shortage of entry-level people.

Problem: Having an adequate pool of candidates for entry-level positions over the next decade

Wild Idea: Use the "NFL draft" approach

Consider college and university degree programs to be like athletic programs as a source of candidates to "draft."

1. **Use Scouts**

Professors—Select key professors on each campus, ones who really understand the industry work environment and can identify the best "athletes," not just the high GPA students.

Campus Facilities Directors—Students are often hired by various facilities, such as the library, cafeteria, and computer center. Directors of these organizations are good resources on students' work habits, ability to apply knowledge, their cognitive ability, attitude, and communication skills.

Recent Graduates Who Are Employees—These people know the "behind-the-scenes" activities and abilities of students with whom they studied and interacted.

2. **Develop Compensation Package**

The NFL management teams develop an integrated package of compensation and playing assignment arrangements. Prospects know their short-term and long-term compensation possibilities. They also know which positions they are being groomed for and what coaches (management) will do to help them prepare for successful careers. Do the same for students being considered for industry jobs.

Problem:	Identifying organizations for outsourcing that are competent and cost-effective
Wild Idea:	Outsource programming to India

Recently, a COBOL programming job was advertised in New Delhi. More than 40,000 persons applied. There is a huge pool of qualified personnel in India, willing to work at wages much lower than those in the United States. I was asked to work with a software firm needing to hire a large number of programmers over the next few years, in a market where the competition for new college graduates was tight. In an idea-generation session I noticed that in the audience of almost 100 managers there were several persons who appeared to be Indian. I suggested the "wild idea" of hiring some of these people to return to India for a period of a year of two to set up groups to subcontract programming tasks from the American software firm. More than half a dozen Indians in the group volunteered; they saw it as an opportunity to return home for a short period while being paid at U.S. levels. The company adopted the idea and the program has been quite successful.

Combining Techniques to Attain Multiplier Effect

The principal reason for use of creativity techniques is to force us to think about the problem or opportunity with a very different perspective than our normal approaches. In fact, the best way to prove to yourself that the techniques are helpful is to use your normal approach to generate ideas, then use a creativity technique to see if it enables generation of additional ideas.

Likewise, the use of creativity techniques in tandem helps expand solution possibilities.

Example of Use of Techniques in Tandem

I'll provide an example of a problem-solving activity in a Fortune 500 firm that was being forced to downsize due to decline in sales. The department in question was forced to make a 30 percent reduction in budget by higher management. All department members were involved in several sessions to derive approaches to reducing the budget. However, this was the third year of downsizing and all the "fat" had been cut from the budget in prior years. The department was having difficulty in coming up with new ideas to reach the additional 30 percent reduction objective without seriously reducing organization effectiveness.

I suggested that they use the Lotus Blossom and Wishful Thinking techniques in tandem to see if additional ideas could be produced. We "peeled back the petals" of the problem to try to better isolate the solution possibilities, using the procedure described in the Appendix. We identified the key resources used by the department, e.g., personnel, computer hardware/software, materials/supplies, facilities, personnel in other departments, company infrastructure. Each resource represented a petal and was recorded in the center of the lower level "blossom" around the perimeter of the Lotus Blossom solution sheet. Then each resource "petal" was further "peeled back" to explore in more depth. For example, the personnel petal was expanded into areas such as prerequisite educational backgrounds, skill specialties, skill levels, cross training avenues, career paths, motivational needs, and opportunities. The exercise produced a detailed look at all the resources used by the department and the characteristics of each resource. This approach identified specific areas for reallocation of resources to be able to cut costs without degrading service levels. A number of ideas were generated that had not been introduced in prior sessions using the department's normal approaches to problem solving.

We then linked to the Wishful Thinking technique to see if the tandem approach would facilitate generation of additional ideas. For example, in the area of personnel resources, some wishful ideas were:

- "I wish I could delegate some of the mundane aspects of my job so I could spend more time on areas that result in more impact on customer service."

- "I wish our group was more familiar with some of the new methodologies, such as information reengineering, so we could take a radical look at the way we operate."

- "I wish we had more powerful computer workstations so we could utilize some of the more sophisticated software available for our work activities."

Some 30 wishful thinking alternatives were generated in this session. The tandem approach was then continued, through use of the Interrogatories techniques to translate these wishful thoughts into something concrete for cost reduction. Note that the wishful thinking session produced ideas that applied not only to cost reduction but also to effectiveness improvement. By taking the perspective of the 5 Ws/H (why, who, where, when, what and how), the wishful ideas were translated into specific ideas for departmental improvement, both in efficiency and effectiveness. For example, the wishful thought of learning information reeingineering methodology was operationalized. Training sessions were held for the entire department and a reengineering project was undertaken that proved highly productive.

Other Examples

In another organization, a mortgage loan department of a bank, the Bug List technique was used in tandem with the IWWMW technique of asking "In What Ways Might We ____." More than 20 bugs were identified through use of the Bug List technique. Then, for each bug, the question was asked: "In What Ways Might We Eliminate the Bug?" For example, personnel in the mortgage loan department had been "bugged" by loan agency delays in responding to a client's request for a loan. In use of the IWWMW approach, they introduced the solution of sending out faxes to each loan agency with the instructions that the first agency that faxed an acceptance to the client's request would get the loan contract. The new approach reduced average delay by three days.

Use of the Nominal Group technique in another organization had produced some useful ideas, but none that were considered "breakthrough" approaches. The problem was project schedule overrun—a problem common to many organizations. I suggested use of the Left-Right Brain Alternation technique to try to better exploit both analytical and intuitive mental processes. The result was quite beneficial; it is explained in the Appendix, under the description of the Left-Right Brain Alternation technique.

Guidelines in Combining Techniques

Any of the 21 techniques described in this book can be used in combination to enhance solution possibilities. Due to the natural inclination of personnel attracted to certain disciplines, there are preferences for starting with analytical versus intuitive techniques. For example, analytically oriented personnel such as engineers or accountants often prefer to begin with an analytical creativity technique. The more intuitively oriented personnel in the sales or human resource departments often prefer to begin with an intuitive technique.

A similar situation exists for the choice of working individually or in teams for creative problem solving. In organizations where more individual activity occurs, group CPS activity is usually a second order process. In organizations where much of the work is done through team processes, team CPS is usually the first choice. However, it is appropriate to use the tandem process in this respect, too. Individuals can use CPS alone before tackling the problem via a group process; or the reverse, the first iteration can utilize the team process, followed by a second iteration of individuals working to refine these ideas then generating additional ideas on their own. As noted on the page which introduces the Appendix, many of the creativity techniques may be used by individuals or groups.

As experience is gained with each of the 21 techniques, personnel begin to seek the multiplier effect of using the techniques in tandem.

"There's no use trying," said Alice. "One can't believe impossible things."

"I dare say you haven't much practice," said the Queen. "When I was your age, I always did it for a half-an-hour a day. Why, sometimes I've believed as many as six impossible things before breakfast."

Lewis Carroll

Conclusion

Professor Henry E. Riggs of Stanford University's Department of Industrial Engineering espouses a view of Japanese versus U.S. creativity that is held by a number of persons: "Japan has demonstrated great abilities in the area of process technology, while the United States has been relatively more capable of product development." Riggs notes that, in almost all fields, the Japanese excel when research targets are clearly defined and fixed, whereas Americans do better when targets are vague, allowing for more personal freedom and individual creativity. Because they are driven by user and in-house suggestions, Japanese companies analyze the limitations of existing processes and make small improvements. They are incrementalists.[58]

One who agrees with Riggs is Sheridan Tatsuno, an American with excellent knowledge of Japanese culture and innovation. He refers to the principal approach to creativity in Japan as *adaptive creativity*. Japanese companies often recycle old customs and ideas, such as miniaturization or multiple use, and combine them with other ideas to develop new ones. Tatsuno gives the example of George C. Devol, Jr., and Joseph Engelberger, who pioneered the first industrial robots in the United States. The Japanese quickly outdistanced the United States in applying this invention, however. "They are using the technology to develop piano-playing robots, sushi-making robots, fire-fighting robots, and hospital-care robots. Their emphasis is not on making breakthroughs but on humanizing and transforming these technologies for applications in everyday life. Japanese creativity is thus highly responsive, eclectic, focused, and practical."[59]

I have taught a course to Japanese business people for a number of years. Many tell me privately that they are highly respectful of the ability of Americans to make quantum leap discoveries and inventions. Most feel that our educational system is superior to theirs, enabling breakthrough-type thinking. In Chapter 3, I discussed some of the reasons that U.S. school children demonstrate less creativity each year they progress through our formal educational programs. Despite this reduction in creative productivity, our citizens are still able to make important creative contributions. The Japanese have now mounted a massive national effort to make their educational system more like ours, to be able to replicate U.S. breakthrough-type thinking.

We must resort to improved approaches to be able to maintain our lead in creativity over the rest of the world. Use of creativity techniques is a proven way to help individuals resurface their innate creative ability.

However, an important ingredient in the creative process is diligence. Raudseep maintains that the popular notion that the creative individual relies mainly on effortless inspiration and unforced spontaneity is "still a widespread misconception." He believes that creative achievement requires "confidence, the maintenance of morale, and long-lasting pervasive excitement to stubbornly resist premature discouragement in the face of difficulties and temporary failures."[60]

Raudseep grants, however, that it is true that some creative persons use the "gestative process of the unconscious to complete ideas for them." This activity does not replace but is used in concert with a "dogged and intense...effort." Yet, "discomfort with persistence or a feeling of flagging interest is often a signal for the need to get away from a problem and to relax for a while.... Creative individuals often find that they can relax by working on another challenging problem. Many of them say that they function best when involved in several undertakings simultaneously, each at a different stage of development, each affording an opportunity to relax when necessary."[61]

John Fabian has developed a table that is a good summary of ways to keep the creative juices flowing, and to combine incubation with idea generation.[62] He refers to the process as *mind-set breaking strategies*. To release energy, he says, three things–storm, calm, and access–need to be combined. *Storm* means provoking a storm of ideas. *Calm* means inducing relaxation; "allowing ideas to percolate in the subconscious." *Access* means tapping intuitive thought. Table 8–1 provides his approach: the left column identifies key idea-generation activities, which are described in the center column. The right column lists his suggested strategy among the three "energy-releasing" activities.

Optimal Team Size

Most of the creativity techniques described in this book can be used by individuals or groups. However, there are optimal group sizes. Some 33 studies of group size have resulted in a data set that shows that the optimal group size is two persons.[63] Dyads were found to be superior because two individuals can achieve rapport more easily,

Table 8–1	Key	Description	Strategy Facilitated
Mind-Set Breaking Strategies	Spark a storm	Using methods to elicit ideas	Storm, Access
	Follow storming rules	Following norms for self-induced or group storming sessions	Storm, Calm
	Tinker with angles	Looking at something from different vantage points	Storm
	Stimulate and relax the senses	Arousing the senses while putting the mind and body into soft focus	Storm, Calm, Access
	Use analogies	Looking for solution clues in analogies	Storm, Access
	Change your form	Getting inside a process or object by taking on its properties, as if it could talk, think, behave	Storm, Access
	Force fit	Connecting the unconnected for novel combinations	Storm, Access
	Take a leap	Pushing the mind to accept big jumps in thinking	Storm, Access
	Access intuition and	Tapping processes usually out of awareness	Access
	Incubate	Letting ideas germinate	Calm

Source: Fabian, J., *Creative Thinking and Problem Solving* (Chelsea, MI: Lewis Publishers, 1990), p. 135.

reaching the level of trust necessary for optimal sharing. Stated another way, it is important for you to find a person with whom you have good rapport to facilitate creativity most effectively. Two persons can bounce ideas off each other in a less threatening, more supportive climate. Figure 8–4 illustrates the close-knit relationship necessary for a dyad to work most effectively.

Vera John-Steiner, in her book, *Notebooks of the Mind,* explains some of the examples of value of dyadic activity.[64] She says that the early French Cubist Georges Braque wrote of the powerful connection between painters as they struggled with their emerging notions: "The things that Picasso and I said to one another during those years will never be said again, and even if they were, no one would understand them any more. It was like being roped together on a mountain."

Another such friendship discussed by John-Steiner was that of Einstein and the mathematician Marcel Grossmann. They met as students at the Zurich Polytechnic Institute, where Grossmann was among the first to recognize Einstein's great talent. He also realized how much Einstein deplored ordinary schooling, and he helped him with the more trying courses and assisted him in finding a job after graduation. The two men continued corresponding after Einstein left

Figure 8–4   An Interactive Dyad Is the Most Productive Group Size

Switzerland, and these letters allowed Einstein to test some of his ideas while they were still in a formative stage. In 1912, when the two men worked together, Grossmann provided the physicist with some important mathematical tools and thus contributed to Einstein's final formulation of his gravitational theory. Their friendship illustrates the continuing need of creative individuals to combine solitary labor with sustaining, nourishing connection with others.

A group size of five was found to be the next most productive. Thereafter the per-person productivity declines as group size increases. However, when teams learn to work well together, the differences in productivity-group size become less significant. Chapter 12 will concentrate on ways that the climate for creativity in an organization can be improved. The better the climate for creativity, the smaller the effect of group size.

Summary

Idea generation is the "fun" phase of the CPS process. Yet, even that activity often needs special approaches to start the juices flowing. Special techniques help us break down our

Figure 8–5   Even on a Moonlit Night like This One in Why, Ariz., 51 Persons Are Constantly
Reminded of the Importance of the "Why" Question for Creativity

normal, traditional way of looking at things, of approaching problem resolution. The objective is to get a free flow of ideas, and that condition requires separation of the idea-generation and evaluation steps. We need to stress the use of the question "Why" in this phase of the CPS process. Recently, I was driving to Mexico from Phoenix and was surprised to find a town named Why. Figure 8–5 depicts a highway sign for the city. I had my friends take my picture in front of the actual sign so I could make a slide as a graphic reminder to my students of the need continually keep the "Why" question in action.

To force ourselves to think in different ways about a problem or opportunity, it is important to ask "Why is it being done the present way?" However, to keep people open and participating in the idea generation process, we must refrain from asking "Why did you come up with that strange idea for a possible solution?" In this phase of CPS it is inappropriate to ask questions that can be interpreting as "shooting down the idea." It is better to ask, "Could you elaborate on that idea?" To help people feel free to share their ideas, to give them assurance that we want to nurture their ideas, we must postpone evaluation until the next phase of the problem-solving process.

A variety of techniques are useful in stimulating the creativity process. Some are straightforward and analytical in approach, such as the techniques of brainwriting, nominal group, and 5Ws/H. Others are more intuitive, such as brainstorming, metaphors/analogies, wishful thinking, and wildest idea. It is often useful to use techniques in combination: Any technique that appeals to the group and is appropriate for the issue at hand.

> Many men stumble over discoveries, but most of them pick themselves up and walk away.
>
> *Winston Churchill*

Exercises

1. Explain the stages in the Wallas model of creativity.

2. Explain the approach of planned incubation.

3. What is the value of deliberate use of humor in the creative process?

4. Some experts consider the nominal group technique to be superior to brainstorming. Why?

5. Under what circumstances can brainstorming be as effective as the nominal group technique?

6. What is the essence of the analogies/metaphors technique?

7. Give an example of how the interrogatories (5Ws/H) technique would apply to an assignment you've had in one of your college courses.

8. Give an example of how the wishful thinking technique would apply to an assignment you've had in one of your college courses.

9. Give an example of how the problem reversal thinking technique would apply to an assignment you've had in one of your college courses.

Internal-Combustion Engine

Patent No. 1,304,808 (1918)
Frederick Henry Royce
Osmaston, Derby, England

"In an internal combustion engine having an induction pipe and means for supply of air thereto, the combination of an air chamber interposed between said pipe and air supply means, an air valve in said chamber and means within the air chamber actuatable by pressure of environment and including an electric circuit and solenoid adapted to cause said valve to assume and maintain an area of opening dependent on the pressure in the chamber: said area of opening increasing if the pressure falls and decreasing if said pressure exceeds a pre-determined pressure."

9

*There are three types of people
in organizations: risk takers,
caretakers and undertakers.*
George Geis

Evaluating,
Prioritizing
Ideas

Evaluating and Prioritizing Ideas

It is important in the idea-generation phase to eliminate evaluation of ideas in order to establish a positive, non-critical climate for idea generation. Evaluating and prioritizing the list of ideas is the task of CPS Phase Four. James Adams reminds us that the convergent thinking associated with decision making is no less critical than the divergent thinking associated with the "production of concepts, since any concept can be killed either by an early decision that it is not acceptable or a later decision that it is too costly to implement."[1]

John Fabian refers to Phase Four as the "measuring tape" phase. "You begin to make the list (of ideas) manageable—sorting and winnowing ideas. The most promising proposals are held up for scrutiny, like a winemaker testing wine. He holds a glass of new wine toward the light to assess its color and clarity, then swishes the wine before sniffing its aroma. The expert finally examines its taste with a mouth cleansed after each sip."[2] We need to use all our six senses in idea evaluation, just as we do in idea generation.

Isaksen and Treffinger say that the purpose of this phase is not to "kill" ideas, but to look closely and critically at the ideas. They list the following tasks for this phase:[3]

- Compare desires (wants) with demands (needs)

- Examine the pros and cons of several ideas

- Narrow the options to a manageable group

- Determine the strengths and weaknesses to help build or develop their best features

- Screen ideas for possible modifications or improvements

- Reject options you do not wish to consider further

- Select or decide upon your most promising possibilities

They remind us that the goal is not just to find the "one best idea," but **to form a good solution** by evaluating, modifying, comparing, assessing, building, and improving. At this stage, they say, "You're using your creative thinking skills to diverge and consider many possible criteria for examining your ideas. You're also using critical thinking abilities." Too often, people associate critical thinking only with very detailed, precise, inflexible, judgmental thinking. "They tend to equate critical thinking with criticism. Of course, the critical thinker must be rigorous, precise and logical; but these skills can be used affirmatively and constructively rather than in a destructive kind of criticism."[4]

We need to creatively design our evaluation process. That is why the symbol of the diamond in the CPS model is used in this phase as well as the others. Although this phase is primarily convergent, it has a divergent aspect as well. There are many evaluation techniques from which to choose, and deciding which to use is an analytical, evaluative process in itself. But the approach to deciding how to evaluate our ideas needs to be creative in order not to eliminate some potentially beneficial ideas. Choosing criteria for evaluation can be a creative process in itself. Criteria are objective standards that measure the value of potential solutions. Useful criteria include time, cost, risk, utility, and performance. Evans suggests we apply the brainstorming principles of deferring judgment and producing quantity in developing evaluation criteria. We then evaluate the criteria and select the appropriate ones: "This reduces the chances of making the wrong decision because of inappropriate criteria."[5]

Fabian suggests that we design our evaluation process by determining how much sifting and screening we will need. "If you are sifting dirt from an archeological digging, you'll probably use a screen with a fine mesh to prevent small artifacts from being lost. If you are laying a foundation of gravel for your new sidewalk, you'll use a screen large enough to allow small to moderate-sized rocks to slip through."[6]

A fair idea put to use is better than a good idea kept on the polishing wheel.

Alex Osborn

Dialogue versus Discussion in Idea Evaluation

Group evaluation can be as valuable as group ideation. Yet, care needs to be taken to ensure productive dialogue and discussion. Peter Senge, in his book *The Fifth Discipline,* talks about the "artistry of dialogue." He says it "lies in experiencing the flow of meaning and saying the one thing that needs to be said now." Like the Quakers, who enjoin members to say not simply whatever pops into their heads but only those thoughts that are compelling (and which cause the speaker to *quake* from the need to speak them), the facilitator says only what is needed at each point in time. This deepens others' appreciation of dialogue more than any abstract explanation can ever do.[7]

As teams develop experience and skill in dialogue, the role of the facilitator becomes less crucial and he or she can gradually become just one of the participants. Dialogue emerges from the "leaderless" group once the team members have developed their skill and understanding. In societies where dialogue is an ongoing discipline, there usually are no appointed facilitators. For example, many American Indian tribes cultivated dialogue to a high art without formal facilitators. Shamans and other wise men had special roles, but the group was capable of entering a dialogue on its own.[8]

In his book, *The Special Theory of Relativity,* David Bohm distinguishes dialogue from discussion.[9] In team learning, discussion is the necessary counterpart of dialogue. In a discussion, different views are presented and defended, and this may provide a useful analysis of the whole situation. Part of the vision of dialogue is the assumption of a "larger pool of meaning" accessible only to a group. This idea, while it may appear radical at first, has deep intuitive appeal to those who wish to cultivate the subtler aspects of collective inquiry and consensus building. In dialogue, different views are presented as a means toward discovering a new view. In a discussion, decisions are made. In a dialogue, complex issues are explored.

When a team must reach agreement and decisions must be taken, some discussion is needed. On the basis of a commonly agreed analysis, alternative views need to be weighed and a preferred view selected (which may be one of the original alternatives or a new view that emerges from the discussion). When they are productive, discussions converge on a conclusion or course of action. Again, dialogues are diverging; they do not seek agreement, but a richer grasp of complex issues. Both dialogue and discussion can lead to new courses of action; but actions are often the focus of discussion, whereas new actions emerge as a by-product of dialogue.

Determining Evaluation Criteria

Davis suggests the following criteria for evaluation of ideas:[10]

- Will it work? Will it do the job? Does it improve present methods?

- Does it reduce costs? Eliminate unnecessary work? Increase productivity? Improve quality? Improve safety? Improve the use of personnel? Improve working conditions? Improve morale?

- Does the idea really "grab" people? Do people ask "Why didn't I think of that?"

- Is it timely?

- Is it a temporary or permanent solution?

- Will it cost too much?

- It is too complicated? Is it simple and direct?

- Is it suitable? Will others accept it (upper management, customers, the union, other groups represented in the company)?

- Are the materials available?

- Is it legal?

- Are we trying to swat a fly with dynamite?

- Are there patent infringements?

Use of objective criteria for evaluation serves several purposes, according to Davis: 1) using criteria helps evaluate ideas, 2) it helps participants learn to evaluate as part of the overall creativity process, 3) it requires people to consider many components of the problem or opportunity, 4) it helps the group explore its own value system relative to the situation at hand, and 5) it can prove that thinking of "silly" and "farfetched" ideas truly can result in good and practical solutions to the problems.[11]

Isaksen and Treffinger have developed a checklist for use in examination of ideas generated in the ideation session. Figure 9–1 provides their criteria checklist. The principal categories are cost, time,

Figure 9–1

Evaluation Criteria
Checklist

Cost–

Will the idea...

1. cost more than our budget allows?
2. reduce costs in the future?
3. cause me to liquidate certain investments prematurely?
4. entail marketing costs?
5. involve many personnel?
6. cost enough to promote the idea of value?
7. provide ways to share cost?
8. have costs that are tax-deductible?
9. have costs that can be planned for over time?
10. provide enough benefit to outweigh the cost?

Time–

Will the idea...

1. be possible to put into operation shortly?
2. allow me to meet my deadline?
3. be timely?
4. be better if done later?
5. be better if done sooner?
6. last or endure?
7. take too long to explain?
8. take too much time in order to achieve quality?
9. be a permanent or long-lasting one?
10. involve a long-term commitment of resources?

Feasibility–

Will the idea...

1. be operationally sound?
2. take more facilities or resources than I have?
3. work in actual practice?
4. do the job?
5. be possible to make happen?
6. be functional?
7. be manageable?
8. get out of control?
9. be suitable?
10. be capable of being deal with successfully?

Acceptability–

Will the idea...

1. be simple, direct and unsophisticated?
2. be compatible with human nature?
3. be acceptable without lengthy explanation?
4. provide some variations in its use?
5. be consistent with accepted values and attitudes?
6. "explode" in people's minds?
7. allow the leadership to go along with it?
8. allow others to endorse it?
9. be a "right" idea or product for the organization?
10. create circumstances that may be difficult to accept?

Usefulness–

Will the idea...

1. meet a real need?
2. provide some long- or short-range benefits?
3. provide some new or original way and at the same time fit into what is currently being done?
4. be profitable?
5. improve methods of operation, conditions, or safety?
6. prevent or eliminate waste or conserve the use of materials?
7. increase production or sales?
8. improve the quality of output?
9. be more efficient to use?
10. prove more advantageous than others?

Other categories–

Will the idea...

1. _____
2. _____
3. _____
4. _____
5. _____
6. _____
7. _____
8. _____
9. _____
10. _____

Source: Isaksen, S. G., and D. J. Treffinger, *Creative Problem Solving: The Basic Course* (Buffalo, NY: Bearly Ltd., 1985), p. 117.

feasibility, acceptability, and usefulness. Within each category, they provide a list of questions to evaluate the various alternatives.

Techniques for Evaluating Ideas

VanGundy identifies a number of approaches for evaluation of ideas.[12] Nine approaches will be summarized and two others will be elaborated on: force field analysis and decomposable matrices.

Advantage-Disadvantage

This is the simplest and most commonly used evaluation technique. It consists of listing the possible alternatives (ideas) and recording the strengths and weaknesses of each.

Battelle Method

The method, named after the originating organization, the Battelle Institute of Frankfurt, consists of three steps of evaluation, called *screens* (for the screening of the ideas):[13]

1. Culling criteria are developed (*e.g.,* "Is the cost prohibitive?")
2. For the items that pass the culling screen, rating criteria are developed; a minimum rating is selected and ideas that rate lower than the minimum are eliminated.
3. Scoring criteria are developed (*e.g.,* poor = 1, fair = 2, good = 3).

A weight is assigned to each factor being considered (*e.g.,* return on investment might be rated six while possibility of no cost overrun might be rated a nine). The score is multiplied by the weight to obtain a total for each idea. A minimum is selected and ideas falling below the minimum are eliminated.

Castle Technique

Three criteria are used to evaluate each idea, using the approach developed by Derek Castle: 1) acceptability (the extent to which an idea satisfies existing goals), 2) practicality (the extent to which an idea satisfies previously established financial and time constraints), and 3) originality (the extent to which an idea makes a significant improvement and provides an elegant solution).[14]

Creative Evaluation

Named by its originator, Leo Moore, the approach uses Roman numerals to categorize each idea in one of three ways: I (simple), II (hard), and III (difficult). Simple ideas are those that can be implemented with a minimum expenditure of time and money; hard ideas require a slightly greater expenditure; and difficult ideas require the greatest expenditure.[15]

Decision Balance Sheet

Developed by I. L. Janis and L. Mann, this approach provides a structured format for exploring all relevant alternatives and evaluating the associated benefits and costs.[16] The process begins with the ranking of ideas, listing the preferred alternative first, the next most preferred second, and so forth. The positive and negative points are listed for each alternative. A balance sheet is then constructed to make it easier to view the positives and negatives.

Idea Advocate

Another Battelle technique, the idea advocate is a person assigned the role of promoting one particular idea.[17] When an advocate is assigned to each idea, the positive aspects of all the ideas will be identified for group examination in order to select the idea that has the highest potential.

Panel Consensus

This approach, developed by Charles Taylor, is based on the concept of an idea funnel.[18] Ideas are randomly distributed to groups or panels who evaluate and assigned weighted values on a scale of five. The best ideas are passed on to additional panels, the number depending on the complexity of the problem/opportunity. The final panel is comprised of upper-level managers. Figure 9–2 shows the use in a complex situation where many persons/panels are used in the evaluation process.

Reverse Brainstorming

The Hotpoint Company developed this approach to try to uncover possible weaknesses of an idea and to anticipate what might go wrong

Figure 9–2   Action Levels of the Panel Consensus Technique

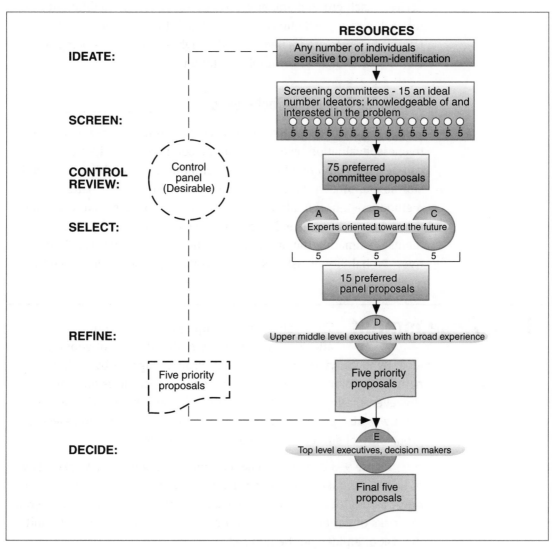

Source: VanGundy, A. B., Jr., *Techniques of Structural Problem Solving* (New York: Van Nostrand Reinhold, 1988).

when the idea is implemented.[19] In this brainstorming session, criticisms are generated instead of ideas. The group then reexamines the ideas to generate possible solutions for each weakness identified.

Sticking Dots

As described by Geschka, this procedure involves giving each group member a fixed number of votes (in the form of self-adhesive, colored dots) and allowing them to allocate the votes in any manner they desire.[20] Each group member receives a sheet of dots (a different color for each person). The individuals stick a dot next to the ideas they favor. The votes are totaled, with the highest-rated ideas being selected for further analysis or implementation.

Combining Evaluation Techniques

Just as creativity techniques can be combined to increase their effectiveness, evaluation techniques can be combined. The idea advocate can be used with any of the other techniques, as can the reverse brainstorming approach. Weighting factors, as used with the Battelle method, are a useful addition to the other techniques. Likewise, any of the techniques can be enhanced by the use of probability assessments—estimating the probability of success of the various alternatives. Probability or risk assessment is the topic of the next section.

Risk Assessment

The evaluation techniques discussed above implicitly attack the task of determining the risk of adopting an idea. By identifying an advantage or disadvantage, or by ranking alternatives, decision makers have good input to their decision process. However, the input would be improved if some explicit risk assessment was also provided. What is needed is an approach to assess the probability of success of the various alternatives.

Figure 9–3 depicts a snake charmer who is not a risk taker. Few of us want to take exorbitant risks; we want to be able to fairly accurately assess them. There are two considerations in evaluating the relative risks of various ideas: 1) the risk that an idea will not work and 2) the risk of an idea not being used.

The management science field has produced many such approaches, varying from such simple approaches as decision trees to complicated techniques such as Markov analysis. One most applicable to evaluation of creative ideas is the Bayesian approach. Developed by Thomas Bayes and adapted to the business field by Robert Schlaifer, the technique is based on the premise that in the absence of more precise data, it is reasonable to use the probability estimates of persons who by virtue of past experience and knowledge can quantify the relative likelihood of events.[21]

Figure 9–3

Figure 9–3

The Objective Is Not to
Avoid Risk but to
Properly Assess It

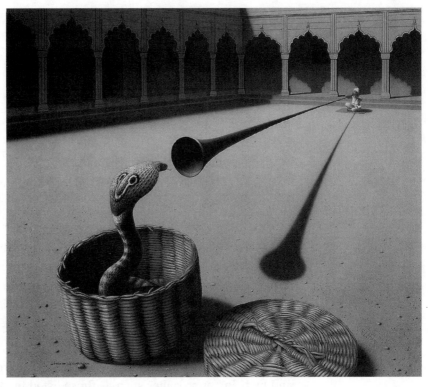

Source: Courtesy of Minolta Corporation.

To illustrate the use of this approach, refer to Chapter 2's example of the associations/images technique. The technique was used to generate many ideas on how to reduce turnover of employees. The ideas were not prioritized in that chapter. When I was consulting with the insurance company in this particular problem, at this point I asked them to prioritize the solutions by their view of the probability of success of each solution. For example, they assigned a probability of 90 percent for the success of the solution, "Help employees understand the true cost of job change." They assigned a probability of 30 percent to the solution, "Try to diminish politics, sheltering employees from these effects." It is not feasible to try to introduce all ideas (in this case about 50 ideas were produced). Assigning probability of success makes better use of scarce resources. Probability can be weighed against the cost of implementation to determine which ideas are cost-effective.

Risks are inevitable in introducing creative changes of more than simplistic scope. Edward de Bono suggests 10 ways of viewing risks:[22]

1. Be aware of possible risks.

2. Design fall-back positions and damage-containment systems.

3. Reduce the risk by testing.

4. Reduce the risk by redesigning the idea.

5. Devise early warning systems.

6. Be as informed as possible.

7. Have insurance.

8. Offer quick reactions and responses.

9. Spread the risk with partners and joint ventures.

10. Assess risk/reward ratios.

The "operating" word for risk taking is "prudent," according to Roberts and Weiss. What is a prudent risk taker? They believe that it is someone who is consciously aware of the risks, who evaluates those risks in terms of the benefit that may be realized, and who then takes measures to try to reduce, minimize, and/or eliminate the risks. However, no decision, especially an innovative one, is risk-free. Risk, however, can be controlled; it can be made tolerable and can even be mitigated.[23]

We can lower the possibility of failure by properly assessing risk and by using approaches such as those listed by de Bono to reduce risk. Nevertheless, many decisions to proceed on an idea require boldness on the part of the decision makers. Soren Kierkegaard summed up that boldness: "To dare is to lose one's footing momentarily. To not dare is to lose oneself."

If we do not take risks, our company is in danger of being outdistanced quickly by our competition, particularly in the present-day business environment of swift and continuous change. Figure 9–4 depicts what happens to non-risk takers—even the giant companies who are leaders in their industry are suffering the same fate as the dinosaurs.

Failure is the line of least persistence.

Alfred W. Brandt

Techniques for Idea Evaluation and Prioritization

Most of the techniques described above are used primarily to evaluate ideas. Some are used to prioritize ideas. Some are used for both purposes. We'll illustrate two evaluation techniques: one that specializes in eval-

Figure 9–4 History Is Full of Giants Who Couldn't Adapt. We Must Overcome Our Natural Tendency to Avoid Risk.

uation (force field analysis) and one that aids in both evaluation and prioritization (decomposable matrices).

Force Field Analysis (FFA) for Evaluation of Ideas

This technique was introduced and illustrated in Chapter 2. The name *force field* comes from the technique's ability to identify forces contributing to or hindering a solution to a problem. Because the field represents a kind of tug-of-war, there are three ways to move the center line in the direction of the more desirable future:

1. Strengthen an already present positive force.
2. Weaken an already present negative force.
3. Add a new positive force.

Force field analysis provides focus for exploring possible solutions. Although its primary use is in idea generation, it is also a good technique to use in evaluating the two ends of the continuum, positive versus negative forces affecting the problem or opportunity. The technique was used in Chapter 2 to improve the probability of a successful implementation of a creativity improvement program. That illustration showed that the tool is also useful for Phase Five of the CPS process, developing an implementation plan. Force field analysis will be illustrated below on another facet of the problem of shortage of entry-level employees. Using this technique helps to identify factors that make it difficult to hire qualified personnel versus factors that improve the company's ability to hire its fair share of the applicant pool. Figure 9–5 provides the results of the force field analysis.

Decomposable Matrices for Evaluating and Prioritizing Ideas

This technique permits participants to undertake quantitative analysis in order to prioritize ideas. The technique was derived from the work of Herbert Simon, Nobel laureate in decision sciences, who believed that complexity in the world has evolved from simple structures organized into progressively formal hierarchic systems.[24] To understand complexity, complex hierarchic systems can be analyzed using a basic property of their structure: near decomposability. The concept of near decomposability refers to the fact that the subsystems of some hierarchic systems maintain some, although not total, interdependence from other subsystems. Decomposable matrices are especially useful for highly system-based problems. The components of each subsystem are listed and arranged within a matrix. Weights are assigned to each of the interactions. Relationships between components can then be selected as the focus for generation of problem solutions. Because this technique forces identification of problem subsystems, their components and how they interact, a clearer picture of important problem elements emerges.

Figure 9–5

Force Field Analysis for
Idea Evaluation

Problem: Meeting need for entry-level personnel over next decade

Catastrophe:

Inability to hire proper number of
qualified personnel

Optimum:

Ability to get our fair share of
applicant pool

Forces

(–)	(+)
Cost-containment policy constrains recruitment	Good working environment attracts good candidates
Limits campus visits	Nice facilities
Limits number of visits to our company	Good communication
Difficult to get release for managers to recruit on campus	Up-to-date tools and techniques
	Up-to-date technology
Selection policies constrain candidate pool	Competitive entry-level compensation package
GPA minimum	
Set of acceptable schools	
Specified field of study	
Difficult to properly assess qualifications	Delineated career paths
	Specified skills
	Training sources
Constraints on reference checking	Mentor program
Inability to properly describe company advantages in training brochure	Sensitized managers
Need attractive brochure	Good behavioral training emphasized on performance appraisal
Need videotape on company facilities/advantages	
Inadequate time for interviews—managerial time constraints	Tuition support for advanced degrees
Inadequate training budget	Interesting work—enhanced through state-of-the-art motivation techniques

Problem: **Rate the value of the ideas produced by the progressive
abstraction exercise, to minimize the effect of the
impending shortage of human resources at the
professional level.**

Figure 9–6 is a matrix that utilizes a variation of the Simon technique
to produce a group consolidation of numeric values for each creative
idea. The 15 alternatives in the solution set (taken from Figure 2–3)
are listed in the first column. Six rating factors were selected for the
evaluation, based on the potential improvement. The first 5 were rated
equally, on a scale of 10 where 10 is high. The sixth rating factor, Ease
in Implementation, was given more weight in the rating; that factor

Figure 9-6   Matrix for Evaluating the Importance of the 15 Solution Approaches for the Problem of Shortage of Human Resources

Solution Approaches (Solution Space)	Rating Factors*								
	1	2	3	4	5	6	7	8	
	Improve Quality of Systems	More Rapid Development of Systems	Leverage Best Performers	Improve Job Satisfaction	Simplify Management Problems	Total	Ease in Implementation	Priority (Col. 6 × 7)	
Improve Creativity	9	9	5	9	9	41	10	410	1
Motivation	8	8	9	9	9	43	8	344	2
Retain High Performers	9	8	9	5	9	40	5	200	3
Delay Retirements	5	5	5	3	6	24	5	120	4
Job Sharing	2	2	4	6	3	17	6	102	5
Simplify Processes	3	9	5	5	8	30	3	90	6
Better Selection	3	2	1	5	5	16	5	80	7
Paraprofessionals	1	5	8	8	3	25	3	75	8
New Tools and Techniques	7	8	9	5	8	37	2	74	9
Improve Recruiting Techniques	2	2	2	1	3	10	6	60	10
Use Part-time Personnel	2	2	5	3	3	15	3	45	11
Automate	8	9	8	4	9	38	1	38	12
Telecommuting	3	4	4	3	3	17	2	34	13
New Hiring Sources	1	1	1	1	3	7	4	28	14
Outsource	5	7	3	3	3	21	1	21	15

*Rating scale = 10 where 10 is high

was multiplied by the total for the other five factors. Of the 15 factors identified as potential ways to increase productivity, the top-ranked factor was Improving Creativity. The bottom-ranked factor was Outsourcing.

The ratings could have been provided by management, or by a project team assigned that responsibility, or by all members of the organization–whichever approach management decides would provide the best information. The probability of success of each approach could also be estimated. Another column could be added to the matrix, containing a probability assessment for each alternative solution. Using the Bayesian estimating technique, the person most knowledgeable about each alternative would estimate the probability of its occurrence.

Evaluating the Creativity of Products and Services

So far we've concentrated on two of the four components of the model of creativity: person and process. Press (environment) is covered in Chapter 11. The fourth component, product, will now be discussed. The majority of the literature on creativity concentrates on three of the four components: person, process, and press. A much narrower set focuses on the topic of measurement of creativity. Of this subset, most of the focus is upon measurement of creativity in the person. According to Brogden and Sprecher, only 14 studies have offered "substantial research" on the measurement of creativity of a product.[25] Even among these studies there was more emphasis upon identifying the creative person than the creative product.[26]

Why attempt to measure the creativity of products or services? I believe that a better understanding of what constitutes a creative product will enable people throughout the organization to participate in product and service improvement.

Determining Product/Service Creativity

At one end of the continuum on criteria for determining creativity of a product are the advocates of a two-criteria measurement. Novelty and utility are the characteristics that distinguish creativity according to this way of thinking. There are a number of two-criteria advocates (novelty-utility).[27] At the other end of the continuum is the Experimental Center for the Advancement of Invention and

Innovation, which identified 33 criteria for evaluating the marketability of new products.[28]

In the center of the continuum is the U.S. patenting process. Although frequently described in the lay literature as consisting primarily of novelty and usefulness, the patent standards are considerably more detailed. Section 3000 of Stringham's patent law [1937] deals with "inventivlevel." According to the law, one who originates novel technology has the right to obtain a patent only if the "quantum of novelty claimed rises to inventivlevel." Inventivlevel is one of the law's standards, or norms or values. The following characteristics used to determine inventivlevel arose from court cases:[29]

1. Qualified intellectual activity *(creative strength)*
2. Usefulness *(Fortschritt*—stride forward)
3. Newness associated with the overcoming of special difficulties
4. An appreciable amount of experimenting before achieving the novel instrumentality
5. Prior skepticism that a development like that of the new instrumentality offered promise of success
6. Unfulfilled desire, which the patent fulfilled
7. Proof of a decided rise in business following the introduction of the patented instrumentality
8. Evidence of the instrumentality possessing novelty—novelty of a combination, novelty of a new application, spatial and kinematic novelty, novelty of a deletion of a useless part, novelty of a substitution. There are certain kinds of novelty that are not associated with inventivlevel: compactness, convenience, change of energy source, perfection of workmanship, and purity of product.

Although the topic of criteria for evaluating creative products has a long history, according to Bessemer and Treffinger, there has not been closure: "There is no conclusive set of criteria."[30]

Measuring Creativity

Creativity tests usually attempt to assess creative ability in the individual on an objective basis. Objective analysis of the product or output of a creative process or behavior attempts to validate the creativity of the output by some standard, verifiable (reliable) measure. Finally, subjective judgments of products or persons as being creative often rely on a panel of expert judges to assess the creativity of the person or output of the creative process. A discussion of each of these three areas follows.

Measuring creativity by administering creativity tests

These studies are in three broad categories: personality inventories, biographical inventories, and behavioral tests.[31] Personality inventories have been used to derive scales for measuring creativity (for example, see Helson and Catell and Butcher[32]).

Another way in which personality inventories have been used is through identifying traits of creative people. For example, Torrance and Khatena gave subjects adjectives to select from in describing themselves, then associated these adjectives with the most creative people based on historic data.[33] Biographical inventories are also used to assess creative ability. The Institute for Behavioral Research on Creativity developed the Alpha Biographical Inventory working with scientists and engineers at NASA.[34] This type of creativity assessment uses an inventory of questions regarding the subjects' biographical background. For example, to assess creativity the inventory includes questions on childhood experiences, hobbies and interests, and notable experiences.

Behavioral tests are the third type of tests used to assess creative ability. These tests are similar to intelligence tests in that they elicit behavioral activity or response from the subject. For example, the Guilford test of divergent thinking based on his structure-of-intellect theory requires the subject to think of as many alternative uses as possible for a common object.[35] The Torrance Tests of Creative Thinking (TTCT) are widely used to assess creativity.[36] The TTCT uses three components: nonverbal tests, verbal tests using verbal stimuli, and verbal tests using nonverbal stimuli. The responses to the test components are scored according to four criteria for creativity adapted largely from Guilford: (1) fluency, related to the number of ideas produced, (2) flexibility, related to the variety of the ideas produced, (3) elaboration, that is, the embellishment of ideas once they are produced, and (4) originality, the use of ideas that tend to be unique or not obvious. Rothenberg has used word-association tests to measure creativity applying a variation of the Kent-Rosanoff word-association test.[37]

While a person's creativity can be assessed by testing, the ultimate criterion by which the person will be judged is usually the substance of his/her output.

Measuring creativity by objective analysis of products

There are few rigorous applications of this approach in the literature of creativity measurement.[38] Ghiselin suggested that determining whether a product is creative can be assessed by evaluating its "intrinsic quality."[39] While this may be true, establishing an objective meaning of "intrinsic quality" is quite challenging. Simonton attempted to assess creativity of music composition by using a computer to analyze musical themes.[40] He was able to objectively determine originality (novelty), but was unable to objectively assess whether the musical theme represented artistic musical value. From the research that has been performed, Amabile believes it unlikely that any acceptable objective measure of creativity can be established without the inclusion of a subjective component.[41]

Measuring creativity by applying subjective judgments of products or persons as creative

Creativity can be subjectively assessed by judging whether a specific person is creative and then making the assumption that the person, if creative, will produce creative things. Creativity can also be evaluated by observing the product of the creative activity and making some subjective judgment regarding that product by applying an agreed-upon definition of what constitutes creativity. The evaluation of the product of the creativity process seems ultimately of more value. A number of researchers have used this perspective in subjective determination of creativity (Sobel and Rothenberg;[42] Jackson and Messick;[43] Amabile[44]).

Example: Measuring the Creativity of Computer Products/Services

It is helpful to understand measurement of creativity in products and services by examining one category of products/services. To this purpose, I will explain a categorization of products and measurement approaches for an Information Systems (IS) organization, then discuss measurement of creativity of software products. Finally, I'll give an example of measurement of software products.

The literature on creativity/innovation in IS is especially sparse. Couger found less than a dozen publications prior to 1991.[45] Only one

Table 9–1

Examples of Information Systems Areas to Measure Creative Results

		IS Activities	Measurement Approach Judging	Metrics
Systems	**New Systems**	Developing Enterprise Model	X	
		Software Development	X	
	Existing Systems	Re-engineering		X
		Problem Solving	X	X
Service	**Software**	Reducing Backlog	X	X
		Fixes	X	X
	Operations	Responsiveness		X
		Defect Reduction		X
Planning	**Opportunities**	Improving Competitiveness	X	
		Improving Scope of Influence	X	
	Capacity	Cycle Time		X
	Functionality	Networking		X
		Image Processing		X
		AI		X

(Higgins, Couger, and McIntyre[46]) provides substantive content on the topic of measurement of creativity. The study dealt with the use of creativity techniques to elicit "more enlightened views of what marketing information should be gathered by an organization." The creative results of three groups using different creativity generation techniques were evaluated by the use of expert judges.

Table 9–1 provides examples of areas in IS where products and services could be evaluated for their creative content. In the area of Systems, under the subheading New Systems, Developing Enterprise Model and Software Development are two examples where creative products are produced. To the right of the listing of activities is the column on creativity measurement. Creativity could be measured by a judging process or by means of metrics. More will be said about the measurement process later.

Table 9–2 provides a second level of abstraction. It contains examples of different levels of creative opportunity for various tasks performed in an IS organization. It illustrates the differences for tasks performed by three job categories in IS: the programmer/analyst, the

Table 9–2   Degree of Creative Opportunity in Information Systems Activities

Low	Medium	High
Programmer/Analyst		
Software Fix	Enhancement	New Development
Budgeting	Project Scheduling	Strategic Planning
Documentation	Proposal Writing	System Development
Attending Status Meeting	Attending Annual Meeting on Company Goals	Joint Application Development Meeting, Goal Setting Meeting
Designing I/O	Designing Processes	Designing Networks, Development Algorithms
Removing Defects in Screen Layout	Removing Defects in Data Validation	Removing Defects in Program Design Stage
Removing Defects at Logical Design Stage	Removing Defects at Physical Design Stage	Removing Defects at Program Design Stage
Systems Manager		
Routine Management	Problem Solving	Planning
Career Planning with Subordinate	Task Assignments	Problem Solving on Subordinate
Managing Standards Adherence	Managing Technology	Managing People
Operations Management		
Managing I/O Functions Managing PCs	Managing Mainframes	Managing Networks
Managing Operators	Managing Schedulers	Managing System Programmers
Improving Capacity	Improving Response	Improving Accuracy, Removing Defects
Identifying I/O Defects	Identifying Processing Defects	Identifying Network Defects

systems manager, and the operations manager. For example, some meetings provide a high level of opportunity for creativity, such as a joint application development (JAD) session or a goal-setting meeting. Status meetings provide minimal opportunity for creative approaches. Locating defects at the logical design stage requires much less creative effort than locating those same defects at the program design stage. Trying to justify to the CEO that the IS function should be elevated in the organization requires much more ingenuity than justifying a salary increase.

Forms design provides less opportunity for creativity than does software design. Deriving ways to improve capacity provides more opportunity for creativity than providing E-mail service, while coming up with ideas to improve response time may necessitate a high level of creative thinking and imagination. However, despite the lessened opportunity for creativity in producing some deliverables, there **is** opportunity in each of the deliverables. Form design may be considered an uncreative task, yet employees who apply themselves can find imaginative approaches to improve the most mundane of tasks. The lack of creativity in present-day forms originates from the belief that the task is uncreative rather than based on facts from discussions with persons saddled with use of poorly designed forms.

Creativity in Software Development

The literature is rich concerning software quality.[47] Criteria have been developed to evaluate software quality.[48] One of the most complete lists of criteria was compiled by Buckley and Poston; it includes economy, integrity, understandability, flexibility, interoperability, modularity, correctness, validity, modifiability, generality, testability, reusability, usability, resilience, clarity, maintainability, portability, and efficiency.[49] The list is comprehensive in evaluating software quality, but it does not fully cover software creativity. There is little question that one of the two factors essential for creativity—utility—has been covered. The majority of the terms in the list relate to utility; none relate to novelty, however. That feature is also excluded from the lists in the other references on quality of software. Does this mean that novelty is not a key concern in software development?

One of the managers I interviewed expressed the belief that novelty has little importance in software, that there should be a single criterion: utility. "If the system meets the needs of the clients, we don't care whether it's a new idea or just the replication of an old idea from another system." Another manager expressed a similar viewpoint and went on to say, "Only developers of proprietary software would have an equal concern for novelty—they have continual need to stay ahead of the competition." A third manager commented that use of the novelty criterion might actually detract from the utility of the application— that the developers might be so intent on producing something new that the utility of the software might be lessened. It would be preferable to use *new* rather than *novel*. To some, the term *novel* emphasizes a search for a different, rather than better, solution. However, the use of the term *novelty* is so ingrained in the creativity literature that I will continue its use.

I believe that novelty is a key concern for all software, whether developed for proprietary or internal corporate use only. Nor is it merely a problem of semantics. The large majority of software has the characteristic of novelty; the debatable issue is merely the matter of degree of novelty. The only software category that has questionable novelty is software "fixes." All additions, changes, and enhancements are characteristic of being new. The change may be similar to that used in another application or even similar to one used in the logic of another module of the application in question—yet it adds something new to the application.

Second, I believe that novelty is essential for software developed internally for a company as well as proprietary software (software developed for sale to other organizations). The problem of using utility as the single criterion is that the emphasis tends to be on short-term benefits. One would have to use supplementary terms, such as short- and long-term utility, to ensure that both needs are properly empha-sized. Use of a joint criterion of novelty, along with utility, promotes (almost forces) an emphasis on more than just the short term.

If one believes it essential to have a single criterion, then perhaps the characteristic should be "robustness." Robust software is powerful-ly built, vigorous, and suited to endurance. Robust software is built for flexibility as well as reliability. The concept of robustness automatical-ly conveys long-term as well as short-term utility. However, the goal of a single creativity criterion is too restraining. Use of both utility and novelty results in better software design, in more robust software. The only problem with the use of the novelty criterion would be a per-ceived need to seek novelty for novelty's sake, rather than to find new and better ways to solve a problem or to meet an opportunity.

Use of the novelty criterion also results in emphasis on extension of the life of the application. A new—and not just utilitarian—solution has higher potential for increasing the life of the application in the highly competitive world in which businesses fight for existence. Even though software developed for internal rather than proprietary use would appear to be less concerned with novelty, the competition is merely indirect rather than direct. If the company's software is not constantly updated (new), the firm will not be successful in its com-petitive environment.

Despite the lack of use of the term in Information Systems, the concept of novelty has always been important. The following are examples or ways novelty in software development is presently expressed:

- New ways to speed up database access

- New algorithms within programs

- New ways to improve response time

- New ways to enrich data, through use of statistical analysis and management science techniques

- New ways to capture and process data and information not previously cost-effective, such as image processing and expert systems

- New ways to link people for information sharing and decision making, such as Group Decision Support Systems (GDSS), networks, and databases.

Next, we will review an example of software that meets the criteria for utility and novelty. For a reference that evaluates the creativity of six different kinds of software, see Couger and Dengate.[50]

MIDS, Lockheed-Georgia

An in-house developed system, MIDS (Management Information and Decision Support system) is used by senior executives at Lockheed-Georgia. The company is a major producer of cargo aircraft, employing more than 19,000 persons at its plant in Marietta, Ga. MIDS provides 710 visual displays for 70 executive users, with a mean number of 5.5 displays viewed per user per day. Executives gain access to the system using a personal computer connected to a mainframe running the MIDS application and, using their unique access password, are allowed access to an authorized set of displays. The displays are accessed through a menu system and the subject area in question can be investigated by functional area, organizational level, and project. Additionally, the user can also enter a keyword that is checked against an index, and a list of all displays related to that keyword are then displayed. Other functions available from within MIDS include a display of a diary of major events and access to electronic mail. There is a great deal of consistency across all displays: standards for color codes, graphic designs, and terminology used. Vertical wording is avoided,

Table 9–3 Criteria for Evaluating Utility of Software Products

Low	Medium	High
Cuts cost 10–20%	Cuts cost 20–50%	Cuts cost > 50%
ROI of 15–20% (cost of capital level)	ROI of 20–100%	Order of magnitude increase on ROI
Helps in retaining a market niche	Gets more penetration of market niche	Helps establish new market niche
Retains present level of customer loyalty	Increases customer loyalty	Locks customer into dependency
Performs functions more efficiently than before be a factor of .5	Performs functions more efficiently than previously by a factor of 1	Performs functions more efficiently than previously by a factor of 2 or more
Performs functions not previously performed	Performs several functions not previously performed	Performs many functions not previously performed
Improves quality	Improves quality and reliability	Improves quality, reliability, and life of application

abbreviations and acronyms are limited to those on an authorized list, and there is a field for explanatory comments. Data to update the screens comes from a variety of sources including internal systems, external databases, customers, and affiliated Lockheed companies. The data are obtained electronically where possible, otherwise, they are keyed into the system. A number of benefits occurred:

1. Executives have access to more relevant, accurate, and timely information than was previously available.

2. There is improved communication. Executives now access identical information; such information can be easily shared with other stakeholders.

3. Among executives, there is an evolving understanding of key information requirements as they are introduced to the system and their familiarity with its capabilities increases.

4. Direct cost reductions were identified, particularly with respect to the development and generation of reports, graphs, and presentation material.

Rating Scales

To assist the judges in the evaluation process, Tables 9–3 and 9–4 were developed. Guidelines for low, medium, and high utility are provided in Table 9–3 while guidelines for low, medium, and high novelty are provided in Table 9–4.

Seven criteria are provided in Table 9–3, beginning with cost. The example is new software that cuts cost 10 to 20 percent for low

Table 9–4 Criteria for Evaluating Novelty of Software Products

Low	Medium	High
Determines new uses for existing technology	Determines how new technology can be applied	Discovers way (approaches) for technology transfer
Introduces an approach, methodology for the first time in a work group	Introduces an approach or a methodology for the first time in the company	Introduces an approach or a methodology for the first time in the industry
Enhances existing applications to perform previously non-computerized tasks or functions	Uses an established algorithm or approach for the first time in this application category	Derives a new algorithm or an original approach for computerization
Conceives of a unique way to present system output for users of the application	Uses conventional technology in an unusual way for this application category	Uses new technology to computerize some tasks that were perceived to be uncomputerizable

utility, 20 to 50 percent for medium utility, and over 50 percent for high utility. Or, the new application may not cut cost at all but may increase return on investment, hence the second guideline: low = ROI of 15 to 20 percent (the norm for cost of capital), medium = ROI of 20 to 100 percent, and high = order of magnitude increase in ROI. The other guidelines deal with retaining market niche, maintaining customer loyalty, performing functions more efficiently, performing functions not previously performed, and improving various characteristics of software. Guidelines for novelty (Table 9–4) deal with how technology and new methodology are used and the type of change introduced.

The components of each software package were separated and evaluated according to degree or level of novelty and utility. Because of space constraints, only the results of the evaluation of MIDS are provided, as an example of how all six packages were evaluated.

Creativity Evaluation: Utility

The value of MIDS is difficult to objectively determine; benefits are mostly intangible. Nevertheless, a number of benefits have been identified that demonstrate the usefulness of the system.

1. Executives have access to more relevant, accurate, and timely information than was previously available. Specific examples are described in the source article.[51] The value of this "better" information is difficult to quantify. However, since management essentially involves making decisions based on the available information, any system that significantly improves the process of providing executives with necessary information plays a very important role in an organization. (Judges' evaluation: **HIGH UTILITY**.)

2. Communication is improved. Executives now access identical information, such information can be easily shared with other stakeholders, and one display screen is dedicated to the display of a diary of special upcoming events. (Judges' evaluation: **MEDIUM UTILITY**.)

3. Use of the system has continually increased since its first implementation with the number of displays, the number of users, and, significantly, the number of display references per user per day all increasing. (Judges' evaluation: **MEDIUM UTILITY**.)

4. Among executives, there is an evolving understanding of key information requirements as they are introduced to the system and their familiarity with its capabilities increases. (Judges' evaluation: **MEDIUM UTILITY**.)

5. Direct cost reductions were identified, particularly with respect to the development and generation of reports, graphs, and presentation material. (Judges' evaluation: **LOW UTILITY**.)

Creativity Evaluation: Novelty

1. This is a large-scale executive information system that works and that is firmly embedded in the organization being used by the top 70 executives, including the president. Additionally, it has been in place for over a decade. (Judges' evaluation: **HIGH NOVELTY**.)

2. MIDS is so easy to use that only 15 minutes of training is provided and user documentation is not necessary. (Judges' evaluation: **MEDIUM NOVELTY**.)

3. Since the beginning of the evolutionary system design process, some insightful decisions have been made. Some of the following characteristics were quite novel when the system was originally developed: 1) a separate terminal was provided for each executive, 2) displays were graphically oriented, 3) intelligent use of color was incorporated, and 4) a set of standards was developed for use across all displays to define screen design and the usage of graphical designs, color, and terminology. (Judges' evaluation: **MEDIUM NOVELTY**.)

Comments on the Evaluation of Creativity of Products/Services _

The preceding example shows how an organization might provide more specific guidelines to foster creativity of products and services. The approach would apply to other internal products, such as accounting systems/procedures, and products made for sale. The activities required to develop a company product can be evaluated in a very similar framework. Likewise, company services could also be evaluated for their creativity. Some are obvious, such as the customer service function of an electronics manufacturing organization. Others not so obvious but just as appropriate for this process would include the order-taking function and how responsive it is to incoming calls, or the accounts receivable organization and how well it manages the follow-up on late payments without alienating customers.

If persons are informed about their native creativity capability, provided processes to facilitate creativity, and supported through a positive climate for creativity, it is logical to assume that creative products and services will result. Nevertheless, employees need ways to measure their results. Employees also need to know what characterizes creative products and services.

Why are these important areas for study? There are three key reasons:

1. Creativity is a key resource in producing competitive advantage.
2. Identifying specific criteria for creativity can lead to greater sophistication in products and services as well as in management techniques.
3. In an era of flattened organizations where career paths are diminished, achievement goals must be substituted for advancement goals. Creativity provides a new category for achievement.

However, the most important reason is the opportunity to tap a previously underutilized resource in business. Behavioral research clearly shows that the native creativity of most individuals is constrained by the emphasis upon conformity in the U.S. educational process and by bureaucracy in the business world. As a result, most of us have felt it necessary to hide this valuable talent, like a gold coin in a safety deposit box. In an era of scarce resources, there is the potential of resurfacing this highly valuable resource—one that will hugely benefit the IS organization. At the same time, in an era of reduced opportunities for advancement and achievement, emphasis upon creativity provides individual employees new challenges and new forms of recognition.

We must beware of what I call "inert ideas"—ideas that are merely received into the mind without being utilized, tested, or thrown into fresh new combinations.

Alfred North Whitehead

Conclusion

The need for thorough evaluation is illustrated by a story of a man at Los Angeles International Airport, standing at the gate for a plane arriving from Tokyo. He sees a Japanese man getting off the airplane with two large bags. The passenger stops, puts down the bags, and looks at his watch. He keys some data into the watch, waits for printout, tears off the printout, and puts it in his pocket. He walks a few feet, hears a beep from the watch, puts down the bags, and listens to a message. He then speaks a response into the watch's receiver device.

The American stops him and comments: "What a marvelous watch. I've never seen any like it. Can you tell me where I can buy one?"

The Japanese man puts down his bags and replies: "No—they are not yet marketed in America."

"Can I buy yours then—I'll pay you double what it cost you," the American responds eagerly.

The Japanese man agrees. He hands over the watch and pockets the money. As the American starts to walk off, the Japanese man points to the two bags and says, "Wait, you forgot the batteries!"

William Miller comments that too many criteria for excessive quantification too early can kill promising ideas or discourage new ones from ever being posed. "Too much quantification can also lead to the creation of data merely to satisfy the system. Conversely, waiting until late in a project's life to apply key criteria can waste valuable resources."[52]

Adams reminds us that we make many of our decisions based on an unconscious mix of experience and emotion: "Our mind is very good at integrating the complexities involved with little conscious intervention. This is the type of decision involved in making 'snap judgements'.... This unconscious approach to problem solving is sometimes called 'hunching' and is not confined to minor decisions.... This intuitive decision-making ability is near and dear to us, as well it should be, because it is based on our life experience and knowledge.... It is a profoundly powerful ability that almost automatically considers preferences, unknowns, probabilities, and data.... However, it is not necessarily consistent with increasing creativity or ability to change.

Unconscious decision making is habitual and, therefore, may destroy new directions."[53]

Caution and care are needed when checking out the worth of ideas, according to Fabian. "Since one of the core rules of (brain)storming is to allow wildness...some of the ideas that are proposed can seem too far out.... An attitude that is heavily critical...could be detrimental. Good but undeveloped ideas or even strange options may have real merit if a little time is taken for greater understanding. Also, overly critical critiquing can cause people to shrivel their creative thinking for the next generation round."[54]

Summary

Figure 9–7 reminds us that even the most up-to-date mouse can still be trapped. We need to be on the lookout to devise ways to avoid mousetraps for the best of our solutions. A careful evaluation process raises the probability that we will select the best solution. A wide variety of approaches exist for evaluating and prioritizing of ideas. This chapter provides a description of 11 different approaches. Sometimes the nature of the problem or opportunity determines which technique might be best. For example, the advantage/disadvantage technique would be satisfactory for a simple problem, while the Battelle Method is more appropriate for a complex problem. Some techniques might be used in combination. For example, the idea advocate could be used along with any of the other techniques.

Figure 9–7

Using an Old Approach to Catch a New Idea

Eeeek!

This chapter also illustrated evaluation of products, the fourth component of the four-component model of creativity. Creative output includes creative ideas and creative products and services. We need to be creative in designing the approach to evaluation and prioritization of creative product. Therefore, evaluation/prioritization have both divergent and convergent elements. As in the case of idea generation, the task of evaluation can be carried out by individuals or by groups. Before groups engage in applying the evaluation/prioritization techniques, they should engage in the diverging activity of dialogue and the diverging activity of discussion.

Once the creative alternatives have been evaluated, we are ready for Phase Five of the CPS process, developing an implementation plan.

> Keep your eyes on the stars but keep your feet on the ground.
>
> *Theodore Roosevelt*

Exercises

1. Why is Phase Four of the CPS process referred to as the "measuring tape" phase?

2. Isaksen and Treffinger identify seven tasks of Phase Four of the CPS process. What are they?

3. What are the five principal categories for evaluation of ideas in the checklist developed by Isaksen and Treffinger?

4. Give one-sentence descriptions of each of the nine approaches for evaluation of ideas identified by VanGundy.

5. One must assess the risk of accepting an idea. Ten ways of viewing risk are identified by de Bono. What are they?

6. Provide a one-paragraph summary of the force field analysis approach.

7. Provide a one-paragraph summary of the decomposable matrices approach.

8. Give one-paragraph descriptions of the three ways to measure creativity.

9. What is the value of establishing criteria for creativity in development of products and services?

Eyeglass Wiper

Patent No. 2,888,703 (1959)

Klara Karwowska of Calgary, Alberta

"The object of the invention is to provide an eyeglass wiper mechanism which will effectively keep eyeglasses clean of rain, steam, or the like...the person wearing the glasses will be able to readily actuate the wipers so as to keep the lenses clean for clear visibility."

*People who say it cannot be done should
not interrupt those who are doing it.*
Anonymous

Developing an Implementation Plan

The final phase in the CPS process is development of an implementation plan. Ideas have been evaluated and prioritized (Phase Four) and now it is necessary to determine how they are to be implemented. This is the neglected step in the CPS process. It appears that most people are excited about generating ideas to solve problems or to identify opportunities, but would rather leave the solution implementation to someone else. Far less has been published on the topic of implementing ideas than on the subject of originating ideas. Some think that there is little creativity involved in this phase. Perhaps the most creativity is needed in this phase! People are naturally resistant to change. It is a real challenge to find creative ways to cause people to want to change their normal way of doing things and to adopt the newly created solution.

The Osborn-Parnes model of CPS labeled Phase Five as "acceptance finding." Their view was that once you gain acceptance for your idea, the plan for implementation is rather straightforward. My version of the CPS model uses instead the Phase Five label "developing an implementation plan." It is broader than the Osborn-Parnes approach, because acceptance is just one component of implementation. Creativity is needed to obtain acceptance of the ideas developed for problem solution and for a new opportunity. Creativity is also needed in deciding how to implement the idea, to make it workable. Therefore, this chapter is separated into the two key components of implementation planning: acceptance planning and action planning.

Hoping to goodness is not theologically sound!

Linus

Have you not learn'd great lessons from those who reject you, and brace themselves against you? Or who treat you with contempt.

Walt Whitman

Acceptance Planning

There are hundreds of stories about reluctance of people to accept new ideas. Clever Trevor's all-time favorite story is about Xerox. Chester Carlson invented xerography in 1938, but more than twenty major U.S. corporations, including IBM and Kodak, showed an "enthusiastic lack of interest" in his system, as Carlson put it. No major corporation or office-supply expert saw a market for xerography. After all, who would buy a copy machine when carbon paper was so cheap and so plentiful?[1]

One of my favorites is about the company reluctant to change button closings on men's trousers. The story goes back to the Hookless Fastener Company (now Talon) in the town of Meadville, Pa. A novice advertising salesman for the old *Saturday Evening Post* stopped in one day to solicit advertising. A Hookless Fastener executive confided in him: "Ninety percent of our zippers go into tobacco pouches. If anything happens to that business, we're out of luck."

The salesman asked where they were selling the other 10 percent. "BFGoodrich is trying some out on footwear and galoshes," was the reply, "and a women's clothing manufacturer is starting to put some on clothes."

The salesman reflected for a moment. "Why not sell them to men's clothing manufacturers to put on men's flies—instead of buttons?"

The idea went to the president of the company, whose judgment was incisive. "I like trousers the way they are. Buttons are safer. We could get into trouble; we might have lawsuits."

It took the company four years to produce the first experimental pair of zipper-fly trousers.[2]

Charles Clark invented Rule 816, which he says has earned its place beside Murphy's Law and the Peter Principle:[3]

Rule 816: Relating to New Ideas

Rule 816 is now in effect until further notice. When confronted with a new idea, vote against it.

Rationale:

1. It is probably not a good idea; new ideas seldom are.
2. Even if it is a good idea, the chances are it will never be tested.
3. Even if it is a good idea and even though it is tested, chances are that it won't work the first time.
4. Even if it is a good idea, and even though it is tested, and even if it succeeds, there'll be plenty of time for thinking up alibis.

Therefore: When confronted with a new idea, the rational action is to take a positive and forward-looking stand against it.

VanGundy describes the problem of acceptance finding activity in this way:

> Numerous obstacles exist in both groups and organizations that can prevent even the best ideas from being implemented. Overcoming such obstacles can be as important as any of the other problem-solving stages. Because of their complexity at the human and technological levels, most organizations have built-in implementation blocks that must be overcome before an idea can be put into action. Some of these blocks are intentional, having been devised to serve as checks to insure the smooth operation of organizational processes; other blocks are unintentional and arise from the peculiarities that emerge from an organization's mythology (culture) .... The third type of block is ... external to an organization ... a change in market demand, for example.[4]

Why People Resist Change

Frustration over people's unwillingness to change is something each of us has experienced. We have vivid ideas of our parents or guardians opposing our "pushing the envelope," trying to get approval to do something that they thought we were too young to do. Yet, when we become parents we find ourselves with the same attitudes about change our elders had. Some of the issues are the same: when our toddlers should have their way about investigating something, when our youngsters should start walking to school by themselves, when teenagers should start dating, when high-school kids should be allowed to make their own decisions about their future.

If we could just examine the reasons that make us hesitate to accept change, we would be better prepared to deal with others who do not accept our ideas as readily as we feel they should.

Figure 10–1 shows Von Fange's graphic illustration of the resistance to change. It portrays the fact that the greater the potential benefit and the more radical the departure from habit and tradition, the greater the difficulty in gaining acceptance for a new idea.[5]

Figure 10–1

The Greater the
Contribution and the More
Habit-Bound the
Organization, the Higher
the Resistance to Change

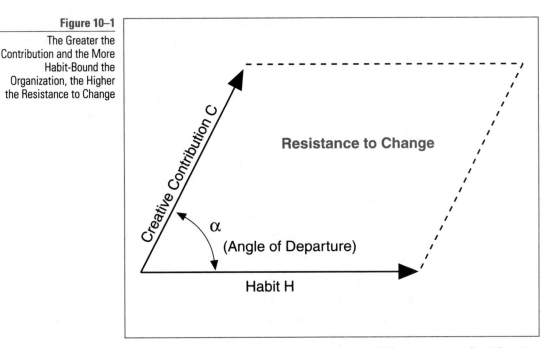

Source: Von Fange, E. K., *Professional Creativity* (Englewood Cliffs, N.J.: Prentice Hall, 1959), p. 27.

Resistance to change is not confined to the non-managerial ranks. Management also can become entrenched and prone to inertia. I received dramatic evidence of managerial resistance in my first year as a manager. Alex Osborn's book on applied imagination had just been published and I read it with great anticipation over its applicability to my own area of responsibility. We had a persistent problem in the manufacturing area that the company had not been able to solve for more than a year. I decided that getting my group together to brainstorm possible solutions might bring up some ideas that had not been considered previously. I took them into the conference room, explained the brainstorming procedure, and was elated at their excitement about the potential for a solution to the problem. People presented their ideas with a lot of exuberance; they were excited in their stimulation from the ideas of their colleagues. We had been at work only 45 minutes, however, before we were interrupted by the secretary of my boss. She handed me a message from him, which said: "This is too long for your whole group to be away from their desks. Please conclude your meeting within the next 10 minutes."

The cause of his concern was the high visibility of my group. The entire administrative offices were in a bullpen arrangement where there were no partitions. The conference room had walls but they were glass, so everyone on the floor could observe who was in meetings and the length of the meetings. My boss was so insecure in his job that he was afraid that the vice president would observe my group having too much fun in our brainstorming session.

With a lot of disappointment, I explained the note to my group and cut the session short. We were told not to use the brainstorming approach again. Fortunately, within six months my boss was replaced with one who was willing to try new approaches; we were able to demonstrate the value of brainstorming such that it became a regular practice in the whole company.

When a change occurs, it may appear as a threat to people's security. In an industrial or business situation, people fear they may lose any or all of the following: 1) earnings (all or part), 2) job, 3) friends, 4) status, 5) recognition, 6) skill, 7) chance for advancement, 8) favorable working conditions, and 9) rights of office.

Psychologist Elliott Smith illustrates the resistance to change by relating the experience of Pasteur.

> The united opposition may be insurmountable even after the discovery is a well-established fact. Thus when Pasteur, looking through his microscope at what had been known for decades—the appearance of active microbes in the course of disease—saw this not as the result of disease but as its cause, he rendered obsolete much of existing medical science. Since he had no formal medical education, he had little internal resistance to overcome. But the announcement of his discovery marshalled against him the organized and bitter opposition of the whole medical profession. Their thinking processes and their practices had all been developed on a different stem. To accept the new point of view involved giving up most of their previous ways of thought and practice, admitting that they had been wrong, and then starting the slow painful path of learning new ones.[6]

Figure 10–2   Trying to Bring About Change Is Often Like Moving a Reluctant Burro

Trying to persuade some people to accept change is like trying to persuade a donkey to go the direction you want it. Figure 10–2 shows
how strong this resistance can be. These five men are depicted in
their unsuccessful attempt to move their donkey during a burro race.
William Miller identifies some of the general reasons that people resist
change:[7]

Integrity.   You might oppose a change out of a sincere belief that it is not
the highest good for the people or the problem. This resistance is strengthened when the status quo would be hard to reestablish if the change
effort failed. You press for a solution that your heart knows is better.

Fear.   You might resist change when you perceive it could threaten
your job, status, dignity, budgets, or relationships. You don't trust that
the change is really in your best interest. Sometimes this fear may be
justified. At other times it may be a "victim" mentality that doesn't like
others controlling your life. Anger and frustration may spring from the
base emotion of fear.

Communication.   A lack of understanding of the need for change can
prevent any serious cooperation, particularly when the price seems too

high. A too-forceful style of telling people what to do can offend, leading to the same result.

History.   You might resist change if you have experienced many meaningless and poorly implemented changes or if you lack confidence in the abilities of the sponsors and change agents to make it work. This resistance is compounded by poor communication.

Pace.   You might resist change when you don't have enough time to grieve the passing of the ways things used to be. The experience of loss and letting go heals at its own pace. Winters are a necessary time and cannot be hurried.

Stress.   You might resist change when there is already too much stimulation for you to manage. You'd rather keep the problems you're familiar with than undergo possible turmoil to get to a "promised land."

I like the wry comment Barbara Johnson makes in her book, *Splashes of Joy in the Cesspools of Life:*

> *The rain falls on the just and also on the unjust, but chiefly the just,*
> *Because the unjust steals the just's umbrella.*

We like to grouse that people rarely will accept our ideas, for a dozen reasons. However, if we spend an appropriate amount of time on acceptance planning, we'll find a sharp increase in the positiveness toward the acceptance of our ideas.

> It takes courage to be creative; just as soon as you
> have a new idea, you're in the minority of one.
>
> *E. Paul Torrance*

Gaining Idea Acceptance

Few persons would attempt to implement a major change without some kind of action plan. Some implementation plans consist of pages of detailed steps to ensure that every related factor has been considered. There is widespread acceptance of the need for implementation planning; not so for acceptance planning. It is amazing how seldom action plans are prepared to gain acceptance of ideas. In 1991 I attended the National Inventors Meeting. Perhaps I should not have been surprised at how much of the meeting time was spent in complaining about people who did not have the insight to accept their inventions. They deplored the lack of vision, stubbornness, narrow-sightedness, "not invented here syndrome," and many other factors that prevented acceptance of their inventions. If equal time had been spent on acceptance planning, it would have been a very productive meeting. Yet when I talked to persons who had attended previous meetings, they said the same kind of behavior occurred year after year. Inventors are interested in discovery but are easily bored when they have to spend time on how to get their discoveries accepted.

Action planning for gaining acceptance is equally as important as implementation planning, but neither are as much fun as coming up with the ideas. If we make a challenge out of the concept of action and implementation planning, perhaps people will be willing to spend more time at it. It is clear that these two activities need creativity, ingenuity, and insightfulness if they are to be successful.

Basadur has developed eight reasons why taking action can be difficult:[8]

1. We find it hard to get started (even when we know exactly what to do). This is called *Procrastination.*

2. We find it hard to get started because our Action Plan is inadequate: either

   - too fuzzy,

   - too complicated,

   - not challenging enough (too easy), or

   - not realistic enough (too difficult).

3. We don't like to carry out some parts of our Action Plan even when we get started.

4. We fear the unknown (which is where our action will take us).

5. We fear our plan might fail.

6. We fear our solution isn't "perfect" (it won't solve the whole problem).

7. We can't say 'no' to other things that are less important but easier and more fun to do.

8. We believe the task is too big to find enough time to do it, so why try?

Balancing Inquiry and Advocacy

Senge talks about the need to balance inquiry and advocacy: "What has become obvious on repeated occasions is that, when there is inquiry and advocacy, creative outcomes are much more likely."[9] He is suggesting that, in seeking advocacy of our ideas, we must also be in an inquiry mode, asking questions to get at the reasons why a person might be opposed to our idea. He has derived guidelines to help us in these two activities.[10]

When advocating your view:

- *Make* your own reasoning explicit (*i.e.,* say how you arrived at your view and the data upon which it is based).

- *Encourage* others to explore your view (*e.g.,* "Do you see gaps in my reasoning?").

- *Encourage* others to provide different views (*i.e.,* "Do you have either different data or different conclusions, or both?").

- Actively *inquire* into others' views that differ from your own (*i.e.,* "What are your views?" "How did you arrive at them?" "Are you taking into account data that are different from what I have considered?").

When inquiring into others' views:

- If you are making assumptions about others' views, state your assumptions clearly and acknowledge that they are assumptions.

- State the "data" upon which your assumptions are based.

- Don't bother asking questions if you're not genuinely interested in others' responses (*i.e.,* if you're only trying to be polite or to show the others up).

When you arrive at an impasse (others no longer appear to be open to inquiring into their own views):

- Ask what data or logic might change their views.

- Ask if there is any way you might together design an experiment (or some other inquiry) that might provide new information.

When you or others are hesitant to express your views or to experiment with alternative ideas:

- Encourage them (or you) to think out loud about what might be making it difficult (*i.e.,* "What is it about this situation, and about me or others, that is making open exchange difficult?").

- If there is mutual desire to do so, design with others ways to overcome these barriers.

The point is not to follow the guidelines slavishly, but to use them to keep in mind the spirit of balancing inquiry and advocacy. Senge suggests, "Like any 'formula' for starting ... they should be used as 'training wheels' on your first bicycle. They help to get you started, and give you a feel for what it is like to 'ride,' to practice inquiry with advocacy. As you gain skill, they can and probably should be discarded. But it is also nice to be able to come back to them periodically when you encounter some rough terrain."[11]

Convincing a person or group of the value of your idea should be just as gratifying as having produced the idea. After all, how much satisfaction is there in saying "I came up with a really good idea the other day, but I couldn't get anyone to agree"? A little care and time in acceptance planning can pave the road to acceptance of your ideas; it also can pave the way to easier acceptance of future ideas. Once people see you have taken the time to consider the ramifications of your ideas, they will have more confidence in you as an idea person.

Isaksen and Treffinger recommend identifying the assisters and resisters in implementation. Table 10–1 shows them using the 5Ws/H technique for this purpose.[12]

Selling Your Ideas

K.T. Connor developed a set of six steps in selling an idea to a specific individual or group. She reviewed the steps in a presentation at the 1991 CPS Institute in Buffalo:

1. Explain the idea and its rationale.
2. Explain the benefits and limitations.
3. Explain the impact on the listener.
4. Ask for reactions and concerns and respond empathetically.
5. Ask for input for resolving these concerns.
6. Agree on the next steps to take.

Table 10–1		**Elements of Assistance**	
Assisters/Resistors in Acceptance Planning	*Who*	People (individuals, groups, organizations, etc.) who might help
	What	Things, objects, or activities that might be helpful in implementing the solution
	Where	Locations, places, or events which might be preferred/or especially useful for the situation
	When	Times or aspects of timing (dates, deadlines, schedules, etc.) which might be beneficial or especially appropriate
	Why	Reasons for implementing the solution, especially reasons that will promote support for the proposed solution
	How	Steps or specific actions which need to be accomplished in order to carry out the solution effectively
		Elements of Resistance
	Who	People (individuals, groups, or organizations) who might oppose, inhibit, or limit the effectiveness of the plan
	What	Things, objects, or activities that might impede progress
	Where	Locations or places that might not be appropriate or helpful in implementing the solution
	When	Particular times to avoid, or aspects of timing which might cause concerns when implementing the solution
	Why	Reason for implementing the solution that might not meet wide agreement; reasons for not accepting the proposed solution
	How	Actions or activities that might operate against the proposed solution or that might promote failure

Source: Isaksen, S. G., and D. J. Treffinger, *Creative Problem Solving: The Basic Course* (Buffalo: Bearly Ltd., 1985), p. 136.

Jack Gibb audiotaped conversations where people were trying to sell an idea. He did content analysis on the tapes and noted where people became defensive. He then analyzed the statements by the person selling the idea that brought about the defensive behavior. He classified the evocative comments into five categories:[13]

1. **Evaluative**—The idea "sellers" made comments like, "Don't be stubborn" or "You may be a little slow understanding this." The same defensive behavior results from overly positive evaluative statements, such as "Oh, you are such a creative person that you'll recognize the value of this idea." Evaluative statements should be avoided.

2. **Controlling**—The seller tries to maneuver a person into accepting the idea. Instead, there needs to be a sensitivity to the other person's needs, to hear what he or she is saying.

3. **Generalizing**—The seller gives general statements like "We can implement this quickly." Instead, there needs to be specificity, such as "This is naturally implemented during the annual revision cycle for performance reviews" or "We'll wait until the month-end reports are completed so the workload is normal."

4. **Indifference**—The seller ignores the feelings of the prospective idea-buyer. "I hear you, but that view is not conducive to the best interests of the company." Instead, the seller needs to show some empathy, "I accept your feelings, although I don't agree with you."

5. **Certainty**—The seller comes across too positively, as if he/she has everything figured out. The seller makes statements like, "I know exactly what you're thinking." Instead, the seller should be tentative, "As far as I can see, this is a good approach." "We're not certain, but the information at hand leads us to believe...."

There are lots of books published on selling your ideas. Almost every sales force has regular meetings emphasizing different approaches in getting people to buy products or services. In trying to gain acceptance for an idea, however, it is much more useful to get other people involved, committed to the idea. The checklist found on page 316 is very helpful in attaining acceptance of ideas.

Enlisting Others' Involvement

A key element in implementation planning is enlisting the involvement of other persons. Joel Weston, Jr., president of Hanes Dye and Finishing Company of North Carolina, developed the checklist found in Table 10–2 to enlist others' involvement.[14] He used the 5Ws/H creativity technique in deriving his checklist.

> Ideas are such funny things; they never work unless you do.
>
> *Herbert V. Prochnow*

Action Planning

Tom Peters, coauthor of the best-selling *In Search of Excellence,* is currently excited about identifying action-oriented companies and the people behind that orientation. He suggests that we may spend too much time in action planning and, in so doing, miss the window of opportunity. He cites the action orientation of MCI employees. "They say there's no one—*i.e.,* boss—to give you the 'final word' on anything. You're routinely supposed to take the initiative, consult with the experts and affected parties on your own. Once you feel that you've gathered a sufficient amount of information, then do something for heaven's sakes. 'Do something' is the constant cry. 'The major sin,' one middle manager said to me, 'is not to make a decision.' Do something, even if it's wrong. That's paramount." [15]

Table 10–2 Checklist to Enlist Others' Involvement	*WHO?*	Who might be involved? What group? Who might make contributions to the achievement desired? Who might be favorably placed, and who might have special talents or resources to help? What special strengths, capabilities, or resources might they contribute? Who might I need to convince of the value of the idea to be implemented?
	WHERE?	Where might you begin for maximum, quick, visible progress? What special places, locations, circumstances, occasions, times, days, or approaches might be utilized for reestablishing and insuring self-generating momentum? What might be a very first step? What other ideas or challenges have you found by answering the "where?" questions?
	WHY?	Why might they freely or willingly lend their support? What might gain enthusiasm for the idea? What opportunities might be provided for them or for you to excel or to shine? In what ways might their participation further their own interests? What might gain support for your aims and activities? How might you demonstrate, dramatize, or visualize the benefits?
	HOW?	How might others be rewarded for supporting the idea? How might you pretest the idea? How might you translate your idea into practice? How might you ensure its effectiveness? How might continual or progressive feedback and corrective action be provided? What might be a possible plan of action? What provisions might be necessary to anticipate and overcome difficulties, obstacles, constraints, limitations, and objections? In what ways might critical factors be controlled?
	WHAT?	What resources (materials, equipment, finances, time, authority, permission, licenses, etc.) might help you to take the necessary steps and to make sure that you succeed? When might they be provided? Where might they be provided? How might they be provided? What new challenges might the idea pose? How might you anticipate and meet these new challenges? How might the idea be improved before it is used in implementation?
	WHEN?	When might the idea be completed? What timing might be used? What might be a suitable schedule or action calendar for necessary steps and events in the implementation? What special days or dates might be helpful in reinforcing your strategy for putting the idea into action?

Source: Raudseep, E., *How Creative Are You* (New York: Perigree Books, 1981), pp. 97–99.

There needs to be a balance between the time spent on implementation planning and the "doing." Peters is not advocating forgoing implementation planning; he is perplexed about the delay in decision making. If an implementation plan is properly done, the decision maker is much more confident about proceeding on the idea.

Meredith classifies implementation failure into three sets of factors: 1) technical—those factors related primarily to the mechanics of implementation, 2) process—those factors concerned with system initiation and use, and 3) inner-environmental—those factors related to the organization's internal environment.

According to Isaksen and Treffinger, the action phase includes the following tasks:[16]

- Putting the plan into action

- Achieving the solution(s)

- Putting it all together so it can actually be accomplished

- Planning to achieve the actual final product

- After action is taken, comparing actions with planned outcomes

- Detecting potential and actual flaws in the plan and making appropriate improvements

- Reviewing actions to determine where or how to proceed

- Knowing how to determine if the plan is successful

Evans stresses the importance of identifying specific sources of difficulty in implementation; demonstrating the use of implementation checklists, key word lists, and implementation stimulators to recognize and overcome possible blocks to implementation; and specifying a plan for facilitating implementation and acceptance.[17]

Improving the Plan

After developing an implementation plan, it is important to check its validity. It takes little additional time and significantly increases the probability of success. Sidney Parnes has developed a 24-point checklist to determine whether the plan can be improved.[18] Parnes asks, "In what ways might I improve the plan?" Table 10–3 provides his responses.

Have you ever had a supervisor dump an implementation task in your lap, saying something like, "I had a good idea yesterday. How about putting it into operation for me?" Such an approach is not nearly

Table 10–3

Can the Plan Be Improved?
A Checklist

- To make it more effective?
- To increase its potential payoff?
- To make it more practical, workable?
- To make it better serve my objective?
- To make it more pleasing to me and others?
- To make it more acceptable to me and others?
- To reap more benefits from it?
- To make it less costly?
- To make it more morally or legally acceptable?
- To get more rewards and recognition from it?
- To require fewer resources?
- To enrich its by-products?
- To increase its appeal?
- To gain more encouragement from others?
- To mitigate problems it might cause?
- To salvage more if it should fail?
- To make it easier to implement?
- To make it easier to follow up?
- To lessen risks or results of failure?
- To give me more confidence in its working?
- To make it more timely?
- To add fringe benefits?
- To make it easier to test?
- To enable taking first steps more easily?

Source: Parnes, S. J., *Visionizing* (East Aurora, New York: D.O.K. Publishers, 1988), pp. 91–92.

as motivating as the supervisor saying, "We've got this challenge facing us and I'm not sure how we can capitalize on it. I'd appreciate your working with me to flesh out the alternatives and then coming up with ideas on how to implement the best alternative." Isn't the second approach much more likely to arouse your interest in the project?

The inventors at the National Inventors' Meeting mentioned earlier need to spend more time in role reversal, putting themselves in the position of a person reacting to their inventions. They could come up with approaches of anticipating and responding to questions that people have about their inventions. Such an activity would result in a much higher acceptance rate of their inventions.

The old adage "The proof is in the pudding" works well for cooks. However, it is much more difficult to apply to business situations. It is too expensive to build a prototype to test every idea. Careful evaluation of the idea, careful thought in obtaining acceptance of the idea, and careful attention to the details of putting the idea to use—all reduce the risk of failure. These tasks may not be as challenging as originating the idea, but they require a lot of ingenuity to make sure the idea works.

I like the Far Side cartoon that shows two cavemen standing next to a mastodon that they have, surprisingly, managed to kill with one arrow. The huge animal is lying on its back with its legs in the air and has the small arrow sticking out of its side. One caveman turns to the one with the bow and says, "Maybe we should write that spot down!" Action planning should include the careful recording of problems that arise in implementation, to facilitate implementation planning for the next idea.

Techniques for Facilitating CPS Phase Five

Just as in the case of each of the other phases of the CPS process, there are techniques useful for facilitating Phase Five. Several creativity techniques are useful in ensuring a successful implementation plan. One was illustrated above, role reversal. Another, the interrogatories technique (5Ws/H) was illustrated twice in this chapter: Weston's checklist for enlisting the involvement of other persons in acceptance planning and the Isaksen and Treffinger sources of assistance and resistance. They suggest brainstorming the factors to be placed in the matrix, then a second session to identify specific steps to take related to the assistance/resistance factors. The 5Ws/H technique is useful in identifying both anticipated implementation problems and the approaches that might be taken to counteract them.

The bug list technique is useful in identifying the factors that "bug" or bother people about accepting the new solution or opportunity. Nominal group, brainwriting, or brainstorming can then be used to come up with approaches to minimize the "bugging" effect of the change. Two other techniques will be illustrated: problem reversal and disjointed incrementalism.

Problem Reversal for Implementation Planning

An approach that has proven effective in testing the validity of an implementation plan is to reverse the problem. After approaching the planning activity from the normal way, "What can we do to get the group committed to this approach?" the group reverses the problem statement: "How could people sabotage our idea?" My experience is that the reversal session always identifies additional alternatives and often ones quite different from those using the non-reversed problem statement.

Combining Techniques

There may have been an implication in the earlier sections of the book that an individual or group should select a single creativity technique for the particular problem at hand. More often, several creativity techniques are used. It is useful to approach the problem/opportunity from several angles, that is, through use of several techniques. It is also useful to combine techniques. Let's review an example of combining the techniques of progressive abstraction and the 5Ws/H. In Chapter 2, I described the use of a creativity technique to attack the problem of software developer reluctance to use CASEtools. This problem has been classified as an example of the proverb of the cobbler's children being the last to be shod. It is enigmatic that software developers, who are constantly trying to get others to use their products to a higher degree, are reluctant to use the computer to a greater extent in their own activities. The earlier exercise illustrated the analogy/metaphor technique in trying to determine the cause of the hesitancy to use CASEtools. The second step derived ways to motivate software developers to use CASEtools. I have used the 5Ws/H on the same problem, also with excellent results. I then combined the use of the progressive abstraction technique to improve the solution, as shown in Figure 10–3.

By abstracting the problem two levels, we significantly increase the opportunity for problem solving. In other words, we expand our solution set substantially. We then can review a body of literature that has been developed on the subject of general resistance to change. Although software developers have some characteristics unique to persons who choose that career field, they also have characteristics in common with the general population. We could examine the literature on people's reluctance to change and approaches to overcoming that reluctance, then apply some of those findings to our problem. By adding that body of material to our solution set, we undoubtedly increase the probability of solving the problem.

The same approach would help in developing an implementation plan. We could concentrate on the reasons people might be reluctant

Figure 10–3   Abstracting a Problem to Higher Levels to Increase Solution Space

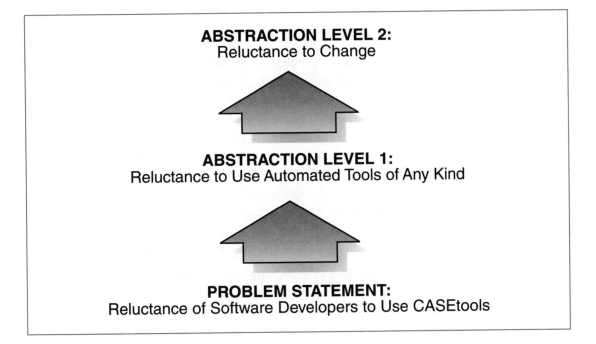

ABSTRACTION LEVEL 2:
Reluctance to Change

ABSTRACTION LEVEL 1:
Reluctance to Use Automated Tools of Any Kind

PROBLEM STATEMENT:
Reluctance of Software Developers to Use CASEtools

to use the particular idea we've generated. However, by also considering the causes for people's hesitancy to adopt new solutions in general, we gain further perspective on the problem.

Using Disjointed Incrementalism

Originated by Braybook and Lindblom, the disjointed incrementalism technique is useful for problem types involving complex decisions and vaguely defined, changing objectives.[19] It produces group synergism. The disjointed aspect of the technique refers to the way in which many policy problems are analyzed at different times in different locations, without any apparent coordinating efforts and without the benefit of relevant past experience. Incrementalism refers to the prescriptions used to compare differences or increments in the consequences of various alternatives with one another and with a present (state) situation. Thus, decisions are made by evaluating the trade-offs possible between an increment of one value and an increment of another value. The technique has the ability of reducing information processing demands made upon a problem solver. It allows a systematic way to restrict the number of alternatives and consequences requiring consideration. The technique can decrease the complexity and uncertainty of a decision environment.

Problem: Improving the selection process

Continuing with our problem of a smaller pool from which to select entry-level employees, selection of personnel who will be satisfactory performers becomes even more important. Bad hiring decisions are very costly, not only the cost to replace the individual, but the costs of poor performance. In addition to the lack of output, poor performers take more managerial time in motivating and counseling. Also, their ineffectiveness must be documented to justify firing. Poor performers also drag down good performers, by their attitude and by not meeting commitments in the essential interactions required for a team. It has been estimated that the cost of hiring, training, and firing is more than double the annual salary of the individual being replaced.

One approach to improving the selection process would be to reduce some of the speculative and intuitive aspects of judging the candidate's qualifications. For example, a study by Wayne Cascio when he was at the University of Pennsylvania showed that the typical interviewer made up his or her mind on whether the candidate was acceptable or not in the first eight minutes of the interview. It is a rare person who can properly assess all the relevant facts and judge the appropriateness for hiring in such a short amount of time. Granted that intuition should play a role in the selection process; however, more complete information should be obtained for a more balanced basis for decision.

Disjointed incrementalism improves the quantitative analysis in such decisions. It begins with identifying the policies.

Step 1.   Delineating the policies regarding selection

Although there are stated policies, such as prohibitions against racial, religious, and political discrimination, unstated policies also need to be clarified. An example is the ability of the candidate to fit into the company and the work group environment. While there are clear-cut policies on things like dress code, where the intent is to have employees meet prevailing norms when they deal with customers, there are also unpublished policies related to attitude about the company—being a "good citizen," having a spirit of cooperation, not always thinking of yourself first. The goal is to clarify the policies so all persons involved in the selection process are consistent in their application of policy.

Step 2.   Breaking the decision to hire into increments for more effective analysis

The position requirements are definitive. To determine the candidates' qualifications to meet those requirements, the following tasks are necessary:

- Evaluating knowledge qualifications
- Assessing desire to work (motivation)
- Assessing probability of longevity (turnover)
- Evaluating technical knowledge
- Evaluating technical ability
- Evaluating communication ability
- Evaluating behavioral skills
- Assessing intelligence (logical ability)
- Assessing creativity
- Assessing ability to "fit in" to the unit and the organization

Step 3.   Evaluating hiring policies

We will take just one of the policies to demonstrate the technique: assessing the ability to "fit in." Interviewers who make up their minds in the first eight minutes of the interview are very confident of their ability to identify "fitting-in" kinds of behavior. Even if interviewers force themselves to continue to gather information about the candidate and to wait until the end of the interview to make a decision, often too much emphasis is placed on the candidate's conformity. Some very creative persons do not "make the cut" because they are so different; they do not exhibit "fitting-in" behavior. Yet, their very creativity is the result of unconventional approaches to problem solving. Their typical interview behaviors are listed below, under the heading of:

"Not-Fitting-In" Behavior:

1. The person's thought process is tangential; tends to go off on tangents and not stick tightly to the point.

2. The individual is deep in the thought process and disregards the body language necessary for good communication.

3. The person appears too interested in the issue for "issue's sake" and not willing to quickly converge on a reasonable answer.

If members of the candidate's work group are open-minded, they will see that a divergent thinker can be a stimulus for new ways to think about problems and opportunities.

Step 4. After the policies have been delineated and evaluated, the other factors in the decision to hire are evaluated and weighted. The result is a significant improvement in the ability to select people who will make the desired level of contribution to the organization.

The society which scorns excellence in plumbing because it is a humble activity and tolerates shoddiness in philosophy because it is an exalted activity will have neither good plumbing nor good philosophy. Neither its pipes nor its theories will hold water.

John W. Gardner

Conclusion

Abraham Maslow has a comment which pinpoints the essence of this chapter:

It is also important for each of us...as students of creativeness with a tendency to deify the one side of the creative process—the enthusiastic, the great insight, the illumination, the good idea, the moment in the middle of the night when we get the great inspiration—and of underplaying the two years of hard and sweaty labor that then is necessary to make anything useful out of the bright idea.[20]

This chapter concentrated on the factors necessary to make something useful out of the bright idea. It is both coincidental and ironic that today, during the writing of the conclusion to this chapter, I found a pertinent quotation in the fortune cookie after my lunch in a Chinese restaurant. It read: "Big changes are ahead for you." My first inclination was "I don't need any big changes in my life—I've got too much on my agenda as it is!" The experience reinforced the problem dealt with in this chapter, the causes behind people's resistance to change. Much of their reluctance to change is well founded; they recognize the work involved and the inevitable debugging time required to implement new ideas. For an idea to justify this kind of effort and commitment, it must be clearly beneficial. An acceptance plan provides the rationale for adopting the idea and the implementation plan provides the most efficient way of putting the idea into operation.

Acceptance of our ideas also requires effective presentations. We should include visual aids so that all will be able to see clearly and follow what we are trying to say. The use of graphs and other charts is beneficial. For the formal presentation, speaker aids that summarize our central theme are very useful in establishing points on which the group can focus its attention. We should make good use of the data, trends, or other stimuli that initially led us to investigate the situation.

Throughout this book I have quoted Arthur VanGundy's fine book, *Techniques of Structured Problem Solving*. He has written several books on creativity. One of his not-so-well-known books is *Stalking the Wild Solution*. In the concluding paragraph, VanGundy reminds us, "Even after you have implemented a solution, you will need to monitor its progress in resolving your original problem. You also should use the implementation process to provide yourself with feedback about how well you performed during Acceptance-Finding. In other words, you should make a conscious effort to learn from your experience. Such learning is a continuous process and will not end upon completion of a formal problem-solving model."[21]

Basadur has developed a list of factors to help build an action plan for implementation:[22]

1. Use the closure principle: get something started, no matter how trivial.
2. Break big tasks down into smaller pieces.
3. Make your action plan simple and specific enough for a child to understand.
4. Make your action plan "challenging but realistic."
5. Use the "Spinach First" principle: do the part you hate the most first to get it out of the way.
6. Write down the worst that can happen (if you fear the unknown); jot down ideas to cope if it does happen.

7. Share your plan with others (if you fear failure). Develop a strategy to minimize your discomfort if the worst does happen and a way to turn failure to your advantage.

8. Ask yourself, "If I wait, how much better will a later solution be?" (if you fear your solution isn't "perfect").

"We should avoid any tendency to attempt rashly to sell our idea," warns Eugene Von Fange, "before we have a definite plan and program worked out to support it. For management very generally (and very properly) will refuse to approve any proposed undertaking that is not well-planned and thought through with regard to the practical details of its execution. Yet, one still finds individuals proposing a project or an idea without having worked out the means of accomplishment, or weighing the actual advantages against the difficulties and costs. This is the difference between a 'well-considered' and a 'half-baked' scheme."[23]

One problem with the CPS model is its implication that the process ends with implementation. It should be shown as circular rather than sequential, indicating continual refinement of the idea. The reason the Japanese are outdistancing the rest of the world in innovation is their overriding stress on continuous improvement, *kaizen*. We need to have a similar mind-set.

When it comes to opening completely new fields, our scientists are still catching up.... However, when it comes to turning new ideas into reality, we have been very successful and very creative.

Akio Morita
President, Sony

Ideas are useless unless used. The proof of their value is in their implementation. Until then, they are in limbo .... Many of the people with the ideas have the peculiar notion that their jobs are finished when they suggest them; that it is up to somebody else to work out the dirty details and them implement the proposals. Since business is a get-things-done institution, creativity without action-oriented follow-through is a barren form of behavior.

Theodore Leavitt

Summary

When you first picked up this book, to which chapter did you turn? I'm sure your starting selection was not Chapter 10, this chapter. Some consider implementation planning a necessary evil. It certainly is necessary if you want to make sure your idea is used. The technique of carefully delineating assisters/resistors is a good way to approach acceptance planning. The plan also must provide for approaches to win support for the idea. The inquiry/advocacy approach is a sound one to facilitate idea acceptance.

Action planning is the other part of the dual tasks essential for effective implementation of ideas. There are excellent checklists to facilitate the task of action planning.

Creativity techniques are useful in this CPS step, as they are in the other four steps. Creative ways are needed to gain acceptance for your ideas and to find the most cost-effective method of implementation.

> Ideas are cheap and abundant; what is of value is the effective placement of those ideas into situations that develop into action.
>
> *Peter Drucker*

Exercises

1. Phase Five of the CPS process includes two major components. Describe each component.

2. Why do people resist change?

3. What can be done to lower people's resistance to change?

4. Explain Senge's concept of balancing inquiry and advocacy.

5. What is the Isaksen/Treffinger recommendation for smoothing the way to acceptance of an idea?

6. What are the factors listed by K.T. Connor for selling an idea?

7. What did Jack Gibbs find when he audiotaped conversations of people trying to sell an idea?

8. The action planning component of Phase Five should include what tasks, according to Isaksen and Treffinger?

9. Summarize the approach of disjointed incrementalism.

10. What combination of techniques is useful for Phase Five of the CPS process as illustrated in Figure 10–3?

Raincoat with a Drain

Patent No. 273,115 (1883)

John Maguire of Toronto, Canada

The object of the invention is to provide a water-proof coat which can be worn in rainy weather without the wearer's legs being made wet from water dripping off the skirt of the coat. It consists of a watertrough or channel to receive the water flowing on the surface of the coat, suitable provision being made to carry off the water away from the legs of the wearer of the garment.

Figure 1 is a view of my improved water-proof coat as it will appear when in use. Figure 2 is an enlarged detail, showing the form of the trough made in the bottom edge of the skirt. Figure 3 is an enlarged sectional detail, showing the arrangement of the spout for carrying off the water from the trough.

Fig. 1.

Fig. 2.   *Fig. 3.*

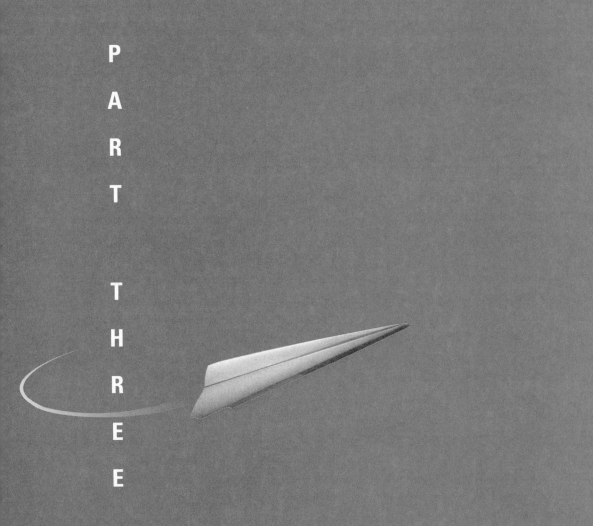

Improving the Climate for Creativity
and Enhancing Personal Attributes

Objectives of Part Three

Even if we work at home, there are factors that either support or detract from our creativity. Perhaps the most important one is the potential for distraction. Children can be a distraction. There are other distractions at home, such as seeing things around you that need done (like mowing the lawn). One of my friends admits that, when he works at home, he always goes out and gets the mail as soon as he hears the delivery truck. He says he can't seem to avoid this distraction, even though he knows it will interfere with the continuity of his planned activity that morning. He also says that he can't help going through the mail immediately instead of laying it aside until he completes his self-scheduled work. If he has a very difficult task, he says he will even start to pay some of the bills that arrive in the mail, fooling himself that he is doing something that must be done instead of directing himself toward solving the problem.

There are also advantages to home work; you can put the phone on record and lock your door, but you can't lock your door at work. Chapter 11 reviews the environment necessary to support creativity. I'll come back to that shortly.

Chapter 12 discusses the attributes of creative persons. One of the most controversial is the relationship of creativity to intelligence. The chapter gives examples of studies on this subject and concludes that the results are contradictory.

Chapter 12 identifies some negative traits characteristic of creative persons, such as stubbornness. The purpose is not to emulate these traits, but also not to allow them to distract us from working effectively with these persons. And those of us who possess these traits need to recognize how they can hinder effective teamwork. We might have difficulty eliminating them, but we can control them when it will result in improved relationships with our colleagues.

There is also a set of positive traits characteristic of creative persons. Some of these abilities, such as flexibility and resisting premature closure, can be acquired. Identifying these abilities helps us know which things are most important in helping us become more creative. Chapter 12 discusses attributes that facilitate creativity and how we can acquire many of them.

Chapter 13 explains how to strengthen your intuitive ability. Business is finally becoming aware that intuition is not a dirty word but a valuable asset in problem solving and decision making. Previously there has been too much emphasis on the analytical approach as the sole method for solution generating. A good balance of the two abilities, a holistic approach, is much more effective. After defining intuition, there is a discussion of the four levels of intuitive awareness: physical, emotional, mental and spiritual. Then, the outlook necessary to improve intuitiveness is described. Specific techniques to aid in improving one's intuitive ability are reviewed: the wise counsel, peaceful setting, and six hats techniques. Finally, there is an explanation of how to integrate reason and intuition.

When our boss has influence over some of the other factors, we can approach him or her to discuss how the climate for creativity can be enhanced. One of the ways to get management's attention is to remind them of the importance of creativity. We are not confined to some ephemeral description; we can illustrate the cost-effectiveness of creativity. For that reason, I included material on cost-effectiveness in Chapter 1. For the same reason, I include some cost-effectiveness material in Chapter 11. I describe the spectacular results possible from management's support of creativity, using the example of a division of IBM where I've served as a consultant. As a result of its creativity, costs have been reduced significantly. It is much more competitive and is growing by leaps and bounds. In Chapter 1, I described the large return on investment characteristic of creativity improvement programs. In those where I've had direct knowledge, the return is a factor of two to six (from 200 percent to 600 percent).

Creativity improvement programs are highly cost-effective. When managers become aware of the potential for cost reduction or profit improvement of creativity, they have the motivation to work diligently to improve the environment for creativity. The following figure illustrates the synergy that results from people sharing ideas in a supportive climate. The posi-

tive climate enables not just an expansion of individual ideas, but stimulates building on each other's ideas to produce a quantum leap result.

Source: Reprinted with permission of Jack Desrocher.

As stated in the Introduction, the majority of this book concentrates on process, the approach to helping people resurface their innate creativity. Although introduced in Part One, the material on person and press is fleshed out in Part Three. The fourth "P," product, is covered where appropriate throughout the book, although given special attention in Chapter 9. If people are provided the tools to resurface their native creativity and are provided with a supportive climate (press), then a creative product can be expected.

There is nothing more difficult to take in hand, more perilous to conduct, or more uncertain in its success, than to take the lead in the introduction of a new order of things, because the innovator has for enemies all those who have done well under the old conditions, and lukewarm defenders in those who may do well under the new.
Machiavelli, (1446–1507) *The Prince*

Improving the Environment for Creativity

Machiavelli's quote reveals that, as early as the Middle Ages, it was apparent that organizational change is difficult to accomplish. Yet, to improve the climate for creativity, most organizations must make changes. Chapter 1 explained the importance of the climate for creativity in an organization, labeled "Press" in the four-Ps model of creativity.

Although persons can be made aware of their innate creative ability and can learn techniques to more easily use that ability, optimal results do not occur unless their company provides a positive climate for creativity. Managers can examine their own practices to ensure that they nurture creativity in subordinates. Teams can evaluate their interaction to determine how to better support creativity among team members. However, even if managers are not providing a creative climate, there are things individuals can do to create a better climate. In this chapter we will review the factors essential for a creative climate. It is management's responsibility to make sure these factors are in place. If management is not meeting that need, a team can nevertheless improve its creative output but not to the level that occurs with good management support.

The team also has responsibility for providing an environment that nurtures creativity. If the team is not supportive of creativity, an individual can nevertheless improve his/her creative output, but not to the level that occurs with proper team support. Both of those situations will be reviewed: the appropriate overall organizational climate for creativity and the appropriate team climate for creativity. We will also discuss how individuals can improve their personal creativity within a less than desirable environment.

The Decline of U.S. Creative Output

Although we will concentrate on an organization's creative climate, it is helpful to understand the factors that have contributed to the decline of corporate creativity in the United States. The facts of that decline are readily available. The number of patents granted by the U.S. government is a traditional test. General Electric held the top spot for 25 years until 1987, when it was supplanted by three Japanese firms: Canon, Hitachi, and Toshiba.[1] In that year, 47 percent of all U.S. patents were issued to foreigners. The Japanese led, with more than 17,000 patents—19 percent of all U.S. patents and a 25 percent increase over the previous year. West Germany acquired over 8,000 U.S. patents and France received 2,990.

In 1991, foreigners also obtained 47 percent of U.S. patents. The Japanese share increased to 22 percent, and four of the top five companies in terms of new patents issued were Japanese-owned. However, a new measure has been developed that indicates that the United States is worse off than before. A company called CHI Research Inc. has developed more sophisticated measures, based on citations of patents as building blocks in new patents. Their "current impact index" measures how often a company's patents are cited relative to those of all other companies. For example, the top company, Toshiba, had a rating of 1.45. This means that its patents are cited 45 percent more than the average. CHI then multiplies the index by the number of patents to get "technological strength." The top five companies and their technological strength ratings were Toshiba (1677), Hitachi (1633), Canon (1201), Mitsubishi (1190), and Eastman Kodak (1186). General Electric was in 9th place with a rating of 1069.[2]

Sheridan Tatsuno, an American of Japanese heritage, has a unique vantage point from which to view the comparison of creative output of the United States versus Japan. In his book *Created in Japan*, Tatsuno explains how the United States "squandered" its technological lead. According to Tatsuno, we became so engrossed with "financial wizardry, short-term profits, fat military contracts, lucrative mergers and acquisitions, and paper entrepreneurialism that we consistently underinvested in long-term education, basic research, and training."[3] As our economy became heavily militarized and inflated, Tatsuno says, product quality plummeted, services deteriorated, and our educational standards "hit rock bottom." Most important, he says, we failed to notice "our Pacific ally venturing out on its own." We preferred to believe the "feel-good" newspaper and magazine articles and management books telling us that Japanese companies are only good at mass production and that the United States was still ahead in basic research and product innovation. We fell asleep at the wheel, according to Tatsuno: "Mesmerized by our own entrepreneurialism and creativity, we couldn't see the competition at our doorstep."[4]

In the first half of the 1980s, Japanese corporate research staffs increased by 42 percent. In 1985 Japanese R&D spending reached 2.77 percent of the gross national product (GNP), exceeding that of the

United States. The Japanese government's goal was to reach 3 percent by the early 1990s and they achieved that goal.[5]

This heavy R&D investment has already paid off handsomely in a flurry of innovative new products. Hitachi launched the "Quiet Lady," a fully automatic washing machine for apartment dwellers who are concerned about making too much noise. Yamaha's digital WX7 looks like a clarinet but plays like a saxophone and can be made to sound like a trumpet, saxophone, piccolo, guitar, or violin. Cosmetic maker Kao Corporation used biotechnology to create "Attack," a laundry detergent four times as powerful as the amount of conventional detergents; Kao racked up sales of $77 million in the first six months of sales to capture 30 percent of the Japanese market. Matsushita Electric and Funai Electric introduced an automatic bread baker that was so popular that they immediately sold out; a $300 million market was created overnight. Sanyo Electric has developed the world's first see-through batteries—translucent amorphous solar cells for use as windows in greenhouses and skylights to absorb natural light and generate electrical power. Perhaps most novel of all is the "Toto Queen," an automated toilet with chips that direct the seat to preheat and to trigger a spray of bottom-washing water during flushing, followed by a blast of hot air and a puff of perfumed mist! It also performs diagnostic processes. It not only generates information on blood pressure, pulse, temperature, urine, and weight, but also processes, stores, and transmits it. It can be viewed on a liquid crystal display, which can be located on the unit or on a nearby wall or shelf. The toilet stores up to 130 days' worth of readings, prints them out, transfers them to a personal computer, or transmits them via modem to a medical service for further analysis. The Japanese are at work on a smart toilet that will be able to differentiate one user's "seatprint" from another's. This growth in paperless toilets is particularly astounding when you consider that as recently as January 1990, only 40 percent of homes in Japan had public plumbing, and bed pans and outhouses are still common.[6]

Tatsuno believes that we are witnessing a historic transformation. "Japan is turning away from the West and reexamining its own cultural roots. It no longer seeks to copy the West, but to develop its own forms of creativity. The Heisei period may well become Japan's 'second Renaissance,' recalling the Heian period (710–794 A.D.) when Japan emerged from the shadows of Chinese culture and created its own culture."[7]

What does this gloomy picture mean to individual companies and the potential of providing a creative climate? Certainly, if our companies allocate fewer dollars to R&D, the United States will continue to lose in the competition to develop new products. Yet, a company can improve its climate for creativity with relatively much less expenditure than R&D allocations. The main factor is not to increase budgets, but to increase management's valuation of creativity. A change in attitude can produce a huge differential. Small dollar investments can be leveraged significantly.

The remainder of the chapter will be devoted to approaches that managers use to foster creativity and approaches used to squelch creativity. By becoming more cognizant of squelching versus supportive actions, management can improve the creative climate. It is hoped that management will also be motivated to do so.

Proving the Cost - Effectiveness of Creativity Programs to Management

Considerable research has been undertaken on the ways that work environments influence creativity.[8] Witt and Beorkrem believe that "an organization's climate for creative productivity is the "organization's set of norms that communicate how the organization values and promotes creativity and innovation."[9]

Perhaps one reason management does not place sufficient priority on climate improvement is the lack of confidence about the cost-effectiveness of creativity. Either they are ignoring the potential creativity of their people, thinking it implausible, or have assumed that they hire creative people. There is justification for both views. Evidence supporting the first view indicates the management is starting to think like the accounting profession, where creativity is considered undesirable. For those who hold this view, "creative accounting" is something to avoid. In one of my presentations to a group of managers on creativity and innovation, one said with great emotion, "We don't want our people to be creative; they can't get work done on time and within budget as it is."

There were agreeing nods from many of his peers in the audience. There is a common view that creativity is expensive: something very desirable but not affordable in this era of declining profits and tightened budgets.

When managers respond this way, I provide some of the hard evidence on the cost-effectiveness of creative activity. I mentioned some of those data in Chapter 1, where I described the return on investment in creativity of a factor of two at minimum to as much as a factor of six. That's 200 percent to 600 percent R.O.I! In the companies where we've implemented creativity improvement programs, we've carefully kept track of the improvements. After four to five months we've performed a cost-effectiveness analysis to determine the level of improvement. Bottom-line oriented managers, like the one quoted above, now have the facts to appreciate the value of creativity improvement programs.

Most organizations would not hesitate to adopt a new methodology or technology if they could be assured of a factor of .3 or 30 percent return on investment. Yet, some managers hesitate to adopt creativity improvement programs because the benefits appear soft. The R.O.I. figures above demonstrate that creativity improvement produces concrete results. To illustrate, I'll provide a brief description of three of the improvements in an IS organization. In each case, I identify the creativity technique used to facilitate the process.

Manufacturing Database Expansion

The manufacturing database was constantly expanding. In order to maintain good response time for database accesses, the database was periodically reorganized. The normal process was to unload the database, make the changes, and then reload the database. This process took around 60 hours to complete. The IS team applied its collective creativity (using the wishful thinking technique) to discover a new way to modify the database size without having to unload/reload the database, reducing the database expansion task to four hours (resulting in a 46-hour time saving). The lotus blossom and 5Ws/H techniques also could have been used on this problem.

Financial Closing Cycle

The monthly financial closing cycle took 24 hours to run the program; moreover, this cycle delayed the output of other important jobs. The financial IS team needed to step back from the way that they were using year-to-date overhead to come up with a new solution approach. They used the interrogatories (5Ws/H) technique to comprehensively examine alternatives. They determined that, since this was a Boolean logic-oriented problem, they could convert two major COBOL programs to

DCL (digital command language) and SQL (structured query language) and reduce the run time from 24 hours to 45 minutes. The lotus blossom technique would have been equally useful for this type of problem.

Bookings Forecast Report

Because the end-of-month booking forecast report normally required six hours of elapsed time to run, the information was not available at the beginning of the new month. To find a better solution, the IS team used the interrogatories technique. One of the resulting alternatives was the use of INGRES (a relational database) instead of RMS (records management services) files. The elapsed run time was reduced from six hours to six minutes, and the CPU time was reduced from 15 minutes to seven seconds, enabling a timely forecast projection. An alternatively appropriate technique would have been nominal group technique.

Although the three examples provided above identified a specific creativity technique used to quick-start the creative process, the process was significantly enhanced by the organization's positive climate for creativity. Before we analyze the factors that provide such a climate, let's review the ways in which managers stifle creativity.

How Managers Stifle Creativity

A manager can create an environment that fosters and encourages creativity among employees. Often, however, just the opposite occurs. Here are some examples of "stifling" comments made by managers in response to subordinates' ideas.

- We've tried that before.

- Our department is not ready for this approach.

- We could never sell it to upper management.

- Your backlog of assignments is too large for me to allow you time to "flesh-out" that idea.

- There's too much risk associated with implementing such an approach.

- I can't argue with that idea—let's look at it again when the pressure has slacked off.

Figure 11–1

Managers Can Stifle
Creativity and Innovation

- That may work; why don't you write me a report justifying the approach?

In addition to stifling comments, some managers use stifling actions to discourage creativity. In most cases, it is not an overt attempt to discourage employees' creativity, but a passive or negligent response to their creative ideas. Figure 11–1 pictures a manager who has the sign "Innovation Stops Here" on his desk. No manager I know would have such an overt statement about his or her hesitancy to adopt new ideas, but many managers implicitly convey this message to their subordinates.

Willingness to Take Risks

As a consultant, I've seen a number of companies—both large and small—where management is very reluctant to take risks. Management in some of these companies is now actively encouraging employees to be more creative, yet they have not changed their own conservatism toward risk. For example, the issue of risk aversion arose in 1993 during a luncheon meeting at a division of a Fortune 500 firm. I had been invited to address a technical vitality session later in the day, on approaches to improve personal and team creativity. The luncheon participants were explaining management's interest in stimulating creativity among employees. Top management had used a number of creative ways to encourage creativity.

I asked about the progress of the program. There was an embarrassing silence until one person responded: "First-line managers haven't changed their attitude about risk; in my group, we got excited about the opportunity to be more creative, began to crank out lots of suggestions, and they got stifled by our manager." Another person commented: "Our manager was supportive but his manager wasn't willing to fund our ideas."

The general conclusion of the group, which had representatives from many organizations within the division, was that top management had done an excellent job convincing the rank-and-file that it wanted lots of new ideas, but that first-line and middle management had not been convinced. The group agreed that two things were probable causes of the lack of success of the creativity program, but was not sure which was the principal cause. Some of the group felt that division management was just passing down the corporate philosophy on encouraging creativity and was not itself willing to take some risks in trying to implement subordinates' ideas. Others felt that top management believed in the value of fostering creativity but had not convinced lower levels of management that they would not be penalized for ideas that did not work out.

Why are middle managers so resistant to change? Because, in the past, a heavy penalty was exacted for mistakes. Peter Senge urges managers to rethink their views on failure. Failure, he says, is simply a shortfall, evidence of the gap between vision and current reality. Senge goes on to say that failure is an opportunity for learning about inaccurate pictures of current reality.[10]

Edward Land, the inventor of instant photography, then founder and president of Polaroid, had a plaque on his wall. "A mistake is an event, the full benefit of which has not yet been turned to your advantage."[11]

Ore-Ida is a company that goes out of its way to create an environment in which experimentation is acceptable. "People were getting the idea as we grew that if they failed, they would be criticized," according to Ralf Glover, general manager for R&D. Ore-Ida gives all idea champions a certificate, regardless of the outcome of their efforts.

With the certificate, Ore-Ida says in effect: "We value your courage and what we have all learned."[12]

Tom Peters always provides earthy, highly pragmatic suggestions to management. In the matter of risk—and of recognition—he suggests that managers create a "small-win environment." Peters urges managers to "induce lots of people to step out, to take a 'minor' risk (to you, not to them), to try something, anything, new. Then find and recognize their 'little' (to you, not to them) success. The peerless grocer Stan Leonard nudges the process along with a 40-page monthly newsletter, recognizing scores of successes at a time. Others are trying similar tricks. Talk it up. Recognize it. Laugh about the little failures and cheer the little successes. Put the 'little' story in the newsletter. Put it on the bulletin board. Put it in the video. Enshrine the winners. Enshrine those who step out. Get focused on—obsessed with—that 'small' win. You'll soon find that small has never been so big."[13]

The esoterics of risk taking can be debated at length. The heart of the matter, however, is the following: "What happens to employees when their ideas are unsuccessful?" I've observed employees who felt they had to change companies because of a mistake resulting from their willingness to try different approaches. They got a lot of negative recognition that they believed they could never live down. They believed that this one mistake would prevent them from career progression in the company. In these companies, employees are heavily penalized for mistakes. Mistakes get a lot more attention than successes!

In other words, if the idea fails, don't hesitate to admit mistakes and move on to other ideas. Herbert Simon reminds us that "the opportunity to be creative can seldom be fully separated from the opportunity to fail."

When management only gives lip service to a creativity improvement program and does not objectively evaluate each idea of subordinates, the program will die on the vine. Employees are quickly turned off from pursuing creativity if very few of their ideas pass the screening test because of management's unwillingness to try new approaches. If management is trying to encourage employees to be more creative in their daily tasks, it must expect that some results will be unsatisfactory. The goal is not risk avoidance but risk assessment.

So far, I've been discussing management's risk-aversion tendencies. It is inappropriate to lay all the blame at management's doorstep,

Figure 11–2   In Japanese, the Two Characters That Represent Creativity Individually Translate to *Dangerous Opportunity*

**Creativity =
Dangerous Opportunity**

however. With the present-day emphasis upon teams, individuals need to feel the support of team members in trying new things. If people believe that team members will chastise them over mistakes instead of encouraging risk taking, they will hesitate to be innovative.

Hesitancy to take risks may be the largest inhibitor to creativity. Figure 11–2 shows the two characters in the Japanese language that represent the concept of creativity individually translate into the words *dangerous opportunity*. The Japanese word for *creativity* clearly acknowledges the element of risk in most improvements. But it also emphasizes that these improvements clearly represent an opportunity. Proper management action is to assess the risks against potential return of the improvement; too many managers are willing only to take minimal risks, thereby forgoing some important opportunities.

When management continues stifling kinds of behavior, employees may stop trying to be creative on the job and apply their natural creativity to after-work hours. We all possess the need to be creative. If our work environment discourages it, we'll find another outlet.

Unfortunately, in such a situation, the company is turning away some excellent resources to maintain competitiveness.

I use several good cartoons on risk taking in my creativity workshop. One is a Gary Larson cartoon that shows the caveman who invented the wheel getting ready for the first test run. The wheel is about eight feet in diameter, carved out of a huge stone, requiring three helpers to push to get it started down a hill. There's a problem in the test design, however. The inventor is sitting on the top of the wheel and has tied himself securely in position for the test run!

I use this cartoon to remind the audience that not all ideas work out. I follow it up with the cartoon of two scientists in a laboratory. One holds up a test tube and asks his colleague, "What's the opposite of Eureka?"

How do managers become less risk-averse? By careful risk assessment. George Geis provides important guidance on this topic: "Successful risk-takers are not wildly passionate about risk per se. Before venturing out on a course of action, they try to seek first to understand and contain risks. If at all possible they try to turn leaps of faith into plays of percentage. Doing so makes them more confident as they move forward."

It does not take a great deal of time to make such assessments. We discussed techniques for determining the probability of various alternatives in Chapter 9. When managers work with subordinates to conduct risk assessment, they do two things: they train employees to become competent in risk assessment so that they understand this essential step in idea evaluation, and then demonstrate to employees that they are willing to consider and act on creative proposals.

Worry is like a rocking chair; it gives you something to do but it doesn't get you anywhere.

Evan Esar

Behold the turtle. He makes progress only when he sticks his neck out.

James B. Conant

Figure 11–3   Companies Need to Regularly Reinforce Their Belief in the Importance of Creativity for Their Employees

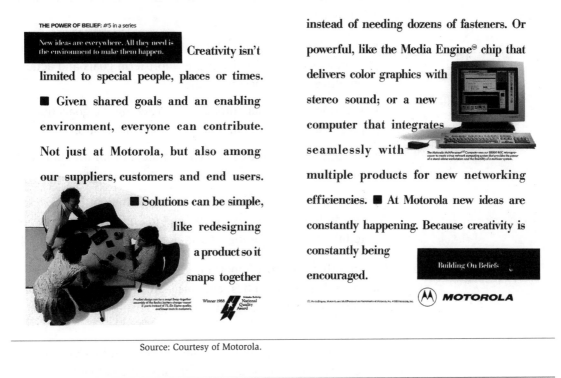

Source: Courtesy of Motorola.

How Managers Can Create a Positive Environment

Some companies work diligently at providing a nurturing climate for creativity. One example is Motorola. Figure 11–3 is an advertisement that shows Motorola's strong emphasis on ensuring a positive climate for creativity.

Abbey and Dickson and Lind and Mumford have found that innovative research-and-design systems are characterized by recognition and reward of superior performance.[14] This is particularly true of the initial exploratory stages of creative endeavors in which the individual's need for acceptance and support plays an important role in motivating further efforts. Taken as a whole, these studies suggest that a climate that facilitates creativity provides a stimulating environment for idea generation and encourages the actions required for implementing these ideas while it demonstrates acceptance and recognition of the individual's creative efforts.

Burnside identified four areas central to improving the climate for creativity, elements that "shape an environment to release the creative energies of employees":[15]

- **Goal Clarity**—includes the long-term goals of the organization; a clear, shared vision; the short-term goals and actions employees are expected to take

- **Freedom**—personal autonomy in reaching the goals that gives full play to the individual's inner motivation

- **Resources**—not only money and time, but information and the assistance and cooperation of other people

- **Encouragement**—the least prevalent stimulant found in his research. It means "to give heart," to encourage employees to take risks in forming, sharing, and trying out new ideas.

Burnside found that the most important obstacles to creativity were status quo, organizational politics, emphasis on standards other than the merit of the work, an excessively critical atmosphere, and a lack of feedback.

Another way of stating similar points is provided by Geis, who identifies the following factors as key to ensuring a creative climate:[16]

- A **secure environment** with minimal administrative or financial interference

- An **organizational culture** that makes it attractive and easy for people to discover and solve problems independently

- **Rewards** for employee performance structured to minimize the chances that intrinsic motivation will be contaminated

- **Managerial willingness to take risks** in the targeted areas for creativity and innovation

- Providing people with formal and informal **training** to enhance creativity

Table 11–1 shows the influence of management, teams, and dyads on the key factors revealed by Burnside's research as affecting the environment for creativity. Management affects all key factors. Even if management is not supportive of improving the environment, your work team can still have influence on five of the factors. Even if the

How to Improve the Creative Climate

Key Factor	Who Has Influence on Attaining Key Factors:		
	Management	Team	Dyad
Goal clarity	X	X	X
Freedom	X		
Proper resources	X		
Encouragement	X	X	X

Obstacles to Creativity

Key Factor	Who Has Influence on Negative Effects:		
	Management	Team	Dyad
Status quo	X	X	
Organizational politics	X		
Emphasis on standards other than the work merit	X		
Excessively critical atmosphere	X	X	X
Lack of feedback	X	X	X

work team is not concerned about the environment, your partner working with you in a creative dyad can help improve four of the factors. Obviously, we would like all three to provide positive support for the climate for creativity. Later in the chapter, more explanation will be provided on how individuals can work to gain an improved climate for creativity despite the lack of management and team support.

Managing Creativity

Kao suggests that creativity can be managed.[17] Yet, what does *managing* creativity mean? Kao explains that creativity "springs" from the inner recesses of human vision, the most intimate reaches of human experience. Creativity is thought by many to be "inspired," its comings and goings unpredictable and highly idiosyncratic. Management seems opposed to creativity, suggesting a valuation of collective attitudes above personal vision. The pragmatic, rational, and judgmental style frequently associated with business management seems at the outset "inhospitable" to creative efforts and threatens to dilute them.

"Why is attention to the management of creativity important?" Kao asks. "Creativity is a competitive issue, not just something nice. It is a valuable resource that must be nurtured, not wasted, given the significant costs associated with creative talent and an infrastructure supportive of creative work."[18]

From a bottom-line standpoint, creative people are an important company asset: the "process" by which a creative "product" is developed or a creative "service" rendered. Managing this human process for maximum effect is vital. Tom Peters believes that reward systems are critical both in monetary and nonmonetary terms. "Signing the painting" is an important source of reward. For example, the Macintosh design team was permitted to sign their names inside the injection molded case of the computer.[19]

Other Factors Affecting the Climate for Creativity

There are some important factors in encouraging and nurturing creativity: trust, positive stress, idea trapping, reflection time, and leadership strategies. We will review each of these factors.

Trust

Fabian identifies several "trust steps." At the lowest end of the trust continuum there is skepticism. Next there is caution. The third level evidences the beginnings of confidence. Finally, trust is realized. It seems to me that the description of levels three and four are not sufficiently different to justify separation. I've summarized Fabian's classifications as follows:[20]

1. **Skepticism**—Proposals and suggestions are met with negative response. The challenge might even come as a hostile outburst, but is more often couched in sophisticated put-downs. Mistakes are taboo. Humor is often a veiled attack, dripping in sarcasm. Good ideas are often kept to oneself for fear of ridicule or having the flaws pointed out. Freedom of the individual or group to think and act alone is curtailed. There is little elbow room for taking chances. Procedures define the range of thinking allowed.

2. **Caution**—Individuals and other work units are treated with a mixture of reactions. They and their ideas are treated cautiously—partly okay, suspiciously not okay. The flow of ideas still is distorted and incomplete; evaluation is quick and judgmental. Questioners seem to be saying, as a preface to their questions, "I want to know if your idea is safe, doesn't threaten the bounds of what I know to be true, and fits my knowledge, discipline, and experience. I want to make sure you know what you are talking about." Non-risky, more commonplace ideas may be acceptable.

3. **Confidence**—People feel good about themselves and those they are around. Because individuals and groups feel honored and safe, any emotions, thoughts, ideas, attitudes, or behaviors are treated with respect. Crazy images, bizarre analogies, spontaneous humor, or wild combinations become natural responses of trusting parties engaged in creative discovery. Expectations are set and individuals and groups accept responsibility for high-quality output in a spirit of dialogue and shared understanding. Then people are free to do their own work, free to be turned on by the challenge of the task, free to take risks and make decisions without heavy supervisory surveillance.

One of the most important teachers and researchers of the role of trust in individuals and organizations is Jack Gibb. In his *Trust: A New View of Personal and Organizational Development,* he writes:

> Trust is a releasing process. It frees my creativity, allows me to focus my energy on creating and discovering rather than on defending. It releases my courage. It **is** my courage. It opens my processes, so that I can play, feel, enjoy, get angry, experience my pain, be who I am. The full life is spontaneous, unconstrained, flowing, trusting life .... When I get into my flow, all of my processes are heightened: my energy and breathing, creativity and imagery, awareness of sights and sounds and smells, courage. I become available to me and to others.[21]

Positive Stress

Usually stress is only viewed in a negative context, something to reduce or avoid. Chris Argyris contends that a commitment to the psychological success of employees is not the same as becoming completely people-centered in the traditional sense of eliminating stress and reducing responsibility and challenge. A certain degree of stress can be correlated with creativity and productivity when the tasks available permit individuals to use their important abilities, when they believe the pressures are legitimate, and when they share in the fruits of success.[22] Studies indicate that healthy individuals seek out responsibility, develop commitments to something outside themselves, and establish personal challenges.[23]

The research of Mihaly Csikszentmihalyi reveals that our periods of struggling to overcome challenges are found to be the most enjoyable times of our lives. This result occurs when "psychic energy is invested in realistic goals and when the skills match the opportunities for action."[24]

Idea Trapping

Charles Clark, in his book *Idea Management,* describes an approach whereby managers latch onto ideas of subordinates and make sure they are properly reviewed. He suggests that management form what he calls an idea trap: a system for catching ideas. He says that, somehow, higher levels of management forget that the persons working on the shop floor, in the receiving room, or on the loading dock are the real experts on their parts of the business. Each person has "ideas galore" on how to make the work easier or tie in better with other parts of the company. They know their jobs better than the persons who send them the materials to work on or the paperwork to process. They know little about the president's job or the vice president's because that work is outside their realm of experience. But each person is an expert on his or her own job.[25]

Clark illustrates with the example of the customer service department of a large office machine firm that faced an embarrassingly high error rate in dispatching customer engineers. Calls for service came through a switchboard, where an operator took down the relevant information. Data on location, type of machine, territory, and customer engineer were number-coded on a card, and the card was sent on a conveyor belt to the radio dispatcher. It was unthinkable, of course, for a leader in the information processing field to get the number codes mixed up, but that was exactly what happened. A dispatcher in the Chicago office came up with the solution: give each customer cards with the correct number codes for their machines. Have the customer read off those codes when calling for service.

Ferguson provides the example of BFGoodrich. The company sent out packages of tire owners' warranties by parcel post, always 50 in a package. Fees varied from 66 cents to $2.35 each, depending on the distance. Someone asked, "Why do we have to send 50 in a package?" There was no reason. Removing four warranties from each package brought the weight down to less than a pound. Now the postage was only 66 cents, regardless of distance, and the hours spent zoning and pricing each parcel were no longer necessary.

An idea trap is any system for catching ideas. Management can use considerable ingenuity in establishing the trap lines. They can be as complex as periodic "take the idea to the top" campaigns or ongoing programs of incentive awards for cost-saving innovations. They can be as simple as a series of idea sessions in each department, using the tools for creativity given in this presession briefing.

Each worker should be considered the expert on his or her segment of the business. The idea traps should be broad enough to draw from all personnel. Not all ideas, of course, will prove valuable. Clark believes that if only one workable idea were mined from each employee, a corporation would be running miles ahead of its competitors.[26]

Time for Reflection

Senge relates the discussion with a manager who was born and raised in India, and who has worked in both U.S. and Japanese firms. She said that when a person in a Japanese firm sits quietly, no one will come and interrupt. It is assumed that the person is thinking. On the other hand, when the person is up and moving about, coworkers feel free to interrupt.

"Isn't it interesting," she said, "that it is exactly the opposite in American firms? In America, we assume that when a person is sitting quietly, they aren't doing anything very important."

How can we expect people to be more creative if they have little time to think and reflect, individually and collaboratively?[27]

Leadership Strategies

In his inimitable style, Peters discusses three leadership strategies to foster innovation and creativity.[28]

1. **Tell stories.** The best leaders—of nations as well as corporations and volunteer groups—have always been the best storytellers. They are masters at passing around the word, by examples of specific deeds, about "what counts around here," "what we cherish," "what we abhor." When it comes to innovation, that means that the

number-one task for the boss is celebrating the renegades, the small wins, the useful failures, the effective cases of bureaucratic rule evasion. Noticing, rewarding, applauding, "going to the side of" a small win producer and holding up that person as exemplar—that's the very essence of leadership to spur innovation.

2. **Talk up innovation.** Hewlett-Packard and 3M, among others, unfailingly emphasize innovation in their annual reports. The best way to "ferret out" a company's strategy is to read its annual report. We assume the annual report is pap, but in fact it tends to emphasize what the chief wants most to brag about (and, by omission, cover up). If the annual report "smells" of innovation, then the odds are rather high that the company does too. In general, if innovation is to be an obsession, it should be a major—even predominant—part of all company media: newsletters, bulletins, memos. A Hall of Innovation Fame is a useful part of the process as well. Start obsessing about quality, and your team (or division or company, as the case may be) will pretty soon be obsessing too. The same holds true for innovation.

3. **Proclaim "life-is-at-bats"/"try it now."** Peters provides another example of the strategy of "ready, fire, aim." Johnsonville Foods boss Ralph Stayer says, "Anything worth doing is worth doing poorly." The first phone, he reminds us, was primitive, as was the first airplane. But without the Wright brothers' plane or Alexander Graham Bell's phone, there would be no Boeing 747, no modern telecommunications system. Put it another way: To start, you've got to start. Talking up life as tries, at bats, is another distinct and special trait of the innovation-inducing honcho. Tout the experiments, big or small, the ones by vice presidents and the ones by receptionists. Shout them to the heavens. Beg for more. "Applauder-in-chief" for innovation is not a bad image.

The following comments are representative of managers encouraging subordinates to be creative:

- That's a good idea. Let's put it on the agenda for further discussion.

- I like it. Document it so I can circulate it and get suggestions for implementing it from the department.

- Good thinking. We can never have too many new ideas.

- I'm sorry your idea didn't work out. Don't be hesitant to come up with other ideas, however. Don't get discouraged. You'll come up with other good ideas.

- Keep the good ideas coming.

How to Be Creative in a Poor Creative Climate

Senge argues that teams, not individuals, are the fundamental learning unit in modern organizations.[29] Whether or not teams and the organization succeed in learning depends largely on whether they achieve a state of "alignment," whereby groups of people function as a whole, toward a common vision. Such alignment is never reached in most organizations. In the view of William Miller, "Most organizations' teams never achieve alignment, but rather a state of 'skilled incompetence,' in which people become highly proficient at self-protection, a major obstacle to learning. This need for defensive mechanisms is prevalent in cultures where the only alternative to winning is losing and where creative ideas, which are inherently safe (unlike actions), are stifled by an exaggerated emphasis on precise thinking. Our full capacity for creativity and problem solving can only be realized where logical, or precise, thinking is practiced in conjunction with intuition and emotion."[30]

Team learning begins with dialogue (creative thinking) in which members freely and creatively explore the issues before them, according to Ferguson. In order to minimize the emotional risks involved, all participants must become equally vulnerable by exposing their feelings and ideas. All ideas must be considered and the participants must suspend deeply held assumptions and resist the temptation to judge. Regardless of the actual position, authority, or expertise of individual members, each must regard one another as a colleague and participate equally within the team environment. Creative thinking is a purely exploratory process in which quantity breeds quality, ideas work in combination, and unfeasible ideas are valuable. The goal is not consensus or agreement but the free flow of ideas and learning.[31] An important finding in my creativity research is that teams, after undergoing creativity training, not only produce many more ideas but are able to implement the majority of the ideas without requesting additional resources. Seventy-five percent of the ideas originated by the team can be implemented at the team level; only 25 percent require additional resources and approval by higher management levels.

Had I been asked prior to the research, I would have estimated that the reverse would occur—that only 25 percent of the ideas could be implemented by the teams without additional resources and higher level approval.

Another surprising result of creativity improvement programs was the ease of implementation. The reason is the bottom-up approach. I had anticipated that a creativity improvement program, like programs such as Total Quality Management, would require a top-down approach to be successful. I had hypothesized that most of the ideas generated by a work unit would require approval and resource allocation at a higher level of management, therefore need top management support. While it is preferable for the whole organization to commit to a creativity improvement program, so it will have broader consequences, individual groups throughout the organization can introduce the program for their group alone, with satisfactory results.

The importance of this finding is the revelation that a bottom-up approach to creativity improvement is possible. Any first-line manager or self-managed team can adopt a creativity improvement program regardless of what is happening in the rest of the company. The group can improve its own climate for creativity and utilize creativity techniques to produce a stream of new and valuable ideas. This finding is important because many programs are "killed off" by middle managers who are apathetic toward the program and who are threatened by it. By working on the factors over which it has control, the team can improve its own subclimate, the factors that most affect its productivity.

Obviously, more widespread benefits would occur if the company as a whole adopted a creativity improvement program. Nevertheless, the individual work unit has the resources and the opportunity to improve its own creativity without waiting for a companywide program to be introduced.

How would the subclimate for the team differ from the positive climate described previously? Very little. The objective is to keep an open, encouraging attitude about acceptance and processing of ideas. The team can use the problem reversal technique to identify all the factors that squelch or ruin creativity. Then the team ranks those factors and agrees to begin a concerted effort to improve the top ten factors. As that set of factors becomes improved, the team can move on to the rest of the list. By the end of the first year, the climate for creativity will be significantly improved.

But what if you cannot even get the team to formally commit to a creativity improvement program? Recall in an early chapter that I discussed the optimal size team for producing ideas. The research shows that optimal team size is two persons, a dyad. You can almost always find someone in your work area with whom you have rapport, then help each other improve your creativity. The sounding-board concept is the key element in the dyad: bouncing ideas off each other. Research shows that two persons can improve their creativity even in a passive environment where others are not yet committed to change. Remember, it is normal to avoid change; only a baby in a wet diaper welcomes change! By patiently working with your dyad partner and beginning to demonstrate an increase in imaginative results, you will begin to pique the interest of other members of the team.

It is a rare occurrence, but there are circumstances where you might be the lone person in your work group interested in finding more creative ways to tackle problems and opportunities. Typically, this situation occurs only in a group where there has been some dramatic problem, such as burnout from overtime work or where there has been a major personality conflict among team members. Setting personal goals to improve your creative ability helps get you through such a period and may even "rub off" on your team members.

Conclusion

Ideally, company climate supports creativity. However, an individual can be shielded from adverse company climate by a supportive team climate and a team by a supportive department climate. See Figure 11–4.

A vivid reminder of how people are turned off by negative comments on their ideas is shown in Figure 11–5. Comments like the ones shown here cause people to gradually lessen their interest in idea generation. By designing this eye-catching advertisement TRW showed that it believes the problem is widespread and that their positive climate for creativity differentiates them from the average company.

I want to conclude this chapter with a look at the past and into the future of the creative climate. John McGowan provides the retrospect, Sheridan Tatsuno the prospect. We begin with McGowan's insight on the past:

> About 9,000 years ago, prehistoric man was suddenly catapulted into history as the result of an astonishing social discovery. Previous to this, small bands

Figure 11–4   Ideally, the Company Climate Supports Creativity. An Individual Can Be Shielded from an Adverse Company Climate by a Supportive Team Climate; a Team by a Supportive Department Climate

of nomadic tribes had roamed ... looking for game and gathering fruits and vegetables wild. Then someone found out that if one domesticated animals and plants, one could have a ready supply of food always at hand .... Thus was agriculture and civilization born .... Fortunately we are on the brink of another momentous discovery which will have even greater impact on cultural and personal escalation.

Heretofore we have harvested creativity wild. We have used as creative only those persons who stubbornly remained so despite all efforts of the family, religion, education, and politics to grind it out of them. In the prosecution of this campaign, men and women have been punished, flogged, silenced, imprisoned, tortured, ostracized, and killed .... If we learn to domesticate creativity—that is, to enhance

Figure 11–5

A Nonsupportive
Climate Can Quickly
Dim Motivation to
Generate Ideas

Source: Courtesy of TRW.

rather than deny it in our culture—we can increase the number of creative persons in our midst by about fourfold. That would put the number and percent of such individuals over the "critical mass" point.

When this level is reached in a culture, as it was in Periclean Athens…and our own Federalist period, there is an escalation of creativity and civilization makes a great leap forward. We can have a golden age of this type such as the world has never seen, and I am convinced that it will occur early in the twenty-first century. But we must make preparations now, and the society we save will be our own.[32]

Tatsuno's views of how the United States is losing its world prominence in innovation/creativity and how Japan is the impetus to that change were quoted at the beginning of this chapter. Another of Tatsuno's quotations is appropriate in this concluding section: his views of the future of the U.S. competitive environment.

> The comfortable stereotype of Japan-as-copycat no longer squares with the technological advances and risk-taking going on in Tokyo. Perhaps we are hearing the sound of one hand clapping—the sound of Americans patting themselves on the back. Or the sound of Japanese creativity falling on ears that are still deaf to new forms of creativity. Our cultural chauvinism—reflected in the Not Invented Here (NIH) syndrome ("If it wasn't invented here, it can't be very good")—is perhaps the main reason for our deafness. The West has been the center of scientific discoveries and technological breakthroughs for so long that most Westerners routinely dismiss signs of Japanese creativity, remaining too busy or too lazy to investigate further .... Japan's push for renewed creativity will shake up relations between the world's interdependent nations. The United States may have been the scientific pioneer, but the baton is being passed to Japan, which is discovering new ways to meld Eastern and Western thinking into a new synergistic approach. Unless we wake up soon to the implications of Japan's latest creative endeavors, the West will be left in the dust as Japan blazes a trail of its own into the twenty-first century.[33]

We need leaders to help revitalize U.S. industry. Warren Bennis set forth a list of characteristics of leaders in the May 1990 issue of

Training magazine. Those leaders must possess the following characteristics, according to Bennis:

- The manager administers; the leader innovates.

- The manager has a short-range view; the leader has a long-
range perspective.

- The manager asks how and when; the leader asks what
and why.

- The manager has his eye on the bottom line; the leader has
his eye on the horizon.

- The manager accepts the status quo; the leader challenges it.

Clear-cut statements on the characteristics of good leaders should be
sufficient to motivate managers to ensure a supportive climate for creativity. However, some managers need bottom-line logic. A representative example occurred in a division of IBM. I've been a consultant to
IBM for more than 25 years; the corporation has sent me to more than
35 countries to work with IBMers and their customers so I've been a
long-time observer of the company. The company has fallen on tough
times because it has moved away from the factors that provided a
strongly supportive climate for creativity in the corporation's early
days. One of the divisions where I conducted my creativity workshops
has a remarkable record of creative accomplishment. At the Lexington
site, all employees are encouraged to utilize their native creativity. The
results are outstanding. This division (which has been organized into a
self-managing subsidiary of IBM) provides computing services to other
organizations, both internal to IBM and external to other companies.
In one year's time the following improvements occurred. **In computer
program code quality**, monthly defects were reduced from 942 to 27
per million function points. **In total systems availability**, defect minutes per month improved from the 99.0 percent level to the 99.96 percent level. This result is even more spectacular when the amount of
system time is understood: 2.2 million minutes per month. **In operations utilization**, MIPs (millions of instructions processed per second)
per headcount improved 28 percent.

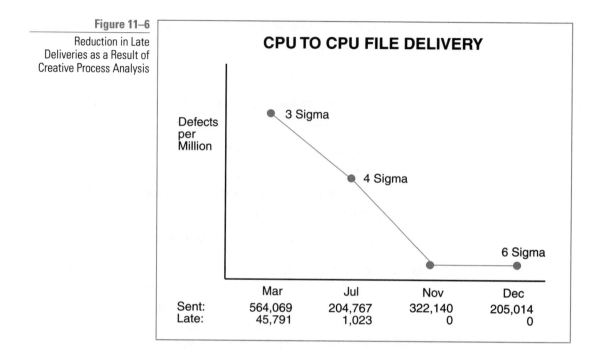

	Mar	Jul	Nov	Dec
Sent:	564,069	204,767	322,140	205,014
Late:	45,791	1,023	0	0

Figure 11–6 illustrates some of these results. **In mainframe to mainframe file delivery**, quality performance moved from three to six sigma level (99.99% defect free). In March, over 500,000 files were sent, of which more than 45,000 (8 percent) were late. By December, there were zero late deliveries. Even though work volume was less than 50 percent of the March workload, considering the huge volume of more than 200,000 files delivered, the improvement in quality performance is outstanding.

Throughout this book, I provided a number of other examples of the cost-effectiveness of creativity improvement programs. The return on investment of these programs is huge. These examples should provide management with lots of incentive to spend time on improving the environment for creativity.

If you go through life convinced that your way is always best, all the new ideas in the world will pass you by. Americans tend to think that the American system is the way things should work all around the

world, but they should not be blind and deaf to how
things are done in other countries.

Akio Morita

Other people see things and say 'Why?'...But I
dream things and say 'Why not?'

George Bernard Shaw

Summary

The fourth "P" in the four-Ps model of creativity, Press, relates to the environment for creativity. Even the most creative persons using the best process will have difficulty producing an optimal service or product if they are not supported by a positive climate for creativity. Some of the positive factors are goal clarity, freedom, encouragement, and recognition. Negative factors include status quo, organizational politics, emphasis upon standards other than merit of the work, an excessive critical atmosphere, and lack of feedback. When the factors that denote positive climate are identified, one sees that the provision of that kind of climate should not be so difficult. It just takes managers who give high priority to ensuring the presence of those factors. Some managers need the motivation of seeing the cost-effectiveness of creative activity. They think creativity is nice to have but not affordable in today's cost-pressure circumstances. There is lots of evidence of the cost-effectiveness of creative thinking; we need to get that evidence into the hands of management.

Once a creativity program is implemented, the evidence of creative results will sustain the interest of management. Maintenance of the positive environment for creativity will continue to be a priority.

There is also evidence that people can be creative in an environment of passivity about creativity. However, creative productivity is less than in a positive environment. With little investment in time and budget, managers can ensure a climate that draws out highly creative activity from subordinates. Not only are employees more productive, they are more satisfied. It is a win-win situation where both company and employee benefit.

Exercises

1. Referring to the section on Objectives to Part Three, how does Chapter 11 relate to the other two chapters in this section?

2. In what ways can management improve the climate for creativity?

3. Fabian identifies factors important in encouraging and nurturing creativity. Explain them.

4. Tom Peters believes there are key leadership strategies to foster creativity and innovation. Explain them.

5. It is possible for a team to be creative even if management is not providing as good a climate for creativity as desirable. Explain how.

6. It is possible for an individual to be creative even if his or her team is not willing to formally commit to a creativity improvement program. Explain how.

7. Managers can be motivated to improve the climate for creativity if they are convinced of the cost-effectiveness of creativity improvement efforts. Based on the information in this chapter, how would you go about convincing management of the value of such a program?

Railroad Hammock

Patent No. 400,131 (1889)
Herbert Morley Small
Baldwinsville, Mass.

"This invention relates to an improvement in hammocks, and has special reference to a hammock so constructed that it can be slung from and used with the backs of the seats of ordinary railway passenger-cars."

Fig. 1.

'Tis never too late to be what
you might have been.
George Eliot

**Personal Attributes and Actions
That Facilitate Creativity**

Surveys reveal that most people do not perceive themselves as creative. Most persons are inclined to believe that creativity is inherited and that we either possess it or we don't. To the contrary, the research shows that creativity is normally distributed; all of us are creative. Enigmatically, we utilize less and less of our native creative ability as we mature and age. Nationwide studies of schoolchildren reveal progressively lower scores on creativity tests as they move through the school system. Unfortunately, the process continues in higher education. University-level studies reveal that first-year students are more creative than seniors. Maslow said, "We are dealing with a fundamental characteristic, inherent in human nature, a potentiality given to all or most human beings at birth, which most often is lost or buried or inhibited as the person gets encultured."[1] Nor does the situation change when college graduates move into industry. Bureaucracy stifles creativity even further.

The evidence indicates, therefore, that without undertaking this study of creativity, most of you never would increase your creative output. Regardless of your age, you would continue to decline in creativity, unless you resorted to some approaches and techniques to improve your creative thinking ability. As described in Chapter 1, there is also evidence that persons who have taken creativity courses have not only halted the natural decline in creativity but have actually increased their creative thinking ability.

It is also valuable for creativity improvement to analyze the attributes of creative persons. Although some of those attributes are inherited, many are not and in fact can be acquired. Rather than think of these as the attributes of creative persons, it is more appropriate to think of them as the attributes of creative thinking. By first identifying the attributes, we can then concentrate on acquiring them.

We will also discuss actions and activities to stimulate creative thinking. Very little of our natural creativity has been lost: it has simply been pushed below the surface by events in our lives and by the educational process that concentrates on imparting knowledge rather than maintaining the inquiry process so natural to us at age five. Think of your creative ability as an iceberg—mostly concealed. You need to elevate it, surface it.

Creativity versus Intelligence

Is creativity tied to intelligence? The results are not conclusive. Insight on the question is provided, however, in three major studies. Davis points out that there are three schools of thought regarding this issue.[2] Some research indicates that creativity and intelligence are moderately related. The second group of research is referred to as the *threshold concept*. Over the wide range of intelligence, from mental deficiency to genius levels, there is a positive and moderately strong relationship between creativity and intelligence. However, at high levels of intelligence (above the threshold of an IQ of 120), the relationship vanishes. The third position, supported by the research of Wallach and Kogan, reveals that when creativity tests are untimed and are administered in a relaxed, gamelike atmosphere, there is no correlation between intelligence and creativity test scores.[3]

Richmond conducted a number of studies comparing creativity in twins. They revealed that differences between the scores of identical twins on creativity tests are similar to the differences between fraternal twins. Therefore, these skills obviously do not have a large genetic component.[4] L.L. Thurstone said: "To be extremely intelligent is not the same as to be gifted in creative work. Students with high intelligence are not necessarily the ones who produce the most original ideas."[5]

Torrance's longitudinal studies support Thurstone's view. The two studies involved high-school students who were tested, then given follow-up tests seven and 12 years later; and elementary students who were followed up 22 years later. Torrance found that life accomplishments supported the earlier test results. For example, with the 22 year follow-up, the "creatively gifted" group exceeded the high IQ group on the "quality of their highest creative achievements, their high-school creative achievements, the number of creative lifestyle achievements and the creativity of their future career choices." He also found that the doubly gifted group (high creativity and high IQ) equaled but did not exceed the creatively gifted group on all five of the criteria for comparison.[6]

The result of the body of tests indicate that creativity is a distinct category of mental functioning that has limited overlap with intelligence, both in the processes used and in the characteristics of individuals who exhibit them.[7]

> Genius is not a gift, but the way one invents in desperate situations.
>
> *Anonymous*

Conditions for Creative Thinking

Carl Rogers identified several important conditions for creative thinking:[8]

1. **Psychological safety.** This is the creative atmosphere, a flexible and receptive environment. It is entirely a matter of attitudes.

2. **Internal locus of evaluation.** This refers to personal characteristics of self-confidence and independence, a tendency to make one's own judgments, and a willingness to accept responsibility for one's successes and failures.

3. **A willingness to toy with ideas, to play with new possibilities.**

4. **Openness to experience.** This includes a receptiveness to new ideas and an attraction to new interests and experiences in the external world. It also includes a willingness to acknowledge internal wants, needs, and habits, some of which may be of questionable social acceptability. For example, a creative male is more willing to accept what at one time might have been considered traditionally feminine interests or behaviors, such as petting a cat, making baby formula, or baking a cake.[9]

Creative Abilities

There are a variety of ways to measure creative thinking ability. While it may be beneficial to take one of the creativity tests, just for personal awareness, I believe it more beneficial to understand the attributes of creative thinkers. In so doing, we can concentrate in adding those attributes to our repertoire of abilities. Figure 12–1 shows that the old adage, "a leopard cannot change its stripes," is not necessarily so; here, a rabbit has added stripes to its appearance! Likewise, we can change some of our attributes in order to become more creative.

George Kneller, in *The Art and Science of Creativity,* defines a number of traits of creative persons; he believes these traits can be acquired.[10] MacKinnon, Torrance, and Davis all have derived lists as

Figure 12–1

It Is Possible to Change
One's Attributes

Source: Courtesy of Andersen Consulting.

well.[11] The composite list of those traits is shown in Table 12–1. An explanation of the traits is provided immediately below the table, borrowing heavily on Davis.

Analogic thinking.   The ability to make analogies, to see familiar things in a new way, to see connections.

Analysis.   The ability to analyze details, to break problems into their constituent components. To be able to ask "Why?" John J. Plomp says: "You know children are growing up when they start asking questions that have answers."

Elaboration.   The ability to expand an idea, which includes developing, embellishing, and implementing the idea.

Extending boundaries.   Thinking beyond the "usual" or "expected," for example, using objects in new ways. Gelett Burgess said: "If in the last few years you haven't discarded a major opinion or acquired a new one, check your pulse. You may be dead."

Flexibility.   The ability to take different approaches to problems, to be adaptive, to view problems from different perspectives.

Fluency.   The ability to generate many ideas.

Table 12–1	Analogic thinking	Originality
Creative Abilities	Analysis	Persistence
	Elaboration	Playfulness
	Extending boundaries	Predicting outcomes
	Flexibility	Regression
	Fluency	Risk-taking
	Imagination	Resisting premature closure
	Intuition	Self-starting
	Logical thinking	Sensitivity to problems
	Metaphoric thinking	Synthesis
	Nonconformity	Transformation

Imagination.   The ability to fantasize, to be original, to form mental images or vision.

Intuition.   The ability to make "intuitive leaps" or sense relationships based upon little, perhaps insufficient, information. A hunch is the start of problem solving, not the conclusion.

Logical thinking.   The ability to separate the relevant from irrelevant, to deduce reasonable conclusions, to evaluate the appropriateness of an idea, product, or solution.

Metaphoric thinking.   The ability to bridge between disciplines, to borrow ideas from one context and use them in another.

Nonconformity.   The ability to be free from the conventional, not bound by accepted rules, beliefs, or practices. A nonconformist feels a compulsion to be different. Mignon McLauglin says: "Every society honors its live conformists and its dead trouble makers."

Originality.   The capacity to produce unusual ideas, solve problems in unusual ways, and use things and situations in an unusual manner. Uniqueness, nonconformity in thought and action.

Persistence.   The ability to focus on a problem and to stick with it until solved. Thaves penned a cartoon that shows Moses holding the two stone tablets on which the Ten Commandments have been carved. He is addressing the huge following after coming down from the mountain where he received the commandments. To his left are about 30 other tablets carved in stone. He tells the Israelites, "These are the command-ments—those over there are the government guidelines that go with them." Creative people keep pushing rules, regulations, and the bureaucracy to get their ideas accepted.

Playfulness. The ability to relax, enjoy one's surroundings and colleagues, and to examine problems in a light-hearted manner. Albert Einstein was once photographed sticking his tongue out as far as possible. Most pictures of Einstein reveal only his serious side. Apparently, he often did silly things to put his colleagues in a playful mood.

Predicting outcomes. The ability to foresee the results of different solution alternatives and actions.

Regression. The ability to think like a child, whose mind is less cluttered by habits, traditions, rules, and barriers; to toy with ideas and to use humor. Arthur Cropley gives the example of the boy, asked by his teacher to describe a polygon, who responds, "It's a dead parrot."

Resisting premature closure. The ability to avoid seizing the obvious or adopting an acceptable idea when many other alternatives should be generated.

Risk-taking. The ability to assess the pros and cons of a project and to take calculated risks. Willing to take risks to achieve desired goals.

Self-starting. The ability to see a problem to solve and initiate action. Doesn't have to be told what to do by others.

Sensitivity to problems. The ability to identify and pinpoint problems, to detect missing information, to see defects in inadequate solutions. De Bono says, "Data become information only when they are looked at through the spectacles of an idea."

Synthesis. The ability to see relationships, to combine elements into a viable whole.

Transformation. The ability to adapt something to a new use; to "see" new meanings, implications, and applications; to borrow an idea from a related problem. In his column in the *Kansas City Star,* Bill Vaughn once wrote, "People learn something every day, and a lot of the time it's that what they learned the day before was wrong."

Personality Traits and Qualities of Creative Thinkers

Davis identifies some personality traits that could be viewed as "creative abilities"—for example, humor; curiosity; artistic interests or talent; tolerance for ambiguity; spontaneity; and perhaps others. Further, there are innumerable learned technical skills and abilities in every social, scientific, business, or artistic field that are essential for creative thinking within that particular area.[12]

Jackson and Messick discuss the qualities of a creative person. One is an attitude of playfulness, "a desire to toy with reality." They talk about the ability of "fusing" of contradictory personal qualities: "There is first the coalescence of personal and universal concerns, with the strangely paradoxical result of losing in self-awareness while gaining in total awareness." A third quality is the alternate blending of working style, "a cyclic pattern of patience and passion, of reflection and spontaneity, a continual shifting from total acceptance of one's ideas and actions to a critical rejection of them." They suggest that a summary of these qualities is illustrated in the word *poetic.* Few business persons would characterize themselves as poetic, or even desire to be characterized in that way. Jackson and Messick cite the *Webster's New World Dictionary*'s definition of *poetic* to support their view: "expressing facts, ideas, or emotions in a style more concentrated, imaginative, and powerful than that of ordinary speech."[13]

For the attributes listed above that you already possess, you can work on honing and applying these creative attributes to problems and opportunities. For the attributes you do not yet possess or possess minimally, you can begin to add to your skill set.

Negative Creative Traits

While we've concentrated thus far on creative abilities, the research shows that it is also useful to identify negative traits of creative thinkers. The list in Table 12–2 comes from the work of both Torrance and Smith.[14] They indicate that these traits are common in creative students. Davis comments that most of these "negative traits" are directly related to creative students' confidence, independence, unconventionality, curiosity, interest in novelty, humor, and persistence. Some are very likely to cause personal or social adjustment problems for the creative person, regardless of age.[15]

Unlike the positive traits, the objective in knowing negative traits is not to emulate them, but to be tolerant of them in our colleagues. How about those traits in ourselves? Should we try to suppress them or change them? Not if we work alone. However, since most of us need to

Table 12–2 Common Negative Traits of Creative Persons	Indifference to common conventions and courtesies

Indifference to common conventions and courtesies

Stubbornness

Resistance to domination

Arguments that the rest of the parade is out of step

Non-participation in class activities

Uncooperativeness

Capriciousness

Cynicism

Low interest in details

Sloppiness and disorganization with unimportant matters

Tendency to question laws, rules, authority in general

Egocentrism

Temperamental

Demanding

Emotional

Withdrawn

Overactive physically or mentally

Forgetfulness, absentmindedness, mind wanders

Sometimes uncommunicative

work with other people, many of the traits would interfere with team cohesiveness: indifference to common conventions and courtesies, non-participation, too emotional, sometime uncommunicative, uncooperativeness, capriciousness, cynicism, egocentrism, temperamental, too demanding, and too withdrawn. Two of the traits might be viewed as useful though not positive: resistance to domination and tendency to question laws, rules, and authority in general. I'll discuss Table 12–2 more fully later in the chapter.

I am embarrassed to recall in my early days as a manager, before I sought any education on the subject of creativity, that I did not appreciate subordinates who possessed these negative traits. In my very first supervisory job, in my mid-twenties, I had been elevated to the position from among my peers. Several were older than I and it took a while for me to feel comfortable in my new position. We had a major project to complete and additional personnel were transferred into my unit. The traits of one of those persons continually perplexed his peers. In meetings when we'd just reached convergence on a solution, he would halt us and say, "I think we ought to consider additional ideas, such as ...." Under the stress of trying to meet budget and schedule constraints, his comments were not appreciated. Finally, the remainder of the group asked to meet with me and requested that I transfer the fellow because he was causing delays by forcing us to consider his disparate viewpoints. Because of my inexperience, I acquiesced and had him transferred. After some education in creativity, I realized that I'd transferred one of my most creative employees. With more maturity in the job, I would have been able to utilize his creative thinking ability without frustrating the rest of the group. In meetings where he wanted to consider yet another alternative, I could have said "O.K., we'll spend another half-hour considering additional ideas on this topic, but must reach closure in order to keep the project on target." Or, I could have asked him to work in parallel with the team on some of his ideas in order to evaluate them more accurately. There were many things I could have done to utilize him more productively and yet not antagonize the remainder of the group. In one sense, I was fortunate to have that experience in my first management job, to prompt me to learn more about creativity early in my career.

> Society has "filters" through which behavior, or even ideas, must pass: Deviance is filtered out.
>
> *E. Fromm*

Activities and Actions to Improve Personal Creativity

Herbert Leff, in his book *Playful Perceptions,* describes 12 creativity aids: things to help us improve our creative thinking. Figure 12–2 depicts these creativity aids. Each will be summarized below.[16]

1. **Think of everything possible that helps you be creative.** After making a list of as many items as possible, vividly imagine what it feels like to experience these things. Examples are being playful, relaxing, not straining, not worrying about criticism, exercising, and reading poetry.

2. **Ask "what if ...?" questions that challenge your usual assumptions or expectations.** If you are envisioning goals, try asking questions to help you envision ways to accomplish these goals.

3. **Explore reversals of your goals or ideals.** For thinking of action strategies, for example, imagine that you are working against your goal. Does this give you insight into some of the opposing forces and how you might deal with them constructively?

4. **Deliberately set out to think of unusual, even nutty, things.** You can call on zany notions to suggest feasible assumption-breakers.

5. **Force yourself to come up with lots of alternative ideas.** The first run of ideas will likely clear out cliché notions and pave the way for imagined improvements.

6. **Imagine you have a magic wand.** What changes or actions would you use the wand to create, especially things that would not normally be possible to achieve? After letting your fancy run wild for a while,

Figure 12–2 Twelve Aids to Creativity

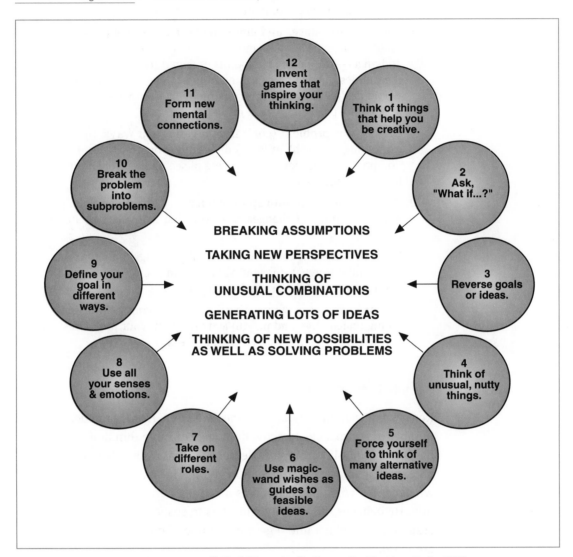

Source: H. J. Leff, *Playful Perception* (Burlington, Vt.: Waterfront Books, 1984).

ask yourself what specific features of the magical wishes particularly appeal to you. Then try to figure out feasible changes or actions that actually embody some of the specific features. Starting with the magic wand should help you get away from old assumptions, and the follow-up steps will help you build on your expanded vision.

7. **Take on different roles as you imagine improvements.** This includes inanimate objects as well as other persons. For example,

imagining yourself as an ice cube might help you think of ways to improve the freezer compartment of a refrigerator.

8. **Use different senses and emotions to suggest new possibilities.** The full range of human emotions—from humor and joy to sadness and anger—can be used as points of departure. For example, what is the funniest tactic you can think of to achieve some change you would desire? How can you constructively channel anger into an attack on a problem instead of on people?

9. **Define your problem (goal) in many different ways.** By expressing the problem (goal) differently, you quick-start the solution process. You begin the process of seeing the problem from different perspectives.

10. **Break the problem into subproblems.** Try focusing on one part at a time and think of changes or actions that would contribute to each part.

11. **Form new mental connections.** Think of things that are in some way similar to what it is you want to change or accomplish, then use them as points of departure for your thinking.

12. **Invent imaginative games that can inspire your thinking.** By combining imaginative and playful activities with your problem solving, you will likely spin off more original ideas.

"What-If" Prompters

Roger von Oech, in *A Whack on the Side of the Head,* provides a number of approaches to activating one's creative thinking. An example is the "what-if" prompter. He believes that asking "what if ..." is an easy way to get our imagination going. These questions can be whatever we wish, just as long as it is not a currently existing situation. He believes this activity allows us to suspend a few rules and assumptions and get into a germinal frame of mind. Some examples are these:[17]

> What if animals became more intelligent than people?
>
> What if human life expectancy were 200 years?
>
> What if bacteria which defecated petroleum were developed?
>
> What if everybody in your company played a musical instrument and you had a concert every Friday afternoon at 3 P.M.?
>
> What if people didn't need to sleep?

Prompter Questions for Personal Opportunity Finding _____

Another important activity is practicing expansion of your divergent thinking. List problems, goals, opportunities, challenges, wishes, dreams, accomplishments, and other fuzzy situations that you sense and you might like to try doing something about. Use the following checklist questions to help you ideate.[18]

1. What do you want to learn? Achieve?
2. What information would you like to get?
3. How would you like to improve?
4. Whom would you like to help?
5. Is there a simpler, less costly method?
6. What would you wish you had more money for?
7. What risks and uncertainties do you face now? in the future?
8. Whom do you need to convince?
9. What changes need to be made?
10. With whom do you want to get along better?
11. What other problems are similar to yours?
12. Where are the bottlenecks?
13. What would make you happy? proud?
14. What makes you worry?
15. What takes too much time?
16. What has bothered you recently?

Using Playfulness to Keep on the Creative Track _____

Sidney Parnes uses cartoons to keep colleagues in a playful mood. He gives, as an example, Burr Shafer's cartoon from *Through History with J. Wesley Smith.* The cartoon shows a man in the wilderness rubbing two sticks together as one would do to start a fire, and saying to a friend, "I was just rubbing these two sticks together and they started to get hot. If I hadn't stopped, they might have caught fire."

Parnes encourages us to become creative-adaptive or creative-innovative persons.[19] He explains the two approaches and illustrates with two more Burt Shafer cartoons.[20]

The *creative-adaptive person* uses creative problem solving, is sensitive to problems and challenges, and creatively solves them by modifying or adapting. But this person may miss far-reaching implications, like a caveman in Shafer's cartoon who has put a wooden axle through a small, round stone shaped like a wheel. He has attached a handle to the axle so one can roll it back and forth. The caption reads, "See, it ROLLS! I told you I'd figure out something to amuse the children."

The *creative-innovative person* deliberately and systematically dreams, envisions, and then uses creative problem solving to turn these images into the best reality he or she can possibly achieve at the moment. The conforming associate looks on without understanding, or often with disbelief. This is exemplified in the Shafer cartoon of two prehistoric men, one of whom is fashioning a large wheel from a stone he is chipping away at. His friend is puzzled. "It looks O.K.," he mutters, "but how are you going to hit people with it?"

Willingness to Risk

Some people are more willing to take risks than others. Risk taking is an attribute of creative people. It must also be an attribute of managers if they are to encourage creativity in their colleagues and subordinates. I've explained risk assessment approaches in prior chapters, to help people be less risk-averse. James Adams provides other incentives. He says if we believe that we are risk-averse and that increasing creativity leads us into increased risk, we have to wonder why any rational person would opt for increased creativity. He believes the answer must "have to do with reward." There must be something in it for us: increased satisfaction, attainment of a goal, avoidance of dissatisfaction, or something else to compensate for the possible losses and the emotional state connected with "leaving an equilibrium state for one with more unknowns." Creativity can be at such a low level that people are frustrated and bored, receiving almost no reward. We all have an internal need for a certain level of creativity in our lives, according to Adams. "If we are below this level we do not speak of rewards, we speak of escape. However, it is more often the case that we are reasonably challenged; change and creativity on the job balanced against that off the job; dynamic activities balanced against static; unknowns balanced against knowns. In other words, life is pretty good. If creativity and change are to be increased in this type of situation, the reward system becomes overridingly important. There must be something in it for us to rock the boat—to take more risk."[21]

Daring ideas are like chessman moved forward; they may be beaten, but they may start a winning game.

Goethe

Conclusion

We all already exert massive amounts of mental effort just dealing with the world, in the view of Marvin Minsky. He says that the difference between those people we regard as geniuses and the rest of us "is exceedingly small, perhaps no more than a froth on the surface of all the rest of our mental activity." The reason that these individuals stand out, according to Minsky, is that they have certain personality traits that drive them to process the products of their imaginations in a particular way."[22]

Many of us are inclined to put the great creative thinkers in a class by themselves—untouchables—and assume we cannot emulate them. We assume that when abilities were passed out, these persons were endowed with an extra helping of creative capacity. To the contrary, many of the persons who have been highly creative were handicapped in one way or another. Albert Einstein is one case in point. Einstein would be classified as learning impaired if he were in school today. He didn't speak until the age of four, and he didn't learn to read until he was nine years old. He had a poor memory. He found it very difficult or impossible to solve mathematical and scientific problems in the usual ways, and because he was very bright, he devised unique ways for himself to do so. Examples of well-known creative persons who were learning impaired but who overcame their handicaps include Thomas Edison, Augustine Rodin, President Woodrow Wilson, General George Patton, Vice-President Nelson Rockefeller, Leonardo Di Vinci, and Hans Christian Andersen. Biological differences such as these have motivated rather than discouraged many successful creative people.[23]

Another example of a person who overcame handicaps to become highly productive is Benjamin Franklin. He had little education but was productive his entire life.

Some people reading this page are doing so with the aid of bifocals. Inventor? *B. Franklin,* age 79.

The presses that printed this page were powered by electricity. One of the first harnessers? *B. Franklin,* age 40.

Figure 12–3 We Need to Overcome the Effects of an Educational Process That Wore Blinders Concerning Creativity

Some are reading this on the campus of an Ivy League university. Founder? *B. Franklin,* age 45.

Some got their copy through the U.S. mail. Its father? *B. Franklin,* age 31.

Now, think fire. Who started the first fire department, invented the lightning rod, designed a heating stove still in use today? *B. Franklin,* ages 31, 43, 36.

Figure 12–3 reminds us that most of us have to overcome the effects of an educational process that "wore blinders" concerning the need to support the natural creativity we possessed at age 5. That same educational process caused us to disdain nonconformists and persons who were impaired.

It has been demonstrated through research that most people are not fully using their native creativity. I believe there are five reasons:

1. Many hold the common view that only a few people are inherently creative. Therefore, they haven't exploited their own potential for creativity.

2. By training, most of us are convergent thinkers, not divergent thinkers. Most education emphasizes early convergence on one right answer instead of divergent thinking.

3. Under the pressure of schedules and standards, business professionals tend to be risk averters, hesitant to try something different.

4. Most college students have not been provided with creativity enhancement techniques. Few schools and universities require a course on creativity. The same applies to industry. Whatever emphasis there has been on creativity has been implicit; there has been an absence of explicit emphasis on creativity by management, either in academia or industry.

5. Perhaps most important, many persons have not been encouraged to seek creative solutions. There is no project milestone for such an activity for the typical work assignment or credit given in the typical classroom assignment.

Each of us has the opportunity to become more creative in our thought process. Like the persons well known for their creativity, named above, we can overcome deficiencies, natural or acquired, because we now possess the knowledge to improve our creativity. Nor do we need to wait for someone else to provide the motivation. There are obvious rewards, both intrinsic and extrinsic. Like the Straw Man in the *Wizard of Oz* (Figure 12–4), who deplored his lack of intelligence until shown that he could improve it on his own, we should not complain about a lack of creativity. We can concentrate on acquiring the abilities proven to be conducive to creativity.

> Freedom is nothing else but a chance to be better.
>
> *Albert Camus*

> Everyone is an artist in charge of designing his or her life. You can also *re*design it over and over again!
>
> *Anonymous*

Summary

Research indicates that native creativity is normally distributed, like intelligence and physical size. The research on the correlation between intelligence and creativity is inconclusive. There is ample evidence of persons far surpassing their native intelligence through motivation and drive. The same is true of creativity. Fortunately, the research also has been able to identify the attributes of creative thinking, such as flexibility, sensitivity to prob-

Figure 12–4

It Is Possible to Improve on
Our Innate Creativity

Source: Courtesy of Lotus Development Corporation.

lems, concentration, elaboration, noncomformity, and playfulness. With that knowledge we can individually pursue a self-education program to acquire those attributes.

There are also negative traits of persons who have proven to be creative thinkers. The researchers who have identified these traits are not encouraging us to emulate them but instead to be tolerant of our colleagues who possess them. Recognizing that these persons are demonstrating creative traits, we can appreciate their contributions and work jointly to improve creative output.

Being aware of the negative traits in ourselves doesn't mean we should suppress them. However, we can recognize how they are "turn-offs" for some of our colleagues and be more sensitive to their effect on others. We can maintain the ones that are essential to our creativity, such as resistance to dominance and the tendency to question laws and rules. We can try to avoid the overt expression of others that detract from our team effectiveness, such as uncooperativeness, cynicism, and indifference to common conventions and courtesies.

In addition to pursuing attainment of the attributes of creative thinkers, there are also personal actions and activities that we can undertake to increase our creative thinking, such as use of prompters. Two lists of actions and activities were provided. In addition, there was a reminder to emphasize "what-if" thinking and playfulness as creative activities.

There is another category of personal improvement that is highly important—improving your intuitive ability. This subject is covered in the next chapter.

Exercises

1. What is the result of the research on creativity versus intelligence?

2. Table 12–1 lists a number of traits of creative persons. Are these traits possessed from birth? Explain.

3. Review the table of creative abilities and identify which you possess. Now identify which ones you might be able to acquire.

4. Which of the negative traits of creative persons do you possess? Should you try to acquire more of these traits? Explain.

5. Leff lists activities to help individuals improve their personal creativity. What are they?

6. Another important activity in expanding your divergent thinking is the use of prompter questions. A checklist of 16 questions is provided. Which ones have you used in the past?

7. Summarize the essence of this chapter.

Bedbug Killer

Patent No. 616,049 (1898)
Frank M. Archer,
New York, New York

"This invention relates to bedbug-exterminators and it consists of electrical devices applied to bedsteads in such a manner that currents of electricity will be sent through the bodies of the bugs, which will either kill them or startle them, so that they will leave the bedstead. The electrical devices used consist of a battery, induction-coil, a switch, and a number of circuits leading to various locations on the bedstead, where are placed suitable circuit-terminals, arranged so that the bugs in moving about will close the circuit through their own bodies."

If you have built castles in the air your work need not be lost; that is where they should be. Now put foundations under them.
Henry David Thoreau

Improving Your Intuitive Ability

In teaching decision making, most business schools concentrate on analytical approaches and techniques; the intuitive aspects of decision making are downplayed or ignored. In the previous chapters, I provided a number of techniques and examples of the use of intuitive techniques, both for idea generation and evaluation. This chapter expands that material, but in the context of improving personal intuitive ability. Chapter 12 was the first of these two chapters that dealt exclusively with personal abilities and activities to become more creative. This chapter deals exclusively with improving intuitive ability.

Perhaps the business-school attitude toward intuition is on the verge of change. Senge reports that, after many decades of being officially ignored, intuition in management has recently received increasing attention and acceptance. "Now numerous studies show that experienced leaders rely heavily on intuition—that they do not figure out complex problems entirely rationally. They rely on hunches, recognize patterns, and draw intuitive analogies and parallels to other seemingly disparate situations … .But we have a very long way to go, in our organizations and in society, toward reintegrating intuition and rationality."[1]

It is enigmatic that intuitive thinking is virtually absent from the business-school curriculum; not only philosophers but scientists have for centuries recognized the importance of intuition. The entire philosophical school beginning with Plato is based on the notion that intuition is a reliable source of knowledge. Aristotle termed intuition a leap of understanding, a grasping of a larger concept unreachable by other intellectual means, yet fundamentally an intellectual process.[2]

Mathematicians, for instance, readily acknowledge the value of intuition in formulating new hypotheses, and use proofs and verification as secondary processes. Likewise in physics and other sciences, it is intuition that provides researchers with new possibilities to pursue with the instruments of science. Weil says that "the history of science shows clearly that great breakthroughs in human understanding have been the result of intuitive perceptions that are only later tested and verified."[3]

Jonas Salk, the discoverer of the polio vaccine, placed great emphasis upon intuition. When studying viruses, for example, he would visualize himself as a particular virus, then intuitively sense how that virus behaved. He would also visualize himself as the immune system to get a sense of how it would battle an invading virus. Only after he envisioned a number of scenarios about a particular situation would he design his laboratory experiments to test his intuitive perceptions.[4]

Salk even wrote a book on the subject: *Anatomy of Reality: Merging of Intuition and Reason.* He supports the idea of encouraging intuitive processes:

> A new way of thinking is now needed to deal with our present reality, which is sensed more sensitively through intuition than by our capacity to observe and to reason objectively. Our subjective responses (intuitional) are more sensitive and more rapid than our mind works. We first sense and then we reason why. Intuition is an innate quality, but it can be developed and cultivated.[5]

Salk goes on to say that intuition may be seen as a continuation or extension of "natural" processes, like instinct, for example. Reason may be seen as that which man adds to explain his intuitive sense. Both intuition and reason play powerful roles in our lives. Salk believes that intuition must be allowed free rein and be allowed to play. Then reason can select from the patterns that emerge.

Nobel prize-winning particle physicist Murray Gell-Mann was an outspoken believer in the necessity of the intuitive process for science. Another well-known physicist, John Howarth, was asked whether it was possible to help students to rely upon intuition as part of their preparation for becoming physicists. He answered:

> Intuitive solution of problems is important. Essentially it is finding the answer to a problem before you have solved it. Students are tempted to believe that physical intuition is something that you either have or don't have. We certainly all have different talents, but the process can certainly be encouraged.[6]

Fritjof Capra, in *The Tao of Physics,* notes: "The rational part of research would, in fact, be useless if it were not complemented by the intuition that gives scientists new insights and makes them creative."[7] Albert Einstein also affirmed the role of intuition in science. "There is no logical way to the discovery of [complex scientific laws]," he explained. "There is only the way of intuition, which is helped by a feeling for the order lying behind the appearance."[8]

Nor is the value of intuitive thought new to government leaders. George Washington used intuition to solve his most difficult problems during the Revolutionary War. He would instruct his orderlies not to let anyone disturb him while he relaxed and intuited decisions. The founding fathers thought intuition so important that they designed the figure on the back of the dollar bill as a reminder: an unfinished pyramid with an eye above it. The pyramid is not complete until the seeing eye is settled in the capstone position; that is, until the intuitive component of the mind plays a major role in developing ideas or making decisions.[9]

> I have had my solutions for a long time, but I do not yet know how I am to arrive at them.
>
> *Karl Friedrick Gauss*

Unwarranted View of the Dichotomy between Analytic/Intuitive

There is an unfortunate tendency to view feelings and thought as mutually exclusive, to force a choice between them. If we focus on one, then we must reject the other. But this viewpoint is mistaken. Feeling and thought are perfectly complementary. Ruggiero points out that "feeling, being more spontaneous, is an excellent beginning to the development of conclusions. And thought, being more deliberate, provides a way to identify the best and most appropriate feeling. Both are natural."[10]

The conflict between intuition and linear, nonsystemic thinking has planted the seed that rationality itself is opposed to intuition. This view is demonstrably false if we consider the synergy of reason and intuition that characterizes virtually all great thinkers. Einstein said, "I never discovered anything with my rational mind." He once described how he discovered the principle of relativity by imagining himself traveling on a light beam. Yet, he could take brilliant intuitions and convert them into succinct, rationally testable propositions.[11]

What Is Intuition?
Intuition is defined as "The power of knowing, or knowledge obtained, without recourse to inference or reasoning; innate or instinctive knowledge; familiarly, a quick or ready apprehension." The word *intuition* comes from the Latin *in-tuire,* which can be translated as "looking, regarding, or knowing from within." In *Awakening Intuition,* Frances Vaughan states that intuition

is the psychological function operative in scientific inventions or discoveries. As a way of knowing, it is experiential and holistic. When one knows something intuitively, one knows it for sure, although one may not be able to explain the feeling of certainty. Intuition is true in the same way that sensation is true: it is your experience, and you know it for what it is. In this sense, intuition is much more than a hunch or vague feeling. It may at times come into awareness only marginally and seem vague but, if given attention, it can become increasingly clear and useful.[12]

The Role of Intuition

Ruggiero posits that intuition is instinctive knowing or perception without reference to the rational process. Of all aspects of thinking, it is perhaps the most dramatic and therefore the most fascinating. History records many cases of important discoveries just "occurring" to people after they have gone through their "preparation phase." They may not even be consciously considering the matter. Then, all of a sudden the answer comes to them, seemingly out of nowhere.[13]

The German chemist Kekule found the solution to a difficult chemical problem that way. He was very tired when he slipped into a daydream. The image of a snake swallowing his tail came to him—and that provided the clue to the structure of the benzene molecule, which is a ring, rather than a chain, of atoms.[14] The German writer Goethe experienced great difficulty organizing a large mass of material for one of his works. Then he learned of the tragic suicide of a close friend. At that very instant the plan for organizing his material occurred to him in detail.[15]

An article in *Science News* gives further evidence of the value of the intuitive. The author, Stefi Weisburd, reported on a symposium at the Smithsonian Institution where artists and scientists gave personal testimonies concerning their creativity.[16] A number of the participants reported that they first prepare their minds with pertinent information, and then allow the intuitive response to "float to the top" toward the solution or discovery. However, often it does take a long time, as in the work of Linus Pauling, who discovered the medicinal properties of Vitamin C. He shared the information that one solution—the alpha-helix structure—took 19 years from the time he learned the necessary factual information to the achievement of the actual solution, and then, the solution occurred while he was lying in bed with a cold.[17]

Fortunately, intuitive ability is not restricted to famous men and women. Most of us have had similar, though less momentous, experiences with it. Ruggiero cautions that "two facts are common to all these experiences, great and small alike. The first is that intuition cannot be controlled; the second is that intuition is not completely trustworthy. Even the strongest intuition can prove wrong. For both reasons, though intuition is always a welcome companion to critical thinking, it is never a substitute for it. This, of course, is no cause for concern because many other skills of thinking can be controlled and developed."[18]

Levels of Intuitive Awareness

The broad range of intuitive human experience falls into four distinct levels of awareness, according to Frances Vaughan: physical, emotional, mental, and spiritual.[19] Although these levels of experience often overlap, they are usually easy to categorize according to the level at which they are consciously perceived.

Shallcross and Sisk prepared descriptions of the four levels. A summary of their descriptions follows.[20]

Physical Level

Tuning in to what the body is telling us can help us make decisions about the situations in which we find ourselves. If, for example, a specific situation consistently makes you tense, you can choose to avoid the situation or make appropriate changes to ease the tension. Paying attention to physical intuitive clues can make a significant difference in how you relate to your environment. Try to think of changes you can make in tension-producing situations to ease them.

Emotional Level

On the emotional level, intuition becomes conscious through feelings. Intuitive cues on the emotional level often involve relations with other people and seem to take on an almost telepathic quality. Have you ever telephoned a friend or relative who was just about to call you? Women's intuition is on the emotional level of intuitive awareness. Traditionally, society was tolerant of women openly expressing emotions but not of men doing the same. This allowed women more freedom to experience the intuitive levels. (Note that Shallcross and Sisk are women.)

Mental Level

The mental level of intuitive awareness often becomes apparent through images, or through what might be called "inner vision." It often occurs in a flash after long, arduous work. First, there occurs an exhaustive application of logic and reasoning, followed by a subsequent intuitive flash. Educated guesses, or the formulation of hypotheses, fall into the category of intuition on the mental level. Einstein was a strong advocate of taking "intuitive leaps." Capra speaks of "spontaneous insight" as being analogous to getting a joke.

The Spiritual Level

Spinoza defined spiritual intuition as the knowledge of God. Bergenthal equates this knowledge with man's experience of his own being and says that man knows God through his deepest intuitions about his own nature. In yoga, spiritual intuition is known as soul guidance—it emerges spontaneously when the mind is quiet. Spiritual intuition is the basis from which all other forms of intuition are derived. Spiritual intuition means focusing on the transpersonal rather than the personal realms of intuition. In Western thinking, the personal is the ordinary waking state of consciousness in which the world is perceived as objects and events existing separately in time and space. The transpersonal means "beyond the personal." In transpersonal consciousness, the ordinary confines of time and space are experientially transcended. Both these realms of human function are available to us. Reason is the mode of knowing appropriate to the personal level. Intuition is the mode of knowing appropriate to the transpersonal level. We need to accept both to actualize our creative potential.

Sensing versus Intuition

Carl Jung, one of the most influential psychologists of our time, focused attention on the role of intuition in intellectual functioning. He stated that information is perceived in two ways: 1) externally, through the 5 senses; and 2) internally, through intuition. Sisk and Shallcross show the differences as follows:[21]

When sensing, you:

- perceive with the five senses
- attend to practical and factual details

- are in touch with the physical realities
- attend to the present moment
- confirm attention to what is said and done
- see "little things in everyday life"
- attend to step-by-step experience
- let your eyes tell your mind

When using intuition, you:

- perceive with memory and association
- see patterns and meaning
- project possibilities for the future
- imagine or read between the lines
- look for the big picture
- have hunches or ideas out of nowhere
- let the mind tell the eyes

Integrating Reason and Intuition

According to an ancient Sufi story, a blind man who was wandering lost in a forest tripped and fell. As the man rummaged about the forest floor, he discovered that he had fallen over a crippled man. The blind man and the crippled man struck up a conversation, commiserating on their fate. The blind man said, "I have been wandering in this forest for as long as I can remember, and I cannot see to find my way out." The crippled man said, "I have been lying on the forest floor for as long as I can remember, and I cannot get up to walk out." As they sat there talking, suddenly the crippled man cried out, "I've got it. You hoist me onto your shoulders and I will tell you where to walk. Together we can find our way out of the forest." According to the ancient storyteller, that blind man symbolized rationality. The crippled man symbolized intuition. According to Senge, who tells this story in *The Fifth Discipline,* we will not find our way out of the forest until we learn to integrate the two.[22]

How does intuition relate to CPS? Sidney Parnes, co-developer of the Osborn-Parnes CPS model, maintains that the intuitive makes explicit and expands "opportunity-finding" processes, providing "sensitivity to objectives or messes." Intuition expands the front end of the

CPS process—opportunity making, the dreaming, the visioning. Then the dreams or visions are engineered into the best reality manageable.[23]

Parnes calls this process "heightened awareness": "I become more aware of something than I was—aware of facts (fact-finding) and/or of ways of viewing a problem (problem-finding) and/or of new connections, associations, relationships (idea-finding) and/or of consequences, repercussions, ramifications of an idea (solution-finding via wide search for criteria), and/or of possibilities for refining and adapting an idea for implementation (acceptance-finding)."[24]

In the processes, according to Parnes, not only can we image existing phenomena from our memory bank, but we can also *transform* these images "kaleidoscopically into infinite new configurations. Probably the most difficult but potentially rewarding transformation is changing a symbolic image (a kind of remote metaphor) into a relevant image to our concern of the moment—like when Kekule transformed his dream of the serpent swallowing its tail into his benzene ring theory."

Parnes advocates *simulated* incubation and *planned* incubation excursions. In planned excursion, persons proceed from examining "what *is*" to exploring "what *might* be," to judging "what *ought to* be," to assessing "what *can presently* be," to deciding "what *I will commit to do now,*" to action that becomes a new "what *is.*"[25]

- "What is" refers to your awareness of the facts or data about a situation.
- "What might be" implies the generation of multiple-viewpoint, forward-thrusting definitions, approaches, and ideas toward the realization of objectives.
- "What ought to be" involves considered judgments about approaches and ideas.
- "What can presently be" refers to your choices and adaptations of approaches and ideas into what seems to be a manageable solution for now.
- "What I will commit to do now" becomes your best plan for gaining acceptance and implementing.
- "Action" becomes your actual *doing, implementing,* including checking results and making adjustments—all of which bring about the new "is."

Analogies can provide a powerful tool to promote this process, such as a pea pod's weakened "seam" designed to allow the peas to easily emerge. The extension to the business world is the built-in weakness in a soda can for ease in pulling it open by a tab. There is also the famous example of Gutenberg obtaining the idea for the printing press from watching how the wine press operated.

Dream Time

We can learn more of intuition from the experience of the Australian aborigine. Pearce relates that the aborigine believed that every man, woman, animal, blade of grass, water hole, or tree had a counterpart, a subtle or dream image.[26] The plan of the world is laid out in this dream form and enacted now, in the physical world. A perfect coordination and cooperation with Dream Time assures man a perfect relation with the force that shapes our world, with creation itself. The aborigine was bonded with the earth. He maintained a state of unity between earth and self. He provided his children with models that stimulated and nurtured intuitive functions at appropriate times in their lives.

Pearce makes a strong point about capitalizing on "prime time" for children's development of intuition. He compares it to Dream Time, a mind-set by which Australian aborigines have operated for more than 30,000 years. By shifting back and forth from the present moment into Dream Time, the aborigine had at his disposal information "closed to our senses five" as the poet William Blake said. This is that capacity of intuition that appears around age four but disappears in Western culture at about age seven for lack of such activities as Dream Time and aborigine-type models. By means of Dream Time, the aborigine knew the location and direction of travel of those animals he was allowed, by his particular clan, to kill, even though those animals might be miles away. He knew where to intercept the animals, and he knew the location of water in the desert, not by some acute ground reading of exterior clues, but by shifting into Dream Time.[27]

To strengthen the disposition to intuitive perception as well as intuitive thinking, MacKinnon suggests teachers emphasize the transfer of training from one subject to another; the searching for common principles in terms of which facts from quite different domains of knowledge can be related; the stressing of analogies, similes, and metaphors; exercises in imaginative play; and training in moving away from just facts in order to see larger contexts.[28]

Vaughan suggests that there are three basic steps in training the mind for optimal development of intuition. The first step is quieting the mind. Any form of meditative discipline will contribute to your ability to do this. Physical relaxation is associated with a quiet mind, thus training in relaxation is an important aspect of this part of the work. The second step is learning to focus attention, or concentrate on that aspect of reality that one chooses to contact at a particular time. The third step is the cultivation of a receptive, nonjudgmental attitude that allows intuition to come into conscious awareness without interference. "You cannot **make** intuition happen, but following the three steps outlined above prepares you to receive and acknowledge it when it does."[29]

How to Improve Your Intuitive Ability

We can learn from other cultures. C.M. Owens compares Buddhism and Zen in their outlook on intuition.[30] In Buddhism, reason is seen as limited, and the knowledge derived from it transient and unreliable. Reason is therefore not considered a trustworthy source of knowledge of the absolute reality underlying a change. The Buddha taught that intuition, not reason, is the source of ultimate truth and wisdom. In Zen meditation, the discriminating conscious mind is quieted, and the intuitive mind is liberated. In the experience of enlightenment the individual returns to the true self or original nature, which is void, and yet contains everything. The student of Buddhism is advised to look into his own mind to find out what is true. The original Buddha nature inherent in all living things is also the true nature of the self; therefore, discovery of one's own true nature is the way to enlightenment of liberation.

Vaughan explains that the philosophical perspective on intuition is currently being investigated in transpersonal psychology. "Recent psychological and physiological research indicated significant differences in the functioning of the right and left hemispheres of the brain." As explained earlier in Chapter 5, the left hemisphere is associated with rational, logical, linear thinking, and is characteristically verbal, while the right hemisphere is associated with intuitive, holistic pattern perception, and is characteristically nonverbal. "The kind of thinking which is attributed to the right hemisphere is sometimes called metaphoric thinking, and is frequently conveyed in images and various artistic forms of expression. As a result of these findings, many educators are becoming interested in learning how to educate the intuitive functions, which have been too long ignored in traditional education. The benefits of educating both sides of the brain, the intuitive and rational, are now widely acknowledged. Those whose formal schooling gave them no opportunity to cultivate intuition are finding ways of developing their intuitive abilities in other contexts."[31]

Robert Ornstein, research psychologist at Langley Porter Neuropsychiatric Institute and professor at the University of California Medical Center in San Francisco, contends that while Western thought is left-hemisphere dominated, oriented toward rational, verbal, linear thinking, Eastern thought is primarily influenced by the intuitive, non-linear mode attributed to the right hemisphere. He also points out that these two modes of knowing are complementary to one another; neither is reducible to the other.[32]

Western psychology has traditionally viewed as normal the rational linear view of reality, which perceives the world as a multiplicity of separate objects and organisms and experiences life as a sequence of events in time. Vaughan believes that this view of reality "posits a duality of subject and object, and a split between spirit and matter." It is based on a mechanistic Newtonian model of physics that is now outdated. Contemporary subatomic physics, on the other hand, suggests a picture of reality that is much closer to the Eastern mystical view of reality, as an interdependent, interrelated unity wherein everything is in a continual state of change and transformation.[33]

The view of Hideki Yukawa, Nobel Laureate in physics, supports the foregoing descriptions. Where the Chinese and Japanese excel, according to Yukawa, and where they pride themselves in excelling, is in the field of intuition—what is called in Japanese *kan*, a kind of sensibility or alertness. On the average, the Japanese would seem to have good *kan*. This has always, however, tended to be seen as opposed to the spirit of science. A thoroughgoing rationalism eludes them. The Indians, on the other hand, though living in the same Orient, are considerably different; mathematics and logic, in fact, were developed in India from an early age.[34] Therefore, it is not completely accurate to use the characterization as Eastern versus Western.

Capra tells us that the universe of the modern physicist, like that of the Eastern mystic, is a system of dynamic, interacting, ever-moving components of which the observer is an integral part. Capra suggests that what is needed is not a synthesis but a dynamic interplay between mystical intuition and scientific analysis.[35] LeShan sees each of these two ways of comprehending reality as appropriate for different things. He says, "The deepest goal is to integrate the two in our lives, so that each viewpoint is heightened and sharpened by the knowledge of the other."[36]

After an extensive study of the process of scientific discovery, Michael Polanyi, distinguished professor of physical chemistry and philosopher, observes:

> And we know that the scientist produces problems, has hunches, and, elated by these anticipations, pursues the quest that should fulfill these anticipations. This quest is guided throughout by feelings of a deepening coherence, and these feelings have a fair chance of proving right. We may recognize here the powers of a dynamic intuition. The mechanism of this power can be illuminated by an analogy. Physics speaks of potential energy that is released when a weight slides down a slope. Our search for deeper coherence is guided by a potentiality. We feel the slope toward deeper insight as we feel the direction in which a heavy weight is pulled along a steep incline. It is this dynamic intuition which guides the pursuit of discovery.[37]

Intuition is not opposed to reason, but works with it in a complementary fashion. Typically, flashes of intuitive insight follow exhaustive use of logic and reason. Capra says:

> Rational knowledge and rational activities certainly constitute the major part of scientific research, but are not all there is to it. The rational part of research would, in fact, be useless if it were not complemented by the intuition that gives scientists new insights and makes them creative. These insights tend to come suddenly, and characteristically, not when sitting at a desk working out the equations, but when relaxing, in the bath, during a walk in the woods, on the beach, etc. During these periods of relaxation

after concentrated intellectual activity, the intuitive mind seems to take over and can produce the sudden clarifying insights which give so much joy and delight to scientific research.[38]

Need for Tolerance for Ambiguity

Chapter 3 described one of the perceptual blocks common to people with business school training and persons of Western culture: an intolerance for ambiguity. We have a strong preference for precise, concrete thoughts. As a consequence, we tend to prematurely reject notions and ideas that do not fit into what we already know, or that are too intangible or elusive to permit immediate comprehension and categorization. Raudseep says that "any vagueness is experienced as a scary, uncomfortable, and sometimes even an irresponsible state of mind by many people because of their predilection for clarity and effortless understanding."[39] The clearly defined and familiar have a powerful hold on most people because the "new" threatens to disturb the secure comfort of the familiar. The hold of the familiar precludes the possibility of permitting the unguided imaginative promptings that emerge during the creative process to have spontaneous free play.

"The truly creative person," Raudseep says, "is not afraid of disorder or ambiguity. On the contrary, he (or she) seems rather attracted to phenomena that are not fully ordered or readily comprehended, and prefers cognitively challenging and complex situations. As a result, he is aware of, and open to, the intricate, confusing and paradoxical qualities of most situations. There is no fear-motivated desire to close out any conflicting or ambiguous elements he encounters. Like all human beings, he seeks integration and order, but he is willing to seek it without shutting out of his awareness the chaotic or the ambiguous."[40]

In their work, creative people are always ready to relax any binding habit patterns, and adhere as little as possible to preconceived plans or stereotyped approaches. They also show "pliability" by being able to simultaneously consider and weigh different or even conflicting concepts and frames of reference. Creative persons also show greater "plasticity and adaptability while creating," and have a healthy respect for "groping and uncertainty while forming and ordering ... thoughts."[41]

Kao depicts the balance of rational and intuitive efforts in Table 13–1. He adds a step—exploitation—to the Wallas model of cre-

Table 13–1	Creativity Stage	Activity	Psychological Style
The Progress Approach to Creativity	Interest	environmental scanning	intuition/emotion
	Preparation	plan the expedition	details/planning
	Incubation	"mulling things over"	intuition
	Illumination	the "eureka" experience	intuition
	Verification	market research	details/rationality
	Exploitation	captain of industry	details/rationality

Source: Kao, J. J., *Managing Creativity* (Englewood Cliffs, New Jersey: Prerntice-Hall, 1991), p. 17.

ativity and shows the activities and psychological styles associated with each step in the Wallas model.[42]

Techniques to Improve Intuitive Ability

Some half-dozen techniques labeled as "intuitive" have been described and illustrated earlier in the book. Three additional techniques will now be described, aimed at improving your personal intuitive ability: wise counsel, peaceful setting, and six hats.

Wise Counsel Technique

Parnes provides a simple, starting type of exercise that helps a person move toward more intuitiveness.[43]

Assume a meditative attitude. Image yourself chatting with a wise person whom you respect. Ask that person for ideas. Listen and interpret the responses for yourself, listing them or translating them into ideas.

Michalko has another version of this technique, called "Creating Your Personal Hall of Fame." The sequence is as follows:[44]

1. **Create your personal Hall of Fame.** Select those people, living or dead, real or fictional, who appeal to you for one reason or another. Following are some of the members of Michalko's personal Hall of Fame:

Ben Franklin	Sherlock Holmes	Jesus Christ
Bill Moyers	Diogenes	Julius Caesar
Mark Twain	Ralph Waldo Emerson	Plato
Clarence Darrow	Andrew Jackson	Shakespeare
Aristotle	George Patton	Sun Tzu

Peter the Great	Robert Frost	Somerset Maugham
John F. Kennedy	Leonardo DaVinci	Eugene O'Neill
Dorothy Parker	Billy Graham	Pearl Buck
Aldous Huxley	Winston Churchill	Abraham Lincoln
Sigmund Freud	Albert Schweitzer	Thomas Jefferson

2. **When you have a challenge, consult your Hall of Fame.** Select an adviser and choose a favorite quotation.

3. **Ponder the quotation.** Write down your thoughts, regardless of appropriateness to the challenge. If you think it, write it. Try to use these thoughts to generate more relevant thoughts. The basic rules are:

> Strive for quantity.
>
> Defer judgment.
>
> Freewheel.
>
> Seek to combine and improve your thoughts.

4. **Choose the thought or combination of thoughts that holds the most promise.** Then restate it.

5. **Allow yourself five to ten minutes to come up with new ideas.** If you produce nothing significant, select another quote or go to another adviser. Keep consulting your Hall of Fame until a quote or passage provokes a train of usable ideas.

Peaceful Setting Technique

The objective of the peaceful setting technique is to enable you to mentally remove yourself from present surroundings so that you have access to a less cluttered, more open mental process. The goal is to try to eliminate the constraints of the normal work environment that impede full use of your native creative ability. By trying to utilize all five senses in this setting (taste, touch, smell, sight, and hearing), you can more easily call on your sixth sense, intuition. I find the technique especially useful on a problem where I've reached an impasse.

Procedure for Use

1. If you cannot shut the door and put the phone on recording position, go to another location where you are less likely to be disturbed, such as the company library, a conference room, or an unoccupied office.

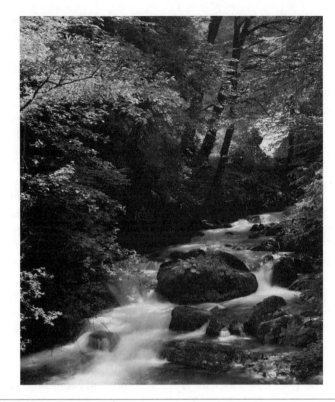

Source: M. Thonig/H. Armstrong Roberts.

2. Now, close your eyes. Get comfortable.

3. Picture yourself at a location where you can be off to yourself, completely alone and peaceful. For me, the location is either on a deserted beach, a beautiful desert island, or in the mountains next to a stream. Figure 13–1 is an example of such a place.

4. Try to experience all five senses in this setting: taste, touch, smell, sight, and sound.

The grass comes to within five feet of the water, with white sand in between. You are sitting in a lawn chair underneath a large tree, completely shaded from the hot sun, facing the sea. You adjust the chair so you can lean all the way back. You are in tune with your surroundings, all five senses are active. First, your sense of sight. You see out into the ocean, noticing the differences in shading as the water becomes deeper. Near the shore, the water is a light green color. It gradually changes shade until a hundred feet or so from the beach where it becomes a darker green. The deepening of shade continues to the furthest distance you can see—it becomes dark blue. With that view lodged in your mind, you begin to experience the other four senses. You are in your swimming suit and feel a warm breeze on your legs and arms. The breeze is gentle and relaxing to you. You next experience the sense of taste. You lick your lips and taste a slight saltiness as the breeze blows the evaporation in from the sea. A jasmine bush winds around the tree under which you are reclining and you smell the sweet fragrance. You are close enough that without opening your eyes you can reach over and pull off a blossom. You raise it to your nose and breath in the fragrance. You put the delicate petals to your tongue, then lower it and rub a petal between your thumb and finger. Your other hand is resting on the arm of the chair and you think of the contrast as you feel the roughness of the wood compared to the smoothness of the blossom. As you relax, you hear the smooth washing of the waves on the beach. Every few minutes, a larger wave comes inland and barely reaches your toes. You enjoy the cool feel of the water. You lie still, completely relaxed. All five senses are in tune with your environment. You have no thoughts but the pleasure of your surroundings.

5. In this relaxed setting, you are able to use your sixth sense more readily. That is your intuitive sense. In this relaxed setting, you should be able to more fully arouse your creative abilities, to apply them a situation that needs improving.

Example of Use

- Think for a few moments about the things you enjoy in your work.

- Think about the people who are a pleasure to work with.

- Think about the parts of the job itself that are enjoyable, that give you a sense of satisfaction.

- Think about the environment, the things the company has done to make your work more enjoyable.

Next, try to channel your creative process into ways to improve a problem that all employees face.

- Think of someone with whom you don't get along very well—not a manager, but a peer, an individual in your work unit or outside your unit.

It is not reasonable to expect to come up with an approach that will cause that person to begin to like you. But it is practical to come up with an approach that will neutralize the problem and enable you to communicate with that person without feeling stressed or angered.

- Think of something you might say to the person to show him or her that you are taking the first step to an improved relationship.

[Examples of things you might think of]:

- A smile when you meet the person in the hall or at the start of a meeting.

- Compliment the person when she or he does something well.

- If you have been openly critical of the person, try to eliminate any personal element of criticism, perhaps apologizing if you think it was received as criticism of the person rather than the idea.

- Think of something you might do for the person that would show you want an improved relationship.

  [Examples of things you might think of]:

- Offer to help in a work assignment.

- Offer to intercede when you have rapport with a person from whom he or she needs help.

- Do something helpful that he or she neither asked for nor expected.

Six Thinking Hats Technique

Edward deBono developed this technique.[45] The method is simple. There are six imaginary hats, each of a different color. At any moment, a thinker may choose to put on one of the hats or may be asked to put on or take off a hat. All people at a meeting can use a hat of a particular color for a few moments at a time. The hats involve participants in a type of mental role playing.

Blue hat thinking:	Facilitates the thinking process
White hat thinking:	An objective look at data and information
Green hat thinking:	New ideas and creative thinking
Red hat thinking:	Legitimizes feelings, hunches, and intuition
Black hat thinking:	Logical negative, judgment, and caution
Yellow hat thinking:	Logical positive, feasibility, and benefits

The method may seem extremely simple and even childlike, but it has proven very effective. It works because it sets the rules of the game, and people then can be asked to play the game. The Six Thinking Hats approach allows us to conduct our thinking as a conductor might lead an orchestra. Like a conductor who points the baton to a specific artist for emphasis at one point in the symphony, we can call forth the needed mode of thinking for the specific point in the problem-solving activity. We can use six hat thinking as individuals as well as within groups.

Western thinking concentrates on the dialectic approach, which is inadequate because it does not provide proper emphasis upon generative and creative thinking. Critical thinking is fine for reacting to what is put before you but does little to produce creative proposals. The purposes of the Six Thinking Hats approach are:

1. *Defined role playing.* According to deBono, the main restriction on thinking is ego defense, which is responsible for most of the practical faults of thinking. Concentrating on the different modes of thinking permits us to think and say things that we could not otherwise think and say without risking our egos. Wearing the clown costume gives you full permission to play the clown.

2. *Attention directing.* If our thinking is to be more than just reactive, then we must have a way of directing attention to one aspect after another. The six hats give us a means for directing attention to six different aspects of thinking.

3. *Convenience.* The symbolism of the six different hats provides a very convenient way of asking someone (including yourself) to switch gears. You can ask someone to be critical or to stop being critical. You can ask someone to be creative. You can ask someone to express his or her purely emotional response.

Use of the Six Thinking Hat approach has the following benefits:

- Simple to learn and use and has an immediate appeal. The visualization of the hats and the colors helps.

- Makes time available for deliberate creative effort. For example, you can ask for "three minutes of green hat thinking."

- Allows the legitimate expression of feelings and intuition in a meeting—without apology or justification: "This is my feeling."

- Allows an "unbinding" of thinking so that each mode gets full attention. It avoids the confusion of trying to do everything at once.

- Provides a simple and direct way of switching thinking without causing offense: "What about some yellow hat thinking here?"

- Requires all thinkers to be able to use each of the hats instead of sticking to only one type of thinking.

- Separates ego from performance in thinking. Frees able minds to examine a subject more fully.

George Bernard Shaw, when asked by a reporter what person from the past or present he would be if he could live his life over, is said to have responded, "I would choose to be the man George Bernard Shaw could have been, but never was." The difference between our productivity and our potential is what we are striving to tap in entirely new ways.

Keep your eyes on the stars but keep your feet on the ground.

Theodore Roosevelt

Conclusion

Some people, however, have little use for intuitive thinking. When faced with a problem, they would rather rely on analytical thinking. They say, "Let's get down to brass tacks." As Karl Albrecht points out, they never give themselves an opportunity to consider steel tacks, copper tacks, plastic tacks, sailing tacks, income tax, syntax or contacts. If you do some intuitive thinking early in the creative process, you may still end up going with the "brass tacks," but at least you will have considered a variety of alternatives. Von Oech feels that "our educational system does a fairly good job of developing hard thinking skills, but there is not much to develop soft thinking." As a matter of fact, von Oech says, "Much of our education is geared toward eliminating soft thinking, or at best, teaching us to regard it as an inferior tool."

Roberto Assagioli, the founder of psychosynthesis (an approach of psychotherapy that stresses that each individual can direct the harmonious development of all aspects of personality), says: "Intuition is one of the least recognized and least appreciated, and therefore one of the repressed or undeveloped (psychological) functions.... Repression of intuition is produced by non-recognition, devaluation, neglect and lack of connection with other psychological functions."[46]

Theologian and artist Catherine A. Kapikian, in an interview by Linda Monk (1988) in *Common Boundary,* responded in this way to the question, "What made you decide to go to the seminary in the first place? Was it a sense that creativity and spirituality were somehow related?":

> I knew, in an intuitive sense, that they were related because the process of creativity, of that private time in my studio trying to create or discover a solution, was the time I always felt closest to my Creator.... It was a meditating time.... I knew deep inside me that it was the most valuable expenditure of my time.[47]

The failure of the educational system in regard to teaching intuitive ability is summarized by Jerome Bruner in *The Process of Education:*

> Unfortunately, the formalism of school learning has somehow devalued intuition. When encouraged to use intuitive thinking or to make "educated guesses," the thinker's results might be right or wrong …. Fostering self-confidence in children is necessary if they are to have the courage and willingness to make some honest mistakes in their efforts to solve problems. Children are unwilling to run the risk of perhaps being wrong if they are insecure or lack self-confidence. Certainly, we need to help children trust themselves and feel confident in exploring their inner knowledge.[48]

There's a *New Yorker* cartoon that shows an executive in his huge office telling his secretary, "Send the press release of my having been made CEO to Mrs. Fletcher, my 4th grade teacher, who once said I would never amount to anything." We can overcome the creativity-retarding effects of our educational process by persistence at achieving a holistic process of thinking.

Bruner refers to the fruits of intuitive thinking as "educated guesses." He believes that encouraging intuitive thinking in children will bear later rewards in "educated guesses," in situations where an immediate right answer is lacking. This theory is supported by the concept that, without practice, the ability wanes.[49]

This conflict between intuition and linear, systemic thinking has planted the seed that rationality itself is opposed to intuition. In the view of Peter Senge:

> People with a high level of personal mastery do not set out to integrate reason and intuition. Rather, they achieve it naturally, as a by-product of their commitment to use all resources at their disposal. They cannot afford to choose between reason and intuition, or head and heart, any more than they would choose to walk on one leg or see with one eye. Bilateralism is a design principle underlying the evolution of advanced organisms. Nature seems to have learned to design in pairs; it not only builds in

redundancy but achieves capabilities not possible otherwise. Two legs are critical for rapid, flexible locomotion. Two arms and two hands are vital for climbing, lifting and manipulating objects. Two eyes give us stereoscopic vision, and along with two ears, depth perception. Is it not possible that, following the same design principle, reason and intuition are designed to work in harmony for us to achieve our potential intelligence?[50]

If one takes the holistic point of view and tries to integrate the two abilities, analytical and intuitive, creative thinking will undoubtedly be enhanced. For those of us who have most of our training in the analytical processes, the enhancement of the intuitive will take some time. We may feel a little foolish at first, but the advantages cited in this chapter, by some of the great minds of our time, provide ample motivation. We should have modest expectations until we have practiced enough to hone our intuitive skills.

> Dreams, not desperation, move organizations to the highest levels of performance.
>
> *Robert Waterman*

Summary

The fact that I left this chapter on intuition until last may imply that the subject is not as important as other subjects covered previously. That is certainly not the case. The last two chapters of the book dealt with personal attributes that could be heightened and personal activities that could be undertaken to improve one's creativity. I felt that those topics could best be appreciated by having the foundation of the prior chapters.

This chapter concentrated on three main points: 1) defining and illustrating intuitive ability; 2) showing that intuition is highly valued by disciplines outside of business schools—and citing the fact that many managers regularly rely on intuitive expression to complement analytical thought; and 3) providing three techniques to facilitate one's intuitive process.

With practice, a person can clearly improve intuitive ability. It is a slow process, however, for those of us who have been educated in schools of business and who are steeped in Western culture. The results unquestionably justify the effort. And, the synergistic benefits of moving into a holistic approach to life are the highest form of motivation.

One of the things I most enjoyed about writing this book was locating the inspirational and thought-provoking quotations. I'll conclude the book with two of my favorite quotes, the first from Dan Bricklin, the inventor of Visi-Calc[51] and the second from Morris Stein.[52]

There is a Jewish parable that says when God made the world, he made it a little bit incomplete so that rather than make bread, there is wheat so we can make our bread. And rather than the earth being made of bricks, it is made of clay so that we can make bricks. Why did he do that? So we can be partners in the act of creation.

Dan Bricklin

The word barah, in the book of Genesis, is used only for God's creative works. It means to create out of nothing. Man is said to make, combine or transform that which already exists into something new. Barah is never used for the novelty that man produces. It is reserved for God.

How things have changed. Once reserved for God we now use creative for new and improved products, for creative cookery (for good as well as bad meals), for creative financing (for questionable deals), etc. We seem to have moved from Genesis Chapter 1 with the story of God's creations to Genesis Chapter 6 with the story of man's creation— the tower of Babel.

Morris Stein

Exercises

1. Why is improvement in intuitive ability not an expected outcome for graduates of U.S. schools of business?

2. Do scientists believe in the value of intuition? Explain.

3. The view of a dichotomy between analytical and intuitive thinking is unwarranted, in the author's view. What is his position on this issue?

4. Explain the concept of intuition.

5. What is the role of intuition in the creative process?

6. Describe the four levels of intuitive awareness as identified by Shallcross and Sisk.

7. What are ways to integrate reason and intuition?

8. What new outlook is necessary to improve one's intuitive ability?

9. Review the peaceful setting technique for improving intuitive ability. Prepare a description of your favorite peaceful setting.

10. Use the wise counsel technique on a problem that you were assigned in one of your college courses.

11. Frances Vaughan comments that taking oneself and one's problems too seriously often interferes with receptivity to fresh, creative possibilities. For example, working with imagery as the language of intuition can be both an entertaining pastime and a powerful means of insight and self-knowledge that can take many forms. Vaughan suggests the following exercise.[53]

For the moment, try playing a game with me. Could you tell me what you are like by using a metaphor? For example, what sort of book would you be? One friend of mine sees herself as a dusty leather-bound Victorian novel. Another fancies himself as a racy paperback. Sometimes I feel like a book of contemporary poetry. What type of book would represent how you feel about yourself at this moment? Learning to describe yourself in terms of metaphors can help you recognize how eloquent the language of imagery can be. Playing this game in a group where each person described others as the cars they appeared to resemble, my friend Jacqueline Larcombe was stunned by what she felt was an amazingly accurate description of herself offered by a twelve-year-old girl she had just met:

"I see you as a dusty-brown Mercedes sedan, four doors, maybe a few dents, definitely not new. You know, it doesn't look so good, but it's got a great motor!"

Sometimes it is interesting to compare your perceptions about yourself with the way others see you. One young man who wanted to be a sleek white Jaguar discovered that others saw him as a Land Rover. My daughter, who sometimes feels like a Porsche, remarked the other day that she was feeling like a beat-up VW bug. The language of imagery can often convey both feeling and insight much more directly than verbal explanations. Thus, imagery serves as an excellent vehicle for conveying intuitive insights which may be difficult to communicate in words.

Anyone can play this game, and of course you can choose, if you prefer, to play it by yourself, or with whomever you want. Learning to play simply means giving yourself the option of using this way to learn more about your intuition. If you limit yourself to casual playing, however, you may find that your interest in intuition remains relatively superficial. It can be fun, but you may also want to explore in greater depth the various ways intuition can expand your life.

12. Eugene Raudseep suggests the following exercise:[54] Remember the famous fable of the five blind men and the elephant? As the story goes, five blind men were trying to describe what an elephant looked like by touching the animal at various points on his body. The first blind man, feeling the elephant's thick and enormous leg, announced that the elephant was rather like a large tree stump. The second blind man, with his hands on the elephant's tail, disagreed, saying the elephant was more like a whip. The third blind man, having felt the elephant's ears, said they were both wrong, that the elephant was shaped like a large lily pad. The fourth blind man, seated upon the elephant's back, said, "No, you're all wrong, the elephant is shaped like a tortoise shell." This announcement didn't sit well at all with the fifth blind man, who had just finished feeling the elephant's trunk, and who thought the elephant to be more like a thick snake.

Now imagine the five blind men touching at various points a cow, a giraffe, a horse, or any animal of your own choosing. What possible images could they form in their minds just through touch?

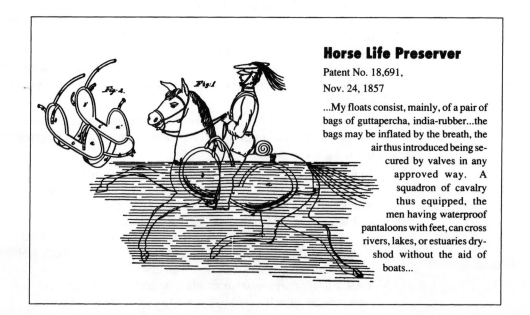

Horse Life Preserver

Patent No. 18,691,
Nov. 24, 1857

...My floats consist, mainly, of a pair of bags of guttapercha, india-rubber...the bags may be inflated by the breath, the air thus introduced being secured by valves in any approved way. A squadron of cavalry thus equipped, the men having waterproof pantaloons with feet, can cross rivers, lakes, or estuaries dry-shod without the aid of boats...

APPENDIX

Twenty-Two Creativity Techniques

Applicability of Creativity Techniques

The majority of the creativity techniques described in the following pages can be used both for individuals and for groups. Groups include dyads as well.

Technique	Analytical		Intuitive	
	Individual	Group	Individual	Group
Analogies/Metaphors			X	X
Attribute Association	X	X		
Boundary Examination	X	X		
Brainstorming				X
Brainwriting				X
Bug List	X	X		
Crawford Blue Slip	X	X		
Decomposable Matrices	X	X		
Disjointed Incrementalism	X	X		
Force Field Analysis	X	X		
Goal/Wish			X	X
Interrogatories (5Ws/H)	X	X		
Left-Right Brain Alternations			X	X
Lotus Blossom	X	X		
Manipulative Verbs			X	X
Morphological Forced Connections			X	X
Nominal Group				X
Peaceful Setting			X	X
Problem Reversal	X	X		
Progressive Abstraction	X	X		
Wildest Idea			X	X
Wishful Thinking			X	X

Analogies/ Metaphors Technique

The use of analogies and metaphors can be a valuable tool in stimulating creativity, both in problem definition and problem solving. Einstein often used these techniques as a way to visualize and solve problems.

The development of the analogies/metaphors creativity technique is generally credited to de Bono (1970). However, Aristotle spoke of the value of metaphor almost 2,200 years ago: "Now strange words simply puzzle us; ordinary words convey only what we know already; it is from metaphor that we can best get hold of something fresh." An analogy is a similarity between two things otherwise dissimilar. Analogies serve to "make the familiar strange and the strange familiar." By the use of analogies, an individual or group can often find a new insight and approach to the nature of a problem and thus its resolution.

Procedure for Use

Analogies

Often one can force analogies (for example, "How is this problem like a time bomb?") to examine and restructure a query. To use the technique of applying analogies:

1. Identify the essence of the query that you are facing (for example, the query might be "How can we improve the way we work with other functions?"). The key to the statement is one of "improving."

2. Create a list of devices and methods that are particularly relevant to the key concept (improving). For example, runners follow a training regimen to improve, which includes a combination of factors (diet, exercise, psychological techniques).

3. Review your specific question in the context of each device or method on your list.

Metaphors

Metaphors can also be applied to gain fresh perspectives on some situation under analysis. A metaphor is a term or phrase that is applied to another, unrelated term or phrase to create a nontraditional relationship. For example, "all the world's a stage."

Metaphors can be used to examine various situations. For example, an organizational environment might be the topic of analysis. One might ask, "How do people in my organization resemble animals in a jungle? How do different animals manage their interactions with each other and how do we translate them into the different leadership styles that are used?" Answering these queries might allow new insight into the situation.

Attribute Association Technique

Originated by Robert Crawford and modified by Arthur VanGundy, the attribute association technique works on the premise that all ideas originate from previous ideas that have been modified in some way. The socket wrench, for example, is an improvement on the wrench. The rachet screwdriver, for example, evolved by changing one of the attributes of the traditional screwdriver to one of pushing instead of turning the handle.

Procedure for Use

The procedure for use of the technique is as follows:

1. State the problem and its objectives.
2. List all of the characteristics of a product, object, or idea related to the problem.
3. Systematically modify the characteristics or attributes to meet the objectives.

Example of Use

1. Problem Statement: Shortage of office space. It will be necessary to rent expensive additional space if a solution cannot be determined for the crowded conditions.
2. Characteristics/attributes: space required for desk, file cabinet, personal computer/terminal, bookcase, chair.
3. Desk: could reduce size if there were more file/storage space above desk. Could think of problem in terms of cubic dimensions instead of traditional approach of square feet of space required per employee.

VanGundy modified procedure for the technique:

1. List all of the major problem attributes.
2. List subattributes for each major attribute.
3. Look at one of the subattributes and write down the first word suggested.
4. Using this word as a stimulus, list the next word suggested and so on until four or five associations have been written down.
5. Repeat Steps 3 and 4.
6. Using the free associations as stimuli, write down any new idea suggested.

Example of Use of the Modified Technique _____

1. Need for additional office space

2. Attributes of desk

   Size: cubic dimension

   Capacity: storage, working space

   Functionality: working space, storage, ergonomic factors, holds things such as telephone, personal computer/terminal, in/out box, calendar

   Weight: heavy, not very portable

   Shape: rectangular, flat on top, kneehole area

   Color: conducive to work area needs

   Degree of personalization: modifiable to meet needs, desires of individuals, such as location of working materials, location of semi-fixed devices (phone, PC, in/out box), space for personal effects (pictures, plants, quasi-functional mementos such as commemorative pen sets, thermometer)

3. Word association with a subattribute

   Personalization: depersonalization

4. Idea stimulus:

   Sacrifice personalization so employees can share desks, avoiding need to rent additional office space (assumes people away from desks often, in meetings, working with customers, clients, business trips)

   Provide enhanced work area to motivate people to share desk: color, furniture design, compatibility of design of work unit combination of desk/bookcase/chair

   Provide enhanced functionality: more powerful PC (e.g., workstation capability telephone with recorder capability)

   Provide storage of personal effects in conveniently reachable cabinets/lockers

   Provide storage of personal files (e.g., locking drawers allocated to each person)

Boundary Examination Technique

The objective of this technique is to restructure assumptions (boundaries to our thinking) and provide new ways of looking at the problem. Another way of thinking about this situation is to try to suspend assumptions. Senge says that "suspending assumptions is a lot like seeing leaps of abstraction and inquiring into the reasoning behind the abstraction." Boundary expansion is used primarily to question various frames of reference in defining a problem. Boundary examinations are based upon the assumption that a problem's boundaries are neither correct nor incorrect. The objective is to restructure the assumptions of a problem to provide a new way for looking at it. The major strengths of the technique are its potential for 1) producing more provocative problem definitions, 2) clarifying often indistinguishable problem boundaries, 3) demonstrating the importance of formulating flexible problem definitions, 4) and coping with management teams that are overly precise in their problem definitions.

Procedure for Use

1. Describe the problem as presently understood.
2. Identify key elements of the definition and examine them to reveal underlying assumptions.
3. Analyze each assumption to determine its causes and effects.
4. Restate the problem based on your deeper understanding of the elements of the problem.

Example of Use

Problem: Smaller pool of candidates for entry-level positions during the next decade

Objective: To expand the boundaries for the traditional candidate pool

Traditional boundaries of candidate pool:

1. A select set of colleges and universities
2. Only specific degree holders
3. Heavy reliance on help-wanted ads
4. Heavy reliance on employment agencies
5. Heavy reliance on college placement centers
6. Minimum GPA of 3.2 or so

Expanded boundaries for the candidate pool:

1. Broaden the set of colleges and universities.
2. Reduce dependence on employment agencies.
3. Consider technical schools and junior colleges.
4. Introduce a rebound program (changing from other disciplines).
5. Place less reliance on GPA.
6. Use other college sources than placement center.
7. Consider niche recruiting.

Brainstorming Technique

Originated by Alex Osborn, brainstorming was designed to separate idea generation from idea evaluation. It has the objective of moving people into an atmosphere of freewheeling thought process whereby ideas are stimulated through hearing others' ideas. The emphasis is on quantity of ideas, using the philosophy that quantity produces quality.

Procedure for Use

William Miller suggests the following ground rules for effective brainstorming:

1. Pick a problem/opportunity where each person has the knowledge/motivation to contribute.
2. Define the problem in neutral terms rather than a preselected solution, e.g., "How do we get this job done?" rather than "How do we get this person or this group to do this job?"
3. Record the ideas on flip charts or large pieces of paper where everyone can see them.
4. Suspend evaluation or judgment until all ideas have been given.
5. Stretch for ideas.
6. When you think you've got all the ideas, go for another round, being even more outrageous in possible solutions.
7. Aim for quantity to help find quality.
8. Accept all ideas, even wild ones.
9. Encourage embellishment and building on ideas.

Example of Use

Almost everyone reading this page has used the brainstorming technique. It would be useful for almost any situation where a multitude of ideas needs to be generated in order to identify two or three useable ideas.

Examples are:

Identifying new products or services

Generating new ways to solve a continual problem or perplexing situation

Finding new approaches to replace old, out-of-date solution approaches

Delineating many alternatives

Brainwriting Technique/(Shared Enhancement Variation)

The distinction in brainwriting is the generation of ideas individually and recording them on a piece of paper. The advantage over brainstorming is reduction in the effect of dominating individuals; brainwriting ensures that all participants have equal opportunity to share their ideas. The other advantage comes from the rotation of ideas among participants with each person expanding and improving the idea. By the time the process is completed, everyone has ownership in the idea. The result is a more mature idea, ready to be implemented, compared to the results of brainstorming where the ideas are mostly immature.

Procedure for Use

The shared enhancement variation uses the following additional steps:

1. The problem or opportunity is recorded at the top of a sheet of paper.
2. Participants record a possible solution on the sheet of paper.
3. The sheets of paper are collected and distributed randomly among participants. (Each time the sheets are redistributed, care is taken to ensure that recipients never receive the same sheet twice.)
4. The recipient of a sheet is asked to record three useful things about the idea.
5. The sheets are collected and redistributed and Step 4 is repeated.
6. The sheets are collected and redistributed and Step 4 is repeated.
7. The sheets are collected and redistributed. Recipients are asked to respond to the question, "What is missing from the idea; what would make it more useful?"
8. The sheets are collected and redistributed and Step 7 is repeated.
9. The sheets are collected and redistributed for the final time. Recipients are asked, "Assume that cost is not a constraint, what has to happen to make this idea work?"
10. The sheets are collected and typed.

The approach normally produces sufficient information for each idea to be forwarded to management for evaluation.

Example of Use

Management of a department wanted to initiate a pilot program on self-managed teams. Another group in the company had introduced the concept without a lot of planning and it had failed. Department personnel were aware of the failure and some were skeptical about adopting the approach. A meeting was held with the group selected for the pilot test. They were trained in the self-managed team concepts/procedures. Next there was a discussion about the problems that had occurred in the pilot test in the other organization. Finally, the brainwriting technique was used to get ideas on how to implement the self-managed team approach. The careful, complete analysis approach of the brainwriting technique resulted in mature ideas that paved the way to successful adoption.

Bug List Technique

According to Henry Petroski, the author of *Evolution of Useful Things,* inventors share the feeling of being driven by a real or perceived failure of existing things or processes to work as well as they might. Fault-finding with the world around them and disappointments with the inefficiencies with which things are done appear to be common traits among inventors. According to Marvin Camaras, an inventor quoted in the same book, "inventors tend to be dissatisfied with what they see around them ... maybe they're dissatisfied with something they're actually working on or with an everyday thing...they say this is a very poor way of doing this." The bug list technique was developed to capitalize on this tendency of faulting things around us—to lead to corrective action.

Procedure for Use of the Technique

1. The group is asked to identify things that irritate or "bug" them. Each person is asked to identify five or 10 bugs.

2. Then the list is consolidated to identify the bugs common to most persons.

3. The group is led through the list and asked to vote.

4. Then the group brainstorms ways to resolve the bugs.

Example of Use

Bug	Solution
"That wretched bookmark fell out of my book again!"	Post-it Note
"Drat! I nicked myself again. This happens every time I change blades."	Electric Razor
"Broke my shoestring again. Wonder if I have an extra pair around?"	Loafers
"This calculator is too bulky to get into my briefcase."	Hand Held Calculator
"Where did I put those extra batteries?"	Solar Powered Calculator
"I can't seem to use carbon paper without getting my hands dirty."	Carbonless Paper
"No matter how careful I am, I still make mistakes on every letter I type!"	Word Processor
"I hate paying a tax accountant to prepare my income tax report."	Tax Prep Software
"I can't remember when I scheduled that doctor appointment."	Computer-based Calendar
"That toilet paper is like sand paper!"	Ever-So-Soft Toilet Tissue

Crawford Blue Slip Technique

This is one of the simplest, yet very effective, creativity generation techniques. It can be used to collect a large number of ideas in a short time. Because the ideas are recorded and shared without the name of the originator, people feel more comfortable about expressing ideas; there is less concern that their ideas will not be considered as useful.

Procedure for Use

Each person receives a stack of blue slips. The leader presents a statement in "how to" form; for example, "How can our company improve its service to its customers?" Persons are urged to write as many answers as possible within a five-minute period. Each answer is recorded on a separate blue slip. Next, the slips are collected and sorted; related ideas are grouped. Then they can be evaluated and regrouped, according to categories related to impact, originality, cost, etc.

Example of Use

C.C. Crawford, originator of the technique, gives the example of gathering 20 people to define the requirements for a new industrial sealant. They wrote independently on six subtargets:

1. Identify customers.
2. Identify experts.
3. Suggest members for a project-management team.
4. Identify possible constraints and limitations.
5. Identify critical success factors.

They then formed groups to sort and evaluate the ideas and decide upon a product definition. Their suggestion was adopted by management and within days the product was in prototype state, significantly reducing product development time.

In another example, a director wanted input from all members of his organization on an issue involving flex time. The organization had adopted flex time two years earlier, and it worked satisfactorily for 18 months. In the past six months, however, there were increasing instances of people taking advantage of the system. People were coming in late, leaving early, and taking extended lunch periods and breaks. Rather than issue a statement that the privilege would be discontinued if these violations were continued, the director wanted to take a more positive approach. At the start of the annual meeting to discuss corporate goals, where all members of his organization were in attendance, he asked them to work with him in deriving approaches to ensure that flex time could be continued with assurance of "a full day's work" from all employees. The Crawford blue slip technique was used to get 100 percent participation. Everyone was asked to record one idea on how the problem could be resolved. Slips were collected. While the presentation on goals was being made, the slips were sorted into categories. After the goal presentation, the blue slip ideas were discussed and voted upon. The technique permitted everyone to participate, drawing attention to the problem and getting group approval. With whole group participation, after the meeting peer pressure began to be exerted on individuals who took advantage of the system. The problem vanished within two weeks.

Decomposable Matrices Technique

This technique permits participants to undertake quantitative analysis in order to prioritize ideas. The technique was derived from the work of Herbert Simon, who believed that complexity in the world has evolved from simple structures organized into progressively formal hierarchical systems. To understand complexity, complex hierarchical systems can be analyzed using a basic property of their structure, near decomposability. The concept of near decomposability refers to the fact that the subsystems of some hierarchical systems maintain some, although not total, interdependence from other subsystems. Decomposable matrices are especially useful for highly system-based problems. Because this technique forces identification of problem subsystems, their components, and how they interact, a clearer picture of important problem elements emerges.

Procedure for Use

1. List the components of each subsystem.
2. Arrange the components within a matrix.
3. Assign a weight to each of the interactions.
4. Select relationships between components as the focus for generation of problem solutions.

Example of Use

Problem: Rate the value of the ideas produced, to minimize the effect of the impending shortage of human resources at the professional level.

Alternatives in the solution set are listed in the first column. Rating factors are selected for the evaluation, based on the potential improvement. Some are rated equally, on a scale of 10 where 10 is high. Other rating factors may be given more weight in the rating; those factors are multiplied by the total for the other factors.

The probability of success of each approach can also be estimated. Another column could be added to the matrix, containing a probability assessment for each alternative solution. Using the Bayesian estimating technique, the person(s) most knowledgeable about each alternative would estimate the probability of its occurrence.

The ratings could be provided by management, or by a project team assigned that responsibility, or by all members of the organization—whichever approach management decides would provide the best information.

Disjointed Incrementalism Technique

Originated by Braybook and Lindblom, the disjointed incrementalism technique is useful for problem types involving complex decisions and vaguely defined, changing objectives. The disjointed aspect of the technique refers to the way in which many policy problems are analyzed at different times in different locations, without any apparent coordinating efforts, and without the benefit of relevant past experience. Incrementalism refers to the prescriptions used to compare differences or increments in the consequences of various alternatives with one another and with a present (state) situation. Thus, decisions are made by evaluating the trade-offs possible between an increment of one value and an increment of another value. It allows a systematic way to restrict the number of alternatives and consequences requiring consideration.

Procedure for Use

1. Delineate the policies involved in the analysis.
2. Break the policies into increments for more effective analysis.
3. Evaluate the policies.
4. After the policies have been delineated and evaluated, the other factors in the decision are evaluated and weighted.

Example of Use

Continuing with the problem of a smaller pool from which to select entry-level employees, selection of personnel who will be satisfactory performers becomes even more important. Bad hiring decisions are very costly, not only the cost to replace the individual but the costs of poor performance. In addition to the lack of output, poor performers take more managerial time in motivating and counseling.

One approach to improving the selection process would be to reduce some of the speculative and intuitive aspects of judging the candidate's qualifications. Disjointed incrementalism improves the quantitative analysis in such decisions. It begins with identifying the policies.

1. Delineate the policies regarding selection.

   Although there are stated policies (such as prohibitions against racial, religious, and political discrimination), there are also unstated policies that need to be clarified. An example is the ability of the candidate to fit into the company and the work group environment.

While there are clear-cut policies on things like dress code, where the intent is to have employees meet prevailing norms when they deal with customers, there are also unpublished policies related to attitude about the company—such as being a good citizen. The goal is to clarify the policies so all persons involved in the selection process are consistent in their application of policy.

2. Break the hiring decision into increments for more effective analysis.

   Examples: evaluating knowledge qualifications, assessing desire to work (motivation), assessing probability of longevity (turnover), evaluating technical knowledge, evaluating behavioral skills, assessing intelligence (logical ability), assessing creativity.

3. Evaluate hiring policies.

4. Evaluate and weight other factors in the hiring decision. The result is a significant improvement in the ability to select people who will make the desired level of contribution to the organization.

Force Field Analysis Technique

The name comes from the technique's ability to identify forces contributing to or hindering a solution to a problem, and can stimulate creative thinking in three ways: 1) to define what you are working towards (vision), 2) to identify strengths you can maximize, and 3) to identify weaknesses you can minimize.

1. At the center of the sheet, write a statement of the problem you wish to solve.

2. Just below, at the left of the sheet, describe what the situation would be like in the worst case—catastrophe.

3. On the same line, at the right of the sheet, describe the ideal, or optimal, situation.

4. The center position represents your current situation. On the right, describe the "forces" tugging right now to move the situation toward the ideal. Then describe on the left side the "forces" tugging right now to move toward catastrophe.

5. The next step is to identify approaches that would improve the situation. Because the typical situation resembles a tug-of-war, use the following three approaches to move the center line in the direction of the more desirable outcome:

   • Identify things that would strengthen an already positive force.

   • Identify things that would weaken an already negative force.

   • Add new positive forces.

Example of Use

Problem: How to ensure creativity techniques are utilized

Catastrophe	**Optimal**
Minimal use of creativity techniques despite training and availability of published materials	Use of creativity techniques in everyday activities, for all employees

Forces

(−)	(+)
Incorporated in standards manual but not enforced	Used in problem-solving/opportunity-finding methodology for all problems
Managers do not use creativity techniques themselves	Managers demonstrate value by use of creativity techniques in their own activities
No change in ways department runs its meetings	Meeting procedures changed to include creativity approaches

Goal/Wish Technique

This technique uses a "departure" method to analyze your goal/wish from a different framework in order to generate new ideas. By using the framework of an "unusual idea," you are forced to consider other alternatives that you might not have thought of otherwise. An example is trying to determine improved approaches for dealing with the most costly turnover problem. For example, the highest rate of turnover for professional employees occurs between their second and third year after entry to the profession.

Procedure for Use

1. Select a goal/wish for an innovative possible solution.

2. Pick a key word (action, concept) from the goal/wish.

3. Think of an example of that key word from a world that is distant from the world of the problem.

4. Forget about the problem and the goal/wish and focus on the example, thinking of associations or images it conjures up.

5. Use these examples to develop unusual ideas to solve the problem.

6. Develop second-generation ideas from any one of the unusual ideas (extracting key principles and applying them in a more realistic fashion without diluting the innovation).

7. Select ideas that have appeal from the second-generation ideas.

Example of Use

1. Select a goal/wish for an innovative possible solution.

   Reduce the turnover of professional employees between their second and third year to the level for other points in their career.

2. Pick a key word (action, concept) from the goal/wish.

   reduce turnover

3. Think of an example from a world that is distant from the world of the problem.

   Hollywood

4. Forget about the problem and the goal/wish and focus on the example, thinking of associations or images it conjures up.

Divorces	**Oscars**	**Movies**	**Critics**
Acting	**Rich**	**Parties**	**Agents**

5. Use these examples to develop unusual ideas.

   Provide Oscars to professional employees.

6. Develop second-generation ideas from any one of the unusual ideas (extracting key principles and applying them in a more realistic fashion without diluting the innovation).

Oscars:	Statues, plaques for high-performance activities
Parties:	Social activities to improve rapport
Divorces:	Keep work demands realistic
Acting:	Try to diminish politics, shelter professional employees from these effects. Let them know the politics essential to their progress.
Agents:	Mentors

Interrogatories (5Ws/H) Technique

The Who-What-Where-When-Why-How questions, or 5Ws/H, aid you in expanding your view of a problem or opportunity, to try to make sure that all related aspects have been considered. By going through several cycles of the 5Ws/H, alternatives related to the problem/opportunity can be explored exhaustively. This technique is one of the most useful of all creativity techniques because it can be used after each phase of the development cycle. By asking Who? What? Where? When? and Why? you have greater assurance that you are covering the full set of alternatives to be considered. The response to the H (how?) question provides approaches to implementing the ideas you have generated with the Ws.

Procedure for Use

1. Develop a question for each of the Ws and the H.

2. Develop responses to each of your questions.

3. Evaluate alternative approaches suggested by your responses to your questions. When an improved approach results, determine its cost-effectiveness; change the problem solution accordingly.

Example of Use

As an example, consider the following responses to the Why question, posed at the conclusion of each phase of development of a computer application:

1. Specification Development: Why does the firm (organization) need this system? Why have you limited the system to this particular set of functions? Why have you selected the specified procedures for accomplishing the tasks of this system?

2. Logical Design: Why is this set of logic the most appropriate for the system? Why have you selected this specific methodology for portraying the system specifications? Why are you dividing the logic among modules in the manner you have chosen?

3. Physical Design: Why are you using traditional life cycle development methodology instead of prototyping? Why have you chosen to use on-line processing (or batch) instead of batch processing (or on-line)? Why are you using database access methodology instead of (relational, direct)?

4. Program Design: Why have you chosen to partition system functions into this particular set of modules? Why not use other optimization techniques for data processing? Why have you selected this programming language?

Left-Right Brain Alternations Technique

The objective is to use a whole-brain approach to attack a problem or examine an opportunity. By focusing upon the different functions performed by each hemisphere of the brain, a more complete, or holistic, solution is attained.

Procedure for Use

The checklist is used to remind us of the different functions performed by each hemisphere of the brain.

Left brain functions	Right brain functions
speaking	awareness without description
reading	seeing whole things at once
writing	recognizing similarities
analyzing	understanding analogies and metaphors
idea-linking	intuition
abstracting	insight
categorizing	gut-level feeling
logic	synthesizing
reasoning	visualizing
judgment	spatial perception
counting and mathematical ability	visual memory
verbal memory	recognizing patterns
using symbols	"feeling" our way
managing time	relating things to the present

Example of Use

A common problem in project management is a plan's failure to meet the desired schedule, either at the initiation of the project or during the course of managing the project.

The problem is explored by alternatively choosing possible solutions from the left brain and the right brain.

Left brain activity	Right brain activity
List the factors that cause the schedule to be overrun.	Obtain team members' feelings, attitudes about the schedule.
Assign team to learn other persons' tasks in order to have backup when people are absent.	Ask team about their willingness to learn other persons' tasks.
Reevaluate the requirements in order to eliminate functions or to delay them to Phase II.	Reevaluate the clients and why they might want certain functions in the system.

Left brain activity	Right brain activity
Analyze the activities on the schedule to see which might be arranged.	Use an analogy of a very different project to see if new ideas for simplifying work might apply (*e.g.*, a chef preparing a many-course meal for a large group).
Think of approaches used on past projects to convince management to increase funding for the project.	Visualize the system in operation to identify benefits that will justify an increase in funding.
Recompute all the time estimates to make sure schedule was calculated correctly.	Hunt for patterns that indicate most promising activities to work on to reduce the time to complete.

Lotus Blossom Technique

The Japanese have developed several creativity techniques that are based on cultural or religious traditions. The lotus blossom is a much-revered flower. Using this approach the petals around the core of the blossom are "peeled back" one at a time, revealing a key component or subidea. This approach is pursued in ever-widening circles until the problem or opportunity is comprehensively explored. The technique utilizes a form that has a core square surrounded with eight circles. This center area is in turn surrounded by eight squares, each containing the core and eight circles.

Example of Use

An example of use is the strategic planning for information systems, where the core issue is "assumptions that tend to constrain our view of the future." The petals represent the categories of assumptions that need to be investigated, such as technology, software, people, and policy constraints. Each of these subject areas then becomes the core of the flower, with petals peeled to reveal subcategories.

For example, in planning for an information systems organization, the software category might have the following assumptions that need to be examined: stay with COBOL as a standard, object oriented programming is too undefined at this point in time, CASEtools are limited to analysis and design and not yet satisfactory in the automatic code generation activity, the present programming standards will continue to be appropriate, packages will be used whenever possible instead of the information systems organization developing applications, users will be able to use fourth-generation languages, etc.

Manipulative Verbs Technique

A checklist generates ideas by taking a verb from the list and "checking" the item against certain aspects of the problem. The comprehensive list of verbs helps reduce the possibility that a solution might be overlooked. You sequentially move through the following list of verbs to suggest possible solutions to the problem.

multiply	distort	fluff up	extrude
divide	rotate	bypass	repel
eliminate	flatten	add	protect
subdue	squeeze	subtract	segregate
invert	complement	lighten	integrate
separate	submerge	repeat	symbolize
transpose	freeze	thicken	abstract
unify	soften	stretch	dissect

Example of Use

A common problem in project management is a plan's failure to meet the desired schedule, either at the initiation of the project or during the course of managing the project.

Approaches to rearrange resources to meet the scheduled date for an information systems development project:

Multiply	Increase the number of personnel Increase the amount of project budget Increase the tools
Eliminate	Eliminate some of the functionality of the system
Subdue	Simplify the design Lower management expectations
Invert	Prototype to test early instead of at end
Separate	Critical from noncritical activities
Unify	Combine modules
Distort	Worst-scenario formulation

Rotate	Personnel
Squeeze	Schedule Resources Requirements
Complement	People skills with computer skills
Submerge	Egos Distractions Less important problems
Freeze	Specifications Personnel (disallow transfers to other projects)

Morphological Forced Connections Technique

A three-dimensional box is used to think of the combining parameters of a problem or opportunity. Examples of parameters are characteristics, variables, or factors. The forced-relationship aspect is the requirement to separate the problem/opportunity into major dimensions, then subdivide into different forms of the dimensions.

Procedure for Use

1. List the attributes of the problem or opportunity.
2. Record below each attribute as many alternates as possible.
3. Make random selections of the alternates, picking a different one from each column to assemble the combinations into entirely new forms.

Example of Use

In designing an information architecture for an organization, the designers have a huge variety of alternatives from which to choose. They could set up a three-dimensional model of the task, on which one dimension was capacity, a second was speed, and a third was flexibility. Each of these dimensions would then be subdivided into as many attributes as possible. By making random selection among attributes, the designers could then assess the resulting capability of the new combination. Usually, the process of evaluating the combination triggers ways to combine other attributes to achieve a solution that would not have been considered under a normal analytical approach to an information architecture.

Nominal Group Technique

Whenever a problem or opportunity involves a new, relatively uncharted scope of activity, it is often useful to use a group technique such as the nominal group technique to generate as many ideas as possible. The philosophy is that ideas beget more ideas, that the process of sharing ideas stimulates additional ideas.

This technique utilizes the positive features of both brainstorming and brainwriting. There is silent generation of ideas in writing, round-robin recording of ideas, serial discussion for clarification, then subsequent rounds of writing. Using this approach, the inhibiting factors of both brainstorming and brainwriting are reduced, while retaining public sharing of ideas to stimulate new ideas.

Procedure for Use

1. Generate ideas silently in writing,
2. Record ideas in a round-robin fashion, or stack sheets in center of room for anonymous listing,
3. Discuss ideas in turn for clarification and stimulation of other ideas,
4. Conduct subsequent rounds of writing and sharing.

Example of Use

Management may be trying to develop a new policy, such as ways to empower employees in order to attain greater levels of commitment to the organization. Nominal group technique provides a way to get everyone to participate. Since all ideas are written down, idea generation time is not dominated by one or more persons. The ideas then can be listed through round-robin sharing, or anonymously shared if a sensitive topic is involved. Other examples are ways to get employees to avoid littering or to improve communication or to contribute to local charities.

Group idea generation is useful for spreading decision making or allowing employees to have a say in adopting new procedures or policies.

Peaceful Setting Technique

The objective of the peaceful setting technique is to enable people to mentally remove themselves from present surroundings so that they have access to a less cluttered, more open mental process. The goal is to try to eliminate the constraints of the normal work environment that impede full use of their native creative ability. By trying to utilize all five senses in this setting (taste, touch, smell, sight, and hearing), they can more easily call on their sixth sense, intuition.

Example of Use

If you cannot shut the door and put the phone on recording position, go to another location where you are less likely to be disturbed (such as the company library, a conference room, or an unoccupied office). Now, close your eyes. Get comfortable. Picture yourself on a deserted beach on a beautiful desert island. Try to experience all five senses in this setting: taste, touch, smell, sight, and hearing.

- Think for a few moments about the things you enjoy in your work.
- Think about the people who are a pleasure to work with.
- Think about the parts of the job itself that are enjoyable, that give you a sense of satisfaction.
- Think about the environment, the things the company has done to make your work more enjoyable.

Next, try to channel your creative process into ways to improve a problem that all employees face.

- Think of someone that you don't get along with very well, not a manager, but a peer—an individual in your work unit or outside your unit—that you have problems with.

  It is not reasonable to expect to come up with an approach that will cause that person to begin to like you. But it **is** practical to come up with an approach that will neutralize the problem and enable you to communicate with that person without feeling stressed or angered.

- Think of something you might say to the person to show him or her that you are taking the first step to an improved relationship.

  — A smile when you meet the person in the hall or at the start of a meeting.

  — Compliment the person when she or he does something well.

— If you have been openly critical of the person, try to eliminate any personal element of criticism, perhaps apologizing if you think it was received as criticism of the person rather than the idea.

— Think of something you might do for the person that would show you want an improved relationship.

— Offer to help in a work assignment.

— Offer to intercede when you have rapport with a person he/she needs help from.

— Do something helpful for them that they did not ask for or expect.

Problem Reversal Technique

One creativity technique that you may find helpful when you are trying to analyze a situation is called the "problem or situation reversal" technique. This technique is particularly valuable for defining a problem in more solvable terms and for finding solutions to everyday problems.

Procedure for Use

We use the following steps in this approach:

1. Write down the problem statement in a question form.
2. Identify the verb, or "action" content, of the statement.
3. Reverse the meaning of the verb or action content and restate the problem in question form.
4. List answers to the reversed problem statement.
5. Reverse the answers you stated in Step 4.

Example of Use

The following example applies the technique following Steps 1 through 5 above.

1. I am always busy, but I don't seem to get the important things done.
2. What can I do to focus my attention on the most important things at work?
3. What can I do to focus my attention on the least important things at work?
4. Just do whatever comes up first when I get to work.

   Always respond to what is requested as soon as I receive a phone call.

   Do the things that are easiest to accomplish.

   Do the things that are my favorite things to do.
5. List and prioritize what I really need to get done.

Use this list as a guide to doing my job.

Progressive Abstraction Technique

The progressive abstraction technique starts with a basic problem description then moves progressively through higher levels of abstraction until a satisfactory definition is achieved. When a problem is systematically enlarged in this way, new definitions emerge that can be evaluated for their usefulness and feasibility. Once an appropriate level of abstraction is reached, possible solutions then can be more easily identified. The major advantage of the technique is the degree of structure provided the problem solver for systematically examining problem substructures and connections.

Example of Use

The baby boom era is past; U.S. population growth is on the decline. Fewer persons entered the workforce beginning in 1992. The second factor affecting the entry-level pool is a reduction in number of persons entering degree programs. The organization defined the problem, therefore, as one of doing a better job of attracting entry-level employees.

However, further analysis showed that the problem is really one of a shortage of professional employees, not just entry-level employees. In a scarcity environment, more personnel turnover occurs. In addition, a problem is occurring at the other end of the employment spectrum; there is an increase in early retirements. These three factors combine to cause a serious shortage of professional employees for at least the next decade.

The first level of abstraction identifies the real problem as one of a shortage of professional employees resulting from the shortage of entry-level employees. The next step is to move to even higher level of abstraction to provide a richer solution space than the original problem definition. This second level of abstraction would be defining the problem as a shortage of human capacity, not just one of headcount. The shortage can be counteracted by increasing productivity. Seven additional solution possibilities emerge: improving motivation, outsourcing, simplifying processes, providing new tools/technologies, improving creativity, automating, and avoiding turnover of higher performers. By moving up two levels of abstraction, the solution space was increased from 3 to 15 approaches.

Wildest Idea Technique

The approach in the use of the wildest idea technique is to move people out of their normal problem-solving modes, which are usually quite conservative, by asking them to try to come up with a "wild" idea. An example was the discovery of radar, which was developed from the bizarre suggestion of a radio "death-ray" for shooting down planes. Instead of rejecting the idea, someone used it as a stepping stone to the concept of radar.

The approach is most useful when an impasse has been reached in problem solving or opportunity identification. Participants need to be jogged out of their mind-set by considering things so remote or unusual that they change their normal frame of reference or paradigm paralysis. It takes a while to get a group into the swing of generating wild ideas. Most of the ideas are impractical, but eventually a useful one emerges. It is usually one that couldn't be produced by one of the more conservative techniques.

Procedure for Use

1. The facilitator selects the first wild idea as a starting point and asks the group to build on the idea.
2. The group continues to explore variations or extrapolations of the wild idea.
3. Then the facilitator asks the group to try to find practical uses of the wild idea.
4. If the results do not meet the problem resolution requirements, the process is repeated on another idea. If no practical ideas emerge, another wild idea is used and the process continues until an acceptable idea is found. This is an important technique because it produces a surge of ideas that are often highly cost-effective.

Example of Use

The technique will be illustrated on another facet of our continuing illustrative problem of shortage of entry-level people.

Problem: An inadequate pool of candidates for entry-level positions over the next decade

Wild Idea: Use the National Football League draft approach

Consider college and university degree programs to be like athletic programs, as a source of candidates to draft.

Use of Scouts

Professors—select key professors on each campus, ones who really understand the industry work environment and can identify the best "athletes," not just the high GPA students.

Campus Facilities Directors—students are often hired by various facilities such as the library, cafeteria, and computer center. Directors of these organizations are good sources on students' work habits, ability to apply knowledge, cognitive ability, attitude, and communication skills.

Recent Graduates Who Are Your Employees—These people know the "behind-the-scene" activities and abilities of students with whom they studied and interacted.

Develop Compensation Package

In the National Football League, management teams develop an integrated package of compensation and playing assignment arrangements. Prospects know their short-term and long-term compensation possibilities. They also know which playing positions they are being groomed for and what coaches (management) will do to help them prepare for successful careers. Do the same for students being considered for industry jobs.

Wishful Thinking Technique

Applied properly, this approach can free you from unnecessary but unrecognized assumptions that you are making about the scenario of concern.

Procedure for Use

Generally, the steps to follow in applying the technique are as follows:

1. State the question, goal, situation, or problem.

2. Assume anything is possible.

3. Using fantasy, make statements such as: "What I really want to do is ..." or "If I could choose any answer to this question, it would be ...."

4. Examine each fantasy statement and, using it as stimulation, return to reality and make statements such as: "Although I really cannot do that, I can do this by..." or "It seems impractical to do that, but I believe we can accomplish the same thing by...."

5. If necessary, repeat Steps 3 and 4.

Example of Use

1. How can I learn more about how customers use my product?

2. I can be any size or shape I want.

3. I will just step inside one of the products shipped today and peer out at my customer and observe how he or she uses the product.

4. Well, I don't think I can accomplish that feat, but I can get a customer's agreement to let me observe my product under use at his or her facility and videotape employees at work using my product.

References

Introduction

1. Rothenberg, A., and C.R. Hausman, *The Creativity Question*, Durham, NC: Duke University Press, 1976.

2. Berlyn, D., *Conflict, Arousal and Curiosity*, New York: McGraw-Hill, 1960.

3. Kanter, R.M., "Change-Master Skills: What It Takes To Be Creative," in *Handbook for Creative and Innovative Managers*, New York: McGraw-Hill, 1988, pp. 91–99.

4. Geis, G.T., "Making Companies Creative," in *Handbook for Creative and Innovative Managers*, New York: McGraw-Hill, 1988, pp. 25–33.

5. Zaleznick, A., "Making Managers Creative: The Psychodynamics of Creativity and Innovation," in *Handbook for Creative and Innovative Managers*, New York: McGraw-Hill, 1988, pp. 35–41.

6. Rhodes, M., "An Analysis of Creativity," *Phi Delta Kappan*, Vol. 42, 1961, pp. 305–310.

Chapter 1

1. Adams, J.L., *Conceptual Blockbusting*, Reading, MA: Addison-Wesley, 1986, p. 10.

2. Ibid.

3. Ibid.

4. de Bono, E., *Teaching Thinking*, New York: Penguin Books, 1976, p. 14.

5. Parnes, S.J., "The Creative Studies Project," in S.G. Isaksen, (ed.), *Frontiers of Creative Research*, Buffalo, NY: Bearley Ltd., 1987, p. 156.

6. Torrance, E.P., "Teaching for Creativity," in Isaksen, S.G. (ed.), *Frontiers of Creative Research*, Buffalo, NY: Bearley Ltd., 1987, p. 191.

7. Davis, G.A., *Creativity Is Forever*, Dubuque, IA: Kendall/Hunt Publishing Co., 1983, p. 202.

8. Bruner, J.S., *Toward a Theory of Instruction*, New York: Norton, 1968.

9. Miller, W. C., *The Creative Edge*, Reading, MA: Addison-Wesley, 1987, p. xvii.

10. Ciardi, J., "What Every Writer Must Learn," *Saturday Review*, Dec. 15, 1956, p. 7.

11. Poincaré, H., quoted in Bruner, p. 59.

12. Freud, S., quoted in Kneller, G. F., *The Art and Science of Creativity*, New York: Holt, Rinehart and Winston, 1967, p. 21.

13. Newell, A., J.C. Shaw, and H.A. Simon, "The process of creative thinking," in Gruber, H.E., G. Terrell, and M. Wertheimer, *Contemporary Approaches to Creative Thinking*, New York: Atherton Press, 1962, pp. 65–66.

14. Hall, A.R., and H.A.F. Smith, "Invention," *The Encyclopedia Americana*, Danbury, CT: Grolier, Inc., 1987, p. 326.

15. Rickards, T., *Stimulating Innovation: A Systems Approach*, New York: St. Martin's Press, 1985, p. 10.

16. Kingston, W., quoted in Rickards, p. 11.

17. Westwood, A.R.C., and Y. Sekine, "Fostering Creativity and Innovation in an Industrial R&D Laboratory," *Research-Technology Management*, July–August, 1988, p. 16.

18. Kuratko, D.F., and R.M. Hodgetts, *Entrepreneurship: A Contemporary Approach*, Chicago: The Dryden Press, 1989, p. 51.

19. Lamb, D., *Discovery, Creativity and Problem-Solving*, Brookfield, VT: Gower Publishing Co., 1991, p. 117.

20. Weisberg, R., *Creativity: Genius and Other Myths*, New York: W.H. Freeman and Co., 1986, pp. 1–3, 12.

21. Clark, C.C., *Idea Management: How to Motivate Creativity and Innovation*, New York: Amacom, 1990, p. 14.

22. Simon, H.A., *Models of Discovery*, Germany: D. Reidel, Dordrecht, 1977.

23. Hall and Smith, "Invention," p. 325.

24. Brown, K.A., *Inventors at Work*, Redmond, WA: Tempus, 1988.

25. Koestler, *The Act of Creation*, New York: Macmillan, 1964.

26. Nayak, P.R. and J.M. Ketteringham, *Breakthroughs*, New York: Rawson Associates, 1986.

27. Ibid.

28. Kidder, T., *The Soul of a New Machine*, Boston: Little Brown, 1981.

29. Raudseep, E., *How Creative Are You?*, New York: Perigee Books, 1981, p. 13.

30. Kiplinger, K., "Beyond 1987," *Changing Times*, 1987.

31. Ruggiero, V.R., *The Art of Thinking*, New York: Harper Collins Publishers, 1991, p. 98.

32. Holmes, F.L., reported in *Notebooks of the Mind*, by John-Steiner, V., Albuquerque, NM: University of New Mexico Press, 1985, pp. 214–15.

Chapter 2

1. Fehrman, C., *Poetic Creation: Inspiration or Craft*, Minneapolis: University of Minnesota Press, 1980, p. 173.

2. Schneider, E., *Coleridge, Opium, and Kubla Khan*, Chicago: University of Chicago Press, 1953, p. 24.

3. Bowra, J., *Inspiration and Poetry*, Cambridge: Cambridge University Press, 1955, p. 3.

4. Pound, E., in *Writers at Work*, Second Series, New York: Viking Press, 1965, p. 39.

5. Harrison, J.A., *The Complete Works of Edgar Allan Poe*, New York: Crowell, 1902, p. 195.

6. Fehrman, *Poetic Creation*, p. 167.

7. Spender, S., *The Making of a Poem*, (1946), reprinted in *Criticism, the Foundations of Modern Literary Judgment*, eds. Schorer, M., J. Miles, G. McKenzie, New York: Harcourt Brace, 1948, p. 189.

8. Bahle, J., "Zur Psychologie des Einfalls und der Inspiration im Musikalischen Schaffen," *Act Psychologica*, The Hague, Netherlands: No. 1, 1936, pp. 7–29.

9. Bahle, "Zur Psychologie," p. 13.

10. Bahle, "Zur Psychologie," p. 12.

11. Ibid.

12. Fehrman, *Poetic Creation*, pp. 173, 188.

13. Simon, H.A., "Understanding Creativity and Creative Management," *Handbook for Creative and Innovative Managers*, Kuhn, R.L. (ed.), New York, 1988, p. 23.

14. Arnold, J.E., "Useful Creativity Techniques," in Parnes (ed.), *Sourcebook for Creative Thinking*, New York: Charles Scribner's Sons, 1962, p. 252.

15. Davis, G.A., *Creativity Is Forever*, Dubuque, IA: Kendall/Hunt Publishing Co., 1983, p. 83.

16. de Bono, E., *Lateral Thinking: Creativity Step by Step*, New York: Harper and Row, 1970.

17. Brightman, H.J., *Group Problem Solving: An Improved Managerial Approach*, Atlanta: Business Publishing Division, Georgia State University, 1988; and Simon, H.A., *The New Science of Management Decision*, Englewood Cliffs, NJ: Prentice Hall, 1977.

18. VanGundy, A.B., Jr., *Techniques of Structured Problem Solving*, 2nd ed., New York: Van Nostrand Reinhold Co., 1988.

19. Miller, W.C., *The Creative Edge*, Reading, MA: Addison-Wesley Publishing Co., 1987, p. 66.

20. Vargiu, J., "Creativity: The Purposeful Imagination," *Synthesis*, Vol. 3, No. 4, p. 23.

21. Davis, *Creativity Is Forever*, p. 83.

22. Geschka, H., G.R. Schaude, and H. Schlicksupp, "Modern Techniques Solving Problems," *Chemical Engineering*, August 1973, pp. 91–97.

23. Kipling, R., *Just So Stories*, New York: Scribner, 1903, p. 86.

24. Lewin, K., *Field Theory in Social Science*, New York: Harper, 1951, pp. 256, 273.

25. Michalko, M., *Thinkertoys*, Berkeley, CA: Ten Speed Press, 1991, p. 232.

26. Gordon, W.J.J., *Synectics*, New York: Harper and Row, 1961.

27. VanGundy, *Techniques of Structured Problem Solving*, p. 127.

28. de Bono, *Lateral Thinking*.

29. Embler, W., *Metaphor and Meaning*, DeLand, FL: Everett/Edwards, 1966.

30. Gordon, W.J.J., and T. Poze, *Strange and Familiar*, Cambridge, MA: SES Associates, 1972.

31. Gordon, W.J.J., and T. Poze, *The New Art of the Impossible*, Cambridge, MA: Porpoise Books, 1980.

32. VanGundy, *Techniques of Structured Problem Solving*, pp. 82–83.

Chapter 3

1. Parnes, S., *The Magic of Your Mind*, Buffalo, NY: CEA and Bearley Ltd., 1981, p. 61.

2. Shallcross, D.J., *Teaching Creative Behavior*, Buffalo, NY: Bearley, Ltd., 1985, pp. 56–59.

3. Adams, J.L., *Conceptual Blockbusting,* Reading, MA: Addison-Wesley Publishing Co., 1986.

4. Ibid; Basadur, M., *Creative Problem Solving,* Ancaster, Ontario, Canada: Center for Research in Applied Creativity, 1989, p. 2.0; Raudseep, E., *How Creative Are You?,* New York: Perigee Books, 1981, p. 100–101; Shallcross, *Teaching Creative Behavior,* pp. 56–59; and Stein, M.I., *Making the Point,* Buffalo, NY: Bearley Ltd., 1984, pp. 13–14.

5. Shallcross, *Teaching Creative Behavior,* p. 58.

6. Adams, *Conceptual Blockbusting,* pp. 56–57.

7. Langer, E.J., *Mindfulness,* Reading, MA: Addison-Wesley, 1989, p. 22.

8. Bianchi, M. D., and A. L. Hampson, (eds.), *Poems by Emily Dickinson,* Boston: Little, Brown and Company, 1957, p. 45.

9. Smith, A., New York: Ballantine Books, 1975.

10. Kuhn, T.A., *The Structure of Scientific Revolutions,* Chicago: University of Chicago Press, 1970, p. 10.

11. Ibid., pp. 157–158.

12. Barker, J.A., *Future Edge,* New York: William Morrow and Co., 1992, p. 37.

13. Ibid., p. 72.

14. Ibid., p. 73.

15. Ibid., p. 35.

16. Raudseep, *How Creative Are You?,* p. 116.

17. Dacey, J. S., *Fundamentals of Creative Thinking,* New York: Lexington Books, 1989, pp. 204–205.

18. Torrance, E.P., "Can We Teach Children to Think Creatively?", *Journal of Creative Behavior,* Vol. 6, No. 2, 1972, pp. 114–143.

19. Dacey, *Fundamentals of Creative Thinking,* p. 205.

20. "Graffiti Gobbler Gets Attention," *Oneonta Star,* 30 November 1981, p. 2. "Crippled Inventor Is Standing Proud," *Oneonta Star,* February 6, 1982, p. 1.

21. Ray, M., and R. Myers, *Creativity in Business,* Garden City, NY: Doubleday & Co., Inc., 1986, p. 92.

22. Ray and Myers, *Creativity in Business,* p. 96.

23. Ray and Myers, *Creativity in Business,* p. 92.

24. Ray and Myers, *Creativity in Business,* p. 93.

25. Raudseep, *How Creative Are You?,* p. 116.

26. Raudseep, *How Creative Are You?,* p. 118.

27. Ruggiero, V.R., *The Art of Thinking,* New York: HarperCollins Publishers, Inc., 1991, p. 94.

28. Ibid., pp. 39–40.

29. Ibid.

30. Quoted in Curtis, C.P., and F. Greenslet (eds.), *The Practical Cogitator,* Boston: Houghton Mifflin, 1945, p. 231.

31. Quoted in Gordon, W.J.J., *Synectics: The Development of Creative Capacity,* New York: Harper & Brothers, 1961, p. 116.

32. Ruggiero, *The Art of Thinking,* p. 80.

33. Clark, C.C., *Idea Management: How to Motivate Creativity and Innovation,* New York: Amacom, 1990, p. 32.

34. Ibid.

35. "Mind Odyssey," *Omni,* February, 1985, p. 16.

36. Bailey, R., *Disciplined Creativity for Engineers,* Ann Arbor, MI: Ann Arbor Science, 1978, pp. 310–311.

37. Shekerjian, D., *Uncommon Genius: How Great Ideas Are Born,* New York: Viking, 1990, pp. 52, 99.

38. Miller, W., *Creativity: The Eight Master Keys to Discover, Unlock and Fulfill Your Creative Potential,* Pleasanton, CA: SyberVision Systems, Inc., 1989. The Innovation Styles® Profile can be purchased from Global Creativity Corp., 4210 Spicewood Springs, Room 205, Austin, TX 78759.

39. Ibid., pp. 45–59.

40. Ibid., p. 56.

41. Barker, *Future Edge,* p. 79.

42. Osborn, A., *Applied Imagination,* New York: Scribner's, 1957, p. 172.

43. Dacey, J.S., *Fundamentals of Creative Thinking,* NY: Lexington Books, 1989, p. 25.

44. Daniel, J., Personal notes on creativity, 1989, unpublished.

45. Tatsuno, S.M., *Created in Japan,* New York: Harper Business, 1990, p. 19.

46. Tatsuno, *Created in Japan,* p. 33.

47. Hanks, K. and J. Parry, *Wake Up Your Creative Genius,* Los Altos, CA: William Kaufmann, Inc., 1983, p. 76.

Chapter 4

1. Descartes, R., *Descartes Philosophical Writing,* translated by E.S. Haldane and G.R.T. Ross, Cambridge University Press, Cambridge, 1911, p. 14.

2. Lamb, D., *Discovery, Creativity and Problem Solving,* Alershot, UK: Gower Publishing Co., 1991, p. 3

3. Simon, H.A., *Models of Discovery,* Dordrecht, Netherlands: D. Reidel Publishing Company, 1977, p. 288.

4. Simon, H.A., *The New Science of Management,* New York: Harper and Row, 1960.

5. Kingsley, H.L. and R. Garry, *The Nature and Conditions of Learning,* Englewood Cliffs, NJ: Prentice Hall, 1957, pp. 421–422.

6. Evans, J.R., *Creative Thinking: In the Decision and Management Sciences,* Cincinnati: South-Western Publishing Co., 1991, p. 91.

7. Osborn, A., *Applied Imagination,* New York: Scribner's Sons, 1953.

8. Parnes, S.J., *Creative Behavior Guidebook,* New York: Charles Scribner's Sons, 1967.

9. Guilford, J.P., "A Revised Structure of Intellect," *Report of Psychology,* Los Angeles: University of Southern California, Vol. 19, 1957, pp. 1–63.

10. Isaksen, S.G., and D.J. Treffinger, *Creative Problem Solving: The Basic Course,* 1985, Buffalo, NY: Bearley Ltd., p. 16.

11. Tatsuno, S., *Created in Japan,* New York: HarperBusiness, 1990, p. 50.

12. Ibid., p. 51.

13. Ibid., pp. 51–52.

14. Parnes, S.J., *Visionizing,* East Aurora, NY: D.O.K. Publishers, 1988, p. 49.

15. Tatsuno, *Created in Japan,* p. 53.

16. von Oech, R., *A Kick in the Seat of the Pants,* New York: Warner Books, 1983.

17. Parnes, *Creative Behavior Guidebook,* p. 43.

18. Ibid.

19. VanGundy, A.B., Jr., *Techniques of Structured Problem Solving,* 2nd ed., New York: Van Nostrand Reinhold Co., 1988.

20. Davis, G., *Creativity Is Forever,* Dubuque, IA: Kendall/Hunt Publishing Co., 1986, p. 72–73.

21. Parnes, S.J., *The Magic of Your Mind,* Buffalo, NY: CEA and Bearley Ltd., 1981, p. 87.

22. Basadur, M., *Creative Problem Solving,* Ancaster, Ontario, Canada: Center for Research in Applied Creativity, 1989.

23. Described by D. Morrison in a July 1991 presentation at CPSI, Buffalo.

24. Isaksen and Treffinger, *Creative Problem Solving,* p. 28.

25. Nayak, P.R., and J.M. Ketteringham, *Breakthroughs,* New York: Rawson Associates, 1986, p. 17.

26. Arnold, J.E. "The Creative Engineer," *Creative Engineering,* American Society of Mechanical Engineers, pamphlet circa 1956, p. 20.

27. Parnes, S.J., *Creativity: Unlocking Human Potential,* Buffalo, NY: D.O.K. Publishers, 1972. Parnes, S.J. and R.B. Noller, *Toward Supersanity,* Buffalo, NY: D.O.K. Publishers, 1973 and *Toward Supersanity, Research Supplement,* 1974.

Chapter 5

1. de Bono, E., *Teaching Thinking,* Middlesex, UK: Penguin Books, 1976, p. 31.

2. Jay, D., *Creativity,* New York: CEA, 1991, p. 77.

3. de Bono, *Teaching Thinking,* p. 33.

4. Ibid., p. 46.

5. Ruggiero, V.R., *Beyond Feelings,* Mountain View, CA: Mayfield Publishing Co., 1990, p. xiv.

6. Ibid.

7. Kubie, L.S., *Neurotic Distortion of the Creative Process,* New York: Farrar, Straus and Giroux, 1966.

8. Ruggiero, *Beyond Feelings,* p. xiv.

9. Springer, S.P., and G. Deutsch, *Left Brain, Right Brain,* New York: W.H. Freeman and Co., 1981.

10. Ibid., p. 37.

11. Ibid., p. 4.

12. Herrmann, N., *The Creative Brain*, Lake Lure, NC: Brain Books, 1990, pp. 8, 9.

13. Ornstein, R., "The Split and Whole Brain," *Human Nature*, 1978, No. 1, p. 79.

14. Ruggiero, *Beyond Feelings*, pp. 13–14.

15. Fabian, J., *Creative Thinking and Problem Solving*, Chelsea, MI: Lewis Publishers, Inc., 1990, p. 39.

16. Ibid.

17. Miller, G.A., "The Magical Number Seven, Plus or Minus Two: Some Limits on Our Capacity for Processing Information," *Psychological Review*, Vol. 63, 1956, pp. 81–97.

18. Craik, F.I., and E. Tulving, "Depth of Processing and the Retention of Words," *Journal of Experimental Psychology: General*, Vol. 104, 1975, pp. 268–284.

19. Walker, A.C., *Psychology and Problem Solving*, Pittsburgh: 1981, pp. 2, 5.

20. Ibid., p. 5.

21. Hayes, J.R., *The Complete Problem Solver*, Hillsdale, NJ: Lawrence Erlbaum Associates, Publishers, 1989.

22. Sperling, G., "The Information Available in Brief Visual Presentations," *Psychological Monographs*, Vol. 74, No. 498, 1960; and Darwin, C.T., M.T. Turvey, and R.G. Crowder, "An Auditory Analogue of the Sperling Partial Report Procedure: Evidence for Brief Auditory Storage," *Cognitive Psychology*, Vol. 3, 1972, pp. 255–267.

23. Klatzky, R.L., *Human Memory: Structures and Processes*, San Francisco: W.H. Freeman, 1975.

24. Hayes, *The Complete Problem Solver*, p. 121.

25. Adams, J.L., *Care and Feeding of Ideas*, Reading, MA: Addison-Wesley, 1986, pp. 31–32.

26. Bettman, J.R., *An Information Processing Theory of Consumer Choice*, Reading, MA: Addison-Wesley Publishing Co., 1979, pp. 143–147.

27. Clemmons, J., *The Art of Creative Thinking*, Philadelphia, PA: 1988, Section C.

28. Ruggiero, V.R., *The Art of Thinking*, New York: HarperCollins Publishers, 1991, p. 9.

29. Dewey, J., *How We Think*, Lexington, MA: D.C. Heath, 1933, pp. 88–90.

30. Adams, *Care and Feeding of Ideas*, p. 73.

31. Ibid., p. 74.

32. Ibid.

33. Glasman, N., R. Koff, and H. Spiers, *Review of Educational Research*, 54, 1984, pp. 461–471; Doyle, W., "Paradigms for Research on Teacher Effectiveness," in Shulman, L. (ed.), *Review of Research in Education*, Vol. 5., Itasca, IL: 1977, pp. 163–198; and Costa, A., *Teaching For Intelligent Behavior*, cited in Grant, p. 34.

34. Grant, G.E., *Teaching Critical Thinking*, New York: Praeger, 1988, p. 35; and Keating, D., "Four Faces of Creativity: The Continuing Plight of the Intellectually Underserved," *Gifted Child Quarterly*, Vol. 24, 1980, pp. 56–61.

35. Ibid., p. 34.

36. Beardsley, M.C., *Thinking Straight*, Englewood Cliffs, NJ: 1966, p. 3.

37. Jay, D., p. 87.

38. de Bono, p. 75.

39. Ruggiero, *Beyond Feelings*, Mountainview, CA: Mayfield, 1990, pp. 112–113.

40. Duncker, K., *On Problem-Solving*, Westport, CT: Greenwood, 1945.

41. Adamson, R.E., "Functional Fixedness as Related to Problem Solving," *Journal of Experimental Psychology*, 44, 1952, pp. 281–291.

42. Torrance, E.P., *Torrance Tests of Creative Thinking*, Chicago: University of Chicago Press, 1984, p. 3.

43. Guilford, J.P., *The Nature of Human Intelligence*, New York: McGraw-Hill, 1967.

44. Davis, G.A. "Testing for Creative Potential," *Contemporary Educational Psychology*, Vol. 14, pp. 257–274.

45. Mayer, R.E., *Thinking, Problem Solving, Cognition*, New York: W.H. Freeman and Co., 1992, pp. 361–362.

46. Ibid., p. 361

47. Chance, P., *Thinking in the Classroom: A Survey of Programs*, New York: Teachers College Press, 1986, p. 133.

48. Polya, G., *Mathematical Discovery, Vol II. On Understanding, Learning and Teaching Problem Solving*, New York: Wiley, 1965, p. ix.

49. John-Steiner, V., *Notebooks of the Mind: Explorations of Thinking*, Albuquerque, NM: University of New Mexico Press, 1985, p.7.

50. Rothenberg, A., and C.R. Hausman, *The Creativity Question*, Durham, NC: Duke University Press, 1976, pp. 311–327.

51. Springer and Deutsch, *Left Brain, Right Brain*, p. 184.

52. Latting, J.E., "Creative Problem-Solving Technique," *The 1985 Annual: Developing Human Resources*, Los Angeles, CA: University Associates, 1985, pp. 163–168.

53. Ornstein, R., *The Psychology of Consciousness*, New York: Harcourt Brace Jovanovich, 1977.

54. Bloom, B.S. and L.J. Broder, *Problem-Solving Processes of College Students: An Exploratory Investigation*, Chicago: University of Chicago Press, 1950, p. 67.

55. Mayer, *Thinking, Problem Solving, Cognition*, p. 363.

56. Parnes, S.J., *Visionizing*, East Aurora, NY: D.O.K. Publishers, 1988, p. 62.

57. Nadel, L., *Sixth Sense*, New York: Prentice Hall Press, 1990, p. 208.

58. Adams, *Care and Feeding of Ideas*, p. 82.

59. Gates, A.I., "Recitation as a Factor in Memorizing," *Archives of Psychology*, Vol. 40, 1917.

60. Michalko, M., *Thinkertoys*, Berkeley, CA: Ten Speed Press, 1991, p. xii.

61. Hanna, E.B., *The Whitechapel Horrors*, New York: Carrol and Graf Publishers, Inc., 1992, pp. 20–23.

Chapter 6

1. Einstein, A., and Infeld, 1938, p. 95.

2. Lyles, M.A., and I.I. Mitroff, "Organizational Problem Formulation," *Administrative Science Quarterly*, Vol. 25, 1980, p. 102.

3. Senge, P.M., *The Fifth Discipline*, New York: Doubleday/Currency, 1990, p. 283.

4. Parnes, S.J., *Visionizing*, East Aurora, NY: D.O.K. Publishers, 1988, p. 16.

5. Brightman, H.J., *Group Problem Solving: An Improved Managerial Approach*, Atlanta: Business Publishing Division, Georgia State University, 1988.

6. Newell, A., and H.A. Simon, *Human Problem Solving*, Englewood Cliffs, NJ: Prentice-Hall, 1972.

7. Ackoff, R.L., "Beyond Problem Solving," *Decision Sciences*, Vol. 5, No. 2, pp. x–xv.

8. Eden, C., "Problem Construction and the Influence of OR," *Interfaces*, Vol. 12, No. 2, pp. 55–60.

9. Evans, J.R., *Creative Thinking in the Decision and Management Sciences*, Cincinnati: South-Western Publishing Co., 1991.

10. Cowan, D.A., "Developing a Process Model of Problem Recognition," *Academy of Management Review*, Vol. 11, No. 4, 1986, pp. 763–776.

11. VanGundy, A.B., Jr., *Techniques of Structure Problem Solving*, Van Nostrand Reinhold Co., Ltd., 1988, pp. 51–53.

12. Evans, *Creative Thinking in the Decision and Management Sciences*, p. 104.

13. Senge, *The Fifth Discipline*, pp. 244–245.

14. Fabian, J., *Creative Thinking and Problem Solving*, Chelsea, MI: Lewis Publishers, Inc., 1990, p. 86.

15. Getzels, J.W., "Creative Thinking, Problem Solving and Instruction," in Hilgard, E.R. (ed.), *Theories of Learning and Instruction*, Sixty-Third Yearbook of the National Society for the Study of Education, Part I, Chicago: University of Chicago Press, 1964.

16. Herron, M.D., "The Nature of Scientific Inquiry," *School Review*, Vol. 79, 1971, pp. 171–212.

17. Thelen, H.A., *Education and the Human Quest*, Chicago: University of Chicago Press, 1972.

18. Guilford, J.P., *The Nature of Human Intelligence*, New York: McGraw-Hill, 1967.

19. Dacey, J.S., *Fundamentals of Creative Thinking*, New York: Lexington Books, 1989, pp. 111–113.

Chapter 7

1. Isaksen, S.G., and D.J. Treffinger, *Creative Problem Solving*, Buffalo, NY: Bearley, Ltd., 1985, p. 45.

2. Raudseep, E., *How Creative Are You?*, New York: Perigree Books, 1981, pp. 133–134.

3. Ibid.

4. Ibid.

5. Ibid.

6. de Bono, E., *Teaching Thinking,* London: Penguin Books, 1976. p. 84.

7. Evans, J.R., *Creative Thinking,* Cincinnati: South-Western Publishing Co., 1991, pp. 99–100.

8. Ruggiero, V.R., *The Art of Thinking: A Guide to Critical and Creative Thought,* New York: HarperCollins Publishers, 1991, p. 110.

9. Kepner, C.H., and B.B. Tregoe, *The Rational Manager,* New York: McGraw-Hill, 1965.

10. Morrison, D., *Creative Problem Solving,* Dallas: Involvement Systems Inc., 1991.

11. Ibid.

12. Isaksen and Treffinger, *Creative Problem Solving,* p. 44.

13. Ray, M., and R. Myers, *Creativity in Business,* Garden City, NY: Doubleday and Co., Inc., 1986, p. 102.

14. Ibid., p. 106.

15. Ruggiero, V.R., *Beyond Feelings,* Mountain View, CA: Mayfield Publishing Co., 1990, pp. 30–31.

16. Ibid., p. 30.

17. Ibid., p. 33.

18. Ibid., p. 31.

19. Ibid.

20. Michalko, M., *Thinkertoys,* Berkeley, CA: Ten Speed Press, 1991, p. 25.

21. Ibid., pp. 197–198.

22. Tatsuno, S., *Created in Japan,* New York: HarperBusiness, 1990, pp. 110–113.

23. Ruggiero, *The Art of Thinking,* p. 97.

24. Interview in *Inc.,* December 1985, pp. 33ff.

25. Michalko, *Thinkertoys,* p. 132.

26. Ibid., p. 25.

27. Ibid.

28. Couger, J.D., "New Challenges in Motivating MIS Personnel," *Journal of Information Systems Management,* No. 4, Fall, 1989, pp. 36–41.

29. Fabian, J., *Creative Thinking and Problem Solving,* Chelsea, MI: Lewis Publishers, Inc., 1990, p. 86.

30. Kilmann, R., *Beyond the Quick Fix,* 1984, p. 50.

31. Ruggiero, *Beyond Feelings,* p. 24.

32. de Bono, *Teaching Thinking,* p. 34.

33. Ibid., p. 75.

Chapter 8

1. Ackoff, R.L., *Art of Problem Solving,* New York: Wiley and Sons, 1978, pp. 3–9.

2. Wallas, G., *The Art of Thought,* New York: Harcourt, Brace and World, 1926.

3. Raudseep, E., *How Creative Are You?,* New York: Perigree Books, 1981, p. 126.

4. Kneller, G., *The Art and Science of Creativity,* New York: Holt, Rinehart and Winston, 1967, p. 49.

5. Henle, M., "The Birth and Death of Ideas," in Gruber, H.E., G. Terrell and M. Wertheimer (eds.), *Contemporary Approaches to Creative Thinking,* New York: Atherton Press, 1962, p. 43.

6. LeBoeuf, M., *Imagineering,* New York: Berkeley Books, 1980, p. 53.

7. Hadamarad, J., *The Psychology of Invention in the Mathematical Field,* New York: Dover, 1954, p. 14.

8. Raudseep, *How Creative Are You?,* p. 148.

9. Ibid.

10. Michalko, M., *Thinkertoys,* Berkeley, CA: Ten Speed Press, 1991, p. 208.

11. Ibid., p. 225.

12. Raudseep, *How Creative Are You?,* p. 148.

13. Ibid., p. 149.

14. Parnes, S.J., *Visionizing,* East Aurora, NY: D.O.K. Publishers, 1988, p. 8.

15. Ibid., p. 42.

16. Michalko, *Thinkertoys,* p. 208.

17. Rosner, S., and L.E. Abt, *Essays in Creativity,* Croton-On-Hudson, NY: North River Press, 1974.

18. Kneller, *The Art and Science of Creativity,* p. 49.

19. Murphy, G., *Personality,* New York: Harper and Row, 1947.

20. Hadamarad, *The Psychology of Invention,* pp. 142–143.

21. Rosner and Abt, *Essays,* p. 196.

22. Poincaré, H., *Science and Mind,* New York: Dover, 1952.

23. Davis, G.A., *Creativity Is Forever,* Dubuque, IA: Kendall/Hunt, 1983, p. 114.

24. Raudseep, *How Creative Are You?,* p. 125.

25. Ibid., p. 127.

26. Guest, E.A., *The Path to Home,* Chicago: Contemporary Books, Inc., circa 1936.

27. Fry, W., *Woman's Day,* March 16, 1992, p. 11.

28. Koestler, A., *The Act of Creation,* New York: The Macmillan Co., 1966, p. 28.

29. Ibid., p. 29.

30. Swindoll, C.R., *Laugh Again,* Dallas: Word Publishing, 1992, p. 20.

31. Peters, L. and B. Dana, *The Laughter Prescription,* New York: Ballantine Books, 1987, p. 8.

32. Swindoll, *Laugh Again,* p. 103.

33. Koestler, *The Act of Creation,* p. 32.

34. Arnold, J.E., "The Creative Engineer," *Creative Engineering,* American Society of Mechanical Engineers, pamphlet circa 1956, p. 20.

35. "Are You Creative?," *Business Week,* Sept. 30, 1985, p. 80.

36. Delbecq, A.L., A.H. Van de Ven, and D.H. Gustafson, *Group Techniques for Program Planning,* Glenview, IL: Scott, Foresman, 1975.

37. Evans, P., and G. Deeham, *The Keys to Creativity,* London: Grafton Books, 1988, p. 143.

38. Osborn, A.F., *Applied Imagination: Principles and Procedures of Creative Problem Solving,* New York: Scribners, 1963.

39. Miller, W.C., *The Creative Edge,* Reading, MA: Addison-Wesley Publishing Co., 1987, pp. 87–88.

40. Parnes, *Visionizing,* p. 26.

41. Evans, J.R., *Creative Thinking,* Cincinnati: South-Western Publishing Co., 1991, pp. 70.

42. Comments made in tutorial session at the National Creative Problem Solving Institute in Buffalo, NY, July 1991.

43. Davis, *Creativity Is Forever,* p. 108.

44. VanGundy, A.B., Jr., *Techniques of Structured Problem Solving,* New York: Van Nostrand Reinhold Co., Inc., 1988, p. 72.

45. Yukawa, H., *Creativity and Intuition,* Tokyo: Kodansha International Ltd., 1973, p. 59.

46. Lamb, D., *Discovery, Creativity and Problem-Solving,* Aldershot, UK: Avebury Academic Publishing Group, 1991, p. 128.

47. Goodman, N., and C.Z. Elgin, *Reconceptions in Philosophy and Other Arts and Sciences,* Routledge, London, 1988.

48. Leatherdale, W.H., *The Role of Analogy Model and Metaphor in Science,* Amsterdam: North Holland Publishing Co., 1974, p. 13.

49. Boyle, R., *The Works of the Honorable Robert,* (Ed.), London: T. Birch, 1772, v. 163.

50. Michalko, *Thinkertoys,* p. 232.

51. Ibid., p. 247.

52. Ibid.

53. Ibid., p. 46.

54. Fabian, J., *Creative Thinking and Problem Solving,* Chelsea, MI: Lewis Publishers, Inc., 1990, pp. 144–145.

55. Ruggiero, V.R., *The Art of Thinking: A Guide to Critical and Creative Thought,* New York: HarperCollins Publishers, 1991, p. 82.

56. Dacey, J.S., *Fundamentals of Creative Thinking,* Lexington, MA: Lexington Books, 1989, p. 124.

57. Glassman, E., *Creativity on the Job,* Chapel Hill, NC: Glassman, 1987, pp. 11–17.

58. Tatsuno, S.M., *Created in Japan,* New York: HarperBusiness, 1990, pp. 16–17.

59. Ibid., p. 17.

60. Raudseep, *How Creative Are You?,* p. 125.

61. Ibid.

62. Fabian, *Creative Thinking,* p. 135.

63. Thornburg, T.H., "Group Size and Member Diversity Influence on Creative Performance," *The Journal of Creative Behavior,* Vol. 25, No. 4, 1991, pp. 324–333.

64. John-Steiner, V., *Notebooks of the Mind,* Albuquerque, NM: University of New Mexico Press, 1985, p. 209.

Chapter 9

1.   Adams, J.L., *The Care and Feeding of Ideas,* Reading, MA: Addison-Wesley Publishing Co., 1986., pp. 191–192.

2.   Fabian, J., *Creative Thinking and Problem Solving,* Chelsea, MI: Lewis Publishers, Inc., 1990, p. 176.

3.   Isaksen, S.G., and D.J. Treffinger, *Creative Problem Solving: The Basic Course,* Buffalo, NY: Bearley Ltd., 1985, p. 117.

4.   Ibid.

5.   Evans, J.R., *Creative Thinking,* Cincinnati: South-Western Publishing Co., 1991, p. 110.

6.   Fabian, *Creative Thinking and Problem Solving,* p. 117

7.   Senge, P.M., *The Fifth Discipline,* New York: Doubleday Currency, 1990, p. 247.

8.   Ibid.

9.   Bohm, D., *The Special Theory of Relativity,* New York: W.A. Benjamin, 1965.

10.   Davis, G.A., *Creativity Is Forever,* Dubuque, IA: Kendall/Hunt Publishing Co., 1986, p. 92.

11.   Ibid., p. 93.

12.   VanGundy, A.B., Jr., *Techniques of Structured Problem Solving,* New York: Van Nostrand Reinhold Co., 1988.

13.   Hamilton, H.R., "Screening Business Development Opportunities," *Business Horizons,* August 1974, pp. 13–24.

14.   O'Rourke, P.J., *The Castle Technique: How to Achieve Group Consensus in a Very Short Time with No Argument,* Lyons, CO: Steamboat Valley Press, 1984.

15.   Moore, L.B., "Creative Action — The Evaluation, Development and Use of Ideas," in Parnes, S.J., and H.F. Harding, (eds.), *A Sourcebook for Creative Thinking,* New York: Scribner, 1962, pp. 297–304.

16.   Janis, I.L., and L. Mann, *Decision Making,* New York: The Free Press, 1977.

17.   Described to A. VanGundy by H. Geschka.

18.   Taylor, C.W., "Panel Consensus Technique: A New Approach to Decision Making," *Journal of Creative Behavior,* Vol. 6, 1972, pp. 187–198.

19.   Whiting, C.S., *Creative Thinking,* New York: Van Nostrand Reinhold, 1958.

20.   Geschka, H., "Methods and Organization of Idea Generation," paper presented at Creativity Development Week II, Center for Creative Leadership, Greensboro, NC, September 1979.

21.   Couger, J.D., *Advanced System Development/Feasibility Techniques,* New York: John Wiley and Sons, 1982, p. 490.

22.   de Bono, E., *Serious Creativity,* New York: Harper Business, 1992, p. 305.

23.   Roberts, R., and A. Weiss, *The Innovation Formula,* Cambridge, MA: Ballinger Publishing Co., 1988, p. 16.

24.   Simon, H.A., *The Science of the Artificial,* Cambridge, MA: MIT Press, 1969.

25.   Brogden, H.E. and T.B. Sprecher, "Criteria of Creativity," in Taylor, E.W. (ed.), *Creativity, Progress and Potential,* New York: McGraw Hill, 1964.

26.   Besemer, S.P., and D.J. Treffinger, "Analysis of Creative Products: Review and Synthesis," *The Journal of Creative Behavior,* Nov. 15, No. 3, Third Quarter, 1981, pp. 158–178.

27.   Rothenberg, A., *The Creativity Question,* Durham, NC: Duke University Press, 1976, p. 6.

28.   Udell, G.G., M.F. O'Neill, K.G. Baker, *Guide to Invention and Innovation Evaluation,* Washington, DC: Superintendent of Documents, U.S. Government Printing Office, 1977.

29.   Stringham, E., *Outline of Patent Law and Guide to Digests,* Madison, WI: Pacot Publications, 1937, pp. 227–245.

30.   Besemer and Treffinger, "Analysis of Creative Products," p. 160.

31.   Amabile, T.M., *The Social Psychology of Creativity,* New York: Springer-Verlag, 1983.

32.   Helson, R., "Childhood Clusters Related to Creativity in Women," *Journal of Consulting Psychology,* Vol. 129, 1965, pp. 352–361; and Catell, R.B., and H.J. Butcher, *The Prediction of Achievement and Creativity,* New York: Bobbs-Merrill, 1968.

33.   Torrance, E.P., and J. Khatena, "What Kind of Person Are You?", *The Gifted Child Quarterly,* Vol. 14, pp. 71–75.

34. Taylor, W., and R. Ellison, "Predicting creative performances from multiple measures," in Taylor, C.W., ed., *Widening Horizons in Creativity,* New York: Wiley, 1964.

35. Guilford, J.P., "The Structure of Intellect," *Psychological Bulletin,* Vol. 53, 1956, pp. 267–269.

36. Torrance, E.P., *Guiding Creative Talent,* Englewood Cliffs, NJ: Prentice-Hall, 1962.

37. Rothenberg, A., "Word Association and Creativity," *Psychological Reports,* Vol. 33, 1973, pp. 3–12.

38. Amabile, *The Social Psychology of Creativity.*

39. Ghiselin, B., "Ultimate criteria for two levels of creativity," in Taylor, C., and F. Barron, eds., *Scientific Creativity: Its Recognition and Development,* New York: Wiley, 1963.

40. Simonton, D.K., "Thematic Fame and Melodic Originality in Classic Music: A Multivariate Computer-Content Analysis," *Journal of Personality,* Vol. 48, 1980, pp. 206–219.

41. Amabile, *The Social Psychology of Creativity.*

42. Sobel, R.S., and A. Rothenberg, "Artistic Creation as Stimulated by Superimposed versus Separated Visual Images," *Journal of Psychology and Social Psychology,* Vol. 39, 1980, pp. 953–961.

43. Jackson, P., and S. Messick, "The Person, the Product, and the Response: Conceptual Problems in the Assessment of Creativity," *Journal of Personality,* Vol. 33, pp. 309–329.

44. Amabile, *The Social Psychology of Creativity.*

45. Couger, J.D., "Ensuring Creative Approaches in Information System Design," *Managerial and Decision Economics,* Vol. 11, No. 5, December, 1990, pp. 281–295.

46. Higgins, L.F., J.D. Couger, and S.C. McIntyre, "Creative Marketing Approaches to Development of Marketing Information Systems," *Proceedings, Hawaii International Conference on Systems Sciences,* January 1990, pp. 398–404.

47. Smith, D.J., and K.B. Wood, *Engineering Quality Software,* London and New York: Elsevier, 1987; Vincent, J., A. Walters, and J. Sinclair, *Software Quality Assurance (Vol. 1): Practice and Implementation,* Englewood Cliffs, NJ: Prentice-Hall, 1988; and Schulmeyer, G.G., and J.I. McManus, eds., *Handbook of Software Quality Assurance,* New York: Van Nostrand Reinhold Co., 1987.

48. Arthur, J., "Software Quality Management," *Datamation,* Dec. 15, 1984.

49. Buckley, F.J., and R. Poston, "Software Quality Assurance," *IEEE Transactions on Software Engineering,* Vol. SE-10, No. 1, 1984.

50. Couger, J.D., and G. Dengate, "Measurement of Creativity of I.S. Products," *Proceedings, Hawaii International Conference on Systems Sciences,* Kona, HI: IEEE, 1992, pp. 288–298.

51. Houdeshel, G., and H.J. Watson, "The Management Information and Decision Support (MIDS) System at Lockheed-Georgia," *MIS Quarterly,* Volume 11, Number 1, March 1987, pp. 126–140.

52. Miller, W.C., *The Creative Edge,* Reading, MA: Addison-Wesley Publishing Co., 1987, p. 192.

53. Adams, *The Care and Teaching of Ideas,* pp. 192–193.

54. Fabian, *Creative Thinking and Problem Solving,* pp. 202–203.

Chapter 10

1. Michalko, M., *Thinkertoys,* Berkeley, CA: Ten Speed Press, 1991, p. 194.

2. Clark, C.H., *Idea Management: How to Motivate Creativity and Innovation,* New York: Amacom, 1990, p. 18.

3. Ibid., p. 19.

4. VanGundy, A.B., Jr., *Techniques of Structure Problem Solving,* New York: Van Nostrand Reinhold Company, 1988, p. 255.

5. Von Fange, E.K., *Professional Creativity,* Englewood Cliffs, NJ: Prentice Hall, Inc., 1959, p. 27.

6. Smith, E.D., "Some Psychological Factors Favoring Industrial Inventiveness," *Creative Engineering,* New York: The American Society of Mechanical Engineers, 1944, p. 19.

7. Miller, W.C., *The Creative Edge,* Reading, MA: Addison-Wesley Publishing Co., 1987, pp. 202–203.

8. Senge, P.M., *The Fifth Discipline,* New York: Double Currency, 1990, p. 200.

9. Basadur, M., *Creative Problem Solving,* Toronto: Center for Research in Applied Creativity, 1989, p. 14–21.

10. Ibid., pp. 200–201.

11. Ibid., p. 201.

12. Isaksen, S.G., and D.J. Treffinger, *Creative Problem Solving: The Basic Course,* Buffalo: Bearley Ltd., 1985, p. 136.

13. Gibb, J., "Managing Creativity in the Organization," in Taylor, C.W., (ed.), *Climate for Creativity,* New York: Pergamon Press, 1972, p. 23.

14. Raudseep, E., *How Creative Are You,* NY: Perigee Books, 1981, pp. 97–99.

15. Peters, T., "Get Innovative or Get Dead," *California Management Review,* Winter 1991, p. 10.

16. Isaksen and Treffinger, *Creative Problem Solving,* p. 135.

17. Evans, J.R., *Creative Thinking,* Cincinnati: South-Western Publishing Co., 1991, p. 113.

18. Parnes, S.J., *Visionizing,* East Aurora, NY: D.O.K. Publishers, 1988, pp. 91–92.

19. Braybrooke, D., and C.E. Lindblom, *A Strategy of Decision,* New York: The Free Press, 1963.

20. Maslow, A., "A Holistic Approach to Creativity," in Taylor, C.W., (ed.), *Climate for Creativity,* New York: Pergamon Press, 1972, p. 293.

21. VanGundy, A.B., Jr., *Stalking the Wild Solution,* Buffalo: Bearley Ltd, 1988, p. 194.

22. Basadur, *Creative Problem Solving,* p. 14–22.

23. Von Fange, *Professional Creativity,* pp. 213–214.

Chapter 11

1. "Eyes on the Prize," *Time,* March 21, 1988, p. 50.

2. "Global Innovation: Who's in the Lead," *Business Week,* August 3, 1992, p. 68.

3. Tatsuno, S., *Created in Japan,* New York: HarperBusiness, 1990, p. 7.

4. Ibid., p. 11.

5. Ibid.

6. Davis, S., and B. Davidson, *2020 Vision,* New York: Simon and Schuster, 1991, p. 16.

7. Tatsuno, *Created in Japan,* p. 12.

8. Bailyn, L., "Autonomy in the Industrial R&D Environment," *Human Resource Management,* No. 24, pp. 478–485; Cummings, L.L., "Organizational Climate for Creativity," *Journal of the Academy of Management,* Vol. 8, September 1965, 220–227; Delbecq, P.F., and P.K. Mills, "Managerial Practices That Enhance Innovation," *Organizational Dynamics,* Vol. 14, Summer 1985, pp. 24–34; Drucker, P.F., *Innovation and Entrepreneurship: Practices and Principles,* London: Heinemann, 1985; Kanter, R.M., "Change Master Skills: What It Takes to Be Creative," *Handbook for Creative and Innovative Managers,* New York: McGraw-Hill, pp. 91–100; Pelz, D., and F.M. Andrews, *Scientists in Organizations,* New York: Wiley, 1966; and Andrews, F.M., "Social and Psychological Factors That Influence the Creative Process," in Taylor, I.A., and J.W. Getzels (eds.), *Perspectives in Creativity,* Chicago: Aldine, 1975, pp. 117–145.

9. Witt, L.A., and M.N. Beorkrem, "Climate for Creative Productivity as a Predictor of Research Usefulness and Organizational Effectiveness in an R&D Organization," *Creativity Research Journal,* v. 2, 1989, pp. 30–40.

10. Senge, P., *The Fifth Discipline: The Art & Practice of the Learning Organization,* New York:Doubleday, 1990, p. 154.

11. Ibid.

12. Peters, T.J., *Liberation Management,* New York: A.A. Knopf, 1992.

13. Peters, T., "Get Innovative or Get Dead," Part 1, *California Management Review,* Winter 1991, p. 21.

14. Abbey, A., and J.W. Dickson, "R&D Work Climate and Innovation in Semiconductors," *Academy of Management Journal,* No. 26, 1983, pp. 362–368; and Lind, S.K., and M.D. Mumford, "Values as Predictors of Job Performance and Advancement Potential," paper presented at the meetings of the Southeastern Psychological Association, Atlanta, GA, March, 1987.

15. Burnside, R.M., "Encourage as the Elixir of Innovation," *Issues and Observations,* Summer 1988.

16. Geis, G.T., "Making Companies Creative: An Organizational Psychology of Creativity," *Handbook for Creative and Innovative Managers,* Kuhn, R.L., (ed.), New York, 1988, pp. 25–33.

17. Kao, J.J., *Managing Creativity*, Englewood Cliffs, NJ: Prentice Hall, 1991, p. 20.

18. Ibid.

19. Peters, T., *In Search of Excellence: The Video*, Waltham, MA: Nathan Tyler Productions, 1985.

20. Fabian, J., *Creative Thinking and Problem Solving*, Chelsea, MI: Lewis Publishers, Inc., 1990, p. 251–253.

21. Gibb, J.R., *Trust: A New View of Personal and Organizational Development*, Los Angeles: The Guild of Tutors Press, 1978, p. 17.

22. Argyris, C., *Integrating the Individual and the Organization*, New York: John Wiley and Sons, 1990, p. 228.

23. Ibid., pp. 4–5.

24. Csikszentmihalyi, M., *Flow: The Psychology of Optimal Experience*, New York: Harper and Row, 1990, p. 6.

25. Clark, C., *Idea Management: How to Motivate Creativity and Innovation*, New York: AMACOM, 1990, pp. 23–24.

26. Ibid.

27. Senge, *The Fifth Discipline*, p. 302.

28. Peters, *In Search of Excellence*, pp. 15–16.

29. Senge, *The Fifth Discipline*, p. 235.

30. Miller, W.C., *The Creative Edge*, Reading, MA: Addison-Wesley Publishing Co., 1987, p. 83.

31. Ferguson, B., "The Creative Environment/ The Learning Organization," *Analytical Support: Series on Innovation*, Stanford Research Institute Report, 1990, p. 6.

32. Gowan, J.C., "Some Thoughts on the Development of Creativity," *The Journal of Creative Behavior*, vol. II, no. 2.

33. Tatsuno, *Created in Japan*, pp. 6–7.

Chapter 12

1. Maslow, A.N., *Toward a Psychology of Being*, Princeton, NJ: Van Nostrand, 1968, p. 138.

2. Davis, G.A., *Creativity Is Forever*, Dubuque, IA: Kendall/Hunt Publishing Co., 1983, p. 53.

3. Wallach, M.A., and N. Kogan, *Modes of Thinking in Young Children*, New York: Holt, Rinehart, 1965.

4. Richmond, B.G., "Creativity in Monozygotic and Dyzgotic Twins," research report from EDRS, 1966 (ERIC Document Reproduction Services of the U.S. Department of Health, Education, and Welfare, National Institutes of Education).

5. Thurstone, L.L., *The Nature of Intelligence*, Patterson, NJ: Littlefield, Adams, 1960.

6. Torrance, E.P., "Some Products of 25 Years of Creativity Research," *Educational Perspectives*, Vol. 22, No. 3, 1984, pp. 3–8.

7. Hensley, P.A., and C.R. Reynolds, "Creativity and Intelligence," in Glover, J.A., R.R. Ronning, and C.R. Reynolds (eds.), *Handbook of Creativity*, New York: Plenum Press, 1989, p. 111.

8. Rogers, C.R., "Toward a Theory for Creativity," in Parnes, S.J., and H.F. Harding, (eds.), *A Sourcebook of Creative Thinking*, New York: Scribners, 1962.

9. Bem, S.L., "The Measurement of Psychological Androgyny," *Journal of Consulting and Clinical Psychology*, Vol. 41, 1974, pp. 155–162.

10. Kneller, G.F., *The Art and Science of Creativity*, New York: Holt, Rinehart and Winston, Inc., 1967, pp. 62–68.

11. MacKinnon, D.W., "What Makes a Person Creative," *Saturday Review*, February, 1962, pp. 15–17 +; Torrance, E.P., "Teaching Gifted and Creative Learners," in Witrock, M. (ed.), *Handbook of Research on Teaching*, Chicago: Rand McNally, 1984; and Davis, *Creativity Is Forever*, pp. 50–52.

12. Ibid., p. 52.

13. Jackson, P.W., and S. Messick, "The Person, the Product and the Response: Conceptual Problems in the Assessment of Creativity," *Journal of Personality*, 1965, 33, pp. 309–329.

14. Torrance, E.P., "Non-Test Ways of Identifying the Creatively Gifted," in Gowan, J.C., J. Khatena and E.P. Torrance (eds.), *Creativity: Its Educational Implications*, Dubuque, IA: Kendall/Hunt, 1981; and Smith, J.A., *Setting Conditions for Creative Teaching in the Elementary School*, Boston: Allyn and Bacon, 1966.

15. Davis, *Creativity Is Forever*, p. 45.

16. Leff, H.L., *Playful Perception*, Burlington, VT: Waterfront Books, Inc., 1984, pp. 88–99.

17. Von Oech, R., *A Whack on the Side of the Head*, New York: Warner Books, Inc., 1983, p. 55.

18. Parnes, S.J., *Creative Behavior Guidebook,* New York: Scribner's Sons, 1967, p. 117.

19. Parnes, S.J., *Visionizing,* East Aurora, New York: D.O.K. Publishers, 1988, p. 20.

20. Shafer, R., cartoons published in *Through History with J. Wesley Smith,* Vanguard Press, 1950, and in *New Yorker Magazine,* 1971.

21. Adams, J.L., *The Care and Feeding of Ideas,* Reading, MA: Addison-Wesley Publishing Co., 1986, p. 140.

22. Evans, P., and G. Deehan, *The Keys to Creativity,* London: Grafton Books, 1988, p. 158.

23. Glassman, E., *Creativity On-The-Job,* Chapel Hill, NC: 1987, pp. 2–10.

Chapter 13

1. Senge, P., *The Fifth Discipline,* New York: DoubledayCurrency, 1990, p. 168.

2. Shallcross, D.J., and D.A. Sisk, *Intuition: An Inner Way of Knowing,* Buffalo, NY: Bearley Ltd., 1989, p. 2.

3. Weil, A., *The Natural Mind,* Boston: Houghton Mifflin, 1972, p. 150.

4. Nadel, L., *Sixth Sense,* New York: Prentice Hall Press, 1990, p. 210.

5. Shallcross and Sisk, *Intuition,* p. 53.

6. John-Steiner, V., *Notebooks of the Mind,* Albuquerque, NM: University of New Mexico Press, 1985, pp. 182–183.

7. Capra, F., *The Tao of Physics,* Berkeley, CA: Shambala, 1975, p. 131.

8. Quoted in Beveridge, W.I.B., *The Art of Scientific Investigation,* New York: Norton, 1951, p. 56.

9. Michalko, M., *Thinkertoys,* Berkeley, CA: Ten Speed Press, 1991, p. 213.

10. Ruggiero, V.R., *Beyond Feelings,* Mountain View, CA: Mayfield Publishing Co., 1990, p. xiv.

11. Senge, *The Fifth Discipline,* p. 169.

12. Vaughan, F.E., *Awakening Intuition,* Garden City, NY: Anchor Books, 1979, p. 49.

13. Ruggiero, *Beyond Feelings,* p. 17.

14. Gerard, R.W., "The Biological Basis of Imagination," *The Scientific Monthly,* June 1946, p. 477.

15. Ibid., p. 478.

16. Weisburd, S., "The Spark: Personal Testimonies of Creativity," *Science News,* November 1987, pp. 298–300.

17. Shallcross and Sisk, *Intuition,* p. 106.

18. Ruggiero, *Beyond Feelings,* p. 17.

19. Vaughan, *Awakening Intuition,* p. 66.

20. Shallcross and Sisk, *Intuition,* pp. 3–6.

21. Ibid., pp. 2–3.

22. Senge, *The Fifth Discipline,* p. 167.

23. Parnes, S.J., *Visionizing,* East Aurora, NY: D.O.K. Publishers, 1988, p. 1.

24. Ibid., p. 60.

25. Ibid., p. 3.

26. Described in Shallcross and Sisk, *Intuition,* p. 47.

27. Ibid., pp. 47–48.

28. Ibid., p. 47.

29. Vaughan, *Awakening Intuition,* p. 34.

30. Owens, C.K., "Zen Buddhism," *Transpersonal Psychologies,* in Tart, C. (ed.), New York: Harper and Row, 1975, p. 156.

31. Vaughan, *Awakening Intuition,* pp. 50–51.

32. Ornstein, R., *The Psychology of Consciousness,* New York: Viking, 1972.

33. Vaughan, *Awakening Intuition,* p. 51.

34. Yukawa, H., *Creativity and Intuition,* Tokyo: Kodansha International Ltd., 1973, p. 56.

35. Capra, F., *The Tao of Physics,* p. 131.

36. LeShan, L., *The Medium, the Mystic and the Physicist,* New York: Viking, 1974, p. 100.

37. Polanyi, M., in Green, M. (ed.), "Toward a Unity of Knowledge," *Psychological Issues,* New York: International Universities Press, 1969.

38. Capra, *The Tao of Physics,* p. 31.

39. Raudseep, E., *How Creative Are You?,* New York: Perigee Books, 1981, p. 136.

40. Ibid.

41. Ibid., p. 137.

42. Kao, J.J., *Managing Creativity,* Englewood Cliffs, NJ: Prentice Hall, 1991, p. 17.

43. Parnes, *Visionizing,* p. 78.

44. Michalko, *Thinkertoys,* pp. 174–175.

45. de Bono, E., *Six Thinking Hats,* Des Moines, IA: Perfection Learning, 1985.

46. Assagioli, R., *Psychosynthesis,* New York: Viking Press, 1965.

47. Monk, L., "Radical Trust in the Creative Process," an interview with C. A. Kapikain, *The Common Boundaries,* Vol. 6, No. 1, pp. 7–9.

48. Bruner, J., *The Process of Education.*

49. Shallcross and Sisk, *Intuitions,* p. 43.

50. Senge, *The Fifth Discipline,* p. 168.

51. *Computerworld,* June 22, 1992, p. 24.

52. Stein, M.I., *Making the Point,* Buffalo: Bearley Ltd., 1984, p. 44.

53. Vaughan, *Awakening Intuition,* pp.44–45.

54. Raudseep., *How Creative Are You?,* p. 130.

Index